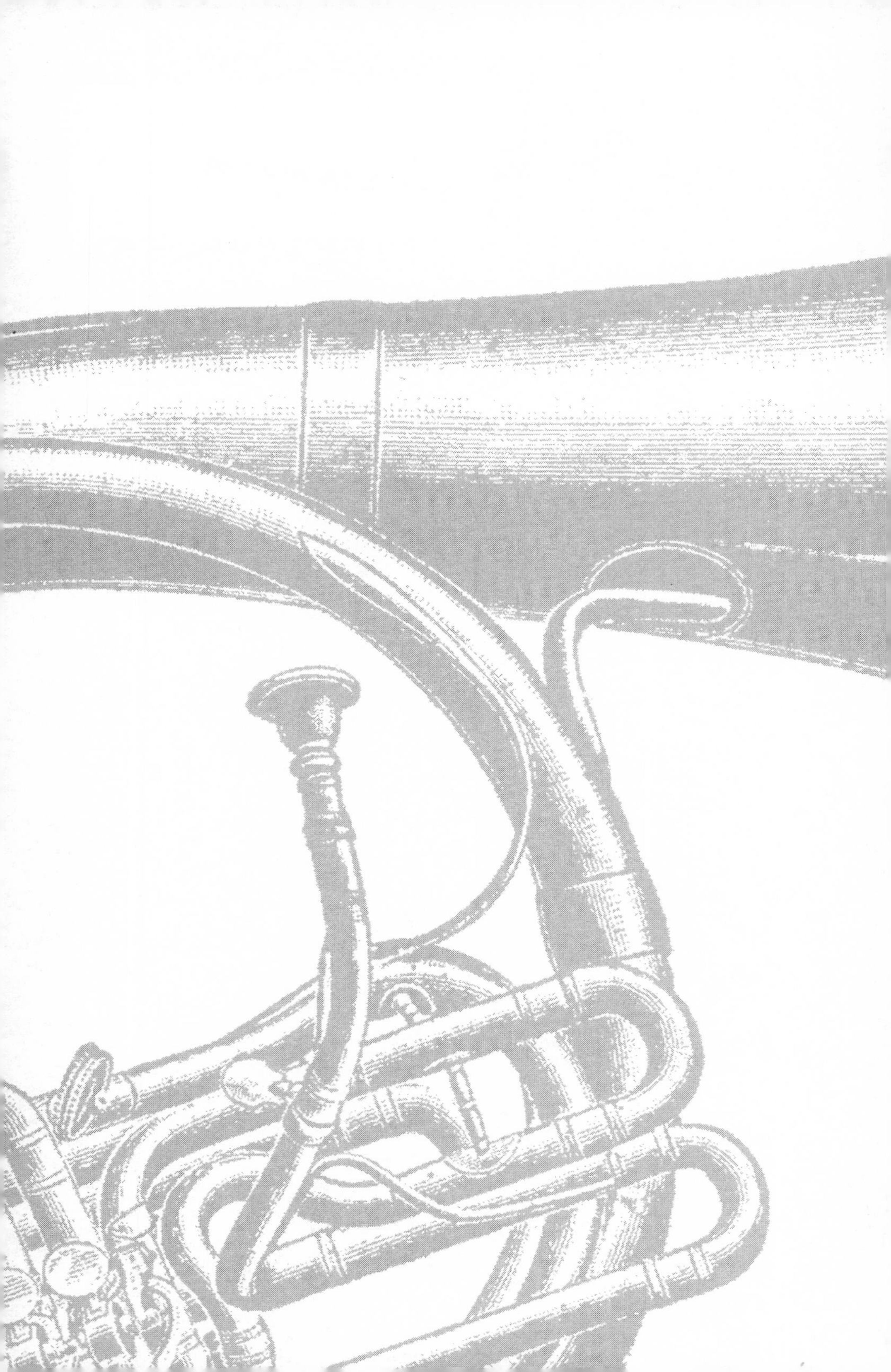

Music FOR THE REVOLUTION

Musicians and Power in Early Soviet Russia

AMY NELSON

The Pennsylvania State University Press
University Park, Pennsylvania

Library of Congress Cataloging-in-Publication Data

Nelson, Amy.
Music for the revolution : musicians and power in early Soviet Russia / Amy Nelson.
p. cm.
Includes bibliographical references (p.) and index.
ISBN 978-0-271-03106-4 (pbk. : alk. paper)
1. Music—Soviet Union—20th century—History and criticism.
2. Music—Social aspects—Soviet Union.
3. Soviet Union—History—1917–1936.
I. Title.

ML300.5 .N45 2004
780'.947'0904—dc22 2003023952

Printed in the United States of America
Published by The Pennsylvania State University Press,
University Park, PA 16802-1003

The Pennsylvania State University Press is a member of the Association of American University Presses.

It is the policy of The Pennsylvania State University Press to use acid-free paper. Publications on uncoated stock satisfy the minimum requirements of American National Standard for Information Sciences—Permanence of Paper for Printed Library Material, ANSI Z39.48–1992.

FOR *Tom and Claire*

CONTENTS

ILLUSTRATIONS

MUSICAL EXAMPLES

PREFACE AND ACKNOWLEDGMENTS

Mention twentieth-century Russian music, and the names of the three "giants"—Igor Stravinsky, Sergei Prokofiev, and Dmitrii Shostakovich—quickly come to mind. Mention artistic life under the Soviet regime, and images of terror, censorship, and the repression of intellectual freedom leap to the foreground. Neither artistic brilliance nor censorship was new to the Soviet period, of course. Through their creative achievements these musicians perpetuated the legacy of Russia's nineteenth-century musical greats—the "Mighty Five" and Peter Tchaikovsky—even as their fraught relationships with Soviet political authority recapitulated many of the prerevolutionary tensions between the aspirations of creative artists and the demands of Russia's rulers.

Yet during the turbulent decade between the Bolshevik Revolution of 1917 and the massive drives for industrialization and the forced collectivization of agriculture that marked Stalin's "revolution from above," Stravinsky and Prokofiev lived abroad, and Shostakovich was just finishing his conservatory training and beginning his meteoric rise to fame. Musical life in early Soviet Russia was rich and diverse, but lacked both the brilliance that had brought celebrity to the Ballets Russes a decade before and the brutal censorship that would attract the world's attention a decade later.

Seen through the prism of what was to come, the twenties often seem to be merely a prelude to totalitarianism in artistic life—the doomed days of artistic pluralism and the twilight of the Russian avant-garde. Yet this was the decade in which the creative intelligentsia defined its relationship with Soviet power and the aesthetic foundations for socialist realism were laid down. This book is about how musicians and Soviet power responded to each other in these formative years, and how these responses as well as musicians' aesthetic preferences helped determine the contours of Soviet musical life. To meet the political demands and ideological challenges of the Bolshevik Revolution, Russia's musicians, most of whom are little known in the West today, grappled with an array of issues affecting musical education, professional identity, and the administration of musical life, as well as the embrace of certain creative platforms and the rejection of others. This is the story of how those debates unfolded and how the musical community helped shape the musical culture of Stalinism.

While writing a book is ultimately a solitary endeavor, the support of many institutions and individuals has been essential to the completion of this one. The dissertation from which this study evolved received generous funding from the International Research and Exchanges Board (IREX), the U.S. Department of Education Fulbright-Hayes Doctoral Dissertation Research Abroad Fellowship Program, the Center for European Studies at Columbia University, the Social Science Research Council, and the University of Michigan. After coming to Virginia Tech, I received funding from the University Creative Match Grant Program, a Pilot Research Project Grant, and several research awards from the Department of History, allowing me to do additional research in Russia and the United States.

As a graduate student at the University of Michigan I was fortunate to find an able advisor in Bill Rosenberg and to benefit from Geoff Eley's steadfast enthusiasm for the project as well as his constant encouragement to refine its analytical framework. Thanks are also due Ron Suny, who was unflagging in his interest in my work, and Jane Burbank and Rosamund Bartlett, for their perceptive comments and willingness to serve as committee members. Over the years, my work and travels in Russia have benefited tremendously from the advice, support, and friendship of Tat'iana Viktorovna Shemakhanskaia and the encouragement of Efim Iosifovich Pivovar. The warmth, hospitality, and creative energy I found in the apartment of Volodia Erokhin and Raia and Iana Gershzon helped sustain me through a particularly difficult Moscow winter. I am indebted to many Russian librarians and archivists, particularly the staff in the First Reading Room of the *Leninka* (now the Russian State Library) and at three archives: the State Archive of the Russian Federation (*Gosudarstvennyi arkhiv Rossiiskoi Federatsii* [GARF]), the Russian State Archive of Literature and Art (*Rossiiskii gosudarstvennyi arkhiv literatury i iskusstva* [RGALI]), and the Glinka State Central Museum of Musical Culture (*Gosudarstvennyi tsentral'nyi muzei muzykal'noi kul'tury im. M. I. Glinki* [GTsMMK]).

I owe special thanks to Corinne Gaudin and Karen Ahlquist for their advice, expertise, and moral support over many years. Portions of the book are also stronger thanks to feedback from members of the "Interdisciplinary

Reading Group"—Jane Aiken, Brian Britt, David Burr, Sue Farquhar, Ann-Marie Knoblauch, and Darleen Pryds. I have come to appreciate greatly the support and friendship of my colleagues at Virginia Tech, particularly Steve Baehr, Mark Barrow, Sue Farquhar, Heather Gumbert, Sharon Johnson, Kathleen Jones, Nyusya Milman, Bert Moyer, Richard Shryock, and Robert Stephens. The encouragement and solidarity of Joseph Bradley, Rosemary Eddy, Sue Fischer, Melissa Johnson, Roy Robson, Christine Ruane, Jeanie and John Weber, and Christine Worobec during the long, and sometimes troubled, gestation of this book has been invaluable.

At Penn State University Press I found a discerning, patient, and humane editor in Peter Potter. Jennifer M. G. Smith contributed her keen copyediting skill to the project. I am also grateful for the perceptive comments of Lynn Mally and Richard Stites, who served as reviewers for the manuscript.

Finally, I am indebted beyond measure to Tom Ewing, whose time in the trenches of this project certainly has exceeded what should reasonably be expected from either a colleague or a spouse. He has read countless drafts and generously brought his keen analytical, historical, and editorial skills to bear on my prose and myriad conceptual and procedural quandaries. His optimism, passion, and patience have inspired and sustained me as we have negotiated the hurdles facing us as partners, parents, and historians over the last several years. This book is dedicated to him and to our daughter, Sinclair, whose enchantment with the world of books, love of music, and delight in the miracles of daily life serve as a constant reminder of the wonders of childhood and the magic of learning. The faults that remain in what follows are, of course, my own.

Portions of Chapters 3, 4, and 8 have been published previously: "Assigning Meaning to Musical Speech: The Theories of Boleslav Yavorsky in the Cultural Revolution," in *Intersections and Transpositions: Russian Music, Literature, and Society*, ed. Andrew Baruch Wachtel (Evanston: Northwestern University Press, 1998), 253–73; "Accounting for Taste: Choral Circles in Early Soviet Workers' Clubs," in *Chorus and Community*, ed. Karen Ahlquist (Urbana: University of Illinois Press, forthcoming); and "The Struggle for Proletarian Music: RAPM and the Cultural Revolution," *Slavic Review* 59:1 (2000):101–32. I gratefully acknowledge the permission of Northwestern University Press, University of Illinois Press, and the American Association for the Advancement of Slavic Studies to use material from these articles here.

Transliteration of Russian words in the main text follows the Library of Congress system, except in the cases of individuals who are better known by the Anglicized version of their name, e.g., Stravinsky, Prokofiev, Lunacharsky, and Tchaikovsky. In the notes and bibliography, Russian language materials are cited using the Library of Congress system; however, names of Russian authors are given as they are spelled in the original material, hence the occasional difference between spellings. Archival references use standard abbreviations for Russian terms: f. for *fond* (record set), op. for *opis'* (subset), d. for *delo* or *ed. khr.* for *edinitsa khraneniia* (folder), l. for *list* (page).

INTRODUCTION

In 1918 Vladimir Lenin offered the writer Maxim Gorky a chilling assessment of the need for violent revolution by paying homage to the power of classical music:

> I know nothing which is greater than the *Appassionata;* I would like to listen to it every day. It is marvelous, superhuman music. I always think with pride—perhaps it is naïve of me—what marvelous things human beings can do! . . . But I can't listen to music too often. It affects your nerves, makes you want to say stupid nice things, and stroke the heads of people who could create such beauty while living in this vile hell. And now you mustn't stroke anyone's head—you might get your hand bitten off. You have to hit them on the head, without any mercy, although our ideal is not to use force against anyone. H'm, h'm, our duty is infernally hard![1]

While this oft-cited quotation provides ample illustration of Lenin's ruthlessness and willingness to use any means to achieve his party's revolutionary ends, it also illuminates the complexities of the subject of this book. Lenin's fear that Beethoven might temper the militancy of the professional revolutionary reflected his regard for the powerful emotional impact of music as well as his appreciation of the sublime beauty of a piano sonata, and, by extension, his regard for the legacy of "bourgeois culture." These attitudes would heavily influence the fate of music and musicians in the early Soviet period—in part because they were shared (if not always acknowledged) by musicians and revolutionaries alike. Also telling is the way Lenin juxtaposes the power of music—a force he finds compelling but ineffable—and revolutionary violence, the potential of which he grasps perfectly. Both kinds of power were instrumental in the early Soviet period, although the coercive dimensions of Soviet

Communism have received far more attention than the ways in which both musicians and Bolsheviks sought to exploit the emotional impact of music.

By examining the first fifteen years of Soviet rule through the prism of music and the activities of musicians, this book offers a perspective on the contours and fate of the Bolshevik revolution that highlights the complexities of the interactions between musicians, politicians, and ideologies. Certainly Lenin's Party-state was very willing to "hit them on the head," and scholars have rightly emphasized the role of repression and censorship in all areas of Soviet artistic and intellectual life.[2] But the development of musical life after 1917 was more complicated than simply a "taming of the arts."[3]

The development of a distinctly "Soviet" musical culture in the twenties and early thirties was guided in many ways by the imperative for cultural transformation that was implicit in the Bolsheviks' political revolution. For as a complement to political and economic restructuring the Bolsheviks also embraced a "civilizing mission" intended to nurture new, socialist attitudes and habits as well as cultural forms that would have broad appeal and reflect the new way of life. As in other areas of artistic endeavor, many attempts to fashion a "socialist" musical culture involved efforts to overcome the divide between elite and popular cultures either by democratizing the "high culture" of the prerevolutionary era or by cultivating new forms of artistic expression.[4] In fact, this study shows how reformers' underlying assumptions and their interactions with their audiences largely determined the fate of these projects.

Although the Bolsheviks consistently displayed their willingness to achieve political and economic objectives with force, persuasion and the accommodation of popular preferences were critical in the battle for the people's hearts and minds, a battle that Lenin and his followers knew they must win if the revolution were to succeed. Accommodation and concession proved to be especially important where music was concerned because of the peculiar qualities of musical creativity. Like writers and artists, musicians such as Dmitrii Shostakovich and Sergei Prokofiev indeed felt the Party's interventions in cultural life and the ravages of censorship. But as recent studies of film, theater, architecture, youth culture, and religion have shown, there were often major contradictions between the Party's conception of policy and its implementation.[5] The responses of musicians (and their audiences) to the project of formulating a "new" musical culture were extraordinarily complex. Exploring the collaborative means by which musical life developed in the early Soviet period reveals the extent to which Soviet culture represented an amalgam of sometimes divergent, but often overlapping, agendas.[6]

The unique qualities of music and musical creativity would be critically important in determining the future of musical life after 1917. Lenin's awe for music's appeal to the emotions and his conviction that this influence could not be countered rationally, but neutralized only with silence, points both to the power of musical expression and to the difficulties of identifying the "content" of music—as opposed to, say, that of literature and the visual arts. It was widely recognized that music did mean something; however, its abstract, non-representational character made that meaning extraordinarily difficult to pin down. In a time when the ideological implications of all artistic forms were subject to fierce debate and intense scrutiny, efforts to identify and create appropriate "music for the revolution" constantly ran up against the intractable difficulties of specifying its content. Musicians, then, were presented with unique challenges and choices.

Music's "abstractness" also meant that it received much less attention (and intervention) from the authorities than areas of artistic endeavor in which political messages were more transparent.[7] While Lenin called film "our most important art," and Stalin would designate writers as "engineers of the human soul," musicians were often castigated for their "backwardness." Throughout the twenties, Party officials and other cultural militants lamented that music and musical life seemed only superficially changed by the revolution. But the low political priority the Party assigned to music also meant that musicians had considerable latitude in regulating their affairs. Their claims to expertise and authority in matters concerning their art were respected in much the same way that the Party respected scientists' assertions that only they could understand and regulate their research agendas. This combination of official neglect and respect for professional expertise meant that musicians were more successful than other artistic groups in promoting their own aesthetic platforms and regulating cultural production and consumption.[8] Although most of them would deny it, musicians themselves assumed a prominent role in the "Sovietization" of musical life.

While the early Soviet musical community displayed considerable aesthetic and political diversity, the challenge of building a new musical culture worked itself out at the hands of musicians who shared assumptions about the nature of musical creativity, the elevating potential of art, and the place of popular culture. In the many issues that dominated musical life in the twenties—from debates about the objectives of conservatory training to efforts to change the musical sensibilities of Russia's masses and campaigns to promote modern music and secure the legacy of the classical tradition—prerevolutionary concerns and dynamics played a prominent role. As Lenin's musings to Gorky suggest, 1917 was a radical turning point defined by violence, destruction, and visions of a brave new world. But prerevolutionary cultural traditions, creative elites, and political dynamics had a profound impact on that new world order.

The dawn of the twentieth century found the Russian autocracy among the most politically antiquated regimes in Europe. Tsar Nicholas II—a devoted family man with little interest in the craft of governing—ruled from an exaggerated but sincere sense of duty to God, country, and the office for which he had been destined by birth. Though he promoted the economic modernization that would ensure Russia's position as a great European power, the last tsar rejected initiatives from his advisors and subjects that would have diluted his autocratic authority, calling them "senseless dreams." State-sponsored industrialization programs in the late nineteenth century, however, stimulated urbanization and the emergence of an industrial working class. Although Russian workers retained economic and familial ties to peasant village communities and the Russian countryside, they also supported the same kinds of socialist and other radical political ideologies embraced by workers in the West. With urban and economic development also came social diversification, as the ranks of professionals and other "middling" orders increased. In the face of the incremental but steady evolution of Russia's public sphere, the tsar held steadfastly to his suspicion of any form of independent civic organization—which only highlighted the obsolescence of the autocracy and the extent to which the country's political system stood ever more at odds with the aspirations and interests of its society.

The social challenges and political tensions of late Imperial Russia extended to cultural and artistic expression as well. At the turn of the century, the Russian school of music composition—embodied in the works of the "Mighty Five" (Mily Balakirev, Aleksandr Borodin, César Cui, Modest Musorgsky, and Nikolai Rimsky-Korsakov) and Peter Tchaikovsky (1840–93), Russia's first professional composer of international repute—confronted new influences from the West, particularly the radical modernism of Richard Strauss and Arnold Schoenberg and the musical impressionism of Maurice Ravel and Claude Debussy. Although guardians of specifically "Russian" traditions held the majority of conservatory posts, and were most prominently represented by the aging Rimsky-Korsakov (1844–1908) in St. Petersburg and by Sergei Taneev (1865–1915) in Moscow, the orbit of impresario Sergei Diaghilev's World of Art (*mir iskusstva*) circle attracted musicians interested in current trends from the West. In both St. Petersburg and Moscow, "Evenings of Contemporary Music" introduced Russians to modern music from the West and to the compositions of Russia's own radicals, Sergei Prokofiev (1891–1953) and Igor Stravinsky (1882–1971).

In poetry and literature, religious and metaphysical perspectives marked the brilliant creativity of what became known as the Silver Age, while iconoclasm and rebellion fueled a stunning burst of innovation in painting and other visual arts. Composers such as Nikolai Roslavets (1881–1944) and Arthur Lourié (Lur'e, 1892–1966) heeded the futurist summons to defy artistic conventions and mock the sensibilities of traditional audiences. At the same time, Alexander Scriabin (1871–1915), a visionary egomaniac entranced by the occult, composed music he hoped would realize the symbolists' hopes for an art that would not only transform the world, but transcend it. Many painters and poets appropriated musical terms such as "sonata" and "symphony" to describe compositions that were fluid, synthetic, or inscrutably abstract, yet the avant-garde in music was less iconoclastic than in these other arts.[9]

Due in part, perhaps, to the relative conservatism of Russian art music at the turn of the century, Russia's educated classes remained staunchly devoted to the elite creativity cultivated in the conservatories and concert halls. At the same time, popular music reflected the increasing complexity of Russia's modernizing society and economy, incorporating foreign as well as indigenous influences. The emergence of short, rhymed ditties called *chastushki* accompanied the growth of working-class neighborhoods in the empire's cities, as did the development of other song genres popular among peddlers, migrant workers, and criminals.[10] The spread of the phonograph and inexpensive sheet music facilitated the dissemination of the "gypsy genre" (*tsyganshchina*), a kind of melodramatic, often frankly sensual song distantly related to both a more elite old Russian sentimental song called the salon romance and the authentic songs of gypsies. The proliferation of cafés, restaurants, and variety theaters provided additional venues for musical entertainment, as did the arrival of movie houses, where pianists or small instrumental ensembles offered live accompaniment for silent films.

A craze for new Western dance music initially infected Russia's social elite, who found ragtime, the cakewalk, and the fox-trot liberating alternatives to the formality of ballroom dancing and its traditional music. The new dance mania also meshed with challenges to convention and traditional values: women and youth embraced the rebelliousness and sensuality of the music and the dance. Passion for the erotic and exotic peaked with the arrival of the tango, whose hypnotic, stylized movements prompted scandal and public debate, and were easily adapted to tragic and even criminal narratives in "Apache" dances and "Tangos of Death."

Traditional peasant culture and music provided inspiration for new kinds of urban entertainment, just as they informed the work of Russia's musical classicists such as Rimsky-Korsakov and modernists such as Stravinsky. Capitalizing on sentimental stereotypes of the peasantry, national pride, and nostalgia for an idealized, bucolic past, Vasilii Andreev's (1861–1918) huge balalaika "orchestra" performed lush harmonizations of folk songs and classics for attentive urban audiences, while Mitrofan Piatnitsky's (1864–1927) song and dance ensemble featured more authentic renditions of traditional songs and epic poems (*byliny*) as well as laments by actual peasant singers.

If the diversity and vibrancy of Russia's musical life were fueled by the interests and aspirations of a rapidly changing society, they also reflected the growing tensions between that society and a regime intent on avoiding political reform. These tensions burst into the open in 1905, as the autocracy struggled to manage a humiliating defeat in the Russo-Japanese War. Mounting pressure from both an increasingly coherent liberal movement and worker-supported revolutionary groups culminated in revolution after troops guarding the Winter Palace gunned down unarmed demonstrators on what became known as "Bloody Sunday." Faced with widespread rebellion in the countryside, debilitating strikes in the cities, and liberal professionals' demands for civil and religious liberties, Nicholas II drafted the "October Manifesto" that provided Russia with a rudimentary, if severely circumscribed, constitutional order. Although the tsar retained his designation as autocrat, the establishment of a national legislative body and the nominal commitment to a rule of law served temporarily to appease liberal and other moderate reformers, thus dividing the forces of the revolutionary movement. For the next decade, Russian constitutionalism relied on a tenuous alliance between the crown and conservative elements in parliament, while the tsar's advisors attempted to deal with economic stagnation and political radicalism in the countryside by repressing rebels and promoting reforms designed to transform the communally-oriented peasantry into freeholding farmers. Naked force also kept the aspirations of the labor movement in check, although repression only enhanced the appeal of insurrectionary political parties—such as the Bolsheviks—to workers.

As would be true later, in the Soviet period, musicians did not take a particularly active role in politics during these chaotic years. Indeed, most felt that the transcendent nature of their creative work divorced them from the political realm. Yet many identified with the reform agenda of the liberal movement, and conservatory professors who chafed under the heavy-handed administration of the Imperial Russian Musical Society lobbied with increasing vehemence for more institutional and professional autonomy. Faculty at both the Moscow and St. Petersburg conservatories signed open letters denouncing the Bloody Sunday massacre and calling for basic democratic reforms and an easing of censorship. Rimsky-Korsakov was dismissed from his post for endorsing the demands of striking students, and several of his colleagues resigned in protest. He returned only when the conservatories were granted limited autonomy and had chosen two of his star pupils, Aleksandr Glazunov (1865–1936) and Mikhail Ippolitov-Ivanov (1859–1935), as their first elected directors. Steeped in the traditions of Russian classicism and respected by their peers, these men would guide the conservatories through turbulent years of war, revolution, and the transition to Soviet rule. Along with their students, such as Aleksandr Gol'denveizer (1875–1961) and Konstantin Igumnov (1873–1948), they made up the generational cohort that would shape the course of musical life in the twenties.[11]

In the aftermath of the 1905 Revolution, many musicians devoted themselves to popular music education activities, the most significant of which was the People's Conservatory organized by Sergei Taneev and other prominent Moscow musicians. Inspired by the model of the Free Music School of the 1860s, the People's Conservatory offered courses in choral singing and elementary music theory to white-collar employees, factory workers, and university students. Like many popular educational initiatives that emerged in this period, the People's Conservatory continued a long-standing tradition of the intelligentsia that called on the privileged to repay their debt to society by promoting the education and "enlightenment" (*prosveshchenie*) of the people (*narod*). This tradition, as well as distinctive Russian attitudes about the moral imperatives of art, dovetailed both with the reform agenda of the liberal movement, which considered education a vehicle for the democratization of society, and with the broader ethos of "culturalism," a commitment to the cultural development and cultural unity of the nation. Although activists in the adult education movement condemned the inequities and oppression created by the political system, most did not consider venues such as the People's Conservatory appropriate arenas for political agitation. Rather, they believed in the power of classical literature and music to improve the individual and transform society as a whole.[12] This commitment to the transformative powers of art would persist across the revolutionary divide, informing a number of agendas affecting music.

The eve of World War I thus found Russian musical society and culture with expanding aesthetic horizons, and grappling with a number of issues that would remain prominent after 1917. These included the tension between advocates of progressive, internationally-oriented modernism and supporters of the classic traditions of the Russian school, as well as concerns about the commercialism, vulgarity, and increasing prominence of urban popular music. Intellectuals, religious officials, revolutionaries, and practitioners of classical music all lamented what they perceived as the degenerative influence of *tsyganshchina*—the "gypsy genre"—and jazz.[13] Even the "folklorism" promoted by Andreev and Piatnitsky attracted criticism from purists who objected to the "corruption" of pristine folk music and from those who opposed efforts to romanticize the primitiveness of Russian peasant life.[14] Some of these critical voices would be lost in the political upheaval of 1917, but others would find an opportunity to act on their objections in the name of creating a socialist culture. The revolution would also ensure that matters of professional and creative identity, particularly questions of academic freedom and the place of the artist in society, would mark the struggles of the early Soviet period.

Historians disagree about the long-term prospects for the survival and evolution of Russia's constitutional order in the absence of a multinational armed conflict, but clearly World War I presented an already precariously balanced polity with staggering challenges. Although "war fever" initially minimized the tensions between state and society, the unity between tsar and people and patriotic support for the war quickly dissipated when what had been envisioned as a limited engagement on foreign territory became a struggle for national survival. The tsar's personal authority eroded under the scandals precipitated by the dissolute Rasputin, whose ability to mitigate the hemophilia of the tsar's son secured his position as advisor to the royal family. Nicholas's decision to assume personal command over the floundering war effort and his steadfast reluctance to accept the counsel of well-intentioned economic and social leaders further undermined his tenuous claims to political leadership. Bread riots in the capital on February 23, 1917, ignited the first spark in a wave of strikes and civil protests that brought down the dynasty eight days later. For the next eight months the Provisional Government struggled to establish itself as a legitimate political authority, address long-standing social and economic grievances, and revive the stalled war effort. Failure on all of these fronts enabled the Bolsheviks to come to power in October 1917 on a deceptively simple platform of "bread, land, and peace." Delivering on these promises after the October Revolution proved difficult, as Lenin's government had to focus initially on extricating itself from the war, fending off counterrevolution, and consolidating its authority as the dictatorship of a proletariat not yet large or politically mature enough to govern itself. But behind the rhetoric of class struggle, building socialism, and redistributing wealth stood a vision of a new way of life that required cultural transformation of the broadest kind, a vision for a new consciousness shaped as much by education and technology as by political indoctrination.

Culture—in the anthropological sense as well as in the sense of artistic creativity and higher learning—would be central to this new way of life. But the Bolsheviks' vision was complex and contested. After an initial period of confusion, the new regime's attitudes toward the prerevolutionary intelligentsia developed along contradictory lines. They were marked, on the one hand, by the desire to control and eventually replace old elites; on the other, they were tempered by a need for the technical expertise necessary to run a vast uneducated country and an appreciation of the cultural capital represented by "specialists" such as scientists, engineers, and accountants, as well as artists, writers, and musicians. The pragmatism underpinning this tension reflected the magnitude of the larger cultural agenda, which called for the creation of a new "Soviet man."[15] Although they knew that this would take time, the Bolsheviks firmly believed that the liberating potential of the revolution would only be achieved with the evolution of a new level of consciousness that involved changes in everything from morality, hygiene, and forms of personal address to education, the use of technology, and new modes of artistic expression. Ultimately, music—and musicians—figured more prominently in various components of the revolutionary project than one might suspect.

What follows gives a new inflection to a largely overlooked story. Chapter 1 begins by considering the initial impact of the October Revolution on musical life and musicians' formative experiences with Soviet power. Despite the turbulence and hardships of the revolution and ensuing Civil War, many musicians embraced the revolution's challenge to democratize "high culture"—often in the tradition of the prerevolutionary adult education movement, but sometimes through projects that were more utopian or iconoclastic. Like those of other educated elites, musicians' early interactions with Russia's new rulers were marked by mutual antipathy and suspicion. However, it quickly became apparent that the Party did not assign the same ideological significance to music that it did to literature, or consider the support of musicians as critical to the national welfare as that of scientists and engineers. This meant that musicians would enjoy more latitude in regulating their affairs and that radical groups would receive less encouragement "from above" than was true in other arenas.

The bulk of this book deals with developments during the period of the New Economic Policy (NEP) (1921–28), when official policies of accommodating the old intelligentsia and supporting artistic pluralism accompanied economic programs favoring limited capitalism and the gradual development of socialist modes of production. Chapters 2 and 3 examine the constituencies and agendas of the two groups whose debates in the musical press have most influenced scholarly assessments of early Soviet music: the proponents of "contemporary" music and the champions of "proletarian musical culture." Because much of the "modern" music of the early Soviet period was proscribed from the thirties to the late eighties, it has been eagerly rehabilitated in both Russia and the West since the advent of the *glasnost'* era. Western observers traditionally have seen the twenties as a time of factional struggle between a noble, but doomed, "avant-garde" and the zealous proponents of "proletarian culture."[16] Yet the politics of the supporters of contemporary music remain largely unexamined, while the difficulties the modernists encountered in promoting "new" music are often mistakenly blamed on their opponents on the musical Left. These advocates of proletarian musical culture were in fact more diverse and marginalized than their reputation as Party-backed "hacks" and proponents of "vulgarized Marxist aesthetics" suggests.[17]

The exploration of the Left's efforts to transform popular musical culture in Chapter 4 highlights the difficulties in changing cultural perceptions, such as musical taste, inherent in reformist campaigns and the persistence of prerevolutionary attitudes toward urban popular culture within the rubric of Marxist ideology. The Left's attempts to overcome the divide between elite and popular music foundered on both an unacknowledged elitism and an inability to offer appealing alternatives for popular songs—including *tsyganshchina*, which were stigmatized as banal and petit bourgeois. But from the efforts to identify appropriately "Soviet" forms of musical expression emerged the concept of the "mass song"—the catchy, often heroic or patriotic, upbeat tunes such as "Song of the Motherland"—which would become the mainstay of popular musical culture in the thirties.

The bureaucratization of Soviet cultural life is often cited as a primary component of the regime's efforts to regulate artistic production and consumption;[18] however, little attention has been devoted to the actual working of various administrative agencies. Chapter 5 shows how the evolution of official musical policy depended heavily on the musicians who staffed the agencies charged with the administration of musical institutions and resources. With few exceptions, these individuals were well-respected, middle-aged, professional men such as Aleksandr Gol'denveizer and Lev Tseitlin (1881–1952), who held faculty appointments at one of the conservatories or directed a major performance ensemble in addition to their positions in the government bureaucracy. They rejected efforts to assign ideological significance to musical creativity, but, as in the prerevolutionary period, they felt obligated to make Russia's cultural heritage, including classical music, accessible to previously disenfranchised groups. Ironically, the archival records of these agencies indicate that musicians who were trying to advance their own aesthetic platforms—and, in most cases, defend the autonomy of their profession and their art—actually assisted in the creation of the official Soviet aesthetic and the regulatory apparatus that enforced it.

The collaborative means by which musicians responded to and sometimes co-opted broader political agendas is similarly in evidence in music education. Chapter 6 examines the intense struggles between faculty, students, and bureaucrats over the objectives of conservatory training and the efforts to democratize access to a type of artistic education that required both talent and lengthy presecondary training. Although cultural radicals saw modest gains in the numbers of workers and peasants who entered the conservatories, efforts to renegotiate the basic mission of the institution and the prestige attached to different kinds of musical specialties were terribly ineffective. As was true before the revolution, most aspiring musicians dreamed of fame as concert pianists or virtuoso violinists, and ability and skill remained far more essential to realizing those dreams than ideology or social origin.

Chapter 7 focuses on the music of 1927. The coincidence of the centennial of Beethoven's death and the tenth anniversary of the October Revolution marked the coalescence of various trends within the musical community, even as changes in the country's domestic and international political situation foreshadowed a shift in cultural and economic policies. The polarized critical response to pieces commemorating the 1917 revolution highlighted the ongoing confusion and dissent over what "music for the revolution" should be about, even as the embrace of bourgeois, Germanic Beethoven as the musical patron saint of the proletarian Russian revolution suggested that preferences for traditional aesthetics and "accessibility" would be central to whatever codes were established.

An assessment of the ambiguities of the Cultural Revolution that accompanied Stalin's forced collectivization of the peasantry and the industrialization drives of 1928–32 concludes the book. As in other areas, the Cultural Revolution in music consisted of officially sponsored attacks on "bourgeois specialists," crude efforts to theorize all dimensions of artistic endeavor in Marxist terms, and the subordination of all creative agendas to the regime's demand for popular mobilization in support of the collectivization and industrialization drives. But although it was marked by the same militaristic rhetoric of renewed class struggle seen across the spectrum of artistic and intellectual life in this period, the Cultural Revolution in music proved to be a largely ephemeral affair. As the waves of radicalism receded in the early thirties, a set of musical aesthetics and institutional practices emerged that bore clear debts to the previous decade's struggles to change musical taste, identify accessible musical forms, and define the place of music and musicians in a socialist society. The musical culture of Stalinism involved far more than official patronage and arbitrary censorship: It reflected many of the agendas and values of the musical community itself.

1

Bread, Art, and Soviet Power
Musicians in Revolution and Civil War

There was no bread, and art took its place. At no time and in no place have I seen people, not listening to, but devouring music with such trembling eagerness, such feeling as in Russia during those years.
—Arthur Lourié

Drag pianos out into the streets
Drums with boathooks from windows dash.
Smash drums and pianos to smithereens,
let there be thunder—
—Vladimir Mayakovsky

By the fall of 1917 the pressures of World War I and political unrest had thrown much of Russian musical life into disarray. Concert halls had been converted to military hospitals, while Sergei Koussevitzky's (1874–1951) orchestra folded after more than half of its members were drafted. Anti-German sentiment led to a virtual ban on performing Wagner, Beethoven, and other German composers. Alexander Scriabin, who initially welcomed the war's potential for a "spiritual renewal," died in the first spring of the conflict, leaving behind an unfinished score for a musical *Mysterium* he hoped would usher in the end of the material world.[1]

Yet on the night of October 25, musical and theatrical performances in Petrograd proceeded without interruption as the Bolsheviks mounted their assault on the tsar's Winter Palace. In the memoir literature, a certain lore evolved around these events that stressed the apparent remoteness of musical life from the revolutionary upheaval. A decade after the fact, the great bass Feodor Chaliapin (1873–1938) proudly recalled that the shocks of the battleship *Aurora*'s cannon fire only briefly disrupted his performance of Verdi's *Don Carlos* at the *Narodnyi Dom*,[2] while conductor Nikolai Malko (1883–1961) emphasized in his memoirs that not a single performance was canceled due to the Bolshevik takeover.[3]

These events and the mystique that surrounds them are both telling and misleading. Western historians have often cited the theaters' uninterrupted routine to accentuate the relative bloodlessness of the Bolshevik coup and to counter the Soviet mythology of the revolution as a mass uprising.[4] Chaliapin's and Malko's testimonies are also revealing because they highlight musicians' perception of the transcendent nature of art, and their insistence that the realm of art is above, if not divorced from, political struggles, even revolutionary ones.

But the memoir lore about October 1917 obscures the complicated, often intense relationship that music and musicians would have with the revolution and its legacy. On the one hand, the development of musical life in the first fifteen years of Soviet rule reflected assumptions about the autonomous nature of musical creativity or its remoteness from everyday life, assumptions held not just by many musicians, but by some of Russia's new rulers as well. On the other hand, the prerevolutionary intelligentsia's concern with developing the cultural sensibilities of the nation's toiling masses as a remedy for "backwardness" would support and even co-opt the Bolsheviks' evolving agenda for cultural transformation. Where music was concerned, that agenda reflected complex, often contradictory attitudes: The scorn many revolutionaries displayed for the culture of the former ruling elite was balanced by the commitment of others who wanted to make the cultural legacy of the past accessible to the proletariat. The Bolsheviks' perception of music as a creative form that had few overt political implications combined with an interest in utilizing the emotional appeal of music in general and the mobilizing potential of songs in particular.

Chaliapin's and Malko's recollections also gloss over the antipathy the Bolsheviks encountered among educated Russians once they came to power. Although Soviet scholars carefully noted that members of "the progressive artistic intelligentsia" supported the revolution, most musicians, as well as other artists and academics, were at least mistrustful of, if not overtly hostile to, the new Bolshevik regime.[5] During the first years of Soviet rule, many of the nation's leading musical lights would leave for the West. The émigrés included composers such as the romantic virtuoso Nikolai Medtner (Metner, 1879–1951), the distinguished composer of sacred music Aleksandr Grechaninov (1864–1956), and George Gershwin's future teacher, Joseph Schillinger (Iosif Shillinger, 1895–1943), as well as a number of younger performers who would have brilliant careers in the West. Among the latter were violinist Jascha Heifetz (1900–1987), pianist Vladimir Horowitz (1903–89), and cellist

Gregor Piatagorsky (1903–76), as well as Isai Dobrovein (1891–1953), the pianist whose rendition of the *Appassionata* prompted Lenin's musings on the seductive potential of the aesthetic experience. Igor Stravinsky and Sergei Rachmaninoff, who already had established international reputations and connections in the West, would make permanent homes abroad where their archly anti-Bolshevik sympathies could be freely vented.[6] Sergei Prokofiev later recalled that Anatoly Lunacharsky (1875–1933), the Bolsheviks' point man for cultural affairs, encouraged him to stay: "You are a revolutionary in music as we are in life. We should work together. But if you want to go to America, I will not stand in your way."[7] Prokofiev left for the United States in May, 1918, in search of more hospitable conditions for his performance career. He would not become a Soviet citizen until the early thirties.

Most musicians did stay, however, and some who would eventually leave, including Chaliapin and Koussevitzky, initially took an active part in the musical life of the fledgling Soviet state. In these early years, Lenin's government was preoccupied with the military challenges, economic hardships, and political fallout of the Civil War, which began in May 1918, soon after Russia's withdrawal from World War I. For nearly three years, the Bolsheviks battled an array of restorationist and anti-Communist forces, including monarchists, foreign interventionists, peasant rebels, and anarchists. With the regime's survival at stake, cultural matters were a relatively low priority. Where music was concerned, the Bolsheviks' primary objective was to establish control of the "commanding heights." This involved nationalizing the conservatories, publishing houses, and theaters, as well as confiscating valuable musical instruments from private collections and aristocrats attempting to flee the country. Lenin's regime was also intent on vanquishing political opposition. For musicians, as for other educated Russians, the civil war years witnessed a number of decisive encounters with Soviet authority that determined the dynamics of *kto kogo?*, a "cursed" question of Russian history that asks, who will beat whom? For musicians the answer would be somewhat equivocal. The Bolsheviks moved quickly to achieve administrative and economic control over musicians and musical life, but had little time or interest in formulating music-related policy itself. As part of an effort to mobilize support for the revolution among Russia's toiling masses and extend the political revolution to the cultural sphere, the government funded an array of programs administered by the Red Army and the Commissariat of Enlightenment (Narkompros, successor to the tsarist Ministry of Education), as well as a vast network of "Proletarian Culture" (Proletkul't) organizations. These programs offered musicians, writers, and artists employment and the opportunity to continue prerevolutionary activities, albeit under radically different circumstances. In music, as in other areas, a main objective of Narkompros was to cultivate old "specialists" and enlist them in the revolutionary project. With some notable exceptions, in these early years musicians found that they had considerable latitude in their affairs. They not only facilitated but largely defined the terms under which musical institutions made their transition to Soviet power and musical life responded to the revolution.

For most Russians, the years of revolution and civil war were haunted by hunger and plagued by terrible material hardship and suffering. Survival became the first priority as musicians began to formulate their creative responses to the challenges raised by the revolution. A few pursued radical creative agendas in an explicit effort to link artistic and revolutionary iconoclasm. Some tried to enlist music directly in the revolutionary struggle and the effort to win the Civil War. But for most, strong threads of continuity from the prerevolutionary period dominated their creative activities and attitudes toward Soviet power.

Kto Kogo? The Conservatories, the Commissar, and Bread for "Bourgeois" Musicians

While the overthrow of the Provisional Government was achieved with relative ease, the Bolsheviks' efforts to consolidate political authority met with considerable resistance. For despite widespread and mounting popular dissatisfaction, the Provisional Government had at least enjoyed some claim to political legitimacy. Most educated Russians saw the Bolsheviks as demagogic rabble-rousers. For instance, a history professor's diary from this period refers to the "gorillas" and "dog deputies" who had usurped the power of the state by force and in defiance of prevailing legal norms.[8] The weeks after the October Revolution were punctuated by waves of strikes and skirmishes between Bolshevik forces and those who opposed their takeover. In Moscow municipal employees went on strike, as did troupes at the state theaters in both capitals.[9] Teachers across the nation refused to work. The universities issued public condemnations of the coup and strident declarations of nonrecognition of the new government.[10] Faculty at the conservatories shared many of the objections articulated by colleagues at other educational institutions and the theaters. But musicians' initial response to the revolution and the developments at the conservatories in the first months of Soviet power indicate how the experiences of musicians would both overlap with and diverge from those of other artists and intellectuals.

Conservatory faculty responded to the revolution much more cautiously than their colleagues at the universities, initially asserting that the conservatories' activities were completely separate from the course of daily life and politics. The faculty council at the Petrograd Conservatory resolved that it would "take no position" on the change in government until it became clear what impact developments in "external life" (*vneshnaia zhizn'*) would have on academic affairs.[11] In Moscow, where the Bolshevik takeover was much more protracted and bloody than in Petrograd, civil unrest closed the conservatory temporarily; two weeks after the revolution, however, the faculty voted to resume classes. On November 25, the day before university professors in Petrograd condemned the Bolshevik takeover as a "calamity," three professors of the Moscow Conservatory held a Bach concert in the school's small recital hall.

Since their founding by Anton and Nikolai Rubinstein in the 1860s, the conservatories had been administered by the Russian Musical Society and a board of directors appointed by the imperial court. Throughout the prerevolutionary period faculty had sought both institutional autonomy and recognition of the professional objectives of conservatory training. The latter quest was part of an ongoing effort to dispel widely held perceptions of musicians as entertainers and music education as a pursuit for "amateur" music lovers, in order to legitimize the place of the professional composer and musician in Russian society.[12]

In some ways, the initial gains toward academic self-rule won after the 1905 Revolution appeared to be broadened in the decree nationalizing both conservatories on July 12, 1918. Ratified by the Council of People's Commissars (Sovnarkom) and signed by Lenin himself, the decree made the conservatories completely independent of the Russian Musical Society but placed them under the direct administration of Narkompros as Institutions of Higher Education (*Vysshye uchebnye zavedeniia* [VUZy]).[13] In two important respects the decree represented a positive development for the conservatory faculty. It relieved them from the jurisdiction of the Russian Musical Society, thus implicitly suggesting the possibility of more autonomy, and it clearly indicated that the new government regarded the conservatories as VUZy, supporting musicians' long-standing efforts to gain recognition as professionals.

But the decree raised alarm as well as anticipation. The most obvious way that "external life" did in fact affect the conservatories was that the Soviet government now held the only purse strings. Like university professors, whose initial dealings with the government had raised anxieties, conservatory faculty noted the Bolsheviks' professed hostility to "bourgeois" institutions such as universities and worried about their intent to open up higher education to Russia's "dark" masses.[14] Concerned about the implications of the July 12 decree, a group of conservatory professors headed by Glazunov asked the head of Narkompros, Anatoly Lunacharsky, to clarify the conservatories' relationship with Soviet power and the extent of Narkompros's authority over their internal affairs. Lunacharsky's response reflected both his commitment to accommodating and winning over the artistic intelligentsia and his role as an agent of the new government. The commissar expressed firm support for "complete autonomy" in academic life, emphasizing how highly he valued the expertise of musical "specialists" and the rights of the conservatory faculty to appoint their own director and other teaching staff. Offering a warning as well as reassurance, though, he insisted that, like the universities, the conservatories must recognize the government's need for some measure of control over educational reform at that pivotal moment. He asserted the Commissariat's right to "regulate" faculty appointments and participate in the drafting of new charters and curricula.[15]

As institutions of higher education, the conservatories were affected directly by the new government's next major reform of higher education. In an effort to democratize access to higher education, on August 2 Sovnarkom opened VUZ admissions to anyone age sixteen or over, and abolished all entrance examinations, requirements for secondary diplomas, and tuition. This decree provoked a storm of protest from the universities; the implications of eliminating virtually all entrance requirements for admissions especially alarmed conservatory faculty.[16] A delegation from the Petrograd conservatory appealed to Lunacharsky, who personally drafted a supplementary order allowing the conservatories in Moscow and Petrograd to admit "only talented individuals."[17] This dispensation nullified the intended impact of the decree, turning a potentially disastrous measure into a boon for the conservatories. Able to maintain admissions standards and freed of the obligation to admit untalented or marginal pupils just because they could afford tuition, the conservatories used the decree to help realize long-standing ambitions to make music education more professional.

Taken together, the decree nationalizing the conservatories and Lunacharsky's support for admissions based on ability illuminate a key dynamic in the evolving relationship between the conservatories and the state bureaucracy. The conservatories' concern to protect institutional autonomy and the special interests of musical education often clashed with the new state's goal of creating a unified, integrated educational system that would meet the needs of post-revolutionary Russia. Though the summer of 1918 would prove to be the high-water mark for Communist toleration of "bourgeois" higher education and willingness to consider autonomy for the universities, the musicians in charge of the conservatories would continue to be able to use widely held assumptions about the ways in which music and music education were "exceptional" to maintain more control over their affairs than the universities and other VUZy.

The delicacy with which Lunacharsky facilitated the conservatories' transition to Soviet rule characterized many of his dealings with musicians and other members of the intelligentsia. Equal parts playwright, literary critic, philosopher, and revolutionary, Lunacharsky was uniquely suited to his post as head of Narkompros. He was married to an actress and had close ties with many luminaries of the artistic world. Before the revolution he had been a main contributor to debates within the Party over "god-building," an attempt to marry Marxism with religion, siding with his brother-in-law Aleksandr Bogdanov in Bogdanov's debates with Lenin over the nature of proletarian culture.

Scholars rightly emphasize the role of this self-described "poet of the revolution" as a Party "specialist" rather than a Party leader, as well as the relative weakness of Lunacharsky's commissariat vis-à-vis other Soviet institutions.[18] Certainly his association with Bogdanov's "Left Bolshevism" hamstrung whatever leadership aspirations Lunacharsky may have had, and his sensitivity to the interests of artists and intellectuals gave his peers ample ammunition to criticize his overly sympathetic treatment of the intelligentsia. Nonetheless, Lunacharsky did have considerable latitude in overseeing cultural affairs, in part because his artistic and aesthetic preferences largely overlapped with Lenin's. He shared both Lenin's unabashed appreciation for Russia's cultural heritage and his interest in preserving it.[19] And like Lenin he placed education and "raising" the cultural level of the Russian people at the center of his vision for cultural change. Lunacharsky's authority over music was much less contested than in other spheres, and his influence was thus more profound in that arena. Welcoming the early support of the artistic avant-garde, he encouraged the efforts of radicals such as the poet Vladimir Mayakovsky and the architect and designer Vladimir Tatlin in hopes that the artistic and political revolutions might fuel each other. But Lunacharsky also proved adept at enlisting the aid of qualified, respected musicians, thus giving them a stake in the new order as well.

As the encounter between Glazunov's delegation and Lunacharsky suggests, the commissar's initial efforts to establish working relations with musicians, sensitive as they were in some respects, ran up against suspicion and indifference in generous measure. After failing to enlist Koussevitzky, whose artistic prestige and administrative skills would have been tremendous assets to his fledging arts administration, Lunacharsky turned to Arthur Lourié to head the newly-formed music department of Narkompros. Lourié was a twenty-five-year-old composer and self-proclaimed futurist with no administrative experience or broad-based authority in the musical community, whose appointment reflects the fact that initially only artistic radicals were willing to work with Lunacharsky.[20] Long vilified by Soviet scholars, and famous in the West for his associations with the futurists and his prewar experiments with microtones and graphic notation, Lourié was friendly with the acmeist poets Osip Mandel'shtam and Anna Akhmatova and the symbolist Alexander Blok.[21] He shared both Blok's mysticism and his equation of revolutionary chaos with "the spirit of music," which initially prompted him to support Bolshevik rule: "You see, this historical process [the revolution] in its entirety was 'music.' It was the agitated element, dark and turgid, which cast up on the shores of life that which was hidden in the abyss of its chaos let loose."[22] Although a contemporary described him as "seemingly exhausted by an excess of culture," Lourié devoted considerable energy to a number of pet projects, including proposals to replace the conservatories with "musical universities" and the aggressive promotion of his own music.[23] Perhaps provoked by Lourié's signature outfit—a bright green suit with huge buttons and an enormous turned-down collar—more staid interests in the musical community resisted the young composer's enthusiasm for radical change and soon seized the opportunity to challenge his authority.[24]

However suspicious they were of Bolshevik motives, many musicians soon joined the efforts to reconstruct musical life that began in the first months following the revolution. Lunacharsky's commissariat rapidly mushroomed in size and organizational complexity, as did Muzo, the music division, which soon formed departments for general and special education, as well as several subdepartments.[25] From an initial staff of twelve in July 1918, Muzo's personnel ballooned to 117 in 1919, and to 184 with an additional 600 to 784 persons "in its jurisdiction" (*podvedomstvennye*) in 1921.[26] The majority of Muzo's activities were coordinated from Moscow, where Narkompros was based after the transfer of the capital from Petrograd in March 1918. A smaller, relatively autonomous division of Muzo continued to operate in Petrograd until May 1921. While the organizational history of Muzo may seem unglamorous, its existence provided musicians with essential resources and opportunities. It enabled them to take an active role in the nationalization, reorganization, and administration of existing institutions and activities, and also provided a forum in which they could pursue creative agendas formed before the revolution. The division's statute for 1918 claimed responsibility for "organizing, regulating and administrating the musical life of the whole country."[27] This authority certainly remained more theoretical than actual in many areas; nonetheless, the scope of the division's activities was impressive.[28]

Muzo oversaw the nationalization of several musical institutions, and established new copyright regulations for music. Although nationalization always involved renaming and frequently entailed restructuring, its continuity, in terms of personnel and activity from prerevolutionary organizations, often was pronounced. Aleksandr Kastal'skii (1856–1926), a distinguished composer of sacred music, was a leading figure in Muzo as well as Proletkul't. He had directed the Moscow Synodal School since 1910, and remained in charge of the newly-organized People's Choral Academy when it merged with one of the choirs of the former Imperial Chapel. The Music and Drama School of the Moscow Philharmonic, which had trained orchestral musicians and actors under the tsars, was reorganized by Muzo and the Commissariat's theater department, into a VUZ known since 1922 as the State Institute for Theatrical Arts.[29] The new State Music Publishing House was established on the premises of Jurgenson's Music Publisher, using the inventory of that firm as well as that of Koussevitzky's Russian Music Press. Koussevitzky's former business manager and artistic director, Pavel Lamm (1882–1951), an early staff member of Muzo, became the director of the new publishing house.[30]

In some cases, the revolution even provided an opportunity to realize objectives defined in the prerevolutionary period. The veneration of science (*nauka*) that so obsessed the academic intelligentsia at the turn of the century had preoccupied musicians as well, informing efforts to institutionalize the study of music theory and musicology in Russia.[31] Although practical subjects such as the theory of composition were taught at the conservatories, debates about the definition and methodologies of what was called "musical science" took place in extramural organizations such as the Musical Scientific Society, founded in 1902 under the leadership of Sergei Taneev. The society amassed the first substantial library of musicological work in Russia, and hoped to found a research institution dedicated to the study of musical science.

Before the revolution, research on music theory had proceeded from Taneev's own study of counterpoint and Boleslav Iavorskii's (1877–1942) modal analysis.[32] While Taneev's work looked back to established practice,

Iavorskii's approach emerged, in part, as a response to impressionism and Scriabin's late style. His theory of "modal rhythm" sought to explain all melodic, harmonic, and rhythmic development in music in terms of the inherent instability of the tritone (the augmented fourth or diminished fifth, e.g., C and F-sharp) and its need to resolve to a more consonant interval (the third or sixth). The dissolution of conventional tonality in late nineteenth-century music, and the possibilities suggested by Scriabin's use of the "mystic chord" (C, F-sharp, B-flat, E, A, D) as an organizing device, inspired other researchers such as Leonid Sabaneev (1881–1968) and Arsenii Avraamov (1886–1944) to explore the potential for new and expanded tone systems.

Much of this work ceased during World War I, but after Narkompros moved to Moscow in 1918, surviving members of the Musical Scientific Society formed the core of Muzo's newly-established "academic subsection" (Ak Muzo).[33] It met in the reading room of the old society's library, and the group's secretary, Mikhail Ivanov-Boretskii (1874–1936), recalled that Ak Muzo even observed the meeting time of its organizational predecessor.[34] Despite considerable material difficulties, Ak Muzo became a bustling center for research in music theory, acoustics, aesthetics, and ethnomusicology. Leonid Sabaneev continued to explore the possibilities of what he called "ultrachromaticism," a nebulously defined fifty-three-step alternative to the twelve-tone scale. In a related field, Nikolai Garbuzov (1880–1956) resumed his research on the acoustic bases of harmony. Meanwhile, the ethnography department attracted the most distinguished ethnomusicologists in the country.[35] When Narkompros was reorganized in 1921, this group was able to create a permanent institutional framework for its activities by reconstituting Ak Muzo as Russia's first full-fledged institute of musical science, known by the acronym GIMN (*Gosudarstvennyi Institut Muzykal'nykh Nauk*).[36]

Among the most influential figures in Muzo was Nadezhda Briusova (1881–1951), who headed both the general and special education sections. Sister of the symbolist poet Valerii Briusov and an ardent supporter of the revolution, Briusova had been an active participant in the People's Conservatory and the prerevolutionary adult education movement. Briusova, who had studied with Iavorskii, now found herself well positioned to influence reforms at the conservatory and in popular music education. She especially wanted to create facilities to train general music teachers and promote popular courses to teach people how to appreciate and respond to classical music. The curriculum and repertoire for these programs relied heavily on Iavorskii's pedagogical method of "listening to music" (*slushanie muzyki*), emphasizing choral singing and folk music.[37] By 1920, seven schools of general music education had been established in Moscow and twenty-five in other cities. The premier school of this type in Moscow was named after Taneev in honor of his long service to the cause of popular music education.

In addition to Narkompros programs, musicians took part in a number of popular educational and "enlightenment" programs for workers during the Civil War. Most extensive were the concert programs and choral studios sponsored by the Red Army, the Moscow and Petrograd Soviets, and above all, the wide network of "proletarian culture" organizations that emerged in the first weeks after the February Revolution. With significant financial support from the Soviet government, Proletkul't, as these organizations were called collectively, expanded its activities throughout the Civil War. By the fall of 1920, as many as 400,000 people participated in Proletkul't theater groups, music studios, artistic workshops, and reading circles across the country. In terms of music, Moscow alone boasted seventeen choral studios as well as a scientific-technical division dedicated to researching a variety of theoretical issues.[38]

Narkompros and Proletkul't provided a forum for musicians to pursue their scholarly and educational interests, but the practical incentives for working for the Soviet state were often equally compelling. The wages and, more importantly, rations from this kind of employment offered musicians some buffer against the difficult living conditions and food shortages that plagued civil war Russia in general and social groups identified as "privileged" under the tsarist regime in particular.[39] Although rationing systems during the Civil War were intended to favor those in whose name the revolution had been won, most academics and employees of Narkompros received more generous allocations than others with similar class backgrounds or occupations.[40] Muzo's rosters indicate that 149 musicians and main coworkers (*otvetstvennye sotrudniki*) were receiving these "academic" rations in February 1921.[41] Wages and rations were also a critical part of intellectuals' attraction to Proletkul't.[42]

Though Lourié later recalled that art took the place of bread in these years, many performers found that their art gave them access to the staples they needed to survive. Chaliapin often insisted that his performance fee be paid in flour and eggs.[43] Pianist Aleksandr Borovskii (1889–1968), who performed for workers and soldiers in the early months of 1918, described the groceries he received as compensation for these recitals as "worth their weight in gold,"[44] and Piatnitsky's peasant choir would perform in exchange for Red Army rations and transportation to the concert.[45] Even those fortunate enough to receive "academic" rations were still preoccupied with finding enough to eat.[46] In May 1920, an obviously exasperated Ippolitov-Ivanov lamented that he would have to miss the opening ceremonies of the new Tchaikovsky museum in order to obtain ration supplements for the conservatory faculty. "If I don't attend to this, it will be me instead of the ration that gets eaten," he declared.[47]

Even for those who "cooperated" with the new government, the civil war years were marked by inevitable and often humbling conflicts between musicians, who belonged to previously privileged social groups, and a regime committed to vanquishing "bourgeois" opponents in a country without a powerful bourgeoisie. Sheila Fitzpatrick and others have identified the importance of the slippery and mutable nature of social identity to understanding the early Soviet period, when a ruling order intent on evaluating its constituency based on rigid conceptions about social class first engaged a complex society where socioeconomic position was not necessarily a reliable litmus test of loyalty and support.[48]

Explicit defiance of Bolshevik authority was rare among musicians, but in many instances their presumed or actual affiliation with forces hostile to the revolution made them the target of measures intended to demoralize Bolshevism's "enemies" and redress past injustices.[49] When Nikolai Miaskovskii (1881–1950), who had abandoned his career as a naval officer to be a composer, was treated like a member of the "exploiting classes" and arrested for refusing to shovel snow in 1921, Muzo canceled a concert in protest.[50] In other cases, association with agencies of Soviet power offered musicians protection from having domiciles and personal property requisitioned, and could even provide access to "treasures" expropriated from others. A graduate of the Corp of Cadets, the music critic and promoter of contemporary music Vladimir Derzhanovskii (1881–1942), was able to keep his spacious five-room apartment (he did have to give one room to his cook) because he worked in both the publication and education sections of Muzo.[51] As head of Muzo's string quartet, Lev Tseitlin received "lifelong" use of a Guarneri violin from the State Ancient String Instrument Collection, a store of rare string instruments confiscated from nobility and émigrés.[52] Chaliapin, who frequently performed for workers and soldiers, marveled at the contradictory experiences of being "bourgeois" on the one hand, which made his wine cellar and silver fair game for requisitioning brigades, and on the other hand a tremendously popular singer, whose fame as an icon of "bourgeois" culture saved him from harsher treatment, opening the doors of even Lev Kamenev and Lenin to his pleas—sometimes successfully.[53]

Music for the Civil War

Like most other Russians, musicians' primary concerns during the civil war years were finding food, staying warm, and coming to terms with Soviet power. Along with establishing working relationships with Russia's new rulers, musicians also had to consider the implications of the revolution for their art. These were by no means self-evident or clearly spelled out. The Bolsheviks came to power with a poorly-detailed cultural agenda, and their energies were consumed by the political, military, and economic challenges of the war. As Marxists, they were committed to restructuring the economic foundations of society in favor of the poorest social groups, the workers and peasants. It was understood that customs would also change, and that the culture of the new socialist society would be different from that of its predecessor. But there was no consensus on how that transformation would come about or on the characteristics of the new culture. Debates over the nature of proletarian culture had divided the Bolsheviks before World War I. Bogdanov and other "left" Bolsheviks believed in the transformative power of ideology and creativity, and insisted that the success of the revolution hinged on the proletariat developing its own ideology, literature, and art. Taking a more materialist approach, Lenin regarded culture as the antipode of "backwardness," something that must be acquired and mastered before a new, genuinely proletarian culture could emerge. Both of these perspectives reappeared after 1917, informing a range of activities and projects intended to bring the revolution to the cultural sphere. The revolutionaries also seized on the mobilizing potential of artistic propaganda, and were unabashed in their convictions that culture and art were valuable weapons in the class struggle.

The imperative for cultural transformation affected musicians as well as other artists, infusing a new political charge into prerevolutionary debates about the trajectory of new music, the nature of popular culture, the value of the classical legacy, and the need for theoretical research. While some musicians tried to carry on their prerevolutionary activities as if nothing had happened, most found themselves caught up at some level in the potentially liberating and democratizing impulses of revolutionary upheaval. Indeed, the most salient images of cultural life during the Civil War include a "frenzy of cultural iconoclasm" as well as "joyous, mass celebrations of the overthrow of the old order."[54] Amidst the frenzy and the joy was an even stronger urge to democratize music and the arts and thus break down barriers between educated Russians and the common people. The revolution inspired musicians and other creative intellectuals to act on long-standing visions of a unified culture, signaling the beginning of a quest for an inclusive art that would breach the divide between elite and popular forms.[55] The mushrooming of popular enlightenment programs in this period was fueled both by the sometimes overlapping but often contradictory objectives of Bolshevik initiatives and by the agendas of the reform-minded intelligentsia. While much of the inclination toward utopianism and iconoclasm would spend itself relatively quickly, the diversity and ambiguity that emerged from musicians' initial efforts to respond to the revolution and from the debates about building "proletarian" culture would continue to inform many of their activities and debates into the twenties.

Proletkul't is often remembered as a hotbed of iconoclasm and revolutionary experimentation because many of its activists embraced Bogdanov's dreams of a unique proletarian culture and his conviction that proletarian consciousness must be cultivated in cultural organizations that operated independently from the political sphere.[56] Scholarship on Soviet music has also emphasized both the amateur and utopian qualities of Proletkul't's broad range of musical activities and the influence of Bogdanov's ideas.[57] But closer inspection reveals a more complex picture of Proletkul't's purview. There was considerable overlap in personnel between Muzo Narkompros, Proletkul't studios, and other organizations. For example, Briusova, Kastal'skii, the composer Reinhold Gliere (1874–1956), and many others worked for both Narkompros and Proletkul't.[58] More importantly, even those committed to creating a distinctly proletarian culture found it difficult to proceed without expert help. To stimulate the emergence of this new culture Proletkul't relied heavily on the expertise and participation of artists and intellectuals whose own agendas and beliefs about cultural change were quite diverse.[59]

Some contributions to proletarian culture did emphasize workers' creativity and the revolutionary struggle. Proponents of what has been called "revolutionary romanticism" encouraged artistic creativity by, for, and about workers, drawing on the images and experiences of modern industrial life and the revolution.[60] Efforts to use music as a mobilizing device to further the revolutionary cause were particularly pronounced in the musical activities in the Tambov Proletkul't. In a stunning gesture of putting new wine into old skins Dmitrii Vasil'ev-Buglai (1888–1956) used members of a former church choir as the foundation for a ninety-voice Proletkul't chorus that toured the front lines agitating for the Bolshevik cause. A graduate of the Moscow Synodal School, Vasil'ev-Buglai used the melodic conventions of liturgical music and traditional folk songs for the agitational and antireligious songs and skits that made up his choir's repertoire.[61]

In Petrograd, the Latvian composer Ianis Ozolin' gave "revolutionary hymns" a central place in the repertoire of the seventy-voice choir he directed.[62] Using the texts of popular Proletkul't poems, such as Vladimir Kirillov's *May Day* (*Pervyi Mai*) and Aleksandr Pomorskii's *The Workers' Palace* (*Rabochii dvorets*), these hymns portrayed a future of grandeur and prosperity built from the rubble of oppression:

> On the dark graves,
> From the roadbed of the Past,
> From the laughter and tears of exhausted hearts,—
> We, the proud ones will build, we, the proud ones will build,
> We will build a Workers' Palace![63]

Kirillov anticipated that these songs were but the first manifestations of a new musical culture: "soon a symphony of labor will ring out, in which the voices of machines, sirens and motors will join in one chorus with the voices of victorious workers."[64]

A second approach to creating proletarian culture promoted avant-garde efforts to break completely with the bourgeois art of the past and find new forms and methods of artistic expression. The possibility of effecting a radical break in cultural forms informed many Proletkul't activities, but was nowhere more apparent than in the theoretical and applied experiments of the theorist Arsenii Avraamov. A graduate of the Music and Drama School of the Moscow Philharmonic Society, Avraamov had been an active participant in both the People's Conservatory and the prerevolutionary debates on chromaticism and the theoretical implications of Scriabin's late style. His work with folk music from the North Caucasus and his assessment of postromantic Western art music led him to investigate alternatives to the traditional twelve-tone tempered scale. The political message of the revolution resonated strongly with his music theories. In 1920, Avraamov reportedly asked Narkompros to confiscate and demolish all pianos as a necessary first step in destroying bourgeois music and the twelve-tone tempered scale.[65] Although this summons went unanswered, he continued to explore alternatives to conventional tone systems during the Civil War. In the technical section of the Moscow Proletkul't's music division, he worked on developing a 17-step tone system with Nikolai Roslavets, and collaborated with Grigorii Liubimov (1882–1934) to develop new tunings for traditional folk instruments and the accordion.[66]

Certainly the most striking of Avraamov's projects was his organization of "symphonies of factory whistles." Inspired by the poetry of Aleksei Gastev, who heard the "song of the future" in the morning calls of city factory whistles, these ambitious experiments exemplified the veneration for technology and the desire to marry it with art that marked many creative endeavors of leftist artists. Avraamov seized on the whistles, horns, and sirens of the modern city as a potential "orchestra" for a new form of mass music. Rejecting the spatial and technical limitations of the "chamber music" of the past, he identified factory whistles as the ideal medium for transforming an entire city into an auditorium. After unsuccessful efforts in Petrograd (1918) and Nizhnyi (1919), Avraamov oversaw a spectacular "multimedia" celebration of the fifth anniversary of the revolution in the Baku harbor on November 7, 1922. The "symphony" used the sirens and whistles of navy ships and steamers, as well as dockside shunting engines, a "choir" of bus and car horns, and a machine gun battery, to evoke the alarm, struggle, and victory of 1917.[67] Cannon blasts and flag directions from a strategically placed signal tower coordinated renditions of *The Warsaw Song* (*Varshavianka*), *The Internationale*, and *The Marseillaise* by these "instruments," a two-hundred-piece band and choir, and a large "whistle main" (*magistral'*) situated on the deck of a torpedo boat (see Fig. 1). The *magistral'* was Avraamov's own creation—a portable "organ register" of whistles, each individually controlled, but working from a common source of steam.[68]

Avraamov's "industrial" iconoclasm and the agitational songs of Vasil'ev-Buglai seem emblematic of an era of revolutionary change, but they did not typify the main thrust of musical activities during the civil war years. Most of the musical programs sponsored by Proletkul't and Narkompros were marked by a preservationist, culturalist ethos consistent with prerevolutionary efforts by educated Russians to use music as a means of developing the aesthetic sensibilities and "raising" the cultural level of the Russian people. Longings for a unified culture that was constructed and imposed from above inspired a range of activities reformers themselves described as *kul'turtregerstvo* ("bringing culture").[69] The hope that art could overcome divisions within Russian society figured prominently in Muzo's declaration of its main tasks: "to break down the walls between professional musicians and the people" and to "join the masses . . . who are pining for music in the depths of their soul."[70]

Yet many Communists active in Proletkul't and the cultural organizations of the Red Army objected to *kul'turtregerstvo* (and its Russified variant, *kul'turnichestvo*) as the ill-conceived project of bourgeois intellectuals who wanted only to bring the treasures of elite culture to uneducated workers and peasants without also engaging in political agitation. Continuing a critique formulated in the prerevolutionary adult education movement, militant activists opposed "abstract

Fig. 1 Symphony of Factory Whistles. Artist's rendition of the Baku Symphony of Factory Whistles and *Magistral'*, 1922. *Gorn* 9 (1923): 110, 113.

enlightenment activity" and "culture for culture's sake" as the remnants of Liberal and Populist agendas that denied the need for education in the class struggle.[71] Tensions between proponents of "education," "enlightenment," and "agitation" would be a critical issue in the reorganization of Narkompros and the creation of Glavpolitprosvet in 1920, a new state agency charged specifically with political enlightenment work. Criticism of *kul'turtregerstvo* by musicians, however, was fairly weak. During the first years of Bolshevik rule the notion of "bringing culture" informed many agendas and cut across other political and aesthetic divisions.

The peasant folk song, the traditions of Western and Russian art music, and training in choral singing occupied a central place in most Narkompros programs. Veterans of the People's Conservatory, such as Nadezhda Briusova and Aleksandr Kastal'skii, used folk songs as the basic repertoire not only for choral training, but for music education as a whole.[72] Kastal'skii maintained that the folk song's "melodic freshness of musical thought" and organic connection to the "people" (*narod*) would help workers understand the rudiments of rhythmic and melodic development.[73] Likewise, the lecture-concert program developed by Sergei Evseev's (1894–1956) chamber ensemble for Red Army audiences was called "Russian Folk Life and Its Reflection in Song."[74]

In a similar vein, Grigorii Liubimov, a veteran of the revolutionary underground and former pupil of Koussevitzky, had begun promoting the domra, a long-necked lute beloved by minstrels in medieval Russia, in conjunction with his activities in workers' education before the revolution. He considered the four-stringed domra to have superior tone quality and range to the modernized balalaikas and three-stringed domras popularized by Vasilii Andreev.[75] As the head of the folk music section of the Moscow Proletkul't, Liubimov promoted "his" domras, which were tuned like the bowed stringed instruments of the classical orchestra but were much easier to play, as ideal vehicles for disseminating music among the masses.

Activists like Liubimov, Briusova, and Kastal'skii considered an appreciation of folk music an ideal foundation on which to develop people's musical sensibilities. From this base, they would then proceed to "more complex" examples of Russian and Western "cultured" (*kul'turnaia*) music.[76] Liubimov hoped that gaining proficiency on his domras would make it easier for workers to learn to play "serious" instruments like the violin.[77] A commitment to teaching workers to appreciate the cultural heritage of the prerevolutionary elite marked many other musical activities of the Moscow Proletkul't. The approved concert repertoire for workers' clubs featured compositions by Bach, Beethoven, Chopin, the German Romantics, Mikhail Glinka, and Aleksandr

Dargomyzhskii, as well as Russian folk songs.[78] Piano lessons and lectures on music history were popular components of a wide array of programs, as was instruction on the domra and other folk instruments. While some efforts to cultivate an appreciation for classical music were almost offensively naive, such as a brochure by Lourié describing an orchestra as "gatherings where lots of musicians play different instruments amicably,"[79] this approach was not the norm. Lunacharsky, who instituted weekly "people's concerts" in Petrograd, exemplified a more typical orientation by insisting that the programs for these events evolve not from "poor" to "good" musical examples, but from "the beautiful but simple to the more beautiful and complex."[80]

Musicians' efforts to make classical music more accessible took many forms. During the Civil War, concert-lectures, which had strong antecedents in the prerevolutionary period, were the most ubiquitous method of *kul'turtregerstvo*. The spoken introductions that preceded these musical performances allowed the speaker to tell audiences how they should listen and respond to the music they were about to hear. The concert-lecture format was used extensively by Proletkul't, Narkompros, and a myriad of official and semiofficial musical ensembles that performed for untutored and unconventional audiences. Some of these presentations, such as the one titled "Spring: How Freedom Began in the Life of Humanity," reflected musicians' perceptions of the liberating, creative potential of the revolution.[81] Others, including those sponsored by the Petrograd Proletkul't with titles like "Beethoven and French Music" and "Russian Composers before Glinka," offered workers a more straightforward introduction to the classical musical tradition in Russia and Western Europe.[82] Given the ambiguity and subjectivity inherent in musical interpretation, the concert-lecture would become a standard feature of musical life in the early Soviet period because it offered a rare, but potentially significant, opportunity to tell audiences what the music they were about to hear "meant."

Underpinning the agenda of *kul'turtregerstvo*, with its emphasis on traditional folk songs and classical music, was a deep-seated hostility to popular urban music and cultural forms intellectuals scorned as "bourgeois." Most musicians felt that bringing "culture" to the people involved the active promotion of certain kinds of music over others. In particular, they objected to most urban popular music, especially *tsyganshchina* and the music of the variety stage. A singer at the Bol'shoi Theater insisted that workers needed "good" music and "real" concerts, rather than "those mixed divertissements where the classics were performed alternately with the accordion."[83] In the spring of 1920, the concert section of Muzo tried to secure a "monopoly" on concerts in Moscow as a way to eliminate the "hackwork" of these "variety" concerts.[84]

Liubimov railed against the petit-bourgeois (*meshchanskie*) songs and the "pot-pourris" from popular operas in the balalaika repertoire disseminated by Vasilii Andreev.[85] Other Proletkul't activists shared Liubimov's conviction that it was their duty to select and cultivate only the truly "healthy" elements of the musical legacy and the current musical culture. At the first Proletkul't conference in September 1918, Boris Krasin insisted that to help the proletariat "master the musical achievements of humanity" workers should be introduced to the "best" examples of musical creativity from the past, as well as the Russian folk song. But at the same time a struggle must be launched against the influence of musical "surrogates," such as the "anti-artistic music of restaurants, cabarets, gypsy music, and so on." In this campaign against truly decadent "bourgeois" music, Krasin saw himself as the guardian and protector of the proletariat, whose undeveloped musical tastes were vulnerable to exploitation. In a critique that foreshadowed one main issue in debates in the twenties he even found the "revolutionary music" of the Petrograd Proletkul't suspect, complaining that "[w]riters of revolutionary songs too often write revolutionary words to the most banal tunes."[86]

Other bearers of culture worried that artistic modernism also threatened to corrupt the masses. Weeks after the October Revolution, Kastal'skii asked the government to preserve and promote folk art in order to protect "the people from modernist and futurist distortions of artistic taste."[87] He championed traditional folk songs as the foundation of proletarian musical culture because they were more accessible to "the toiling masses" than the "modish chromatic delicacies" served up by "our exhausted artistic epicures."[88]

As Lynn Mally has suggested, the conflicting strategies and approaches to developing "proletarian culture" pursued in Proletkul't studios were a source both of dissent among the movement's organizers and of Proletkul't's popularity with workers.[89] The variety of work pursued in the music studios was remarkable, defying simple categorization, even for the work of certain individuals. For example, the "modern," "industrial" iconoclasm of Avraamov was anchored in a deep and sophisticated appreciation for traditional folk music. His research with Liubimov on retuning the domra fostered at the same time the development of new means of musical expression and the cultivation of an instrument inextricably bound to the antiquated, or "feudal," social and economic structures of the peasantry. Nor were the "revolutionary romantics" in Petrograd purists. The same organization that promoted "revolutionary hymns" and strolling choirs as the true expression of workers' creativity also sponsored concert-lecture series to train working-class audiences to appreciate the elite musical culture of the past.

The contradictions within and between various visions of cultural change, as well as the new state's reluctance to sweep away the old culture in its quest for a new one, go far in explaining the eclecticism, somewhat chaotic improvisation, and utilization of particularly resonant examples from the musical legacy of the past that characterized many efforts to address the revolution with music during the Civil War. Transgressing and redefining spatial hierarchies were central not only to visions of revolutionary theater and mass spectacle, but also to efforts to democratize classical music.[90] This involved bringing the masses to previously sacred "temples" such as the concert halls in Moscow and Petrograd, and even the Hall of Arms in the Winter Palace, where a concert commemorating the first anniversary of the revolution included Stravinsky's *Firebird Suite*, a revolutionary hymn composed by Chaliapin, and Lourié's *Our March* (*Nash Marsh*)—a spoken declamation of Mayakovsky's poem with band accompaniment. But extraordinary efforts also went into bringing music to the masses with concerts in working-class neighborhoods, army barracks, riding schools, and cafeterias. Following Mayakovsky's poetic summons and Avraamov's wishes, many pianos were requisitioned from their owners and dragged "out onto the streets," where they were loaded up onto a cart carrying a singer, a pianist, and perhaps more instrumentalists.[91] Rather than being smashed as a step toward destroying bourgeois music, the newly mobile pianos helped bring it to workers and soldiers.

Unlike the concert in the Winter Palace, the repertoire for most programs relied heavily on classics from the Russian and European repertoire. In contrast to the visual arts, where the revolution inspired a genuine flood of creativity, few original musical works appeared during the Civil War.[92] Musical offerings to audiences of this period were incredibly diverse, but from the first days of Soviet power, Beethoven's and Mozart's music was identified with the spirit of the revolution. Beethoven's works were staples on programs for the musical celebrations and popular concerts organized by Narkompros, the Moscow Soviet, the Commissariat of War, and various Trade Union organizations.[93] And the exultant refrains of the *Ode to Joy* and the heroic passion of the Third and Fifth Symphonies elicited enthusiastic responses from listeners of all social backgrounds.

While Bolshevik hostility to organized religion made sacred and liturgical music politically suspect, religious music not tied explicitly to the Orthodox church provided the solemnity and ritual mystique needed to legitimize the new regime. Beginning with the May Day festivities of 1918, Mozart's *Requiem* became de rigueur in commemorations honoring revolutionary martyrs. The piece made an "indelible" impression on the deputies of the Petrograd Soviet who listened raptly to its performance in Party headquarters on the first anniversary of the revolution.[94]

The eclecticism of concert programming in these years reflected the multiple and often contradictory agendas within the musical community. But it also indicated a lack of consensus on what "the revolution" meant. Indeed, this was one of the key issues of the Civil War. As part of the "symbolic language of the revolution," certain songs became standard features in concert programs.[95] Music had played an important role in the revolution since the fall of the autocracy. Singing had united demonstrators in 1917, and specific songs became revolutionary symbols that transcended Party divisions.[96] During the Civil War, the performance of these songs demonstrated solidarity with the revolutionary cause, even if the nature of that cause was contested.

Ironically, few of these songs were new, although new revolutionary texts were often set to old melodies. Those songs with the most valence and popularity came from either old Russian popular culture or the revolutionary underground. Whereas the abstract nature of instrumental music left its content open to debate, lyrics made the meaning of songs more concrete. Many of the most frequently performed songs came from the international revolutionary movement.[97] These included the Polish *Warsaw Song* (*Varshavianka*), with its intense martial rhythm and dramatic call "to bloody battle, holy and righteous," and *The Red Banner* (*Krasnoe znamia*), which came to Russia by way of Switzerland and France, and was sometimes sung in Polish. Of the songs distinctly associated with the Russian revolutionary underground, the jaunty determination of *Boldly, Comrades, in Step* (*Smelo, tovarishchi, v nogu*) was among the most commonly heard, together with the haunting lyricism of *You Fell Victim* (*Vy zhertroia pali*), the lament sung to honor those who died fighting for the revolution. Concert programs also regularly featured old Russian songs about hardship and rebellion, such as *Sten'ka Razin*, a ballad lauding the exploits of the seventeenth-century Cossack rebel, *The Cudgel* (*Dubinushka*), an homage to hard labor that had been the most popular protest song during the 1905 Revolution, and the melancholy barge haulers' songs, *We Cry Out* (*Ei, ukhnem*).

The search for a new national anthem also highlights the ambiguities of the revolution and the importance of Western influence on early Soviet culture. Both main contenders came from France, suggesting a larger emulation of symbolic traditions associated with the French Revolution, as well as conscious efforts to appropriate the traditions of the international revolutionary movement. *The Marseillaise* had emerged as the anthem of the February Revolution. Sung by crowds denouncing the tsar, it was performed at all official events, as well as at funerals and before theater performances after the overthrow of the autocracy. The original French anthem appealed to "citizens" for national unity and patriotism. But the form of the song common in Russia after February was often identified as the "*Workers' Marseillaise.*" It was slower, and followed a slightly different rhythm from the French original. Its lyrics clearly identified it as a song of social protest that summoned "working people" and called for a destruction of the "parasites" and the "vampire-tsar."[98]

Lenin disliked the *Workers' Marseillaise* due to its association with the "bourgeois" French republic and the Provisional Government. He preferred *The Internationale*, the anthem of the European socialist movement written by Pierre Degeyter to commemorate the French Commune of 1871. *The Internationale* was relatively unknown in Russia before 1917, but its popularity increased considerably in the months following the February Revolution. The Bolsheviks, as well as other socialist parties, embraced the song's insurrectionary call to "arise, you wretched of the earth" as well as its messianic promise that "we have the right to rule the earth."

At Lenin's initiative, *The Internationale* became the new state's national anthem in the summer of 1918. Kastal'skii completed an arrangement of the piece for mixed chorus within weeks of the October Revolution, which was published early the following year. Whereas Degeyter's song was originally written as a jaunty march in 2/4 tempo, the Russified version of the piece was slower and more solemn.[99] By the first anniversary of the revolution, the bells in the Kremlin tower that had chimed *God Save the Tsar* and the Orthodox hymn *Kol' slaven* for the Romanovs had been reset to play *The Internationale* and the revolutionary funeral march *You Fell Victim.*[100] But both anthems continued to be performed. A concert sponsored by the Moscow Proletkul't commemorating the first anniversary of the revolution featured a domra ensemble and choir directed by Liubimov that performed *The Internationale*, *The Marseillaise*, and *Boldly, Comrades, in Step*, as well as folk songs.[101]

Numerous accounts reveal that whatever the program, audiences in these years were diverse and appreciative. Years later, Leonid Sabaneev recalled that despite the terrible cold in the concert halls, and despite the wants and hunger of the musicians, musical performances somehow flowered nonetheless.[102] Recognizing the positive effect that music had on popular morale, Lenin thwarted efforts to close the theaters in Moscow during the heating crisis of 1919.[103] Soldiers listened raptly to Chaliapin, even when he performed in an unheated riding hall. And concerts at the Moscow Conservatory were always well attended, although everyone, including the conductor, kept their coats and hats on. For audiences and performers, music was eagerly devoured soul food in times of physical hunger and terrible hardship.

Consolidation and the Transition to Peace

By the fall of 1920 it became clear that the Bolsheviks would win the Civil War. Having vanquished the various forces that mobilized against Soviet power on the battlefield, the Bolsheviks now became more involved in the struggle for the "third" or "cultural" front, where the revolution's enemies were the cultural "backwardness" of the masses and the old intelligentsia.[104] Broad, often contradictory patterns of retreat and consolidation motivated administrative and institutional reforms and the first official pronouncements on cultural policy as the regime began to shift its energies away from immediate military crises and toward the no less daunting challenge of building socialism in peacetime.

After the initial flurry of conferences and decrees in 1918, the Civil War forced the Bolsheviks to shelve plans for reforming higher education. But with peace at hand, a University Charter was issued in 1921 that formally abolished autonomy for these institutions by mandating Party-state appointment of rectors and administrators. Even as the Party took preliminary steps to establish its dominance over the universities, the intelligentsia, and the professoriate, however, the conservatories carried on with little intervention from the government and largely sympathetic treatment from Narkompros.[105] Although the former rectors of the Moscow and Petersburg universities were among the 200 academics deported by the Bolsheviks in August 1922, Ippolitov-Ivanov, like Glazunov in Petrograd, stayed on as the Moscow Conservatory's director.[106] Party members were appointed to the administrative boards of the conservatories, but they had little influence on the institutions' affairs. The first Communists came to the conservatories only in 1920, and Party organizations were not founded there until 1922.

The conservatories thus assumed a position not unlike that of the Academy of Sciences, which retained much of its independence until the late twenties.[107] Obviously the Bolsheviks attached far less significance to the accomplishments of musicians than they did to the expertise of the academics at the Academy of Sciences. But like science and technology, music seemed to be more ideologically neutral than other forms of artistic expression or intellectual endeavor.

The fall of 1920 found Lunacharsky increasingly under fire from influential Party leaders for being too conciliatory toward the old intelligentsia, resisting educational reforms, lavishly subsidizing Proletkul't, and wasting money on the former Imperial theaters to the detriment of the revolutionary and experimental theaters. In November, the Politburo charged Evgraf Litkins with reorganizing Narkompros in order to streamline the bloated bureaucratic apparatus, cut costs, and limit Lunacharsky's influence as much as possible. The work of Litkins's commission and a subsequent commission headed by Iurii Larin cut the number of Narkompros employees by more than half, but also produced a crazy quilt of agencies with conflicting jurisdictions and confused hierarchies.[108] Lunacharsky remained in charge of a commissariat whose financial resources shrank considerably as the government adopted the market-based fiscal policies necessary to restore economic order. The struggles to reform the administrative apparatus for education and the arts ended the autonomy of Proletkul't and produced official statements that became the foundation for cultural policy in the twenties.

Proletkul't's existence as a mass organization essentially independent of state and Party control ended abruptly in December 1920, when it was subordinated to Narkompros and publicly censured by the Central Committee.[109] Many scholars have explained the movement's collapse in terms of the ideological disputes between Lenin and Bogdanov and Proletkul't's endorsement of "futurist" efforts to wholly reject classic artistic traditions and achievements. But as the work of Proletkul't's music divisions suggests, iconoclastic artistic radicalism was by no means the only, or even the dominant, influence shaping Proletkul't activity. Indeed, the diversity and eclecticism of artistic endeavors pursued under Proletkul't auspices largely invalidates the charge of iconoclasm as well as efforts to identify Proletkul't as "Bogdanov's organization."[110] Lynn Mally convincingly argues that the real motivations for subjugating Proletkul't to Party and state organizations were more political than ideological. The movement's insistence on autonomy, its broad base of support among rank-and-file workers, and its theoretical authority over a wide network of cultural and educational organizations made it a potentially formidable source of opposition to a regime still consolidating political control.[111]

Concurrent developments in the music division of Narkompros indicate how important personality could be in the realigning of forces that took place in this period. As the head of Muzo, Arthur Lourié actively promoted the cause of modern music, including his own. Muzo concert programs relied heavily on the works of Scriabin, Ravel, and Debussy, while the publishing subsection used its scarce resources to print Lourié's own compositions, including some that were overtly religious. In fact, auditing agencies suspected corruption in the way the section's financial affairs were handled.[112] Lourié's colleagues complained that he set the programs for Narkompros concerts without consulting them, and that by promoting music for "experienced listeners" he betrayed the department's commitment to make music more accessible to the masses.[113] The young iconoclast's efforts to overhaul music education prompted Ippolitov-Ivanov and Gol'denveizer to complain to Lenin about the "meddlesome" musical commissar.[114] Lourié also antagonized musicians in the newly formed Trade Union of Art Workers (Rabis) by criticizing the low professional standards and petit-bourgeois ideology of orchestral musicians.[115] In the fall of 1920, Rabis launched a noisy campaign against inefficiencies and corruption in the Muzo bureaucracy. In October, Lunacharsky called for a joint meeting of the Narkompros Art Section Collegium and the Rabis leadership. At the same time, the Workers' and Peasants' Inspectorate (Rabkrin) launched a full investigation of Muzo's activities.[116]

The statement that emerged from discussions between Narkompros and Rabis became the cornerstone of official policy in the cultural sphere, retaining considerable validity throughout much of the Soviet period. Drafted by Lunacharsky and Rabis leader Iuvenal Slavinskii, the "Theses on the Bases of Policy in the Area of Art" supported much of the Proletkul't agenda, particularly those elements associated with *kul'turtregerstvo.*[117] The Rabkrin report on Muzo echoed the same concepts in all major respects.[118] Both documents asserted that the proletariat must have all of the past achievements of world art at its disposal and insisted that the art of the future could only be built on the foundations of the past. They called for workers to have access to artistic higher educational institutions, such as the conservatories, as well as amateur musical activities and popular (mass) programs that promoted cultural development. The Rabkrin report even cited Proletkul't concerts as a positive counterpoint to Muzo's programs, which "in no way take into account the demands of the revolutionary moment and revolutionary mood."[119] Both of these documents also suggest a strong preference for a cleansed bourgeois legacy as the basis for the musical culture of the future. The Rabis statement expressed a concern for excising all traces of decadence and depravity as well as the vulgar debris of "boulevard pornography," while the Rabkrin inspector lamented that in the absence of genuine revolutionary hymns the proletariat still relied on popular street songs (*chastushki*).[120]

But although the Rabkrin report and statement on artistic policy endorsed many Proletkul't activities, they rejected all claims to autonomy in artistic affairs. In a temporary measure that was part of a broader struggle to define agendas and delineate bureaucratic turf for the state agencies charged with educational, propaganda, and "enlightenment" activities, the statement on artistic policy placed Rabis and the Narkompros arts sector under the supervision of a newly-formed Party organ, the Main Political Enlightenment Committee (Glavpolitprosvet). For Muzo this was, in part, punishment for not having fulfilled its responsibility to direct musical affairs for the entire republic. The Rabkrin report admonished that Muzo's significance as an "all-republic" organization existed only on paper.[121]

Although the Moscow Proletkul't continued to function, albeit on a significantly reduced scale, after the events of October through December 1920, the majority of musicians working in its music studios joined the music division of Narkompros, forming the core of the musical science institute, GIMN. In the aftermath of Rabkrin's investigation of Lourié's administration, Boris Krasin (1884–1936), who had headed the music studios of the Moscow Proletkul't, became head of the Narkompros music division.[122] Soon after, Lourié joined the musical emigration, moving first to Berlin and then Paris before settling in the United States in 1941.

Krasin never belonged to a political party but had been active in the revolutionary movement since 1905.[123] To his position at Narkompros he brought experience directing choral circles and scholarship in Mongolian folk music, as well as a passion for the newly emerging electronic instruments.[124] He became ubiquitous in the musical bureaucracy, joining, and often directing, virtually every state agency with a music division during the twenties. In temperament and musical predilections it is difficult to imagine a more pragmatic, uninspired contrast to the effete, mystical Lourié, who would later assert that "[i]n the early days of the upheaval . . . art occupied an aristocratic, privileged position . . . [and] musical creation was untouched by politics."[125] In most instances, however, the musicians who worked in the bureaucratic successor to Muzo found less to object to in Krasin's administration than they had in Lourié's.

The demise of Proletkul't as an independent organization by no means signaled the end of any of its primary strands of activity or the resolution of the debates fueling the movement's diversity. All of the primary organizers of the Moscow music division continued their research and educational activities and assumed active roles in the administration of musical institutions and state agencies. The legacy of Proletkul't's eclecticism and struggle to reach a consensus on the methods and nature of cultural transformation constantly resurfaced in the debates between the emerging factions in the musical community. As the varied paths taken by many Proletkul't activists suggest, in music, as in other areas, the iconoclasm that was inspired both by the revolution and by the artistic innovations of the turn of the century was often at odds with the fundamentally traditional conceptions of culture (*kul'tura*) and "enlightenment" held by the reform-minded intelligentsia. Nadezhda Briusova became the architect of the most critical reforms affecting the structure and content of music education. Aleksandr Kastal'skii abandoned his prerevolutionary work as a composer of religious music, falling back on his expertise in folk music to embrace the agenda of the newly formed Russian Association of Proletarian Musicians (RAPM) before his death in 1926. Folk instrument expert Grigorii Liubimov also lent his expertise to RAPM, while his research partner from Proletkul't, Nikolai Roslavets, worked as a censor at the state publishing house, becoming RAPM's arch enemy. Arsenii Avraamov joined Boris Krasin on the staff of the state agencies responsible for administering musical institutions, and continued his work on new tonal systems, including 48-tone scales, at the musical research institute, GIMN.

For musicians, the first years of Soviet power witnessed dramatic changes, but also considerable continuity. Through institutional reform, musicians' attempts to continue their prerevolutionary activities, and the regime's efforts to mobilize support for the revolutionary cause, the salient terms of the relationship between musicians and Soviet power had been established. Indeed, the basic tenets of the emerging relationship between the regime and the intelligentsia were evident in the Bolsheviks' willingness to feed and support those who did not work openly against them. As the country moved toward peace, it was clear that despite the Bolsheviks' professed hostility to bourgeois culture and institutions, musicians would have considerable influence in the shaping of Soviet musical life.

2

The Peculiarities of the Soviet Modern

NEP Culture and the Promotion of "Contemporary" Music

If it is art it is not for all,
if it is for all it is not art.
—Arnold Schoenberg

Art belongs to the people. Its roots should be deeply implanted in the very thick of the labouring masses. It should be understood and loved by these masses.
—Vladimir Lenin

The disparate trajectories of the Proletkul't activists after the Civil War reflect the vibrancy and diversity that are the most commonly cited and striking qualities of Soviet musical life in the twenties.[1] Despite all of the losses due to emigration, considerable talent remained in the classical musical community, including Miaskovskii, the prolific symphonist Shcherbachev, who developed a distinctive linear style, and Roslavets, who has been called the Russian Schoenberg. The new generation, with Dmitrii Shostakovich (1906–75) at its fore, also numbered Aleksandr Mosolov (1900–1973), Gavril Popov (1904–72), and Leonid Polovinkin (1894–1949) in its ranks. Like the literary and artistic scene, the musical world had its share of experimenters and visionaries. Joining Avraamov in the effort to marry music with technology was Lev Termen (Theremin, 1895–1993), who developed one of the world's first electronic instruments while trying to repair a radio in 1920.[2] In Leningrad, Georgii Rimskii-Korsakov (1901–65), grandson of the famous Nikolai, also experimented with electronic instruments and microtonal music, forming a Society for Quarter-Tone Music and organizing performances of his own quarter-tone pieces and the music of Alois Hába and other pioneers in this area. Constructivism found its musical incarnation in the work of Vladimir Deshevov (1899–1955) and Aleksandr Mosolov, who used "instruments" such as corrugated sheet metal, whistles, and saucepans as well as "prepared" pianos to evoke the aural environment of the machine age in their music. Other endeavors, notably Persimfans (derived from *Pervyi simfonicheskii ansambl'*, the First Symphonic Ensemble), the conductorless orchestra sponsored by the Moscow Soviet, reflected collectivist and egalitarian impulses directly inspired by the revolution.

Perhaps most importantly, after years of war- and revolution-induced isolation, Russian musical life rejoined the international music scene. Composers from Western Europe, including Darius Milhaud, Franz Schreker, and Alban Berg, came to Soviet Russia to conduct their music, along with a host of distinguished conductors and soloists. Some Russian musicians made the pilgrimage to Europe and many more had their works published abroad or performed at international music festivals.

While the vibrancy of musical life in the twenties suggested a wide-ranging and genuine diversity, in general terms musicians fell into one of three main categories of artistic and political preference. The first category included advocates of tradition and the "Russian school," such as Aleksandr Glazunov, Mikhail Ippolitov-Ivanov, and Reinhold Gliere. Although they had no formal organization in the twenties and rarely entered into the polemical debates that dominated the musical press, these men retained control over key academic and administrative posts. Many of them displayed attitudes consistent with nineteenth-century liberalism. Their commitment to preserving and cultivating the artistic traditions they considered among humanity's finest achievements extended to a deeply-held belief in the intrinsic value of education and knowledge. While denying the political dimension of artistic creativity, they often supported efforts to enhance the access of previously disadvantaged social groups to the artistic heritage of the former elite. They continued to look askance at much of the new music promoted by their prerevolutionary rivals from the "Evenings of Contemporary Music," who resumed and broadened their activities through the Moscow-based Association of Contemporary Music (ASM, *Assotsiatsiia sovremennoi muzyki*) and two kindred organizations in Leningrad that promoted the most recent and innovative music from the Soviet Union and Western Europe. Some adherents of these groups, the second major category of postrevolutionary development, tried to link their innovations in harmonic language to a radical political agenda. The most flamboyant and intriguing example of this tendency was Nikolai Roslavets, who cited Leon Trotsky's theories of cultural transformation to identify his own work as the harbinger of an as yet unborn, "proletarian" culture. But for the most part the modernists were "fellow travelers" who neither embraced completely nor rejected the revolution. Nor was Roslavets' artistic radicalism representative of an aesthetic spectrum in which fairly conventional preferences figured much more prominently.

Musicians committed to the multiple and often contradictory definitions of "proletarian culture" made up the third major group. Initially represented by the Russian Association of Proletarian Musicians (RAPM, *Rossiiskaia assotsiatsiia proletarskykh muzykantov*), the musical Left soon split into two rival organizations. Members of RAPM and the Organization of Revolutionary Composers (ORK, *Ob'edinenie revoliutsionnykh kompozitorov i muzykal'nykh deiatelei*) defined themselves as the alternative to the "bourgeois decadence" of the modernists of the second group. Their commitment to democratizing access to musical institutions and using music to strengthen popular support for Soviet socialism was also embraced by a group of composition students at the Moscow Conservatory who formed a "production collective" (Prokoll, *Proizvodstvennyi kollektiv studentov-kompozitorov*) in 1925.[3]

RAPM lobbied for official support throughout the twenties, finally receiving it during the Cultural Revolution that accompanied the drives for collectivization and industrialization at the end of the decade. Given RAPM's official backing during the Cultural Revolution, the subsequent dissolution of the ASM, and the excision of much of its music from the officially recognized corpus of Soviet music in the mid-thirties, scholars have viewed the musical scene of the twenties almost exclusively in terms of warring factions. Assessments of the ASM and RAPM and the shrill polemics between the proponents of "contemporary" and "proletarian" music have very much reflected the political persuasions and disciplinary preferences of the observer. Using much of the derogative vocabulary formulated by RAPM, Soviet scholars condemned the ASM's international orientation, elitism, and "formalist" interest in innovation and compositional technique, which they considered only slightly more threatening to the treasures of the cultural legacy and development of Soviet music than the "vulgarized" Marxism and "sectarianism" of RAPM.[4] Western musicologists, intrigued by the creative diversity and Western leanings of the ASM, lamented the persecution and ultimate repression of Russia's musical modernists by RAPM, the zealous handmaids of a crude Stalinist program for bringing the arts to heel.[5]

This interpretive framework remained essentially unchallenged even as some Soviet scholars began a cautious reappraisal of the early Soviet musical legacy in the mid-seventies.[6] Increased access to archival materials and growing interest in the first musical victims of Soviet cultural policy that accompanied *glasnost'* further fueled efforts by Russians and Westerners to recover and assess the music of Russia's modernists.[7] A growing spate of recordings, newly-published scores, and music festivals as well as several scholarly studies have now brought composers such as Nikolai Roslavets and Aleksandr Mosolov to the attention of the international musical community.[8]

Interest in reviving the modernist music of the Soviet twenties stemmed both from what one musicologist has called the "romance of repression" and from the apparent affinities between the composers affiliated with the ASM and the Western avant-garde musicians who so profoundly influenced the course of "serious" music in the twentieth century.[9] These assumptions underlie scholarly studies that examine the uniqueness of Soviet modernism, the originality of a "Leningrad school" centered around Vladimir Shcherbachev (1889–1952), the legacy of Scriabin, and the evolution of serial and other nontonal techniques and their relationship to the Second Viennese School. Focused as it is on specifically musical issues, this literature leaves the paradigm of victimization and competing factions largely intact, with RAPM and the musical Left as neglected and stigmatized as the "modernists" are valorized and rehabilitated.

As a complement (and perhaps counterpoint) to efforts to recover the musical legacy of Russian modernism, this study presents an alternative view of the modernists' activities and their fate. By examining the promotion of new music in terms of the ambiguous position of the creative intelligentsia in the early Soviet period and in the context of a broader crisis of reception that affected new music throughout the West, this chapter identifies the strengths as well as the weaknesses of the modernists' endeavors. It positions the successes of "contemporary music" in terms of powerful, if informal, networks of patronage and institutional support, and acknowledges the significant role played by well-placed individuals such as Boris Asaf'ev and Nikolai Roslavets. This conceptual framework suggests that while the dogmatic opponents of modernism, such as RAPM, were certainly one source of vulnerability for the ASM, many of the concerns raised by the musical Left spoke to more generalized problems facing composers of new music in this period. Factional struggle did play an important role, but so too did the aesthetic and political perspectives of the modernists.

Musicians and the Cultural-Political Dynamics of the Twenties

The diversity of early Soviet musical life, which holds such interest for musicians and musicologists, points to the toleration of artistic and intellectual pluralism and the accommodation of the bourgeois intelligentsia that many historians have identified as the cornerstone of an official policy often referred to as the "soft line."[10] As proposed by Sheila Fitzpatrick, this framework for understanding the cultural policies of the twenties emphasizes the Party's commitment to raising the cultural level of the masses, its refusal to give preferential treatment to artistic groups claiming to represent proletarian interests, and the link between Stalin's consolidation of power and the sudden deterioration of official policy toward the old intelligentsia in 1928–29. Faced with the task of governing an undereducated and underdeveloped country, the regime needed the talent of creative intellectuals as well as the more practical skills of scientists and other "specialists."[11] It also badly wanted the prestige associated with preeminence in any artistic or scientific field. Policy toward music reflected the preference for expertise over ideology in the Party-state's priorities. Most aspects of musical life fell under the administrative purview of Narkompros, where Lunacharsky's commitment to winning artists and intellectuals over by persuasion was unflagging.

Yet more ominous dynamics were also at work. If the intelligentsia was necessary, it was also suspect. Since it was the only remaining prerevolutionary elite, the real and perceived possibility of dispossession made its position terribly precarious. The New Economic Policy (NEP), which was adopted in 1921, endorsed limited capitalism and implicitly allowed for more conciliatory policies to nonproletarian groups, including the intelligentsia. Like the accommodation of the peasantry and the toleration of private trade that defined NEP, the commitment to cultivating good relations with the "bourgeois specialists" was a pragmatic concession on the part of the regime, a compromise that was resented in many quarters and never envisioned as permanent. For the majority of Bolsheviks NEP was a distasteful package of concessions to the enemies of the revolution. Its adoption beset many in the Party with anxieties about the regime's ideological legitimacy, breeding determination to overcome this "disciplined retreat" from revolutionary purity as soon as possible.[12] The institutionalization of censorship bodies, the limits placed on private publishing, and the ever-expanding bureaucratic involvement in cultural affairs indicate the guardedness and uncertainty with which the Bolsheviks regarded artistic and intellectual freedom.[13] Indeed, a recent study of the Higher Party Schools, which were to be the training grounds of the "red intelligentsia," highlights how the Bolsheviks' commitment to replacing the bourgeois specialists with their own "red experts" solidified in the first years of Soviet rule.[14]

Given the brutality with which artists and intellectuals were repressed in the thirties, it is understandable that so many analyses of music and literature have focused on the inherent tension between the Soviet regime's ability or aspiration for control and the amount and nature of artistic freedom in the

NEP cultural order. The crude, and often erratic, incursions of the Soviet regime into artistic life also inform a huge biographical literature that charts the negative effects of censorship on the life and work of famous musicians, especially Shostakovich.[15] For all of its merits, however, the emphasis on the dynamic of control versus freedom overlooks other significant factors.[16]

These factors include the Bolsheviks' contradictory methods and objectives in the cultural sphere, as well as musicians' own efforts to secure influence and support. In his examination of the Higher Party Schools, Michael David-Fox shows how Bolshevik political, social, and cultural agendas intertwined in kinetic and often contradictory ways. Arguing that the Party's objectives on the third front were guided by two interwoven trajectories of cultural revolution—a positive program of enlightenment, education, and moral improvement, and its militant, antispecialist, antibourgeois antipode—David-Fox rejects the notion of a soft line on culture that was abruptly abandoned in 1928, instead positing that an "inner cultural revolution" was accomplished in the twenties that conditioned the "great turn" at the end of the decade.[17] This perspective goes far to clarify the often bewildering complexities of the Bolsheviks' simultaneous effort to transform themselves and the society around them, and serves as a valuable guide to the ways in which cultural policy was linked to other programs.

The appeal of this interpretation, however, stems from its focus on the institutions founded by the Party to train its own intellectuals. But while the "totalizing aspirations" of the revolutionary Party may have been writ large at the front lines of the Communist Academy and Red Professors' Institute, a different view emerges when the twenties are considered from the vantage point of music and musicians, where there is little evidence for Party aspirations of any sort—limited or totalizing—much less the will to implement them. Unlike literature, which had obvious ideological significance and attracted interest from the Party's highest echelons, or film, which Lenin recognized as a powerful tool for the education and political indoctrination of a largely illiterate population, music was commonly recognized as a low priority among other third front missions.

Musicians were also a peculiar type of creative intellectual. They were clearly representatives of the old cultural order, but the intractability of identifying musical "content" made their creativity seem more ideologically "neutral" than that of writers and visual artists. This discrepancy was an important factor in their relations with Soviet power. Certainly the Bolsheviks' contradictory attitudes toward specialists and what they represented affected musicians as well as other intellectuals. As representatives of the culture of formerly privileged groups, musicians were the object of indifference or hostility from the Party's rank and file and its youth organization, the Komsomol, while members of the Party leadership who were themselves either products of a privileged upbringing or had acquired "bourgeois" sensibilities in their studies abroad clearly valued musicians' accomplishment and cultural sophistication. But at no time was there any concerted interest in training "red musicians." Indeed, the Party had a hard time getting its members to accept posts at musical institutions such as the conservatories. Because the ideological implications of musical creativity were far from obvious and because musicians were not essential to the economy, they were not just accommodated, but were left on their own, relatively free of the interventions that occurred in literature. As we will see, the radicals on the musical Left received little in the way of official support or even encouragement in the quest to make music and its institutions more accessible to the proletarian masses. Yet throughout the twenties the proponents of modern music and the more aesthetically conservative representatives of the musical "establishment" enjoyed the state's favor and funding. Musical life during NEP reflected many of the contradictions and struggles that indicated the tenuousness of the Party-state's commitment to accommodation on the third front. It also serves as a shining example of the soft line in practice, as well as demonstrating an arena in which the intelligentsia "won" a fair amount of the time and even managed to co-opt whatever mission the Party had to their own ends.[18]

The musical intelligentsia's successes in this area came in part as a natural by-product of what Barbara Walker has called "the patronage contract." Rather than focusing on the presence or absence of artistic freedom in an authoritarian system, Walker posits that the literary intelligentsia's relationship with the government is best understood in terms of the intelligentsia's quest for material resources and support for their creative endeavors and the state's willingness to provide them in exchange for political acceptance.[19] As we will see, most of the musicians involved in the promotion of modern music in the twenties were well integrated into the patronage networks and institutions that formed the backbone of musical life. The leaders of the ASM were on the faculty of the conservatories and musical research institutions, and were employees of the State Publishing House and the Narkompros agencies charged with the administration of the arts.[20] They maintained strong ties with progressive music circles in the West and their activities were well supported by the state, which demanded little in return.

The delicacy of the modernists' position derived from the kind of music they promoted and the way they promoted it. As was true in the West in this period, "new music" met stiff resistance from many musicians and the concert-going public. This crisis of reception, which would have profound repercussions everywhere, was particularly acute and complex in the Soviet Union, where the revolution's democratizing impulses stood in sharp conflict with the increasingly elitist thrust of classical music.

The politics of engagement were thus terribly significant. In keeping with traditional attitudes toward Western art music, many musicians insisted that their art was autonomous from its social context. However, the assertion that music was "apolitical," or above politics (and fashion), was itself a political statement given enormous significance by the political environment.[21] The modernists responded to that environment in varied ways. Many directed their energies toward composing and performing their music with as little attention to the "outside" world as possible. Others, such as Asaf'ev and Roslavets, worked closely with Soviet power in an attempt to shape an emerging culture according to their own visions of cultural transformation.

This reassessment of the modernists is by no means an attempt to deny the tragic fates of musicians like Roslavets and Mosolov, or to minimize the impact of aesthetic regimentation on Soviet music. It does, however, suggest that these developments be seen from a perspective that considers the actions and agendas of individuals not just as casualties of Soviet cultural politics but as factors that influenced their development.

"Contemporary" Music in Moscow and Leningrad

Organized efforts to promote new music first congealed in 1923, but they built on endeavors from the prerevolutionary and civil war periods. While working at Narkompros, Arthur Lourié established an Association of Contemporary Music, intended to propagandize modern music and publish its members' work. In 1919–20 the association sponsored a number of chamber concerts, including a series of "musical exhibitions" showcasing the work of Debussy and Scriabin in the small hall of the Moscow Conservatory.[22] In Petrograd, two efforts to establish concert organizations for new music in 1922 collapsed almost immediately. The Society for the Propagation of Contemporary Russian Music (*Obshchestvo Propagandy Sovremennoi Russkoi Muzyki*) folded after sponsoring two concerts of chamber music, and conductor Emil Cooper's attempt to set up a Leningrad affiliate of the International Society of Contemporary Music failed when he emigrated in the fall of that same year.

More viable developments began when the main supporters of musical modernism from the prerevolutionary period resumed their activities after the end of the Civil War. In Moscow, the impetus came from the music critic Vladimir Derzhanovskii, who had organized the Evenings of Contemporary Music in 1909 together with his wife, the singer Elena Koposova-Derzhanovskaia (1877–1942), and the conductor Konstantin Saradzhev (1877–1944). In Petrograd, the cause of promoting new music was most successfully advanced by Boris Asaf'ev (1884–1949), a philologist, composer, and music critic whose prerevolutionary reviews had applauded the radicalism of Prokofiev, Stravinsky, and the early work of his boyhood friend Nikolai Miaskovskii.

In 1922 Derzhanovskii took a position at the export publishing house, International Book (*Mezhdunarodnaia kniga*), and soon established a mutual trade agreement with the Viennese publisher Universal Edition. Returning to his prerevolutionary endeavors, he organized a series of concerts in 1923–24 in conjunction with an exhibit of music and music books published in Germany and Russia since the beginning of the war.[23] Leonid Sabaneev, who now headed the music section of the State Academy of Artistic Sciences (GAKhN, *Gosudarstvennaia akademiia khudozhestvennykh nauk*), offered to sponsor similar performances on a regular basis at the academy. Through the efforts of Derzhanovskii and Sabaneev, the new Association of Contemporary Music (ASM) was formally organized on November 29, 1923.[24]

The double meaning of the adjective "contemporary" (*sovremennyi*) in Russian reflects the ASM's interest in music that was either "contemporary" in the sense of being recently composed or "modern" and thus innovative in compositional style. A commitment to propagandizing new music from the West as well as from Russia was the most salient feature of the ASM, but this did not mean that the organization promoted the kind of iconoclasm espoused by Avraamov during the Civil War. Although many have seen the ASM as a tragically repressed avant-garde, it is better understood as a progressive but fairly well integrated section of the musical establishment. Emphasizing the distinction between creativity that is stylistically "modern" and the ideologically confrontational stance that distinguishes a genuine "avant-garde," Richard Taruskin has characterized the ASM's music as "elite modernism" that extended and intensified existing practice without signaling a radical departure from it.[25] As a whole this depiction holds true, although individuals such as Roslavets certainly displayed many of the ideological and creative attributes associated with avant-gardism in other fields.[26] The majority of the organization's members displayed little of the hostility to traditional artistic institutions and audiences and virtually none of the aesthetic of negation and rupture with the past that characterized avant-garde movements in the visual arts.[27] The artistic radicalism represented in Mosolov's constructivism and Georgii Rimskii-Korsakov's work with microtones was more than balanced by the creative conservatism of such prominent figures as Miaskovskii and Aleksandr Gedike (1877–1957).

Some proponents of the ASM's music linked progressive musical style to revolutionary politics. But the modernists had no ideological platform. In fact, one scholar has characterized them as "ideologically free."[28] A veteran of the association later described the ASM as a "society for music lovers," whose diverse membership had no interest in ideological platforms or politics.[29] But the association did have to respond to critics who made claims about the "class content" of particular pieces of music. Perhaps the most emphatic rejection of crude efforts to evaluate musical content was presented by Leonid Sabaneev, who insisted that music functioned in a sphere completely separate from the political world: "[M]usic IS NOT IDEOLOGY which is somehow attached to it. It is a pure construction of sound. . . . [M]usic does not express ideas, it does not express 'logical' constructions. Rather it has its own musical aural world, its own musical ideas, and its own internal musical logic. It is a closed world, and the gulf between it and logic and ideology usually can only be breached in a forced and artificial way."[30]

Until his emigration in 1926, Sabaneev was among the most prominent proponents of the ASM's music. Like other influential figures in the association, composing was not his primary activity. Vladimir Derzhanovskii resumed his prerevolutionary leadership of the Moscow modernists, serving with Sabaneev and the musicologist Viktor Beliaev (1888–1968) in the ASM's administration and on the editorial board of the organization's journal. The conductor, Konstantin Saradzhev, also figured significantly in guiding and promoting the organization's activities, as did Pavel Lamm, an editor and musicologist who restored Musorgsky scores and taught chamber music at the Moscow Conservatory.

At the outset of NEP, Lamm remained the head of the State Music Publishing House, which was incorporated into the administrative orbit of the State Publishing House, *Gosizdat*, late in 1922. He headed an editorial board dominated by conservatory faculty, including ASM members Miaskovskii and Gedike. Beliaev served as his assistant, providing an important link with musicians and publishing activities in Leningrad. In April 1923, several months before the official establishment of the ASM, the State Publishing House launched a journal devoted to new music, *To New Shores of Musical Art* (*K novym beregam muzykal'nogo iskusstva*), edited by Derzhanovskii and Beliaev. Articles included translations from the German musical press, discussions of polytonality, quarter-tone systems, and regular reports "from abroad," including a letter from Prokofiev and news about Medtner and Stravinsky.[31] The centerpiece of the final issue was Nikolai Roslavets' introduction (the first in Russian) to *Pierrot Lunaire*, Schoenberg's celebrated chamber work in which the half-spoken, half-sung technique of *Sprechstimme* decenters the role of pitch.[32]

In addition to being well connected to domestic and foreign publishing channels, the cause of promoting "new music" was embedded in long-standing social networks deeply entrenched in the musical establishment. The core of the ASM, which had about sixty members, came from two artistic-social circles, one that met weekly in Pavel Lamm's quarters in the faculty apartments adjacent to the conservatory, and a second that revolved around Derzhanovskii and his wife.[33] Both of these circles functioned as informal networks of mutual support that gave their members access to resources and privileges and sheltered them from the impersonal market forces they disdained.[34] The effectiveness of these networks depended on personalized relationships between a circle's members and individuals with state power. As we will see, these patronage networks were powerful because many of their members either had some measure of state power (i.e., as an official of a state agency) or were on good terms with someone who did.

The core membership of the circle around Pavel Lamm and his wife consisted of senior faculty members such as Miaskovskii, Saradzhev, Gedike, the theorist Georgii Katuar (Catoire, 1860–1926), and the pianists Aleksandr Gol'denveizer and Konstantin Igumnov, both of whom would serve as directors of the conservatory during NEP. Younger faculty included Anatolii Aleksandrov (1888–1982), a pianist and composer best known for his song cycles of *Alexandrische Lieder*, and Samuil Feinberg (1890–1962), a distinguished performer of Bach and modern piano music, whose own densely textured piano compositions conveyed a dark pessimism and a clear debt to Scriabin.[35]

Meetings at the Lamms' revolved around performances of symphonic pieces transcribed by Lamm for two pianos, eight hands. The repertoire consisted of nineteenth-century classics, as well as newly composed work by the circle's members, especially Miaskovskii.[36] The group's energies focused on the creative efforts of its male members, but women also made important contributions to the group, which insiders affectionately dubbed "*Lammsimfans*," a play on the acronym designation of the conductorless orchestra, Persimfans. Aleksandrov's wife, Nina Georgevna, was an accomplished singer, an early promoter of Delcrose's rhythmic gymnastics, and the unofficial head of the Lamm circle's "women's group." Lamm's sister, Sofia Aleksandrovna, managed the logistical details of receiving and feeding guests.

The music and personality of Nikolai Miaskovskii figured prominently both in *Lammsimfans* and the second group of ASM members that gathered on Sundays at the Derzhanovskiis' spacious apartment near the end of Ostezhenka Street to select pieces for the ASM's programs. A gifted symphonist whose style became more conservative as he matured, Miaskovskii had become friends with the Derzhanovskiis after his symphonic poem *Skazka* was performed at one of their concerts in 1911. Through them he also met Pavel Lamm, becoming close friends with the musicologist when they both worked at Narkompros during the Civil War. Miaskovskii and Lamm thus formed the nucleus of the overlapping subset between the two groups, which also included Dmitrii Melkikh and Miaskovskii's student Vissarion Shebalin. Miaskovskii's friendships with former classmates and colleagues in Petrograd/Leningrad also made him a bridge between the progressive musical communities in the two capitals.

As in Moscow, the social roots for the official promotion of new music in Leningrad came from two informal salons, one that met at the house of Anna Vogt and one sponsored by Boris Asaf'ev at the State Institute of the History of the Arts (GIII, *Gosudarstvennyi institut istorii iskusstv*).[37] Vogt's circle revolved around Boris Asaf'ev and the composer Vladimir Shcherbachev, the most committed proponents of musical modernism in the former capital.[38] Recently appointed to the faculty of the conservatory and to GIII, Shcherbachev brought a number of students and followers into the salon's orbit, making his role in Leningrad comparable to that of Miaskovskii in Moscow.

As St. Petersburg, Leningrad had been the seat of modernism in the prerevolutionary period, but disputes over the extent to which "contemporary" music should be innovative delayed and compromised efforts to establish an organization comparable to the ASM for several years. Aesthetically conservative "Korsakovists" led by Maksimilian Shteinberg (1883–1946) and Aleksandr Ossovskii (1871–1957) remained committed to the compositional language and pedagogical traditions of the Russian national school. They opposed Shcherbachev's and Asaf'ev's efforts to reform the conservatory's composition department and expose Russian musicians to progressive music from Western Europe. Both factions wanted more opportunities to hear recently composed music, but they had dramatically different assessments of particular pieces and compositional techniques, and each group interpreted the adjective "*sovremennyi*" according to its own aesthetic preferences. The Leningrad Association of Contemporary Music (LASM, *Leningradskaia assotsiatsiia sovre-*

mennoi muzyki) was formed in January 1926 as a joint endeavor involving an almost equal number of "modernists" and "traditionalists."[39]

When traditionalists gained control of the LASM's first administrative board and artistic council,[40] Asaf'ev set up his own organization, the New Music Circle (*Kruzhok novoi muzyki*), to promote "music [that is] new and modern in essence—not chronologically, but ideologically: music in which the composer expresses new ideas in a new language."[41] From its base at the Fourth Musical Technicum (a vocational school for music teachers and chorus conductors), the New Music Circle sponsored "concert-exhibitions" of new music like those organized by Asaf'ev and Roman Gruber at GIII.[42] The group also put on a series of closed performances for its members and as many as seventy "student affiliates" from the technicum.[43]

It soon became clear that neither organization was viable on its own, and the New Music Circle rejoined the LASM a year after its founding. But the divisions between conservatives and modernists remained, and the LASM folded in 1928. To its credit, in 1926 the association sponsored several chamber music concerts as well as the premiere of Shostakovich's First Symphony under Malko's baton on May 12. But in 1927 the LASM's offerings dwindled to only four performances. The increased programming of twentieth-century scores in Leningrad, which became especially pronounced after mid-decade, was primarily due to the influence of Asaf'ev, Shcherbachev, and Malko on the repertoire committees of the theaters and philharmonic.[44]

In Moscow, however, the ASM became a major force in the city's concert life. From an initially modest offering of six chamber music programs in 1923–24, the organization expanded its activities to encompass a series of seven symphonic concerts, an equal number of chamber music recitals, and a four-part Beethoven series in 1927–28. The recital hall at GAKhN served as the venue for most chamber music and solo performances, while symphonic concerts were held in the Large Hall of the Moscow Conservatory, the Theater of the Revolution, or, less frequently, the Hall of Columns. In addition to compositions by contemporary Russian composers, audiences heard recent works by émigrés Sergei Prokofiev and Igor Stravinsky. The work of Arthur Honegger, Paul Hindemith, Béla Bartok, and Zoltan Kodaly, as well as Darius Milhaud, Erik Satie, Maurice Ravel, and Francis Poulenc kept Soviet musicians apprised of current tendencies in central Europe and France.[45]

In conjunction with its concert activities, the ASM put out its own bulletin, *Contemporary Music* (*Sovremennaia muzyka*), which, like its concerts, was subsidized by Narkompros.[46] Though it was billed as a "monthly," the journal appeared irregularly in thirty-two issues between 1924 and 1929, with a print run of 1,500. *Contemporary Music* covered events on the domestic and international music scene, maintained a high level of scholarship and writing, and, particularly in its early years, featured many contributions from foreign music critics and composers. Reports from Leningrad modernist organizations were a regular feature, as were sections on the activities of the International Society of Contemporary Music (ISCM) and a calendar of musical events in Moscow.

The ASM's international orientation and links with the European music community enhanced its prestige in some quarters during NEP and attracted volumes of abuse during more xenophobic periods of Soviet history. The organization saw itself both as part of an international community of progressive musicians and as the guardian and perpetuator of a distinctly Russian musical tradition. Many ASM members traveled to Europe in the twenties, including Miaskovskii, Asaf'ev, Feinberg, and Saradzhev. They also maintained contact with Russian émigrés such as Medtner, Cherepnin, and especially Prokofiev, who was considered a member of the Lamm circle even though he lived abroad for the entire decade.[47] Transnational empathies and explicit desires to identify with progressive musicians elsewhere informed the self-perceptions and representations of practitioners of "contemporary" music in Soviet Russia. In Moscow, Shebalin and his friends at the conservatory dubbed themselves "the Six" after the band of French modernists led by Erik Satie and championed by Jean Cocteau.[48] An anthology of new music from Leningrad featuring the work of Shcherbachev, Popov, and Deshevov was entitled *Northern Almanac* in homage to the *Album* by Les Six—who had named themselves after the Russian Mighty Five![49] Contacts between the ASM and the modern music scene in Western Europe were enhanced further by the mutual trade agreement between the Soviet State Publishing House and Universal Edition, and by Derzhanovkii's position at *Mezhdunarodnaia kniga* and affiliation with the All-Union Society of Cultural Relations Abroad (*Vsesoiuznoe Obshchestvo kul'turnoi sviazi s zagranitsei*).[50]

Critical response to the ASM's concerts was mixed. Not surprisingly, contemporary music received ample praise in the modernists' own publications, as well as from some critics outside the association.[51] But negative reviews, frequently couched in a crude Marxist framework, often outnumbered favorable assessments. Both the modernists and their critics responded to the dissolution of conventional harmony and musical form in European art music after Wagner and Scriabin. But while many proponents of "contemporary music" saw the breakdown of traditional harmonic language as a new point of departure,[52] others saw a "state of decay" that was part of the broader cultural crisis of the bourgeoisie. For these critics, many of whom aligned themselves with the proponents of "proletarian music" on the musical Left, so-called contemporary music was the decadent, creative tailings of a class in decline—the "last word of a dying culture."[53]

Modernism's critics from the musical Left found evidence of the degenerate nature of modern music in the poverty of this music's "content." They branded the modernists as "formalists" who neglected content in their search for new methods of organizing sound and alternatives to conventional harmony.[54] These critics attached signal importance to music's ability to influence emotions and create moods, equating musical "content" with the ability of a given piece to elicit certain feelings or to strengthen a particular worldview or ideology. They claimed that the modernists, in their quest for technical innovation, had mechanized creativity and stripped music of its emotional appeal.[55] By focusing on how a work was written rather than on its content or appeal to others, the modernists exaggerated the intellectual dimension of composing music and perverted the creative process. The result was overly cerebral music, created by the mechanical application of theoretical rules. Critics argued that the modernists' veneration of this impoverished mode of creativity reflected the individualistic, spiritually enervated culture of the bourgeoisie. Extending to music a charge initially leveled against futurist poetry and the constructivist paintings of Chagall, critics from the proletarian camp claimed that

> all the wrong notes of the modern composers (Schoenberg, Stravinsky, Roslavets) are no more than the fixation of tones in an unorganized, chaotic style that is intelligible to absolutely no one besides the artist who discovered them. . . . Constructivism in its extreme manifestation (intellectualism, formalism, fetishization of creation) is the delayed product of a dying culture and an uncomfortable shield for those who are against the building of a new life.[56]

Following logically from this critique were charges that musicians remained an "artistic aristocracy" and were alienated from their audiences. Rather than "crossing the Rubicon of the cultural October" to address the needs of Soviet Russia's "new consumers," the modernists focused their attentions on the capitalist West and on Russia's musical émigrés, especially Prokofiev and Stravinsky.[57] Many critics insisted that dissonance and complexity made much recently composed music inaccessible to audiences. They claimed that proletarian listeners in particular had difficulty relating to music that was overly complicated, not obviously "beautiful," and seemingly remote from the demands of building socialism. Indeed, some charged that composers' elitism was deliberate, insisting that they feared "the simplicity, accessibility of melody, harmony and form" that would win success with a broad public.[58]

Critics from the musical Left were particularly troubled by the "individualistic" concerns and lack of social responsibility they identified among young composers, including Aleksandr Mosolov, whose work they denounced as "utterly alien to our Soviet reality."[59] At issue were two of Mosolov's vocal chamber works: *Three Children's Scenes* (Op. 18), and *Newspaper Advertisements* (Op. 21). The former depicted a child tormenting a cat, as well as the naturalistic grunting of a naked toddler. In the latter a "serious" and finely crafted score satirized banal newspaper announcements about a lost dog, a rat exterminator, and the sale of leeches. While the modernists' journal praised Mosolov's talent, mastery, and innovation,[60] leftist critics condemned his work as morally bereft, goalless mischief whose naturalistic excesses fell short of the task of genuine art, which was to direct attention to significant and important ideas.[61]

The inaccessibility of contemporary music to proletarian audiences may have been widely accepted, but it was not uncontested. Iuliia Vainkop reported that workers and trade union members preferred music by Mosolov, Stravinsky, and Hindemith to older music, because it "stirred the imagination" and was "more interesting."[62] Other critics asserted that workers had a natural empathy for new music, especially compositions that invoked the aural environment of the industrial city such as Deshevov's percussive piano piece, *Rails*. A critic for the LASM emphasized the enthusiasm expressed by working-class audiences for music that imitated the noises of factories and the hubbub of city streets:

> What is closer to the proletariat, the pessimism of Tchaikovsky and the false heroics of Beethoven, a century out of date, or the precise rhythms and excitement of Deshevov's Rails? During the playing of Beethoven, the workers were utterly bored, and patiently waited for the music to end. But contemporary Soviet compositions aroused contagious emotion among the audience. Proletarian masses, for whom machine oil is mother's milk, have a right to demand music consonant with our epoch, not the music of the bourgeois salon which belongs in the era of the horse and buggy and of Stephenson's early locomotive.[63]

Taken at face value, negative assessments, many of which came from proponents of "proletarian music," comprise the most compelling evidence of "factional struggle" within the musical community, and seem to exemplify the peculiarities of early Soviet cultural politics. Certainly this perspective has its merits. But when the crude Marxist rhetoric is stripped away, the objections to new Soviet music parallel concerns raised elsewhere in this period. Situating the "new Soviet music" of the twenties in a broader context suggests that other dynamics also made the promotion of new music a perilous endeavor.

As the ASM and the Leningrad modernists moved from the isolation of salons and informal circles into the realm of concerts and published programs, they encountered the prevailing dynamic governing the consumption of "serious" music in this period, which perpetuated a canon of works by dead composers and was highly resistant to new music. In Russia as in the West, the nineteenth century had witnessed significant changes in the attitudes of European audiences and composers. A moral critique of commercialism had evolved into an idealist musical aesthetic that identified music as a "high" art that was distinct from and superior to simple entertainment.[64] The noisy bustle of eighteenth-century musical theater audiences gave way to the reverential silence of bourgeois patrons of "absolute" symphonic music. Performances became rituals honoring high art, the concert hall a temple for a subjective, individual musical experience.[65] To emancipate music from the whims of the marketplace and fashion, proponents of musical idealism looked to the past for the standards of musical taste, settling on Bach, Handel, Mozart, Haydn, Beethoven, and Weber, and eventually Mendelssohn and Schumann as a pantheon against which all new work must be judged. In Russia, the works of Glinka and the Mighty Five shared this veneration as masterworks. While reverence for masterworks initially shaped a standard of taste that supported composers like Schumann and Wagner, this taste became increasingly intolerant of new music as the century progressed.[66]

Changing attitudes toward music worked in concert with the evolution of the repertoire itself. After Beethoven, the demands serious music made of orchestral musicians and audiences increased steadily. Symphonic music increased in length, formal sophistication, and technical difficulty, requiring more rehearsal time from orchestras and a more developed musical memory from audiences. An experienced ear was necessary if the problems posed at the beginning of a major work (such as an opera by Wagner) could be heard to have been resolved convincingly at its end.[67] By the turn of the century, the system of tonality that had formed the foundation of Western music for nearly three hundred years was under great strain. The music of Wagner and Scriabin had expanded the system to its breaking point, and composers were in search of new organizing principles. A new creative conjuncture coincided with and exacerbated a crisis involving composers and their audiences. In 1913, riots broke out at performances of Stravinsky's *Rite of Spring* in Paris and Alban Berg's *Altenberg Lieder* (Op. 4) in Vienna. As their music provoked scandal and moral outrage, avant-garde musicians began to reject public taste and define a separate social and musical role for themselves.

In 1918 Arnold Schoenberg founded the Society for the Private Performance of Music to give musicians the opportunity to hear their work performed according to the most rigorous professional standards and without the intrusion of the public.[68] Concerts were unpublicized and admission was by invitation only. No critics were allowed. This was a defensive move that enabled composers to bring their music to the "small enlightened public that would understand it."[69] A few years later, Schoenberg supported the establishment of the International Society of Contemporary Music (ISCM), a prestigious vehicle for promoting new music that remains in existence to this day. At its inception, the ASM became an informal affiliate of the ISCM, and the Soviet organization's contacts with the European organization intensified throughout the decade.[70] The ASM sent representatives to the ISCM's annual festivals, publicized the society's activities in its journals, sponsored performances of new Soviet music in Western Europe, and forwarded scores of recently published Russian music to the ISCM's London headquarters.

Like the ISCM and Schoenberg's Society for Private Performance, the ASM musicians tried to establish arenas in which "new" music could be presented, if only to an inner circle of colleagues and friends.[71] While the crisis of reception for modern music extended far beyond the Soviet Union, it would be particularly problematic there given the imperatives of the revolution, for Lenin had insisted that "art belongs to the people." In order for "contemporary" music to be truly in consonance with contemporary life, it had to have broad appeal.[72] To be sure, not all of the music programmed by the ASM was as challenging to audiences and performers as the innovations of the Second Viennese School. But the association's organizers acknowledged that its public performances attracted only a sophisticated musical public and students from the conservatory.[73] Leonid Sabaneev freely confessed that his music was known only to an isolated circle, adding that "the kind of creativity I am capable of can never be geared for the recognition of the 'broad masses.'"[74] Like the New Music Circle in Leningrad, the ASM also sponsored "closed concerts" featuring new works, that only members of GAKhN and their guests could attend.[75] Programs for all of the ASM's events emerged from the salons that met weekly at the Derzhanovskiis' and Lamms'. The wisdom of attempting to keep the alienated and uninitiated away seemed to be borne out when a reviewer of Roslavets' work ridiculed his "futurist system" that was "intelligible only to himself."[76] When officials at Narkompros urged the ASM to try to broaden its constituency, Derzhanovskii protested that not just the masses but even musicians put up obstacles (*prepriatstviia*) to the kind of music the organization promoted.[77]

Clearly this orientation was incompatible with broader efforts to democratize access to elite culture. Yet modernism not only survived but flourished during NEP. This success was only partly attributable to the soft line. When neither the masses nor fellow musicians would support modernism, it became the responsibility of well-placed individuals to defend this kind of music and make it relevant to Soviet reality.

Art, Politics, and the Importance of Personality

Boris Asaf'ev in Leningrad and Nikolai Roslavets in Moscow were among the most significant forces in articulating and defending the varied tasks and goals of contemporary music in the twenties.[78] Both men had completed their professional training and established a place for themselves in the musical scene before 1917. In the twenties they were much more vocal in their promotion of new music than younger representatives of the modernist camp such as Mosolov, Shostakovich, and Shebalin. Their aesthetic and political orientations differed from each other in important respects and their perspectives were just part of a wide and nuanced discourse about music in the twenties. But brief consideration of their positions in the musical community reveals much about the ambiguities of "contemporary music" and the contradictory influences of new political and artistic conjunctures.

Considered the "father of Soviet musicology," Boris Asaf'ev was a guiding spirit of musical life in Leningrad in the twenties.[79] In addition to a post at the Leningrad Conservatory and leadership of the New Music Circle and LASM, he served as the dean of the Music History and Theory Department at GIII, an institution that he had helped to establish. Under the pen name "Igor Glebov," he contributed to a wide range of musical and artistic journals, including Leningrad's daily newspaper. He edited the LASM's journal, *New Music* (*Novaia muzyka*, 1927–28), as well as the yearbooks published by the music division of GIII.[80] The contents of the latter indicate the range of Asaf'ev's interests as a musicologist and as a composer—from quarter-tone systems and electronically generated music to old Hebraic psalmody and the music of Lully, Glinka, Musorgsky, and Scriabin.

Trained as a philologist as well as a composer, Asaf'ev received degrees from the University of St. Petersburg in 1905 and studied at the St. Petersburg Conservatory with Rimsky-Korsakov and Anatolii Liadov. He began to publish as a music critic in 1914, and on the eve of the revolution came into the orbit of the writer Maxim Gorky, one of the most influential practitioners of networking and patronage among the intelligentsia. In his work for Gorky's journal, *New Life* (*Novaia zhizn'*), Asaf'ev met the poet Mayakovsky as well as Lunacharsky. He formed a lasting friendship with the future head of Narkompros that would influence his own political views and the evolution of state policy toward music throughout the twenties.[81]

Asaf'ev's critical writings from the twenties reflect a variety of influences. A traditional training in the Rimsky-Korsakov method and respect for the work of Vladimir Stasov and Aleksandr Serov, two nineteenth-century founders of Russian music criticism, imbued Asaf'ev with a veneration for the totality of Russia's musical heritage as a unique but affiliated branch of the Western musical tradition. At the same time he was intrigued by and supportive of the innovative potential of the harmonic and rhythmic experimentation taking place in Russia and Western Europe. He maintained an active correspondence with Alban Berg in 1928–29, and reviewed Shcherbachev's symphonies, Honegger's *Pacific 231*, and the operas of Berg and Ernst Krenek in *Contemporary Music*.[82] In these years he also published the first analysis of Stravinsky's music, as well as his major contribution to Soviet music theory, *Musical Form as Process*.[83] Like Iavorskii, whose work on mode was a formative influence, Asaf'ev's exegetical texts are discursive and heavily dependent on neologisms, making assessment and even comprehension of his ideas extremely difficult.[84] Asaf'ev was not a Marxist, but (again like Iavorskii) would find the vocabulary of dialectical materialism appropriate to a system of thought that reflected numerous influences, including Russian symbolism, Hegel, Kant, and the intuitive philosophy of Henri Bergson.[85]

Asaf'ev was committed to publicizing new Western music, but also demonstrated concern with the place of "new music" and its proponents in Soviet society. In keeping with prevailing attitudes about musical taste and the Russian intelligentsia's deep-seated aversion for the market, he asserted that composers had to believe they were creating music that would be embraced in the future, or they would be little more than slaves to the marketplace and dictates of fashion.[86] At the same time, Asaf'ev recognized the potency of modernism's critics, and addressed their concerns head on. He urged composers to acknowledge the crisis of new music and meet the challenge of the revolution by writing music with broad appeal. They should "hurry" to abandon the "closed spaces" of the concert hall and find new theatrical forms that would break down the wall between art music and the people, bringing music "into the free expanses."[87] The needs of the "new musical consumer" commanded his attention, yielding essays on "revolutionary folklore" and the relevance of Mozart and Schubert to contemporary audiences.[88]

While Asaf'ev objected to the "agitational music" and utilitarian aesthetic of the musical Left, he was eager to identify common ground where it existed. When Kastal'skii, who was the only seasoned composer to join the militant proletarian group RAPM, died in 1926, Asaf'ev penned eulogies praising the composer's mastery of choral writing and devotion to folk music.[89] Despite Kastal'skii's long association with the Orthodox church, Asaf'ev insisted that he not be regarded as a composer of applied sacred music. He asserted that the composer's pieces with religious themes transcended the church as musical treasures with appeal and value to the Communist state, as did Mozart's *Requiem*, Beethoven's *Missa Solemnis*, and Bach's cantatas.[90] A sophisticated champion of new as well as old music, Asaf'ev proved adept at weathering every storm the Soviet cultural scene produced.

The same cannot be said for Nikolai Roslavets, whose career never recovered from the setbacks he experienced at the end of the twenties. Also unlike Asaf'ev, whose theoretical work and music criticism far outlived his limited compositional endeavors, Roslavets was a composer first and a music critic second. He was a member and supporter of the ASM, but did not belong to its major social circles, nor was he on the faculty at the conservatory. A unique and compelling figure, Roslavets was one of very few musicians who worked to join radical political and creative agendas, and the only professed Marxist in the modernist camp. While many in the intelligentsia petitioned the state for support and preference in this period, Roslavets was in a position to help determine the shape of policy toward music in general, and his music in particular. An influential and outspoken proponent of his own vision of cultural transformation, Roslavets was an individual who both influenced and responded to the ambiguous and often treacherous political dynamics of the NEP order.

On the eve of World War I Roslavets had developed close ties with the artistic avant-garde, and developed a nondiatonic method of composition called the "New System of Tone Organization," based on "synthetic chords," the first mature elaboration of which is found in the *Sonata No. 1* for violin and piano (1913). Bearing some debts to Scriabin, but decidedly unique,

Roslavets's twelve-tone system evolved independently and nearly a decade in advance of Schoenberg's.[91] His music came to the attention of Derzhanovskii's circle, where he made the acquaintance of Sabaneev and Miaskovskii, who praised Roslavets's music in the journal, *Muzyka*.[92]

Roslavets's political sympathies before the fall of the autocracy are unclear, but the kaleidoscopic evolution of his political allegiances during 1917 suggest both the initial breadth of the revolutionary movement and the speed with which that spectrum narrowed. When the autocracy fell, Roslavets initially inclined toward anarchism, then led a local organization of the peasant party, the Socialist Revolutionaries (SRs) in Elets, briefly identified with the Left wing of the SRs, and then joined the Bolsheviks![93] In addition to his work with Proletkul't, Roslavets was among the founders of Rabis, represented that organization in the Moscow Soviet, and worked under Lourié at Muzo.

In 1921, Roslavets resigned from the Party and many administrative positions to devote more time to composing, but he remained an influential figure in musical life and the state bureaucracy throughout NEP.[94] After a brief stint teaching at the music academy in Khar'kov and working for the Ukrainian Narkompros, he returned to Moscow in 1923 and became a political editor (censor) at the newly-formed Main Committee on Repertoire (Glavrepertkom, *Glavnoe upravlenie po kontroliu za zrelishchami i repertuarom*), the censorship organ for the performing arts, film, music, and records.[95] He would retain this position until 1930, representing an agency that consistently challenged the conciliatory policies in the arts supported by Narkompros.[96] Indeed, soon after its formation, Glavrepertkom attacked the repertoire of the Bol'shoi Theater, denouncing scenes in *The Queen of Spades* and *The Night Before Christmas* as "monarchist propaganda."[97] Whereas proponents of the soft line at Narkompros may have been conflicted or ambivalent, the censorship bodies (Glavrepertkom's companion agency for the press was Glavlit) consistently championed the need to regulate and control literature and artistic productions, maintaining that artistic merit never mitigated problematic content.[98] Roslavets was no exception in this regard, but his own artistic orientation made him the champion, rather than the denigrator, of music that radicals on the musical Left rejected for its "formalism" and inaccessibility to the masses.

In the fall of 1923, the Party organization at the State Publishing House closed down *To New Shores*, had Pavel Lamm arrested and temporarily detained, and drove off many of the musicians who had been working with the publisher since the Civil War. The editorial board of *Musical Virgin Soil* (*Muzykal'naia nov'*), the journal that replaced *To New Shores*, was dominated by Communists whose critique of affairs in the conservatories and concert halls quickly alienated the musical community.[99] Early in 1924, Roslavets became the head of the publisher's political section. While the almost studiously apolitical tenor of *To New Shores* had precipitated intervention by Party members who resisted the old intelligentsia's influence and stimulated the formation of the proletarian musicians' organization, RAPM, the general tone of the soft line demanded that efforts be made to win over the musicians, not terrorize them into silence. The head of the publishing house, Otto Shmidt (1891–1956), charged Roslavets with the task of winning the ASM members back over and founding a musical journal that would be Marxist in orientation and explicitly address the implications of the revolution for music.[100] This mission to attract the support of other musicians who wanted to work together with the Party on the cultural front bore many similarities to that of Aleksandr Voronskii, the editor of *Red Virgin Soil* (*Krasnaia nov'*), who cultivated the support of literary "fellow travelers."[101]

In July 1924 the first issue of *Musical Culture* (*Muzykal'naia kul'tura*) appeared under Roslavets's editorship, with the assistance of the ASM leaders (Beliaev, Derzhanovskii, and Sabaneev), as well as Asaf'ev and Boleslav Iavorskii. Like *Contemporary Music* and *To New Shores*, the new journal featured sound scholarship and focused on the contemporary music scene. Unlike the other two publications, it gave considerable emphasis to recent technical and theoretical developments. Quarter-tonal, atonal, and machine music received extensive coverage, as did Georgii Konius's "metrotectonic" method of formal analysis.[102] What most distinguished *Musical Culture*, however, was its explicit concern with the relationship between radical art and politics.

Roslavets defended avant-garde music, which seemed so inaccessible to mass audiences, in the context of Trotsky's theories of cultural transformation. Citing Trotsky's *Literature and Revolution* (1924), Roslavets asserted that a specifically proletarian culture would never exist because the proletarian dictatorship was transient.[103] In the period of its dictatorship the Russian proletariat would, of necessity, focus on economic and political concerns.[104] As the dominant class, the proletariat would destroy the culture of its former oppressors and then build the culture of socialism. But to do so, the "youthful" culture of the Russian bourgeoisie must first be understood and mastered. This could not be achieved by "simplifying" music to correspond to the current level of the cultural development of the masses. The aesthetic preferences of workers and peasants in this transitional era reflected a "nonculture" that was the product of social, economic, and political oppression rather than the offspring of a new artistic awareness. The building blocks of truly revolutionary music were the new tone systems being developed by composers like Roslavets, not the peasant folk song and traditional forms (particularly sonata-allegro form) idealized by RAPM.[105] Roslavets was unabashed in confessing that he was not a "proletarian composer." On the contrary, he insisted,

> I am so "bourgeois" that I consider the Russian proletariat—the lawful inheritor of all of the culture that came before him—to be worthy of that culture's best musical part. And therefore it is specifically for him that I write my symphonies, quartets, trios, songs and other "head smashing" works, . . . being completely convinced that I will live to see the day when the proletariat will find my music as intelligible and accessible as it is today to the best representatives of Russia's progressive musical society.[106]

Through the lens of Trotsky's Marxism, Roslavets defended the inaccessibility of his work and displayed one component of a more widespread element of the European avant-garde's ideology that defined artistic value in terms of future tastes. Alienation from the general audience proved the value of his work.[107]

While working as a political editor Roslavets continued to compose using the New System of Tone Organization. In his compositions he used the six to nine pitches that comprised the "synthetic chord" horizontally, in order to construct melody, as well as vertically, to create harmony. A work's opening synthetic chord also assumed some of the functions of the tonic, often reappearing at the end of the piece.[108] The centrality of harmonic fields to his music made the immense range and technical capabilities of the piano a particularly attractive instrument for Roslavets. In the twenties he wrote several piano sonatas and completed a number of vocal and chamber pieces, and also worked on several large-scale symphonic works, many of which were lost or never finished. There was a rational slant to Roslavets's system, which also had much in common with Scriabin's mystically inspired work. Refuting charges that the modernists had "fetishized the creative process," Roslavets vigorously denied the presence of any external "inspiration" for his music, asserting that composition was purely an intellectual activity: "I know that the creative act is not some 'mystical trance' or 'divine discovery,' but rather a moment of the highest exertion of the human intellect, as it strives to transform the unconscious (subconscious) into a form of consciousness."[109]

Although he felt his music belonged to the future, Roslavets was also dedicated to developing the musical sensibilities of the masses without patronizing them. He made numerous contributions to the "revolutionary-agitational" literature designed for use in workers' clubs. These songs, many of which employed a modified version of the New System of Tone Organization, aroused scorn from the musical Left and are a source of embarrassment to those currently eager to revive interest in his "serious" music.[110]

In his quest to realize the cultural transformation he believed must accompany the revolution, Roslavets used his position as political editor to involve himself in a number of debates on concert policies, publishing practices, and strategies for composing "mass songs." These activities, combined with his promotion of his own "music of the future" and the influence he exercised as censor, earned him the unqualified enmity of the musical Left.[111] He became a lightning rod for attacks on "head smashing" formalist music that was too preoccupied with technique to convey an idea.

Roslavets displayed some of the aesthetics of negation and much of the vanguard, interventionist political rhetoric that characterized the avant-garde in other artistic fields. He was, however, rather atypical of the Soviet modernist musical community as a whole, in which the eclectic flirtation with atonality, the interest in neoclassicism, and the self-conscious appropriation of urban popular music that typified musical modernism elsewhere in this period was also found. The referential framework for the ASM and the Leningrad modernists was not the artistic avant-garde whose tragically successful quest to establish a truly revolutionary culture has been delineated by Boris Groys and Katerina Clark.[112] Instead, musically as well as ideologically, the musical modernists were fairly well integrated members of the musical establishment, and official policy supported and was defined by these groups rather than the militants on the musical Left. While "traditionalists" from the old Russian school were put off by the dissonant percussiveness of Prokofiev and the naturalistic effects and vulgar "ultrarealism" of Mosolov's *Three Children's Scenes*, they shared the ASM's desire to have contact with the West and its interest in promoting recently composed music. Members of the ASM did their best to exploit their influence in musical institutions and the bureaucracy for their own personal, political, and aesthetic benefit, doing so with considerable success. This accomplishment was facilitated by the creative weaknesses and ideological shortcomings of their shrill critics on the Left.

Soviet musical modernism was strongest when it was defined and promoted by an individual rather than an organization—through Asaf'ev's critical writings or Roslavets's polemics, politics, and compositions. But even the movement from the individual to the salon and association was a source of debate and then weakness. The broader public realm was even more treacherous, not because of official policy or the influence of RAPM and the musical Left, but because of the dynamics governing the reception of "contemporary" music.

3

The Three Faces of the Musical Left

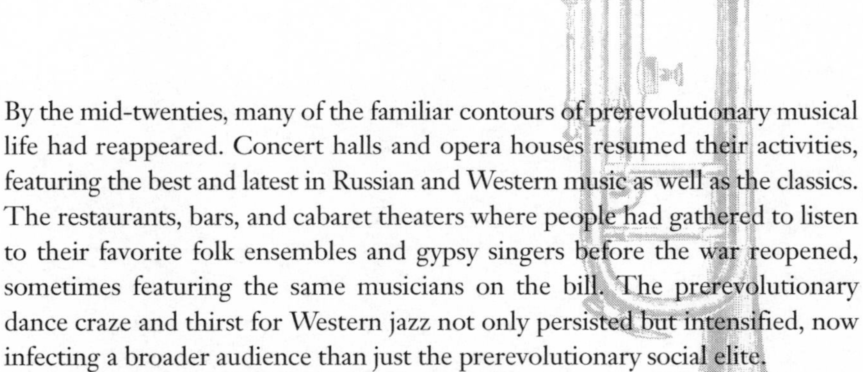

We need for musical creations to become a part of life, and therefore it is necessary to achieve a harmonious union between genuine artistic music and the demands of the masses. I would say that we do not even need music that simply satisfies the wants of the masses, but music founded on what is heard in the unique rhythms of these masses, in the unique musical consciousness they carry with them.
—Anatoly Lunacharsky

By the mid-twenties, many of the familiar contours of prerevolutionary musical life had reappeared. Concert halls and opera houses resumed their activities, featuring the best and latest in Russian and Western music as well as the classics. The restaurants, bars, and cabaret theaters where people had gathered to listen to their favorite folk ensembles and gypsy singers before the war reopened, sometimes featuring the same musicians on the bill. The prerevolutionary dance craze and thirst for Western jazz not only persisted but intensified, now infecting a broader audience than just the prerevolutionary social elite.

But while most musicians and educated Russians cheered the revival of musical life, others took this renewal as an ominous sign that music remained beyond the reach of the revolution. They asserted that in most respects, music was still a "fine" art, a leisure pursuit for the social and aesthetic "elect." In the concert hall the same audiences of old, with the undistinguished addition of private entrepreneurs known as Nepmen, heard the same (bourgeois) music as before the revolution, while workers and peasants still listened to music in bars or on the street, often accompanied by the creaking twang of the accordion. Professional art music seemed to offer little to the toiling classes. And, aside from the occasional charity concerts they gave for working-class audiences, most art musicians remained remarkably detached from and untouched by the ideological challenge of 1917. Popular education programs initiated during the Civil War continued, but were peripheral to most musicians' concerns.

The three groups that comprised the Left wing of the Soviet musical scene in the twenties pursued a number of strategies in an effort to bring the revolution to music. Members of the militant "proletarian musicians" organization, RAPM, the more utilitarian "revolutionary composers" affiliated with the Organization of Revolutionary Composers (ORK), and the conservatory students in Prokoll all developed Marxist methodologies for analyzing music and musical life, worked in popular music education programs, and wrote music they hoped would appeal to the broad masses of Soviet society and further the cause of the revolution. Although their tactics varied, all three groups worked to create a musical culture that would be, in Lenin's words, "deeply implanted in the very thick of the labouring masses."[1]

Given RAPM's polemics with the modernists during NEP and its dominance of musical life during the Cultural Revolution, both Western and Soviet-Russian scholarship have emphasized its importance in the factional politics of the twenties and inevitably condemned its members as musical "hacks" or advocates of "vulgarized" Marxist aesthetics.[2] Recent examinations of the organization provide more nuanced assessments of its significance for Soviet musical culture and its role in the Cultural Revolution.[3] The official support that RAPM enjoyed during the years of the Great Break at the end of the decade naturally has prompted scholars to focus on the group's earlier radicalism, ambitions, and rivalry with the ASM, but this perspective distorts RAPM's significance and its place in the twenties. By overstating RAPM's influence it overlooks the diversity of the musical Left, minimizing the importance of RAPM's rival, ORK, as well as the activities of Prokoll, a group of composition students at the Moscow Conservatory.[4] This diversity was significant in itself, and each of these three groups had a distinct place in the factional politics of NEP. They shared common objectives, but the ways in which their agendas and the support they were able to mobilize for them differed had important implications for the development of Soviet musical culture.

Proletarian Musicians and Revolutionary Composers: Ideological Orientations, Membership, and Creative Platforms

The impetus to form the Russian Association of Proletarian Musicians, RAPM,[5] came from a handful of Communist musicians who felt that music had remained largely unaffected by the revolution. When the association was founded in June 1923, its organizers issued a proclamation condemning the "apolitical reserve of the musical environment . . . the musical tastes of NEP . . .

and the complete absence of a class approach to musical enlightenment" in schools and the conservatories.[6] Consisting initially of a mere seven people, RAPM was based at the agitation-enlightenment department of the music division of the State Publishing House, *Gosizdat*. David Chernomordikov (1869–1947) headed the association's first governing board, assisted by Lev Shul'gin (1890–1968) and Aleksei Sergeev (1889–1958).[7] The organization grew slowly throughout the twenties, reaching a peak enrollment of about sixty during the Cultural Revolution.

The Proletarian Musicians envisioned themselves as a counterbalance both to the elitism of the ASM and the degenerate "hackwork" of the Association of Moscow Authors (AMA), which promoted the publication and dissemination of popular songs, fox-trots, and *tsyganshchina* (often referred to collectively and disparagingly as the "light genre"). The association looked to the Russian Association of Proletarian Writers (RAPP) as its organizational model, and maintained a close affiliation with RAPP throughout its existence. At the organization's inception the Proletarian Musicians had neither an ideological platform nor a coherent program. The group's first declaration made no mention of "proletarian music" per se, but lamented the "chaos" and lack of direction in concert repertoires and music publishing and the "ideological instability" of young musicians.[8]

The organization's beginnings coincided with the launching of the journal *Musical Virgin Soil* (*Muzykal'naia nov'*) at the State Publishing House. Although its title was clearly an homage to *Red Virgin Soil*, the literary journal edited by Voronskii that cultivated non-Party and fellow traveler writers and poets, the new journal had a much more practical and overtly politicized approach than its predecessor, *To New Shores*. Edited by Chernomordikov, Sergeev, and Sergei Chemodanov, *Musical Virgin Soil* featured articles on "revolutionary music," concert policies, affairs at the Moscow Conservatory, and repertoire for workers' clubs, trade unions, and the Komsomol organizations. In their quest for "genuine new shores of communication and collaboration with the proletariat,"[9] RAPM's leaders called on "all progressive and creative forces" to join in the struggle against the isolation and backwardness of the "musical front."[10] But although the list of "collaborators" for the early issues of *Musical Virgin Soil* included a number of prominent musicians, beneath this token support lay suspicion, if not hostility, toward a group poised to challenge widely accepted notions about the social and political significance of music and the foundations of musical life. When Roslavets launched *Musical Culture* and *Musical Virgin Soil* became the official organ of RAPM in 1924 (issue 6–7), the names of many earlier supporters were missing from *Musical Virgin*

Soil's cover page. From the beginning, the Proletarian Musicians struggled with both a real and imagined position as outsiders in the corridors of bureaucratic power and musical society.

While respected pillars of the musical community headed the modernist ASM, the founding members of RAPM were either just beginning advanced musical training or had been more active in revolutionary politics than in the mainstream of musical life. David Chernomordikov and Lev Shul'gin had completed degrees in composition at the St. Petersburg Conservatory before the outbreak of World War I, but then had left the capital. After joining the Bolsheviks in 1905, Chernomordikov published Russia's first anthology of revolutionary songs, including the first Russian version of *The Internationale.*[11] During the Civil War he worked in popular musical education and musicians' unions in the Caucasus. In 1923 the Party assigned him to the State Publishing House. Shul'gin became a Party member in 1917 and left his position as a choir director in Rostov-on-the-Don to teach music in the Red Army's political enlightenment administration during the Civil War. In these years he also headed the information division of Proletkul't and worked in the ethnography section of Narkompros. In April 1921 he became the head of the agitation-enlightenment department of the music division of the State Publishing House, a position he held until 1933. His efforts there were supported by Aleksei Sergeev, a "political editor" and composer with some musical training from the Moscow Synodal School. RAPM's youngest members, Lev Lebedinskii and Sarra Krylova, had just entered the Moscow Conservatory as party nominees at the end of the Civil War.

As well as a somewhat inexperienced membership, RAPM also suffered from internal strife. By the end of 1924 the organization's membership had grown to twenty-six, but ideological differences over the nature of proletarian versus revolutionary music and the best tactics for creating it caused a split in ranks.[12] The final issue of *Musical Virgin Soil* in 1924 announced that six people, including Sergeev and Shul'gin, had withdrawn their membership.[13]

The departure of Shul'gin's group allowed what was left of RAPM to set out a more coherent program. It was always easier to identify what the association opposed than what it supported, and disagreements within the group persisted. But those who remained adopted an ideological platform based on a Marxist interpretation of the musical legacy.[14] Evaluating music in terms of the social and economic context in which it was created, the Proletarian Musicians' platform asserted that two types of music existed before the revolution: the folk music of the exploited classes and the bourgeois music of the exploiters. It maintained that music written when the bourgeoisie was an ascendant class struggling to overthrow feudalism (i.e., Beethoven's music written in the era of the French Revolution) was healthy and progressive. But contemporary art music and "written, cultured" music from the more recent past, which the ASM promoted, reflected the decadence of an exploitive class in decline. The platform also condemned urban popular music, especially that associated with cabarets and the variety stage, as well as Western dance music, as a degenerate, bourgeois influence on the sensibilities of the working class.

If the Proletarian Musicians' preferences for "healthy" bourgeois music required a fairly elaborate rationale, their attitudes toward folk music were even more complex and contradictory. The folk song's association with the (politically backward) peasantry prevented them from openly embracing it as the foundation for the proletarian musical art of the future. Yet they clearly valued this music. They tried to salvage parts of it by distinguishing between "good" songs about work, robbers, and rebels, which they associated with the poor (exploited) peasantry, and the "bad" patriotic and religious songs supposedly sung by kulaks.[15]

RAPM maintained that the development of proletarian music had been retarded by the oppressive conditions of capitalism and the hegemony of bourgeois culture. The group's primary objectives were to nourish the nascent "sprouts" (*rostki*) of proletarian music by working with the music circles of workers' clubs, promoting efforts to make the conservatories more accessible to workers and peasants, and debating with other musical groups, and to create new methods of composing music. Until the Cultural Revolution, RAPM focused its energies on the first of these tasks, which is not surprising given that most of its members were aspiring musicologists and critics, rather than composers. For the most part the association left the more difficult and nebulously defined challenge of composing "proletarian" music aside, instead emphasizing the importance of "ideological leadership" and the "re-education" (*perevospitanie*) of musicians for creating the environment from which proletarian music would emerge. The group was most noted for its polemical exchanges with modernist musicians who sought to link artistic innovation with political radicalism and for its efforts to "proletarianize" the conservatories.

After the secession of Shul'gin's group, the leadership of the Proletarian Musicians' association passed to less experienced hands. Lebedinskii soon became the head of the organization, assisted by Sarra Krylova, who edited the association's journals. The only singer and one of the few women in the group, Krylova was invited on several occasions to perform for Lenin. Lebedinskii came from a doctor's family that supported the Socialist Revolutionaries. He had run away from home at fourteen to fight in Mikhail Tukhachevsky's unit of the Red Army, joining the Bolsheviks in 1919. He worked for the secret police and in a steel factory before asking the Party to support his desire to pursue musical studies.[16] An orator of considerable skill and boundless enthusiasm, he received his degree in musicology in 1930.

Lebedinskii's background and training typified that of the most visible and well-known cohort of RAPM's membership. Consisting of fewer than a dozen people, this group was young (most were born in 1900 or later), predominantly male, and in the process of achieving professional status.[17] Most completed a degree at the Moscow Conservatory in the late twenties or early thirties, many as musicologists. Several, including Lev Kaltat (1900–1946) and Iurii Keldysh (1907–95), were students of the Florentine-trained historian, Mikhail Ivanov-Boretskii.[18] Six became full members of the Party in the thirties or forties. Although RAPM was committed to promoting proletarian composers, the social origins of these RAPM members, many of whom were the sons of rural doctors or clergy, were typical of the radical intelligentsia and the leadership of other artistic groups such as the militant writers' association, RAPP, which were "proletarian" in name only.[19]

Despite the homogeneity of the most prominent part of the association's membership, the artistic and social profile of the organization as a whole was more varied. Aside from conservatory students with Communist political inclinations and professional aspirations, the organization also attracted leaders of music circles in workers' clubs who had little or no formal musical training: in 1928 more than one-third of RAPM's membership had no special qualifications as musicians.[20] Although the group's founding membership was dominated by veteran Party members in their thirties, by the end of 1924 only 20 percent of RAPM's members were Communists.[21]

From 1924 until the Cultural Revolution there were only two composers of note within the group's ranks.[22] M. M. Lazarev was the son of a poor church cantor who had served in the Red Army and Proletkul't before joining Georgii Katuar's composition class at the Moscow Conservatory. Lazarev soon vanished from the musical scene, but RAPM boasted of his social background and considered his vocal pieces, such as *Party Membership Card No. 224332* (*Partbilet No. 224332*), examples of genuine proletarian music.[23] In *Pound the Hammer* (*Bei molotom*), as seen in Example 1, Lazarev deployed up to six vocal parts in a pulsing declamation inspired by the sounds of the industrial workplace:

> Pound, pound the hammer!
> Pound, pound the hammer!

Pound!
Our faces are flushed with the blaze of the heat,
Iron we melt in the flames of the furnace,
Our hands work so nimbly, so nimbly, so nimbly,
And echoing them are the panting bellows:

A far more significant contribution than Lazarev's short-lived efforts was made by Aleksandr Kastal'skii, who became a professor at the conservatory after the Moscow Synodal School merged with that institution. Given his background as a noted composer of religious music, Kastal'skii would appear to be an unlikely ally of the Proletarian Musicians. But his previous activities with the People's Conservatory and Proletkul't indicate the depth of his commitment to promoting Russian folk music and popularizing choral music. He supported RAPM out of sympathy for its democratic orientation and his interest in using Russian folk music as the source for a new mass, revolutionary art.[24] Before his death in 1926 he composed several choral pieces on revolutionary themes, including *Song about Lenin* (*Pesnia pro Lenina*) and *To V. I. Lenin* (*V. I. Leninu*), which commemorated Lenin's death.

Kastal'skii's interest in folk motifs and melodies took him beyond overtly political themes. In works such as *Sten'ka Razin* he employed a more customary style of adapting folk melodies to a choral setting. Using the rich vocabulary associated with fishing and a balalaika accompaniment, *The Angler* (*Rybolov*) described a poor fisherman's comic attempts to steal from a wealthy peasant and their painful consequences. Works such as these, which related the exploits of robbers and rebels, exemplified the "healthy" folk song approved by RAPM. But despite his conservative musical predilections, Kastal'skii also experimented with unusual vocal effects and instrumentation. In *Troika* (Example 2), cymbals, triangles, and trumpets accompanied the chorus's tribute to "sun-legged" chargers pulling a speeding sleigh:

Whistling over the field, under the tattered knout,
Wind from the right, wind from the left, and from behind,
As though the wings of a hurricane carried them
These red, sun-legged chargers.

Hey, fly, charge forward, a shot in the wild night.
Russian sledge under a silver yoke
The path churned up by horseshoed hooves
Rear up, rear up, by the moon in the deserted night.

Example 1 M. M. Lazarev, *Pound the Hammer* (*Bei molotom*). For unaccompanied mixed chorus. RAPM called Lazarev's evocation of a hammer striking an anvil in the opening bars an example of "the masterful conveyance in music of the production process." Moscow: Muzsektor gosizdatel'stvo, 1924; K., "M. Lazarev," *Muzyka i Oktiabr'* 4–5 (1926): 12.

Kastal'skii's most distinctive large-scale work from this period was the *Agricultural Symphony* (*Sel'skokhoziaistvennaia simfoniia*), which was commissioned for the opening of the Moscow Agricultural Exhibition in 1923. More cantata than symphony, the work used traditional folk songs and dances for thematic material, and was scored for a full symphony orchestra, choir, and two soloists, as well as a domra quartet.[25]

The creative pursuits of Grigorii Liubimov provided an additional dimension to the Proletarian Musicians' activities. In the twenties Liubimov continued to promote the four-stringed domra (which came to be known as the "Liubimov" domra), publishing anthologies of music for domra ensembles and giving concerts in the Soviet Union and abroad with his domra quartet, whose members also belonged to RAPM.[26] He worked in the ethnographic section of the research institute, GIMN, and from 1926 to 1932 taught courses on folk instruments at the Moscow Conservatory.[27] In recognition of the domra ensemble's popularity with audiences and the high quality of its performances, Lunacharsky awarded Liubimov the title "honored artist of the republic" at the ensemble's tenth jubilee.[28]

While the main thrust of RAPM's activities in the twenties was on criticism and popular education, those who left the organization to form the Organization of Revolutionary Composers (ORK)[29] felt compelled to write music "for the revolution," even if it could not yet be considered "proletarian." While they shared many of RAPM's views on the musical legacy (including a veneration of Beethoven),[30] contemporary art music, and the current condition of popular musical culture, members of the Revolutionary Composers felt that critique and reform were not enough. Rather, they saw the composing and disseminating of songs on revolutionary themes as an essential part of the education and consciousness-raising that would eventually produce genuine proletarian music.[31]

The Revolutionary Composers never adopted a formal platform, contenting themselves instead with vaguely worded proclamations similar to that which heralded the founding of RAPM. A "preliminary" platform published in the first issue of the organization's journal, *Music and Revolution* (*Muzyka i revoliutsiia*), stressed the need for music to facilitate the broader tasks of cultural revolution,[32] as did an unpublished document preserved by Shul'gin's widow: "We public-spirited musicians pose as our goal the construction of a new life and a new culture based on communist ideology. . . . We consider that at the present time, musical influence should take a direction that facilitates the strengthening of the ideology of the proletariat and fights for a new, better, communist form of life."[33]

Although comparable in size to RAPM, the Revolutionary Composers were older (none born after 1900), less professionally qualified, and even less Communist. More than half were indeed composers, although only four had conservatory degrees, and none of these were from Moscow. Like their counterparts in the Proletarian Musicians' association, most ORK members took some part in the musical activities of workers' clubs, the Red Army, or other

Example 2 A. Kastal'skii, *Troika*. For mixed chorus, three trumpets in C, triangle and cymbals. Text by the peasant poet Petr Oreshin. Published in *Krasnyi Oktiabr'*, an anthology of revolutionary music commemorating the sixth anniversary of the revolution. Kastal'skii uses vocal glissandi and hissing to evoke the winds that sweep a speeding Russian troika to a great destiny, in a manner reminiscent of prerevolutionary road songs and the coda of Gogol's *Dead Souls*. Moscow: Muzsektor gosizdatel'stvo, 1924.

community organizations. With the exception of their leaders, Shul'gin and Sergeev, few were Party members in the twenties.[34]

The Revolutionary Composers acknowledged the distinction between their music, which was published by the "agitational" division of the State Publishing House, and music promoted as "artistic literature." Often referred to as *agitki*, a label developed for the agitational art and poetry of the Civil War, most of these pieces were written for solo voice or vocal ensembles. They were utilitarian, and had a specific, fairly modest purpose. According to Shul'gin, "[i]t will be enough, at first, if we manage to rivet attention to certain themes and moods, and if we can satisfy musical needs and play a certain musical-educational [*vospitatel'naia*] role for the proletariat."[35]

In terms of quantity, the Revolutionary Composers' efforts were impressive. Throughout NEP, the output of the agitational division increased constantly, from ten choral anthologies and 104 individual pieces in 1923 to over 300 titles in 1926. ORK's compositions favored romantic, revolutionary themes, often using texts by the proletarian poets affiliated with *The Smithy* (*Kuznetsy*) for hymns extolling the glory of the revolution, visions of happiness for all, or the joys of free labor. The group also found lyrics in the poetry of Dem'ian Bednyi, Vladimir Mayakovsky, and Aleksandr Bezymenskii. Their music was usually festive and often bombastic and overwrought. The uneven quality of these pieces concerned other musicians, the puritans in RAPM, and even Lunacharsky, who once mocked the *agitki* as "homebred simplifications" that either "forged" old music or flaunted inappropriate decoration, "like wearing earrings in one's nose."[36] A contemporary critic has called them "cold, complicated monster songs."[37]

Songs and choruses by Mikhail Krasev (1897–1954) exemplified the deficiencies of agitational music, and typified ORK's creative output. Krasev was by far the most prolific member of the group, publishing more than 250 choruses in five years. Although the Revolutionary Composers boasted of his productivity and the fact that he had only a minimum of formal training,[38] the Proletarian Musicians and others felt that Krasev's music epitomized all that was wrong with ORK's orientation and the dangers of writing music "to order" (*po zakazu*) (Example 3).[39] Like most of his colleagues, Krasev used his compositions in his work with music groups in workers' clubs and orphanages. He also began studying the folk music of the Caucasus and Crimean Tatars and wrote a number of pieces for children.[40]

Although less productive than Krasev, other members of ORK also devoted considerable energy to composing. Sergeev and Shul'gin published an occasional piece, but were mainly occupied with their duties at the publishing house. Among ORK's more active composers was Grigorii Lobachev (1888–1953), who had participated in Proletkul't and was a founding member of the music research institute, GIMN. In the twenties Lobachev continued to work with choirs in workers' and Red Army clubs and published arrangements of folk songs as well as agitational songs, such as *Il'ich Lived* (*Zhiv Il'ich*) and *A Call to Rebel* (*Zov miatezhnyi*). The latter used fanfares and dotted rhythms to create the martial, heroic mood that was Lobachev's trademark.

Klimentii Korchmarev (1899–1958) was one of the only ORK composers who wrote both "artistic" and "agitational" music. His opera *Ivan the Soldier*

Example 3 M. Krasev, *The Communard's Song* (*Pesnia kommunara*). For mixed chorus and piano. Text by S. Zaiatskii. The unremarkable voicing for the choir is overshadowed by a lumbering piano accompaniment with jarring dissonances created by poor voice leading. The martial feel of the piece is at odds with the 3/2 time signature. Moscow: Muzsektor gosizdatel'stvo, 1925.

Flames glitter over the walls,
Terribly rages the blaze.
All Paris to the barricades,
I am a young Communard!

(*Ivan soldat*, 1927) and the ballet *Serf Ballerina* (*Krepostnaia balerina*, 1927) were among the first works on Soviet themes written for the musical stage. Among his agitational pieces are *Left March* (*Levyi marsh*) and a number of settings of Bezymenskii's Komsomol poems.

In this rather motley collection of revolutionary composers, some individuals stood out more than others. By far the most prominent and skilled composer in ORK was the Proletkul't veteran Dmitrii Vasil'ev-Buglai, who had also defected from RAPM. In the twenties Vasil'ev-Buglai continued to compose on revolutionary themes and work with amateur choruses, directing the musical activities of the clubs affiliated with the All-Russian Central Executive Committee.[41] Like Kastal'skii, who had been his teacher at the Moscow Synodal School, Vasil'ev-Buglai often used folk melodies and dances as the foundation for his pro-Soviet songs. He was also drawn to the short, rhyming form of the *chastushka*, whose name means "often" or "repeatedly." The experiences of the Civil War provided a common theme for many of his pieces, including his famous arrangement of the recruitment song *Send Off* (*Provody*), which satirized traditional peasant values and celebrated the Bolsheviks' cause, and *Red Youth* (*Krasnaia molodezh'*), which valorized courage and sacrifice (Examples 4a and 4b). Vasil'ev-Buglai also continued to write the antireligious, satirical songs that his Proletkul't choir had performed at the front. These included *Priest-Drones Living by Cheating* (*Popy-trutni zhivut na plutni*) and *The Church Service* (*Tserkovnaia sluzhba*), an extended musical "fresco" based on cartoons and poetry by Dem'ian Bednyi published on the front page of *Pravda* on January 6, 1923.[42]

Noncomposers also made important contributions to the activities of the Revolutionary Composers organization. Shul'gin's wife, Elena Shul'gina (née Miamlina, 1888–?) served as the corresponding secretary of the organization's journal, *Music and Revolution*. She contributed regularly to the journal, often in pieces coauthored by Shul'gin or Efim Vilkovir, whose proposal prompted the establishment of the workers' faculty (*rabfak*) at the Moscow Conservatory. Mattias Sokol'skii (real surname "Grinberg," 1896–1977), a graduate of the Kiev Conservatory, was an active music critic, contributing regularly to *Music and Revolution* and a number of other journals, including the prestigious weekly, *Life of Art* (*Zhizn' iskusstva*). Sokol'skii held a number of administrative positions in the twenties and was head of music programming for the Moscow Trade Unions' radio station. Nikolai Dem'ianov (1888–1961) and Vladimir Dasmanov (1896–?) strengthened the Revolutionary Composers' connection with popular education programs and cultural activities. Dasmanov directed

Example 4a D. Vasil'ev-Buglai, *Send Off* (*Provody*). Text by Dem'ian Bednyi. Vasil'ev-Buglai's music is an adaptation of the Ukrainian folk tune *Oi, shcho zh to za uchinivsia. Antologiia sovetskoi pesni. 1917–1957*, vol. 1, ed. Viktor Belyi. Moscow: Gosudarstvennoe muzykal'noe izdatel'stvo, 1957.

When my very own mama sent me to the fighting
Then my very own kinfolk came a running.
Then my very own kinfolk came a running.

Where on earth you going guy?
Where on earth?
Oh, don't go there Johnny, into the army.
Oh, don't go there Johnny, into the army.

Example 4b D. Vasil'ev-Buglai, *Red Youth (Krasnaia molodezh')*. The simple couplets of this solemn hymn reflect the influences of traditional soldiers' songs. Rossiiskaia assotsiatsiia proletarskykh muzykantov. *Tvorcheskii sbornik*. Moscow: Gosudarstvennoe muzykal'noe izdatel'stvo, 1931.

We go on without fear,
We go on without fail,
We go on to meet the awful foe.

The cause of the oppressed is the cause of youth.
Woe to those on yonder dark shore.

the music programs of "Polenov House,"[43] which organized cultural programs for the countryside surrounding Moscow. Dem'ianov taught choral singing and music theory in a number of Moscow music schools (technicums) and was an instructor for leaders of music circles affiliated with the Trade Unions' workers' clubs.

The leaders of the Revolutionary Composers organization would rejoin RAPM during the Cultural Revolution, but for the remainder of NEP they played an important part in the factional politics of musical life and pursued a unique strategy for changing musical culture. While the Proletarian Musicians have borne much of the blame for the hastily written "revolutionary" music of the twenties, ORK, much more so than RAPM, was the haven for "almost illiterate, amateurish composers."[44] The differences between the two organizations may seem slight, and their ideological positions did overlap more than either side would admit. But, as is often true of schisms, the enmity between former comrades ran deep and intensified with time. The rift between the Proletarian Musicians and the Revolutionary Composers had important consequences for the future of Soviet music and made the tactical choices for other activists on the musical front more complex.

Prokoll

Although it shared many of the objectives advanced by RAPM and ORK, the third group on the musical Left launched an independent quest to address the needs of an audience much broader than the traditional musical public. In the spring of 1925 several composition students at the Moscow Conservatory organized a "production collective," or Prokoll, in order to write music that would be both artistically valuable and accessible to a mass audience. The idea to organize the group emerged in the fall of 1924 during a competition for pieces commemorating Lenin. Aleksandr Davidenko (1899–1934) and Boris Shekhter (1900–1961), who both won prizes, had realized the need for this kind of creative organization as they worked on their entries.[45] Additional impetus came from students who, in completing their required practicums in workers' clubs, found the repertoire for the clubs' choral circles inadequate, antiquated, or politically inappropriate. Prokoll was also an effort to counterbalance what its organizers perceived as the apolitical and cliquish stance of the young composers affiliated with the ASM.[46] In addition to Davidenko and Shekhter, Prokoll's initiative group consisted of Viktor Belyi (1904–83),

Genrikh Bruk (1905–?), and Vladimir Tarnopol'skii (1897–1942). Others soon joined, including Marian Koval' (1907–71), Nikolai Chemberdzhi (1903–48), Zara Levina (1907–71), Vladimir Fere (1902–71), Sergei Riauzov (1905–83), Zinovii Kompaneets (1902–87), Daniel Zhitomirskii (1906–92), and Nikolai Chaplygin (1905–87). The group also included Dmitry Kabalevsky (1904–87), the famous composer of children's piano music.[47]

Prokoll described its main task as the "creation of artistic musical literature saturated with the ideas of Soviet revolutionary public opinion." It sought to realize this objective in two ways: first by "searching for new musical forms in consonance with contemporary reality" using the musical achievements of the past and present as a foundation; and second by creating musical forms (marches, mass songs, etc.) suitable for mass performances.[48] The group worked primarily in the area of vocal and choral music, and developed a system of rigorous peer review for their compositions. They focused on short vocal pieces because they felt this music best met the current needs of the "mass audience." Recognizing that "Soviet revolutionary public opinion" might have little in common with the tastes of traditional consumers of classical music, they subjected their work to "social trials" by factory workers and students, soliciting written and verbal feedback after each performance. They also held public debates on such topics as "Decadence and Music" and "The Jazz Band."[49] All of the group's members worked directly with workers in some capacity, either as leaders of choral circles or as accompanists in factory clubs.

The profile of Prokoll presents a sharp contrast to both the Proletarian Musicians and the Revolutionary Composers. Virtually all of the group's twenty-odd members were born at the turn of the century or later.[50] All received a conservatory degree or its equivalent, the vast majority in composition. Although only Marian Koval' and Viktor Belyi belonged to the Komsomol during their conservatory days, a third of the group became full-fledged Party members in the late thirties or forties.

In keeping with the group's spirit of collectivism, Prokoll did not have an official "leader," but Aleksandr Davidenko was the "soul and cement" of the enterprise.[51] The orphaned son of an Odessa telegraph operator, his musical abilities were first noticed in the mandatory singing classes of the seminary where he was sent after his parents died. He studied briefly at the Odessa Conservatory in 1918 before being drafted into the Red Army. After being demobilized in Kharkov he worked as a railroad janitor, continuing his musical studies with Joseph Schillinger at the Kharkov Musical Institute. When Davidenko came to Moscow in the early twenties Aleksandr Kastal'skii and Reinhold Gliere took the young man under their wing, helping him gain provisional admission to the conservatory and jointly enroll in the People's Choral Academy (which Kastal'skii directed).

Like the ASM, Prokoll united people already linked by social ties as well as artistic and ideological sensibilities. Davidenko shared Odessan origins with his closest friend Boris Shekhter and the pianist-composer Zara Levina, whose acquaintance he had first made at the Odessa Conservatory. Like Davidenko, Daniel Zhitomirskii had made his way to the Moscow Conservatory from Kharkov, as did Viktor Belyi, who had also studied with Schillinger. The core of Prokoll—Davidenko, Shekhter, Belyi—along with their wives and Zara Levina, navigated the adventures and hardships of student life together as only close friends can.[52] With few exceptions, Prokoll's commitment to collectivism did not involve joint authorship, but rather collective editing of pieces written by individuals. Discussions at the group's weekly meetings were frequently intense, and criticism direct and unceremoniously harsh. Yet by all accounts participants rarely felt the comments were petty or unjustified.

When evaluating its members' work, the group also debated the appropriate ways to reach the mass audience it so idealized. Davidenko and others, such as Marian Koval', strongly felt that vocal forms should be foremost in the group's attention because text provided a concrete link between music and social reality.[53] Davidenko insisted that every member write songs geared to a mass audience, even threatening those who failed to produce such pieces promptly with "formal reprimands." With what Daniel Zhitomirskii described as "fanatical straightforwardness," Davidenko hoped to elevate songs and mass music in general to "full value" (*polnotsennye*) forms of musical creativity.[54] But while many Prokoll members regarded what they called "pure," or instrumental, music with suspicion, others, including Zhitomirskii and Nikolai Chemberdzhi, felt that an exclusive focus on vocal forms would doom Prokoll's members to "hackwork." They insisted that proficiency with sonatas, symphonies, and quartets was essential to every professional composer.[55]

Nevertheless, songs and choruses made up the overwhelming majority of Prokoll's output.[56] Even Viktor Belyi, who had previously written almost exclusively for the piano, shifted direction under Davidenko's influence. In the search for "monumental" revolutionary art, Davidenko did take on larger projects using vocal forms, such as *The Year 1919* (*1919 g.*), an opera about the Civil War. The group's most celebrated undertaking was a "collectively composed" oratorio, *October's Path* (*Put' Oktiabria*), commemorating the tenth anniversary of the revolution in 1927.[57]

Like ORK's *agitki*, Prokoll's compositions dealt with a discrete set of themes: the revolution and its heroes, the Civil War, building socialism, and the country's "new heroes," Soviet youth. The group's most successful compositions from the twenties dealt with the events and heroism of the Civil War. Prokoll members drew on a diverse range of sources for their music, including contemporary (anonymous) revolutionary songs, songs from the Red Army, *chastushki*, contemporary art music, and the aural palette of the modern urban environment. While they struggled to avoid an "uncritical" use of the Russian peasant folk song,[58] some, especially Davidenko, used the melodic and formal conventions of Russian folk music and studied the music of the country's ethnic minorities.

The different levels of accessibility and sophistication present in Prokoll's compositions indicate the problems the group encountered in attempting to both reach a mass audience and achieve artistic significance in their work.[59] A few songs, such as Davidenko's *Budennyi's Cavalry* (*Konnaia Budennogo*) (Example 5a) and *The First Cavalry* (*Pervaia konnaia*), and Shekhter's *The Young Guard* (*Molodaia gvardiia*) (Example 5b), were catchy and could be quickly picked up by the untrained ear. The ease with which these songs were taken up by soldiers, the Komsomol youth, and others earned them the designation of "mass songs," a concept that would be much debated in the second part of the decade.

But most of Prokoll's vocal pieces were too complex and too closely tied to the recital hall to allow for quick assimilation by the musically untrained, and were unsuitable for collective performance. Despite its understated, direct appeal and melodic references to a Siberian vagabond song,[60] Davidenko's *Mother* (*Mat'*) falls into this category, as do Shekhter's prize-winning entry from the 1924 Lenin commemorative competition, *When the Leader Dies* (*Kogda umiraet vozhd'*) and Belyi's vocal monologue *The Twenty-Six* (Example 6). In an effort to overcome the distance between performer and audience Prokoll made good use of the engaging potential of the half-spoken, half-sung form of the vocal monologue. The earliest and best known effort in this area was Davidenko's vocal placard, *About Lenin* (*Pro Lenina*), which earned him a scholarship to complete his conservatory studies.

Prokoll's artistic orientation and struggle to remain independent of other musical organizations indicate the complexities of musicians' political and aesthetic allegiances in this period. Davidenko's group admired and was drawn to the music promoted by the ASM, including that of Aleksandrov and Miaskovskii, as well as Prokofiev, Stravinsky, Hindemith, and the French "Six." Several Prokoll members, Viktor Belyi, Vladimir Fere, Dmitry Kabalevsky, Marian Koval', Zara Levina, and Boris Shekhter, were students of Miaskovskii, who occasionally brought them to the Sunday meetings at

Example 5a A. Davidenko, *Budennyi's Cavalry* (*Konnaia Budennogo*). For a cappella voice and chorus. Text by N. Aseev. A bold, jaunty verse that segues to a rollicking chorus provides the musical framework for recounting Budennyi's epic Civil War victory. The strophic structure and couplet verse form of this marching song are typical of the traditional soldiers' songs and folk dances to which it is related. *Antologiia sovetskoi pesni. 1917–1957*, vol. 1, ed. Viktor Belyi. Moscow: Gosudarstvennoe muzykal'noe izdatel'stvo, 1957.

From heaven's mid-day scorching rays there was no approach.
Budennyi's cavalry spread out across the steppe.
Budennyi's cavalry spread out across the steppe.
Budennyi's cavalry spread out across the steppe.
Spread out across the steppe.

Derzhanovskii's.[61] Belyi, Fere, Kabalevsky, and Koval' all played in or had their work performed at the ASM's concerts.[62] At the debate on "Decadence and Music" Prokoll members defended Stravinsky and Prokof'ev from attacks by RAPM representatives who championed Beethoven and Musorgsky.

But the group's utilitarian concern with meeting the musical needs of what they called the "mass audience" and commitment to practical work with the music circles of workers' clubs also made Prokoll sympathetic to the orientation of RAPM and ORK. Both of these organizations identified a kindred

Example 5b B. Shekhter, *The Young Guard* (*Molodaia gvardia*). Text by S. Tret'iakov. Shekhter's march provides an uplifting, bold affirmation of the "young guard's" commitment to the Soviet state. Rossiiskaia assotsiatsiia proletarskykh muzykantov. *Tvorcheskii sbornik.* Moscow: Gosudarstvennoe muzykal'noe izdatel'stvo, 1931.

Iron reservists, we grew up everywhere
By our oath we'll be first in battle, in building, and in labor.

We are the young guard of an invincible camp.
We are the young guard of workers and peasants.

spirit in Prokoll and courted its young members. Viktor Belyi and Marian Koval' published attacks on ASM composers and jazz, which were applauded by both the Proletarian Musicians and the Revolutionary Composers.[63] But as "serious" composers, Davidenko's group rejected the deliberately simplified style promoted by ORK. Prokoll objected to the distinction between agitational and artistic music, insisting that the mass audience deserved and demanded a music incorporating the best qualities of contemporary art music as well as the classical legacy.[64] Throughout the twenties, Davidenko insisted that the group maintain its independence and unique position among other musical groups. Prokoll declined the ASM's offer of a merger in January 1926, and most of its members refrained from participating in the internecine disputes and polemics that commanded much of RAPM's attention. Only with the advent of the Cultural Revolution did politics win out over artistic preferences. In 1929 Davidenko and the core of Prokoll joined RAPM, becoming the creative nucleus of that organization.

Factional Politics and Outsiders

The creative potential and political orientation of Prokoll made the ASM, RAPM, and ORK see Davidenko's group as an attractive potential ally. The other organizations on the musical Left, however, were much less sought after. RAPM's split with ORK and the resulting disputes over tactics and ideology had far-reaching repercussions for both groups that were especially damaging to the fortunes of the Proletarian Musicians. For the rest of the twenties the organization's small size, squabbles with other musicians, and inability to secure adequate institutional and financial support compromised its effectiveness. Although the Revolutionary Composers had a stable institutional base for their publishing activities, their music failed to gain popularity with its intended audience (workers, soldiers, and peasants) or win acceptance from other quarters in the musical community. For different reasons and to varying degrees both groups remained marginalized from the mainstream of musical life until the Cultural Revolution.

From its inception RAPM found itself on the defensive in its dealings with the State Publishing House and the bureaucratic apparatus of Narkompros, the latter of which was staffed predominantly by well-trained, professional musicians.[65] While the bureaucracy for the most part ignored rather than opposed RAPM, the organization encountered genuine enmity at the State Publishing House from Nikolai Roslavets, who used *Musical Culture* to promote his own conception of revolutionary music—a vision completely at odds with the evolving "back to Beethoven" program of RAPM. As political editor of the music division, Roslavets had censorial control over *Musical Virgin Soil* that could only partly be mitigated by Chernomordikov, Sergeev, and Shul'gin. When RAPM launched a direct attack on the views set out in "his"

Example 6 V. Belyi, *The Twenty-Six* (*Dvadtsat' shest'*). Text by N. Aseev. Skryabinesque influences (which, as with RAPM, were controversial among Prokoll members) lend expressiveness to the piano part of this tribute to the twenty-six commissars from Baku martyred during the Civil War. Rossiiskaia assotsiatsiia proletarskykh muzykantov. *Tvorcheskii sbornik*. Moscow: Gosudarstvennoe muzykal'noe izdatel'stvo, 1931.

And do not wash the rouge from the face
And do not bury from fear in the earth
The one who betrayed Shaumian,
The one who betrayed Dzhaparidze.
Ahhh.

journal, Roslavets exercised this authority freely, prompting the Proletarian Musicians to appeal to "higher authorities."[66] Both sides lost. The Party organization at the publishing house decided to close down both journals at the end of 1924.

This decision, which dealt a staggering blow to both RAPM and Roslavets, coincided with an administrative restructuring of the Music Division that integrated its affairs more closely with those of the State Publishing House.[67] The administrative shakeup continued the centralizing and rationalizing processes begun at the end of the Civil War and made music publishing subject to the principles of "cost accounting" (*khozraschet*) that were to strengthen the country's economy. It also further attenuated the influence of ASM members (Lamm, Miaskovskii, Roslavets) who were active in the Music Division's affairs, causing the ASM to protest the restructuring.

Those involved responded to these measures because of their impact on musical life, but developments outside the musical community were also decisive. The suspension of both journals and the concurrent bureaucratic reshuffling stemmed at least partially from the Party's reluctant intervention in the campaign that the proletarian writers organization, RAPP, waged against Voronskii's support of loyal, non-Party writers throughout 1923. The press section of the Central Committee first drafted a statement on literary policy in a two-day meeting in May 1924. The main tenets of this policy were ratified at the Thirteenth Party Congress a few weeks later, and elaborated upon extensively in the Central Committee Resolution on Belles Lettres of July 1925.[68]

The Central Committee's resolution framed the debate in literature in terms of ongoing class struggle and its extension to the cultural front. It welcomed the advent of artistic groups representing proletarian interests and acknowledged the historic rights of these groups to cultural hegemony. At the same time, the resolution dictated that "fellow travelers" should be tolerated and encouraged, as their support was essential for the building of socialism. The Party thus gave implicit encouragement to proletarian groups but declined to give them a monopoly on the press or intervene directly in debates about artistic form and style. Although the policy set out in the resolutions of 1924–25 addressed literary issues, it had obvious implications for the other arts, and formalized the Party's commitment to preserving the cultural legacy and supervising publishing enterprises and relations between rival aesthetic groups.

These developments exacerbated the tensions within RAPM and contributed to the split in ranks. Taking a cue from the Party's directive to be more tolerant and accommodating of specialists and "fellow travelers," Shul'gin's group supported a proposal to replace *Musical Virgin Soil* and *Musical Culture* with one journal edited by Roslavets with the assistance of RAPM representatives. The future ORK members also pressured RAPM to disband as an official organization registered with Narkompros, and become an informal circle (*kruzhok*) of the agitation department, a suggestion RAPM rejected out of hand.

At the end of NEP, Lebedinskii bitterly remembered this time as the darkest hour of his organization's history.[69] RAPM managed to retain its formal independence, but lost its base of operations. In 1926 it succeeded in publishing five issues of a journal called *Music and October* (*Muzyka i Oktiabr'*) with a private press, but was unable to sustain the journal. Kastal'skii's death in 1926 deprived RAPM of its one professional composer, and when David Chernomordikov received a diplomatic assignment in Greece that same year it lost the only "Old Bolshevik" from its founding group.

Although scholars have long maintained that RAPM's influence increased during the twenties, a chronic lack of financial resources and an inability to broaden the scope of their activities plagued the Proletarian Musicians throughout the decade. Despite its designation as the "Russian" Association of Proletarian Musicians, RAPM remained a Moscow-based organization. Affiliates formed in Leningrad and other provincial cities but had only a shadowy existence until the advent of the Cultural Revolution. With little official support and no journal, the group turned much of its attention to practical work with clubs and amateur music groups. The Moscow Trade Unions nominally supported these efforts, but RAPM was less successful in forming an alliance with the Komsomol, whose agendas often mirrored those of RAPM and whose political position became stronger as the decade progressed.

As we will see, RAPM took advantage of those opportunities that did present themselves. The organization played an active part in the debates on the "mass song" in 1926 and made every effort to capitalize on the commemorative activities surrounding the centennial of Beethoven's death in 1927. It was a force to be reckoned with at the Moscow Conservatory, where it lobbied for reform of the curriculum and admissions policies and was often backed by the Conservatory's Party and Red Professors' Organizations.

With the closing down of *Musical Virgin Soil* and the reorganization of the publishing house, the Revolutionary Composers also went through a difficult period of retrenchment. But Shul'gin's and Sergeev's continued employment at the State Publishing House gave their group the institutional base that the Proletarian Musicians sorely lacked. ORK members continued to publish their work in ever-increasing quantity. When the Music Division again sponsored a journal in 1926, Shul'gin was its main editor. *Music and Revolution* appeared monthly until 1929 and was the most substantial "thick" music journal in the twenties.

The success of *Music and Revolution* reflected both the stability of official policy toward the arts following the Central Committee's 1925 decree and the political savvy of the journal's editors. In keeping with the official policy of cultivating "fellow travelers" and gathering all sympathetic forces to the lines of the third front, *Music and Revolution* covered a wide range of issues and involved participants from many sectors of the musical community. It reported on the classical music scene in the Soviet Union and abroad, as well as the activities of workers' clubs, music schools, the conservatories, and research institutes. Along with articles by members of ORK, the journal featured contributions from leaders of the modernist organizations (Sabaneev, Beliaev, and Asaf'ev, but never Roslavets), the distinguished historians Ivanov-Boretskii and Konstantin Kuznetsov, and the theorist Nikolai Garbuzov. The good scholarship of many of these articles, along with the diversity of the journal's offerings, have earned *Music and Revolution* and ORK the reputation of being more "tolerant" of the Russian and Western modernists than their rivals in RAPM.[70] But the journal is better characterized as being eclectic or even contradictory in its position. Articles by ORK's Sokol'skii praised the talent and promise of Dmitrii Shostakovich and Sergei Prokofiev, calling for the latter's return to Soviet Russia.[71] Yet lead editorials frequently set out caustic diatribes against contemporary music and foreigners, sometimes directed at their own contributors.[72]

Thus, ORK was a much stronger presence on the NEP musical scene and the diversity of the musical Left was more significant than scholars have recognized. Official response from the Party and the State Publishing House to the factional struggles of the early twenties narrowed the field of debate, but also eventually supported a more inclusive journal. Contradictory as its contents often were, *Music and Revolution* became an important part of the forum in which musicians addressed the ideological challenges of the revolution. The issues raised by RAPM, ORK, and Prokoll were debated from a range of perspectives in the musical press and addressed concretely in popular education and enlightenment programs for workers, youth, and soldiers. An examination of these activities reveals the dilemmas musicians of the Left encountered in their quest to find an audience for their music and to reform popular musical culture.

4

Of "Cast-Off Barroom Garbage" and "Bold Revolutionary Songs"

The Problem of Popular Music, 1923–1926

Наше оружие—наши песни.
Наше эолото—эвенящие голоса.
—В. Маяковский

Our songs are our weapon,
Ringing voices our gold.
—V. Mayakovsky

The musical Left's debates with other musicians and their efforts to reform the content of and access to music education created a struggle for the "commanding heights" of musical culture. This battle occupied much of the Left's energy, but was only part of a broader campaign to bring the revolution to music. Efforts to cultivate a new kind of musical culture from the bottom up were even more central to the program of the Proletarian Musicians (RAPM), the conservatory students in Prokoll, and especially the Revolutionary Composers (ORK). These groups strove to reform popular musical culture in the early years of NEP.

The musical Left pursued a number of strategies to eliminate the divide between elite and popular musical culture, all of which involved a rejection of popular urban music as it currently existed and the cultural influences that fostered it. As part of their effort to instill workers with an appreciation for particular kinds of music (their own, or selections from the classical repertoire), reformers campaigned against songs and dances they called "NEP music." Their specific objections to this music reflected a hostility to NEP itself that was shared by many activists on the cultural front. The Left understood their struggle against the banality and philistinism (*poshlost'* and *meshchanstvo*) they felt this music fostered as part of a war on the manifestations of degenerate bourgeois culture that corrupted the sensibilities of workers and peasants. Because workers were the most attractive constituency and because cultural work in the countryside was minimal in the years after the Civil War, these groups concentrated their attentions on music in the daily life (*byt*) of the working class in Russia's urban centers. Only in the second part of the decade did their efforts extend to provincial towns and the countryside.

Music's ability to influence the emotions and its nonrepresentational qualities presented these groups with unique challenges. The tensions between intractable musical preferences and reformers' rejection of most music that enjoyed widespread popularity undercut the effectiveness of their efforts to bring the revolution to popular music, as did their inability to offer appealing substitutes for what they criticized. A commitment to democratizing select portions of the legacy of European art music counterbalanced their dismissal of genuinely popular forms, indicating an unacknowledged elitism at odds with their nominal commitment to develop a genuinely proletarian musical culture. The Left's attempts to transform musical creativity and its milieu failed in the short run, but by framing the question of "revolutionary" or "proletarian" music in terms of accessibility and a distinction between desirable and objectionable musical styles, these musicians left a lasting mark on Soviet musical culture and laid the foundations for the Cultural Revolution in music.

What Was "NEP Music"?

What the musical Left stigmatized as "NEP music" was rich in variety, for beyond the walls of the concert hall and operatic theater, Russians listened to, played, sang, and danced to a wide range of music. Traditional folk songs retained their appeal, as did songs of the revolutionary movement, which were genuinely revered in certain quarters and enthusiastically promoted by the authorities. But the presence and popularity of many other kinds of music in the twenties—from "gypsy" romances and street songs, to tangos, fox-trots, two-steps, and *chastushki*, "rhymed ditties"—more fully reflected the diversity of Russia's modernizing urban culture.

In the twenties the gypsy genre (*tsyganshchina*) remained popular and was dispersed through sheet music, on records, and from the same stage venues as in the prerevolutionary period. *Tsyganshchina* generally conveyed one of two ranges of emotions—a feeling of abandon, recklessness, or lawlessness, or one of disappointment in love, spiritual crisis, jealousy, and hopelessness.[1] Some of the most popular "gypsy" songs of these years, such as *Gypsy Girl* (*Tsyganochka*), directly linked these feelings to exotic, romanticized images of gypsies. Others, such as *Little Bells* (*Bubentsy*) and *Cut-Glass Tumblers* (*Stakanchiki granenye*), associated commonplace items (a broken glass or sleigh bells) with lost love and regret for the past.[2]

Along with the gypsy genre, dance music, much of it imported from the West, enjoyed tremendous popularity. The prerevolutionary enthusiasm for the tango and fox-trot persisted, as did a hearty appetite for the latest in Western jazz. Travelers and touring groups such as The Chocolate Kiddies and Benny Peyton's Jazz Kings acquainted eager audiences with new dances and music. The mid-twenties found Russians wriggling to the shimmy and the Charleston, and savoring wildly erotic revivals of dances associated with the decadence of high society before the revolution. In Apache dances rakishly clad mobsters preyed on unsuspecting females, while death's-head masks concealed the faces of the male seducer in Tangos of Death.[3] The demand for live jazz enhanced the market for sheet music. Dance tunes (primarily waltzes, but also fox-trots, shimmies, two-steps, and so forth) were published in considerable quantity by private firms such as the Association of Moscow Authors (AMA) as well as the State Publishing House. To promote sales of newly-published dance music, the AMA also sponsored a jazz band led by Aleksandr Tsfasman from 1927 to 1930.[4]

Profiling the audience for and popularity of particular kinds of urban music in this period has its challenges. Although the constituencies of certain types of music were determined partly by sensibilities and resources, many songs and dances gained a general popularity that defies simple categorization. Thus, while ragtime and fox-trots had originally been a leisure pursuit of the upper classes, in the twenties a thirst for the new dance music seized broad sections of the urban population, becoming particularly insatiable among young people, including working-class youth and Komsomol members. Similarly, while the gypsy genre continued to appeal to people with middle-class sensibilities and access to guitars, pianos, phonographs, and money for buying sheet music, it also reached a more varied public in cafés, at parks, and at popular stage venues such as Moscow's Palace theater and the Aquarium music hall. Some *tsyganshchina*, especially pieces advertised as "songs of the new way of life," gained popularity among workers and even found an audience in the countryside.

"Songs of the new way of life" sometimes used the musical style of *tsyganshchina* (and critics often lumped the two together), but took the revolution or its impact on everyday life as their main theme. The most successful composers of these kinds of songs got their start writing for the variety stage, often in southern Russia or Ukraine. Three songs about the revolution that earned a permanent place in the popular repertoire were written by *estrada* musicians during the Civil War. After being drafted into Budennyi's First Cavalry, Dmitrii Pokrass put his background as a pianist at Rostov's Crooked Jimmy theater to good use in composing *Red Cavalrymen* (*Krasnye kavaleristy*) (Example 7), a jaunty tribute to these legendary fighters.[5] His brother Samuil composed *The Red Army Is Stronger Than All* (*Krasnaia armiia vsekh sil'nei*) in 1920 to rally resistance against Pyotr Wrangel's last offensive in the Crimea. That same year, Iulii Khait crafted the uplifting strains of the future anthem of the Soviet air force, *Aviamarsh*, better known as *Ever Higher* (*Vse vyshe*) (Example 8) after a demonstration of military planes at the Kiev Aerodrome.[6]

During NEP, songwriters such as Khait, the Pokrass brothers, Matvei Blanter, and Valentin Kruchinin published much of their work with the AMA, which became a primary source of "light genre" music—a catchall designation for *tsyganshchina*, dance tunes, and songs of the new way of life. The mood of songs like *Tambourine's Jingle* (*Bubna zvon*) by Samuil Pokrass and Khait's *No Need to Meet* (*Ne nado vstrech'*) fit comfortably with the *tsyganshchina* tradition of restlessness, melancholy, and disillusionment with love. Other pieces such as Khait's *The Young Successors* (*Smena*) and Valentin Kruchinin's *Mine No. 3* (*Shakhta No. 3*) evoked the hopes and travails of a distinctly Soviet context, becoming popular with a range of audiences. But of all the songs of the new way of life, Kruchinin's *Little Bricks* (*Kirpichiki*) was unsurpassed in its success with audiences of all social backgrounds.[7]

Pavel German wrote the text for this lively, pro-Soviet ditty about love and revolution in a brick factory for a variety show at the Peacock's Tail theater in 1923. Valentin Kruchinin's musical accompaniment was an adaptation of *Two Dogs* (*Dve sobaki*), a popular German waltz tune by S. Beilinzon, also used in Meierhold's production of Ostrovsky's *The Forest* (*Les*) in the 1924–25 season. A topical, sentimental story and catchy tune quickly made *Little Bricks* a hit. Sheet music sales ultimately totaled almost a million copies before the piece was banned during the Cultural Revolution. The song inspired both a film and a play, and lent its name to at least two songbooks. It entered the song repertoire of factories, mines, and the countryside, where numerous textual adaptations emerged reflecting the particular circumstances of, among other places, a cloth factory and a coal mine.[8] Its popularity was matched, however, by an overwhelmingly negative response from critics who found its text banal and its music reminiscent of a hurdy-gurdy (Example 9). As we will see, *Little Bricks* and its success became emblematic of just about everything that reformers thought was bad about "NEP music."

Example 7 D. Pokrass, *Red Cavalrymen* (*Krasnye kavaleristy*), 1920. Text by various authors, including A. Frenkel'. Also known as *Budennyi's March* (*Marsh Budennogo*), the song lost its association with the composer as it became popular. Shul'gin transcribed it as an "anonymous" revolutionary song in a Moscow workers' club in 1922. The State Publishing House put out this four-part setting by S. I. Pototski in 1924, two years before the AMA published the first version attributed to Pokrass. Evidence of the composer's dance hall experience is found in the rhythm and repeated eighth-note melody of the verse.

We are the Red Cavalrymen
About us epic story tellers spin this tale:
About how on clear nights
About how on rainy days
We proudly and boldly go off to fight.

Example 8 Iu. Khait, *Ever Higher* (*Vse vyshe*). For voice with piano and accordion accompaniment. Although youth responded to the utopianism of Pavel German's text, critics found Khait's music overly sentimental, banal, and too reminiscent of a cabaret tune. Moscow: Muzyka, 1966 [1920].

We have been born to make fairy tales come true,
To overcome distances and space.
Our minds have given steel wings to our hands
In place of a heart, a pulsing motor.

A final category of urban popular music consists of several largely unpublished genres that had emerged in the decades prior to the revolution. This music included "cruel romances," "underworld" or "street" songs, and *chastushki*, and circulated primarily among the less affluent and less educated. "Cruel (*zhestokie*) romances," such as *Marusia Poisoned Herself* (*Marusia otravilas'*) and *The Grave* (*Mogila*), were distinguished by their overwrought, trite music and ironic, melodramatic lyrics about illicit love, betrayal, or infidelity. "Underworld" (*blatnye*) or "street" (*ulichnye*) songs told of the woes and exploits of homeless children, criminals, and the down and out. The bands of children left homeless by the economic and social upheaval of the revolution claimed *Forgotten, Abandoned* (*Pozabyt, pozabroshen*) as their anthem. It was among the most popular street songs during NEP and was later immortalized in the 1931 film, *Road to Life* (*Putevka v zhizn'*).[9] Other underground and street songs commented more directly on the daily life that inspired them. The narrative verse and sales cry refrain of *Bagels* (*Bublichki*) lent the song to endless repetition and variation by a street vendor:

> Come buy these little buns, these little tasty buns
> Bring all your rubles here, come right away.
> And on this bitter night, look at my bitter plight
> Have pity on this private peddler girl.

Some street songs were more lighthearted, such as *Chicken* (*Tsyplennok*), which parodied the internal passport system and the corruption of the police:

> Boiled chicken,
> Roasted chicken,
> Chickens also want to live!
>
> We will catch him
> And then arrest him
> He'll hardly have a passport to show.
>
> No passport?
> Give me some coin!
> No coin? Off with your coat![10]

Short (usually four-line) rhymed songs called *chastushki* originated in the countryside, but were also sung and composed by urban workers, whose creations then drifted back to the village. Like the cruel romance, *chastushki* were

Example 9 V. Kruchinin, *Little Bricks* (*Kirpichiki*). Text by Pavel German. The most common version of the song traces the fortunes of a poor girl whose love for Stenka, a fellow brick factory employee, survives strikes, war, and revolution. Returning to the devastated factory after the Bolshevik victory, the couple rebuilds the brickyard and Stenka becomes the new factory director. Leningrad and Moscow: Russkoe izdatel'stvo, 1924.

On the outskirts of some forgotten town
I was born to a poor family.
Woe was me I thought, when at age fifteen
I was sent to the brickyard to work.

especially popular among women. Many were about love, but they also provided a constantly evolving commentary on current events. In the early Soviet period ethnographers and other researchers monitored them closely for political content. The best-known, pro-Soviet *chastushka* in this period was the Civil War soldiers' song, *Little Apple* (*Iablochko*):[11]

> Hey you, little apple,
> Apple with a spot of green,
> Kolchak won't be allowed
> To get beyond the Urals.

As with other types of "NEP music," the appeal of *chastushki* stemmed, at least in part, from their topicality and versatility. Paradoxically, the accessibility and variety of this music were a source of concern for would-be reformers.

Confronting Musical *Byt*

As was true elsewhere in the twenties, popular music in Soviet Russia faced criticism from a number of quarters. Just as hostility to jazz united moral and aesthetic crusaders in the United States, so were concerns about some of the music of daily life (*byt*) in the Soviet Union shared by broad sections of the creative intelligentsia, significant numbers of musicians, and even some political authorities. The criticisms of the musical Left overlapped those of others who objected to music they considered politically or aesthetically unacceptable. But the Left was unique in that they tried to correct what they criticized.

Leftist musicians' critique of popular music and strategies for changing it reflected a complex blend of ideological and cultural preferences. Their analysis of musical culture arose from their faith in Marxism and the conviction that art reflects and advances the ideology of the class that creates it. Their belief in "class" art also obliged them to try to define, identify, and help create a proletarian music. But given the absence of a clear position on music in the oeuvre of Marxist theorists and the challenges of formulating ideological evaluations of nonrepresentational artistic expression, the musical Left's "Marxist" perspective never achieved coherence. Instead, elements of class analysis, speculation about music's function in the ideological superstructure, and a certain amount of utopianism blended with deeply ingrained aspects of the Russian intelligentsia's beliefs about culture to yield distinctive, often contradictory diagnoses of what was wrong with music and how to fix it.

Activists in RAPM and ORK frequently noted that unlike the other arts, especially literature, music and musical life seemed virtually unaffected by the revolution. The music played in the capitals' concert halls still reflected the preferences of the former elite, while popular music either continued prerevolutionary traditions or was imported from the decadent, capitalist West. They explained this "backwardness" in terms of the "conservatism" of musical culture, which they maintained stemmed from the nature of musical creativity itself.[12] The abstract nature of musical expression set it apart from other artistic forms that relied on more concrete language and images. Convinced that art could not be "neutral" or "classless" (until a classless society had been achieved), the musical Left nonetheless admitted that music did not lend itself readily to ideological analysis, because (again in contrast to literature) musical perception involved the emotions more than the intellect.

And yet the qualities that made music "backward" also made it incredibly attractive to revolutionaries and reformers, for the musical Left well understood that music's influence on the emotions made it a powerful mobilizing device. Songs had been valuable allies to the revolutionary movement. They should continue to serve as powerful weapons in the class struggle and become important tools of the proletariat in building Communism. In their debates with other groups and in their efforts to attract more official support for their programs, activists frequently insisted that music was not just entertainment or amusement (*razvlechenie*). It was a medium for training one's aural perception of the world. By properly influencing people's emotions it should strengthen elements of proletarian ideology in the masses.[13] The fact that the proletariat had yet to establish cultural hegemony, combined with the reformers' understanding of the reasons for music's "backwardness," made it easy for members of the Left to admit that little, if any, truly "revolutionary" or "proletarian" music existed as of yet. Their challenge was to create the conditions under which such music would emerge.

The first step was to evaluate the current state of affairs. Condemnation of persistent bourgeois influences that it felt prevented the proletariat from establishing cultural hegemony underwrote the Left's critique of NEP musical life. Musicians of the Left persistently applauded what they perceived as an increase in the masses' attraction (*tiaga*) to music since 1917,[14] but insisted that *tsyganshchina* and fox-trots were as objectionable as the "head smashing" compositions of modernist composers because they spoiled workers' sensibilities. They felt that songs and dance tunes published in the "light genre" category were degenerate influences on the laboring masses, often dismissing them as musical "surrogates" or "cast-off barroom garbage."[15] A writer for RAPM's journal, *Musical Virgin Soil*, characterized the problem as follows: "To this day workers do not know big and real music. But their thirst for [*tiaga k*] music, for singing and dancing, is huge. Previously as well as now, this thirst has been satisfied mainly by musical surrogates that corrupt [*rasvrashchat'*] the worker."[16] To the musical Left, the popularity of *Little Bricks*, with its sentimental lyrics and lilting waltz tune, indicated how susceptible the masses were to petit-bourgeois "survivals" (*perezhitki*) masquerading as revolutionary music.[17] Some even faulted Narkompros for ignoring this issue, and proposed that these songs be banned.[18] *Chastushki* and other unpublished genres of "urban musical folklore" (including cruel romances and underworld songs) also came in for criticism, both for their ideologically objectionable lyrics and their banal, overly sentimental accompaniment. Although some maintained that street songs merited study and collection,[19] most considered all urban popular music the product of the working class's assimilation of the second-rate music of the bourgeoisie. If this music warranted study, it was only in order to understand how to eradicate it, thereby purifying "proletarian musical consciousness" for the reception of "healthy, good music."[20]

Convinced that music was indeed an ideological weapon, one that not only reflected but also influenced its environment, the musicians of the Left attributed a range of defects in working-class *byt*, or daily life, to light genre music. The light genre, they maintained, had a subtle, narcotic effect on those who sang, listened to, and danced to it.[21] *Tsyganshchina* and fox-trots provided diversion and entertainment for workers and Komsomol members, but dulled their militant, revolutionary aspirations and dampened their enthusiasm for "social work." Elaborating on the oft-heard denunciation of the light genre as "surrogates" for "real" music, ORK leader Lev Shul'gin criticized "petty-bourgeois" (*meshchanskie*) songs for their "narrow, individualistic character," and the way they dealt with "base feelings" or "naked sensuality." Banal, sentimental lyrics, or simple coarseness, made these songs very "accessible," and thus prevented people from searching out more sophisticated musical material: "Thanks to their accessibility, these songs divert our perception to the side, away from the real artistic, healthy song. They atrophy our ability to go over to the side of more developed musical material, and thus are one of the strongest brakes on the musical cultural enlightenment of the masses."[22]

Clearly, the lyrics of longing, unrequited love, revenge, and melancholy that typified *tsyganshchina* were incompatible with the wholesomeness that RAPM and other cultural puritans associated with building socialism. But the musical Left found the music even more harmful, because it intensified the effect of the text it accompanied. During NEP, its condemnation of the actual music of "gypsy" songs remained fairly vague, focusing on the alleged negative influences of this music without identifying the precise musical components of *tsyganshchina*'s "narcotic" effect and appeal. But suggestions of the more thorough critique that would coalesce during the Cultural Revolution did appear. When evaluating its own compositions, the Left criticized pieces that employed harmonies with suspensions, modulation from a major key to its parallel minor, and particular melodic conventions (*oborota*), pointing out that these musical devices were hallmarks of the *tsyganshchina* style.[23] Musicians of the Left especially disliked melodic chromaticism, identifying it as the musical component of the sentimentality that they found so objectionable in *tsyganshchina*. The *tsyganshchina* "sound" even made them suspicious of songs with impeccable political pedigrees. When Prokoll edited an anthology of songs collected from the Society of Former Political Prisoners and Exiles, the group debated the necessity and methods for eliminating the melodic "sugariness" (*slashchavost'*) and "vulgarity" that were traits of *tsyganshchina* and cruel romances from these melodies.[24] Revolutionary Composer leader Aleksei Sergeev initially opposed the publication of the popular revolutionary *Song of the Commune* (*Pesnia kommuny*) (Example 10), because he was "embarrassed" by the "sentimental and chromatic phrase" accompanying the lyrics "the whims of fate have no power over us."[25]

Given their concern with music's psychological influence, which it held to be at least as powerful as the more specific message conveyed by words, the musical Left, especially the Proletarian Musicians, developed an unbridled hostility for what it called "pseudo-revolutionary music." This category included many pro-Soviet songs written by composers affiliated with the AMA, such as Iulii Khait, Matvei Blanter, and the Pokrass brothers. Musicians on the Left conceded that many of these songs, such as Khait's *Ever Higher*, had perfectly acceptable lyrics. But their music, which often had the sound of the gypsy genre or a cabaret dance tune, undermined or even sabotaged the meaning of the words. During the Cultural Revolution these songs would come under particularly relentless attack. But during NEP, the musical Left focused its criticism on the common practice of "updating" an old, familiar melody by setting it to a revolutionary text. Most of these adaptations dated to the Civil War and were among the most popular revolutionary songs, especially with youth.[26] The example of "pseudo-revolutionary" music the Left criticized the most during NEP was a favorite fighting song-hymn of the Red Army, *We Will Go to Battle Boldly* (*Smelo my v boi poidem*) (Example 11), whose melody bore clear debts to the prerevolutionary salon romance, *Fragrant Clusters of the White Acacias* (*Belaia akatsiia grozdi dushistye*).

A strong vein of prudishness also underscored the Left's critique of light music. It objected to many "gypsy songs" and the most popular dance music

Example 10 A. Mitiushin, *Song of the Commune* (*Pesnia kommuny*). Text by V. Kniazov. Sergeev objected to the G-sharp (which is necessary for the cadence) in the sixth (full) measure. Moscow and Petrograd: Gosudarstvennoe izdatel'stvo muzykal'nyi, 1923.

We're not broken by need
Poverty won't drive us off.
The whims of fate have no power over us
Never, no, never, no
Never, no, never, no
The communards will never be slaves.

of the twenties—the fox-trot, tango, shimmy, and Charleston—for their erotic overtones and associations with public drinking and the seamier aspects of romantic love. The Left's critics insisted that both the text and music of *tsyganshchina* identified it as the music of prostitutes and bars. They felt that both the liberties taken with tempo and melody and the melodramatic hand-wringing and rolled eyes associated with singing gypsy music facilitated efforts by female singers to captivate and sexually arouse their (largely) male audience.[27] Sensuality and eroticism were even more pronounced, and therefore objectionable to the Left, in popular dance music. The American-European origins of the fox-trot and shimmy made them all the more suspect.[28]

Popular music was problematic for RAPM and ORK precisely because it was genuinely popular. As the decade unfolded their concerns intensified as their efforts to replace *tsyganshchina* and fox-trots met with minimal success. For now their explanations for the appeal of the light genre focused on broader, controversial aspects of Soviet life, particularly the capitalist conditions fostered by NEP. It was more comfortable to blame a lack of alternatives and the corrupting influence of commercialism for the popularity of music the Left despised than to fault workers for their preferences. The financial success of composers affiliated with the AMA further fueled the Left's railings against light genre music. Like other members of the creative intelligentsia, these musicians harbored a deep antipathy toward commercial influences in the cultural arena.[29] They felt that their education, moral commitment, and ideological charge to improve the lives of the previously disadvantaged made them the best arbiters of cultural values, not the greedy private publishers and self-seeking musicians they denounced as "hacks."

Theoretical Solutions

The musical Left's objections to popular music as it currently existed stressed the evils of "bourgeois" influences, but it also necessarily involved a rejection of the broader cultural patterns that nourished this music. The popularity of petit-bourgeois (*meshchanskaia*) music among the working class indicated that the more fundamental problem was the cultural level of that class. Like militants in the Komsomol, activists on the musical Left constantly bemoaned the "low cultural level" of most of the working class.[30] To get rid of *tsyganshchina* the sensibilities of workers had to be changed (a process activists always described in terms of "raising") so that they would want to sing and listen to something else.

Example 11 *We Will Go to Battle Boldly* (*Smelo my v boi poidem*). Also known by its refrain, *For Soviet Power* (*Za vlast' sovetov*). *Antologiia sovetskoi pesni. 1917–1957*, vol. 1, ed. Viktor Belyi. Moscow: Gosudarstvennoi muzykal'noe izdatel'stvo, 1957.

Listen, all workers
The war has begun!
Throw down your tools
And prepare for the campaign.

Boldly, we'll go to battle
For Soviet power
And as one we'll die
In that struggle.

In the musical community as a whole there were a few iconoclasts who saw in the revolution an opportunity for a radical break with the cultural forms of the past and the promise of a proletarian culture created by workers and peasants themselves. But Aleksandr Bogdanov's approach to cultural transformation found virtually no adherents among the musical Left. As was true of many Bolshevik theorists on culture, activists in RAPM, Prokoll, and ORK usually failed to appreciate the relativity of their own internalized "bourgeois" values vis-à-vis music, literature, and art. Seeing themselves as "cultured" and discriminating, in contrast to the unsophisticated, "backward," and uncritical working class, they identified their mission as leading and guiding the proletariat to a "higher" level of artistic appreciation and cultural development.[31] They scorned the apolitical agendas of *kul'turtregery* but shared (along with Lenin and many other Old Bolsheviks) much of their cultural conservatism and (bourgeois) biases. Blind to the limits of their own tastes and values, these activists saw the task of cultural transformation in the musical sphere in terms of the transmission (*peredacha*) of the "best" of musical culture to the masses.[32]

That "best" was itself "bourgeois," consisting of select aspects of the nineteenth-century European and Russian art music tradition, with special reverence accorded to the music of Beethoven and Musorgsky. In keeping with the Party's directives on literature of 1920 and 1925, the musical Left considered the artistic legacy of the past an important component of the musical culture of the future. But it found only certain parts of the musical legacy acceptable. Unlike the "decadent" music of the late nineteenth and early twentieth centuries, they felt Beethoven's music reflected the positive strivings of the bourgeoisie when it was the bearer of cultural and economic progress. Identifying Beethoven as the musical voice of the "struggling" bourgeoisie, the Left thought his music could provide the proletariat with a healthy foundation for the music of the future.[33]

RAPM's emphasis on the importance of the "healthy" part of the musical legacy (a part that got smaller as the decade unfolded) was especially strong. But all three groups were convinced that "mastering" at least an attenuated version of the "best" of the bourgeois musical legacy was essential not just for overcoming the "backwardness" of popular musical culture, but for creating the music of the future. "Transmitting" the musical culture of the past to the masses was only the first step to "mastering" and "overcoming" it.[34] "Not back to Musorgsky, but forward from him!" rang out the rallying cry of the Revolutionary Composers.[35]

The Left's definitions of proletarian music were even more muddled than its perspectives on proletarian culture, but the Proletarian Musicians and

Revolutionary Composers agreed that genuine proletarian music did not yet exist.[36] RAPM maintained that it was present only in nascent form, as "sprouts" (*rostki*) in workers' songs and a few pieces by Kastal'skii, Lazarev, and Vasil'ev-Buglai.[37] Both RAPM and Prokoll condemned the Revolutionary Composers' agitational music as being simultaneously overly complicated and banal.[38] ORK's members defended the revolutionary music that they wrote for today by distinguishing between it and the proletarian music of the future that was yet to come. Their *agitki* provided an alternative to *Little Bricks* and *White Acacias*. But they insisted that agitational music was destined to become "revolutionary proletarian music" as the cultural level of the masses evolved.[39]

All three groups agreed that revolutionary music was vocal music.[40] Undoubtedly this was partly because the presence of text provided one reasonably secure anchor for identifying musical meaning. The importance of songs like *Boldly, Comrades, in Step* and *The Warsaw Song* to the revolutionary struggle was also not lost on them. But they were especially drawn to the song because its emotional appeal and potential for collective participation perfectly suited it to bring people together and create a sense of unity. Activists on the musical Left saw singing as a central part of the revolutionary experience: "The proletariat wants to sing. Street demonstrations are saturated with songs. The ranks of the Red Army close tightly with song."[41] Now that the revolution had been won, they had an ambitious vision of the song's role in building socialism: "Formerly the song was the constant work and life companion of workers and peasants. Now its arena is broadening. It should become a bright expression of class consciousness; it should participate in socialist construction, playing the role of agitator. It should be caustic satire and an emotional confirmation of the new way of life."[42]

The programmatic statements of all three groups spoke of the challenges of composing instrumental music for the revolution, and the Revolutionary Composers and Proletarian Musicians spent much time debating this issue with musicians outside of their groups.[43] But the Left made few efforts to write instrumental music, preferring to leave the challenges of truly abstract creativity for the future. An early RAPM sympathizer insisted that "music born in the fire of revolution cannot, in its first years of existence, be absolutely instrumental."[44] Vasil'ev-Buglai made a more prescient observation in discussing the musical work of the Central Executive Committee's workers' club: "The Kremlin doesn't like pure [instrumental] music."[45]

As noted above, the Left appreciated the connection between work and song in traditional life. Its musicians felt that music was the natural companion of manual labor, and praised songs such as *The Cudgel* and the barge haulers' song *We Cry Out*, which were closely connected with the work process.[46] In their search for the musical material that would nurture the development of proletarian music, their attention naturally turned to the peasant folk song, a traditional focus of interest for Slavophile ethnographers and composers of Russian art music. The ideological implications of the peasant folk song's musical characteristics and sociological origins became the subject of extensive debate, and RAPM became less enamored of it as the decade progressed.[47] But in the early twenties, many assumed that proletarian music would bear clear debts to the folk song.[48] RAPM member and Proletkul't veteran Grigorii Liubimov saw folk music as "our musical mother lode" whose tradition of anonymous, collective composition guarded against degeneration and individualism.[49] Others felt the folk song had artistic value "because it was a genuine expression of the everyday life (*byt*) and ideology of a whole class, developed over the course of centuries."[50] They lamented the "corruption" and "perversion" of the folk song that accompanied economic modernization and urbanization, and worried that the urban music they so despised was making headway against traditional music in the countryside.[51] Using "broad, bold" folk songs in workers' clubs was advocated even by those who cautioned that "mournful songs depicting the centuries-long oppression of the peasant masses" and "sad songs on the heavy part and sorrowful plight of women" had "nothing in common with our current reality."[52]

Appreciation for the folk song was shared by the Left's best composers. Kastal'skii had pursued research on the influences of folk music on Russian church chant in the prerevolutionary period,[53] and in 1923 published *The Peculiarities of the Russian Folk Music System*. After the People's Choral Academy was absorbed by the Moscow Conservatory in 1922, he worked to integrate the study of folk music into the conservatory's curriculum. He published several adaptations of folk songs during his membership with the Proletarian Musicians. Folk songs also provided the foundation for the music lessons he designed for music circles in workers' clubs.[54] Kastal'skii's pupils, Vasil'ev-Buglai and Aleksandr Davidenko, were true to their mentor, often writing in an idiom with clear debts to the Russian peasant folk song.[55]

Workers' Clubs, Revolutionary Music, and Proletarian Instruments

The Revolutionary Composers were astonishingly prolific, but in terms of actual members, the groups of the musical Left remained small during NEP.

Implementing these groups' programs to "transmit" musical culture to the masses required that they work with other organizations, such as the Komsomol and the trade unions, whose agendas often overlapped and overshadowed their own. Popular music was, of course, closely entwined with many aspects of people's lives. But the cafés, bars, and theaters where most people listened and danced to music during NEP were scorned by the musical Left as hotbeds of the crass philistinism that was so despised. Activists from all sectors of the musical community looked to the radio as the ideal means for educating and entertaining a mass audience, especially in the countryside. But the radio industry in the Soviet Union was still in its infancy and most musicians preferred direct contact with their intended audience. Besides schools and the armed forces, the context where reformers saw the best opportunity to influence the musical culture of the working class somewhat insulated from the pressures of commercialism were the workers' clubs funded and administered by the trade unions.[56] Although the trade unions and Glavpolitprosvet supervised the clubs' activities and had a decisive influence on the content of their programs, most RAPM, ORK, and Prokoll members undertook some kind of work in the clubs' music circles. The choirs and instrumental ensembles of these clubs thus provided them with a forum and laboratory for implementing and evaluating their program.[57]

The programs for the music circles were shaped by the broader objectives of the clubs, which were changing at the time that RAPM and ORK were founded. As John Hatch has shown, during 1924 Proletkul't's conception of the clubs as "the 'forges' of a new proletarian culture" gave way to the more tutelary objectives of the Party and trade unions, which viewed them as "instruments" of Communist education.[58] This new emphasis is evident in the way activists described the objectives of the clubs' music circles after 1924. The purpose of the clubs, they acknowledged, was one of political education (*vospitanie*). But the club should also help workers mold a new way of life (*byt*) and overcome the old one. They repeatedly insisted that musical activities were not merely entertainment or a means of relaxation for tired workers. Rather, the objective of musical work was to prepare politically conscious citizens and to overcome bourgeois musical tastes as well as bourgeois ideology.[59] Music in the clubs advanced the broader objective of the cultural development of the working class, also serving an agitational function. Music was to awaken collective feelings, glorify the heroism of the working class, and help emancipate workers from the grip of religion and other vices.[60] It was in the clubs' music circles that the battle against NEP music was to be fought and won. Here workers would acquire musical, as well as political, literacy. The music circle would provide musical education and upbringing (*vospitanie*) for "backward" workers, bring "joy and liveliness" to the club's overall work, and support the activities of its other divisions. Outside the club, the choral circle was also to be a conduit of musical culture out into the masses by spreading healthy, proletarian music[61]—quite an ambitious program.

The music circles, especially the choral groups, were among the clubs' most popular activities.[62] They attracted music lovers and people who liked to sing, but who usually knew little about music. Instrumental music circles were less popular, primarily because participation usually required some prior expertise and access to an instrument. Most of the instrumental circles consisted of ensembles of folk instruments, including domras, balalaikas, and mandolins, as well as guitars and accordions. Some clubs had bands, and a few even had a jazz band. While most choral circles included men and women, the instrumental ensembles were overwhelmingly male. Regardless of what the organizers intended, many people participated in music circles because they liked to sing and enjoyed public performance, not to become more politically literate and culturally sophisticated.[63] This was but the first of many obstacles hindering the circles' effectiveness.

The second was the instructors of these groups. The Left's activists constantly bemoaned the shortage of qualified instructors for music circles. They complained that many leaders of choral circles either shared the same "bad" musical tastes as their members or were former directors of church choirs.[64] An instructor with the appropriate musical skills and political orientation was essential if the music circles were to spread musical literacy, develop socialist values, and raise political awareness among their members.[65] Although courses and seminars offered by the Moscow Trade Union Soviet (MGSPS), the Krasnaia Presnia School of Music Instructors, and the Choral Department of the Moscow Conservatory tried to address this problem, "good" music instructors remained in short supply. The problem of bringing qualified instructors into the music circles was intractable during NEP and would become a key area of concern during the Cultural Revolution.[66]

The Left placed heavy emphasis on the importance of "musical literacy" to the overall objective of developing workers' musical preferences and "general cultural literacy."[67] The task of the circle leader was to train (*vospitivat'*) workers' tastes so that they could distinguish between bad, bourgeois urban music and music that was "fresh, healthy, and valuable."[68] What "musical literacy" meant varied. It often included the ability to read music and proficiency at the rudiments of ear training such as recognizing intervals, cadences, and scales and taking rhythmic dictation. The Left's programs for teaching musical literacy in the clubs emphasized active learning using familiar tunes, especially folk songs and revolutionary songs.[69] Boleslav Iavorskii's method for "listening to music" (*slushanie muzyki*), which taught people to follow the phrasing and respond to the mood of a given piece, was also widely used.[70] Some activists also staged demonstrations that compared "good" revolutionary music with the gypsy genre and "pseudo-revolutionary" music. Whatever the method, the objective and underlying assumptions were the same: Knowledge was essential to overcoming a liking for music that was too sentimental, trite, sensual, or coarse. Directed listening, a basic awareness of the mechanics of musical language, and exposure to "good music" would make workers more discriminating in their musical preferences.[71]

The Left's "civilizing mission" focused on, but was not restricted to, the confines of the club. Its members retained a veneration for the citadels of elite musical creativity, and lobbied Narkompros to provide workers with discounted or free tickets to concerts and operas. RAPM advocated teaching people how to appreciate classical music and opera, using modified (or simplified) examples of classical music in workers' clubs. Shul'gin's emphasis on the centrality of high culture to the cultural development of the masses reveals much about the Left's personal frame of reference: "We can't move forward . . . unless the masses can become familiar with the same, excellent, positive examples of music (from the past and present) that, in their time, the broad circles of the intelligentsia learned. . . . As music lovers (not specialists) they had the opportunity to develop their taste by going to the serious concert stages. The masses should now have the same opportunity."[72]

But while the musicians of the Left felt that visits to the Bol'shoi or performances by Persimfans were important, they looked to the clubs as the real crucible of change. It was in the music circles that the challenges posed by people's existing musical preferences and the problems with the Left's own creative work first appeared, only to remain intractable.

The instrumental groups were especially problematic in this regard. Given ORK's and Prokoll's emphasis on vocal music, complaints about the shortage of new and suitable repertoire for these groups were common. Commentators from the musical Left acknowledged the problem but did little to solve it. They applauded folk ensembles who enriched their traditional repertoire with arrangements of good "artistic" music by Wagner, Schubert, and Grieg.[73] A domra orchestra that performed the overture from Bizet's *Carmen* received special praise.[74] But the Left objected to the prevalence of hackwork (*khaltura*), the waltzes and polkas that were in the repertoire of many bands, and the very existence of jazz bands and noise orchestras in clubs. By catering to existing tastes, the Left insisted that these groups entertained workers at the expense of their cultural development. The fact that many instrumental groups also played for hire outside the club was even more worrisome.[75] Aside from concerns about repertoire, some activists questioned the overall value and purpose of the instrumental groups. While the ability to play an instrument was one measure of cultural sophistication, some felt that it was better for workers to hear instrumental music performed by professional musicians than to listen to the inferior, amateur efforts of the club ensembles.[76]

The question of which musical instruments best served the broader objective of developing people's musical sensibilities was itself contentious. Traditional folk instruments, such as the domra and balalaika, had their advocates. Other reformers insisted that workers receive instruction on "cultured" instruments such as the piano and violin. Cost, availability, and the need for extensive training on the latter made them impractical choices. Many folk instruments were also in short supply and had harmonic or mechanical limitations. In the effort to identify and promote the ideal "proletarian" instrument, a number of ingenious and controversial proposals emerged. Some activists looked to a new generation of "modern" instruments, such as the eerie-sounding electronic Termenvox, as the mass musical instrument of the future. Others advocated a return to the most basic materials. At Polenov House, Vladimir Dasmanov insisted that a series of water-filled bottles would make an ideal "instrument" for peasants. But of all the strategies suggested and pursued, those involving the accordion were the most debated and significant.

Discussion of the accordion's place in the development of Soviet culture began in 1924 and was addressed in the pages of RAPM's journals.[77] But the main impetus to promote the instrument came from the Komsomol, which began to use the instrument in its cultural and political education work in 1926. The musical Left supported this campaign, applauding both the Komsomol's efforts to involve accordionists in organizations of "rational leisure and entertainment" (clubs) and the accordion's potential to develop the musical tastes of workers and peasants.

Activists' interest in the accordion stemmed mainly from the instrument's widespread popularity among workers and peasants. A regular feature of musical life in urban working-class districts, the accordion was also the most popular instrument for weddings, dances, and other festivities in the countryside. The Komsomol poet Aleksandr Zharov celebrated its potential as a "stirring, intelligible agitator."[78] Like the piano, the accordion had both melodic and harmonic capabilities; however, it was cheaper, easier to learn, more portable, and required less maintenance. Some even suggested that instruction in the accordion be offered at the conservatories.[79]

The success of initial efforts to promote the accordion surprised and encouraged reformers. At the end of 1926, the Komsomol, aided by the trade unions and various state agencies as well as ORK and RAPM, sponsored competitions for the best accordionist, first in Leningrad and Moscow, and then in cities across the country.[80] These events proved to be enormously popular. Thirty thousand listeners attended the 1926 competition in Moscow, which attracted nearly 1,200 contestants. The competition was adjudicated by a distinguished panel of faculty from the Moscow Conservatory that included Mikhail Ippolitov-Ivanov, the institution's current director Konstantin Igumnov, Persimfans founder Lev Tseitlin, and Nadezhda Briusova. Finalists and winners presented a showcase concert to a full house at the Bol'shoi Theater. Publicity for the competitions attracted newcomers to the musical activities of workers' clubs. Within a year, more than one hundred "accordion circles" had formed in Moscow's clubs.

Reformers rejoiced in their success in using the accordion as a mobilizing device, but found that the instrument's popularity was both an asset and a reflection of the cultural patterns they most wanted to change. The accordion had its critics as well as its champions, and even its supporters struggled to overcome the instrument's technical shortcomings and its association with undesirable music and behavior. For most musicians and many activists on the cultural front, the accordion was an "uncultured" instrument, bound up with the coarse, boorish (*khamskii*) backwardness of working-class and peasant life (*byt*) that the revolution had promised to overcome.[81] These sentiments were advanced most prominently by Dem'ian Bednyi, whose satirical poems indicted the accordion for its association with drunkenness and hooliganism and echoed the criticisms of musicians who objected to the instrument's limited harmonic capacity and ugly, "creaky" sound:

> It shrieks, it thunders, it whines.
> To finish off Russian song is its design
> [. . .]
> When our country is richer,
> Becomes musically cultured
> And our culture is on the rise,
> The accordion will fall silent, shrill fool.
> Silent and dead with its true friend,
> The tavern, destroyed by the club circle [. . .][82]

Musicologists also faulted the accordion for its German origins, offering "genuine" Russian folk instruments like the domra and balalaika as more desirable alternatives.[83] Like Bednyi, they blamed the accordion for the ruin of traditional forms of folk singing, especially peasant "wailing" songs, which had been an exclusively vocal genre.

The accordion repertoire caused even more hand-wringing among reformers. More than three-quarters of the participants in the first Moscow accordion competition, including the winner, played either *Little Bricks* or the equally objectionable *Gypsy Girl.* A small percentage played Russian folk songs, and even fewer performed revolutionary songs. Only a handful of contestants chose "artistic" works from the classical repertoire.[84] Furthermore, most accordionists lacked the formal training and ability to read music that reformers equated with "musical literacy." The overwhelming majority of accordionists were self-taught and played by ear. Less than two percent of competitors in the first Moscow competition could read music.[85]

Given these concerns about the accordion's technical deficiencies and negative influence on musical culture, reformers adopted a stance of compromise on the instrument's promotion and use in popular educational activities. The Proletarian Musicians and Revolutionary Composers agreed to "cultivate, then eliminate" the accordion, hoping to use the instrument to bring about its own obsolescence. Together with the Komsomol they successfully lobbied for commissions to develop the instrument's repertoire and technical capabilities at the Moscow Conservatory and the State Institute of Musical Science (GIMN) and established a course for accordion teachers at the Krasnaia Presnia Music School. Working first for the technical improvement and mass distribution of the accordion, the Left hoped that as musical literacy and education in the classical musical tradition spread and the resources of the Soviet state improved, workers and peasants would then embrace the piano and violin.[86]

The accordion campaign and work with the clubs' instrumental circles had their challenges, but they consumed only part of the musical Left's energies. A great deal of the Left's attention centered on the activities and repertoire of the choral circles. Initially, the choral circles' programs were fairly self-contained. The choruses performed for other club members and gave recitals, sometimes in conjunction with political meetings, demonstrations, or other club-sponsored events. As the decade unfolded, however, circle organizers focused more on providing music for other club activities and less on trying to emulate professional music-making in the form of independent concerts. In part this shift reflected evolving attitudes about the nature of amateur (*samodeiatel'nyi*) artistic programs in the clubs.[87] But it was also a response to the fact that the club members who most liked to sing and listen to music usually joined the choral circles, leaving few appreciative listeners in the audience.[88] By 1925 choruses were often enlisted to provide music for skits, plays, and "living newspapers" (dramatic commentary on current events) put on by the clubs' drama circles.

Activists constantly worked to regulate the choruses' repertoire for these auxiliary activities, as well as the circles' independent performances, trying to balance the musical preferences of the singers and their audiences against their own sense of appropriate music. The Left encouraged club leaders to ensure that the music for any activity was selected and prepared in advance, since spontaneous music-making in the club or choral circle inevitably consisted largely of songs like *Little Bricks*, fox-trots, and other music reformers found objectionable.[89]

The music adopted by most choral circles divided into three main categories. Revolutionary music, including old revolutionary and prison songs, as well as ORK's *agitki*, made up a large portion of the choruses' fare, along with an eclectic assortment of "classics." Folk songs, especially "artistic" arrangements of well-known melodies (by Glazunov, Tchaikovsky, Borodin, Musorgsky, etc.) rounded out the choral circles' repertoire.[90]

Unfortunately for the Left, and the Revolutionary Composers in particular, chorus members and audiences responded much more positively to folk music and "classics" than they did to most revolutionary music. Their favorite pieces were arrangements of folk songs, such as Liadov's *Ring Dance* (*Kolodets*) and Glazunov's setting of the barge haulers' song, *We Cry Out* (*Ei ukhnem*). Old revolutionary songs and Civil War favorites like *Send Off* were still popular in many quarters, but people became bored with them as the immediacy of the war years faded. New revolutionary music that the choruses did like, such as Davidenko's *Budennyi's Cavalry* and Vasil'ev-Buglai's *Blood and Snow* (*Krov' i sneg*) and *About the Past* (*O proshlom*), invoked the style of a folk song.

But for the most part, singers and audiences found much of the "acceptable" revolutionary music too hard, too clichéd, or just not very interesting. Although many of Davidenko's pieces were well received in clubs and by the Red Army, the difficulty of many of Prokoll's works was problematic. As for ORK's *agitki*, singers complained that they "all sounded alike," and rejected newly-composed pieces as "the same old stuff."[91] They felt that Lobachev's work lacked variety, and that Krasev's pieces, especially the piano accompaniments, were too difficult. Some thought Aleksandr Titov's piano parts were acceptable, but his chorus writing was bad.[92] Early in 1926, Nikolai

Dem'ianov acknowledged that audiences were bored with *agitki*, although their interest in ideologically suspect "revolutionary folklore" and "songs of the new way of life" was increasing.[93]

Aside from issues of style, certainly a major cause of the failure of the *agitki* and many of Prokoll's compositions to compete successfully against songs like *Little Bricks* for a mass following lay in the technical requirements and intended performance mode of this music. In emulating "artistic" vocal music, the ORK composers (and some Prokoll members) made their pieces too difficult. Most of the *agitki* were four-part choruses with moderately difficult piano accompaniments. They were designed for stage performance, and not easily picked up and "dispersed" among the masses. Like many other activists in the music circles, Dem'ianov linked the failure of the *agitki* to find a loyal following to a need for more accessible "mass songs," a concept that had been used in the most general way since the early days of the revolution.[94] Criticisms of the *agitki* began to appear even in ORK's journal, where choral circle members called for "bold, revolutionary songs" with simple melodic lines and no accompaniment.[95] These requests echoed other calls for better, easier pieces that would truly be "mass songs," for at the same time official agencies began to show some interest in musical affairs.[96]

The 1926 Conference on Musical Enlightenment Work

Marginalized as they were from the bureaucratic patronage network that held the purse strings in Narkompros, the Left blamed many of its difficulties on the government's lack of support and interest in mass musical enlightenment work.[97] But in 1925, Glavpolitprosvet, the state's organ of Communist propaganda charged with co-coordinating the political enlightenment work of Narkompros, the All-Russian Executive Committee, and the Komsomol, seemed to hear their pleas.[98] In conjunction with intensifying efforts to bring political education to the countryside, and its increasing role in the workers' clubs, Glavpolitprosvet became more concerned with the overall objectives of political enlightenment work. Although its primary focus was the theater, problems with the "musical front," which the leader of the art section described as "our most backward," also demanded attention.[99] In the fall of 1925 Glavpolitprosvet held a series of meetings on the question of "music for the masses" and the activities of the State Publishing House. Although Roslavets attributed all of the music circles' difficulties to the poor quality of the *agitki* and the Agitational Section's unwillingness to enlist the help of leading ("good") composers, others felt that the situation was more complex and required broader discussion.[100]

Glavpolitprosvet convened the First Conference on Musical Enlightenment Work on March 13, 1926, to address a range of issues. Many were practical, such as the shortage of instruments and qualified instructors and the challenges of expanding musical enlightenment work to the countryside. But more fundamental was the need for a coherent approach to "mass music" and the ideological principles guiding musical enlightenment work.[101] More than half of the 150 participants were leaders of local music circles, and a number of musical institutions sent delegates to the conference, which was held at Polenov House. But speeches by the Proletarian Musicians' leader, Lev Lebedinskii, Revolutionary Composer head Lev Shul'gin and the censor Nikolai Roslavets dominated the agenda and formed the foundation for the conference resolutions.

Like many such events, this conference produced fabulous manifestos and detailed programs for change, many of which were realized only partially, if at all. But the resolutions are significant because they conferred, for the first time, the official approval of certain musical qualities and the rejection of others. They presented a preliminary formulation of the characteristics of the "mass song" that would become the backbone of state-sponsored popular music in the 1930s. They also reinforced the division between RAPM and ORK and set the stage for the Cultural Revolution in music three years hence.[102]

The practical measures proposed in the resolutions echoed proposals put forward by and long associated with the Proletarian Musicians, and generally supported by their rivals in the Revolutionary Composers' association. They called for the establishment of more music circles, the publication and promotion of simplified examples of classical music for these ensembles, the mass production of instruments like the balalaika and accordion, the proletarianization of musical education, and increasing the number of workers' faculties (*rabfaki*).[103] The resolutions' emphasis on "inculcating composers, young musicians, and musical masters with new ideology and Communist influence" clearly reflected RAPM's input.

But the theoretical statements that designated the creation of mass songs "saturated with proletarian-Soviet ideology" as the "first and most pressing task" and that delineated the characteristics of these songs were much more contentious. These resolutions described the "proletarian-soviet mass song" as one that correctly portrayed the life and was "saturated with the mood and ideas of its class." It would provide the foundation of mass musical culture and the opportunity to replace musical deformities (*urodstva*) with genuine artistic compositions. A mass song could be assimilated by the broad masses "without special effort" and was performed in everyday life. Mass songs often served a particular social function. They were closely connected with the processes of everyday life, such as work (*The Cudgel*), social rituals such as dances or weddings, or the revolutionary struggle (*Boldly, Comrades, in Step* and *The Warsaw Song*). The resolutions also stipulated particular characteristics that were essential to the mass song. These included the subject of the text and the use of accessible language that clearly expressed the song's mood (sorrow, joy, heroism, etc.), as well as a clear, singable melody, simple, lively rhythm, and an affinity with the "harmonic conventions [*oborota*] employed by the masses until now."

While the Proletarian Musicians would hardly quarrel with the promotion of songs that "correctly" portrayed the mood and experiences of the proletariat, or the need for "artistic" compositions, they rejected the idea that a song's potential for assimilation "without special effort" was a sign of its good quality. After all, was not the ease with which people picked up *Little Bricks* part of what made the song so harmful?[104] They also opposed the emphasis on mass music (or revolutionary music) rather than proletarian music. Furthermore, they denounced the effort to reduce the mass song to a "recipe" of desirable traits, insisting that the Revolutionary Composers had already been using this approach for years and it clearly wasn't working. As one exasperated member of RAPM put it: "Everyone is bored with the composers at *Muzsektor*. They want to talk about simple rhythm, but the masses are bored with that too. Give them a song, not rhythm. The masses want to sing."[105]

The resolutions on the mass song advanced a position put forward by Shul'gin shortly before the conference virtually point for point.[106] They implicitly acknowledged some of the shortcomings of the *agitki* (their difficulty and low quality) and proposed a modified strategy for writing revolutionary music. But ORK's belief that a song must be easily accepted and understood ("mastered without special effort") highlighted the deepening rift between Shulgin's group and RAPM. For if the Revolutionary Composers felt that workers would not embrace songs they did not understand, Lebedinskii and his comrades maintained that the backwardness of working-class *byt* guaranteed that a genuine proletarian song would not meet with immediate success. Indeed, resistance was a partial measure of authenticity. Real proletarian music would find acceptance only when the degenerate influences in working-class culture had been eradicated.[107]

Despite the high esteem that both RAPM and ORK had accorded the peasant folk song, the resolutions of the musical enlightenment conference suggested that, for ideological reasons, its contribution to the music of the future needed to be carefully circumscribed. After an extended debate on "musical populism," the conference adopted a resolution that stipulated that while mass songs should use "familiar" harmonic conventions, they were not to imitate the traditional peasant folk song. It was too closely bound to prerevolutionary peasant ideology, the resolution maintained, further warning that the "despair, passivity, and ignorance" reflected in the folk song could have no positive influence on the psyche of the modern worker.[108] Here were the first signs of the (short-lived) hostility to traditional folk music that would come into full flower during the Cultural Revolution. But the impetus to identify composers who relied too heavily on the melodic, harmonic, and rhythmic conventions of the folk song as "musical populists" and "formalists" at this point seemed to come not from RAPM or ORK, but from Glavpolitprosvet representative Simon Korev (1900–1953) and the Left's nemesis Nikolai Roslavets.[109]

In the aftermath of the conference, the scope of musical enlightenment work expanded in urban centers and began to extend to the countryside. But practical concerns about the shortage of instructors, instruments, and music for these activities persisted. The problem of finding songs with ideologically acceptable texts and music that could rival *Little Bricks* for popularity remained especially thorny. The musical Left made little or no headway against the popularity of "NEP music" in the clubs or elsewhere. The enthusiasm for jazz increased as indigenous ensembles led by Alexander Tsfasman, Leopold Teplitsky, and others formed in the wake of touring groups from abroad.[110] Although the conference resolutions signaled a shift in ORK's theoretical approach, the nature and reception of its music changed little after 1926. The ORK composers continued to be incredibly prolific. In 1927 alone Vasil'ev-Buglai published nearly eighty pieces, and Mikhail Krasev twice that many. But only isolated pieces such as Vasil'ev-Buglai's *Harvest Dance* (*Urozhainaia pliasovaia*) and Korchmarev's antireligious musical skit, *About the Sexton* (*Pro d'iaka*), gained even limited popularity.

The genuine popularity of the music the Left found objectionable and an inability to offer appealing alternatives to *tsyganshchina* and "pseudo-revolutionary" songs compromised reformers' efforts change popular music in these years, as did the unacknowledged elitism of their agenda. But in their activities with workers' clubs and their debates with each other, the musicians of the Left helped lay the foundations for both the Cultural Revolution and the popular music of Stalinism. The challenge of democratizing the culture of former elites versus the need for a new one would be a recurring theme in many areas during the Cultural Revolution, as would assaults against cultural practices and creative forms associated with petit-bourgeois banality and philistinism. The Left's critique of light genre music articulated the latter prejudices especially potently, and was partially upheld in the cultural mélange of the thirties. Similarly, the Left's interest in the mass song was shared by others searching for effective mobilizing devices during the years of the Great Break and for appropriate forms of entertainment in the thirties when "life became more joyful." Although the composers of ORK and Prokoll would not make their careers writing them, the mass songs that became the officially promoted alternative to sentimental tunes such as *Little Bricks* in the 1930s displayed the characteristics formulated at the 1926 conference.

5

Politics and Patronage

State Agencies and the Development of Cultural Policy During NEP

I hold that music is given to us to create order.
—Igor Stravinsky

Both the institutional and the ideological legacy of the Civil War determined the shape that cultural policies took during NEP. At the level of official policy, the debate over Proletkul't and the futurists set a strong precedent for the state to refrain from backing a particular artistic faction, even when the attempt was made to link artistic and political radicalism. Indeed, the rejection of a "cultural October" in 1920, combined with an ambivalence about the extent to which the state should interfere with independent creativity and scholarship, became the foundation of cultural policy in the twenties. While the 1920 resolution on artistic policies asserted that the arts were subject to supervision by both the state and the Party, musical institutions and organizations were administered and funded by the former. In 1924 Lunacharsky emphasized the importance of this distinction. Although the Party might support and encourage particular tendencies or artistic groups (such as RAPP), the task of the state was to remain as neutral as possible in the ongoing struggles between different artistic groups.[1] Party leaders such as Bukharin and Trotsky did play a conspicuous role in the debates on literature and proletarian culture. But in music, the staff and policies of the state agencies exerted a much more palpable influence than debates within the Party. The most important statement by the Party on artistic affairs, the Central Committee Resolution on Literature of 1925, had almost no impact on musical education, performance, or research. Briefly acknowledged in the musical press and in the resolutions of the Conference on Musical Enlightenment Work, the decree is not even mentioned in the protocols of the various music sections of Narkompros.

The state agencies that administered musical institutions in the twenties were descendents of Muzo and other divisions of Narkompros formed during the Civil War. Despite efforts and intentions to the contrary, the structural overhaul of the Commissariat early in 1921 failed to produce a centralized arts administration.[2] During NEP the administrative improvisation and constant reorganization of the Civil War gave way to interagency competition and bureaucratic overlap, as policy was hammered out for individual organizations and groups in the musical sections of several distinct agencies. Virtually every musical institution, organization, and performance ensemble was under the jurisdiction of at least one of these central boards (*glavki*). With their authority over the allocation of fiscal, material, and human resources, the Narkompros agencies played a crucial role in the life of the conservatories, research institutes, professional orchestras and choirs, and associations like the ASM and RAPM. Indeed, the survival of a given institution or organization often depended wholly on administrative support.

The size and pervasiveness of the state bureaucracies offer an important rationale for Christopher Read's assertion that by the beginning of NEP, cultural life increasingly was subject to state control, exercised through the expanding "tentacles of the Central Committee."[3] Certainly the bureaucratization of all areas of Soviet life in the twenties presents an inescapable and uncomfortable counterpoint to the accommodation and artistic pluralism traditionally associated with NEP culture. But while the Soviet state clearly did have a predilection for centralization, and administrative consolidation was unlikely to be compatible with artistic diversity, focusing on the apparatus of control overlooks several important characteristics of the bureaucratic dimension of artistic life in this period.

The organs of the state were ubiquitous, but their powers were by no means clearly defined or uncontested. Administrative supervision was not necessarily synonymous with control over artistic or musical life. Narkompros, whose various divisions were directly involved with virtually every aspect of arts administration, was the ultimate "lightweight" of Soviet administrative organs.[4] The Commissariat's head, Lunacharsky, had a history of political unorthodoxy and a reputation for being overly conciliatory toward the old intelligentsia that permanently compromised his ability to gain power or influence not only beyond, but sometimes even within, his own sphere of the third front.[5]

Furthermore, the structural complexity and inadequately defined hierarchy of the Commissariat ensured that administering a unified music policy would have been all but impossible, even if one had existed. Three of Narkompros's semi autonomous agencies, the State Academic Council (known by its acronym GUS, *Gosudarstvennyi uchenyi sovet*), the Main Administration of Scientific and Artistic Institutions (Glavnauka, *Glavnoe upravlenie nauchnymi,*

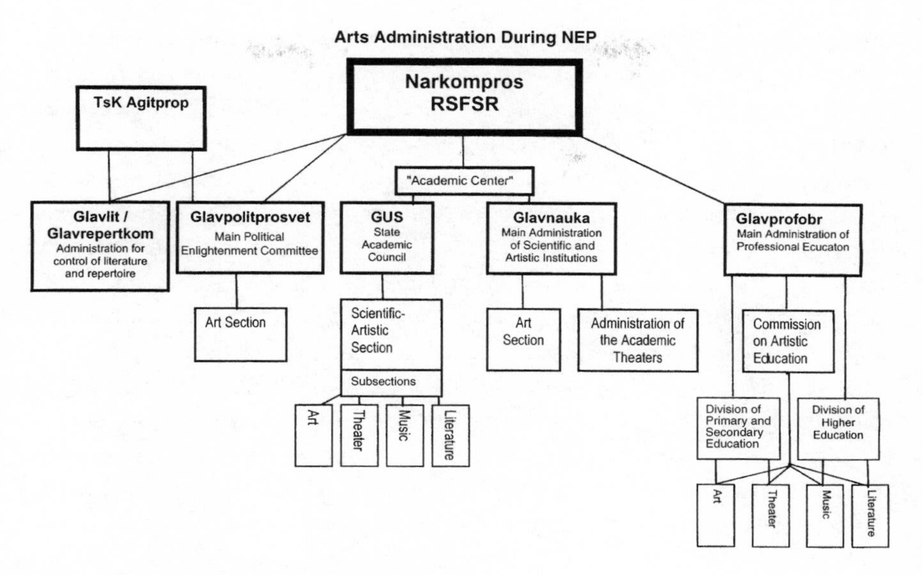

Fig. 2 Arts Administration During NEP.

muzeinymi i naucho-khudozhestvennymi uchrezhdeniami), and the Main Administration of Professional Education (Glavprofobr, *Glavnoe upravlenie professional'nogo obrazovaniia*), supervised the budgets, curriculum, repertoire, and staff of musical research institutions, conservatories, performance ensembles, and musical associations. In addition, a broad range of musical activities fell within the jurisdiction of the music division of the State Publishing House, Glavpolitprosvet, and the censor, Glavlit/Glavrepertkom. While technically under the jurisdiction of Narkompros, the latter two agencies also reported to the Party's Committee for Agitation and Propaganda (Agitprop), whose objectives frequently ran counter to those of the soft-liners at Narkompros (Fig. 2). To further complicate the picture, both Glavnauka and Glavprofobr sponsored standing committees on key musical issues such as reforming the conservatories and defining policies for research institutes and performance ensembles.[6]

The overlapping jurisdictions of the Narkompros agencies prompted frequent complaints about "parallelism" and "bureaucratic chaos" from the entire musical community, but especially from the Left, as well as from the ranks of the state agencies themselves.[7] Although each agency took the task of shaping the ideological and material development of the institutions and organizations in its charge seriously, the absence of clear directives for formulating and implementing policy, particularly when more than one agency was involved (which was most of the time), made this assignment extraordinarily difficult. Nor did the *glavki* manage their routine affairs with any semblance of efficiency. Far from being models of bureaucratic proficiency, they spent an astonishing amount of time generating paperwork and defending bureaucratic turf. In many respects, these problems replicated those associated with the overgrown bureaucratic apparatuses that plagued every aspect of Soviet life in the twenties. But this chapter will show that the administrative overlap and lack of clarity in these agencies' roles and jurisdictions were also a function of the Party's ambivalence about the state's role in the administration of artistic and scholarly life, and a reluctance to dictate artistic policy.[8]

It was the staff of Narkompros agencies that most directly affected the fortunes of musical organizations, institutions, and musicians. Drawn almost exclusively from the musical professoriate, members of the musical divisions of GUS, Glavnauka, and Glavprofobr were predominately established pedagogues, performers, and composers. Though they were employed as representatives of Soviet power, above all else they were musicians—specialist intellectuals, devoted to their art, for whom prestige, influence, and power were more important than any specific ideology.[9] Their policy decisions more often reflected institutional and aesthetic loyalties than conformity to bureaucratic hierarchy or allegiance to ideological principles. Throughout the twenties they protected and cultivated the institutional and creative legacy of the prerevolutionary social order, while trying to make this legacy more accessible to previously disadvantaged social groups.

A mere eight people held virtually all of the key musical positions at GUS, Glavprofobr, and Glavnauka: Boleslav Iavorskii, Nadezhda Briusova, Aleksandr Gol'denveizer, Boris Krasin, Nikolai Miaskovskii, Lev Tseitlin, Arsenii Avraamov, and Konstantin Igumnov. All of them were in their forties, and none were Party members during NEP.[10] Many had been active in the prerevolutionary adult education movement, especially in the People's Conservatory. During the Civil War, they had continued this kind of work in the studios, choirs, and instrumental ensembles of the Moscow Proletkul't. With the notable exception of Arsenii Avraamov, they were not iconoclasts or radical innovators, but were committed to the traditional values of the nineteenth-century reform-minded intelligentsia, particularly "raising" the cultural level of the masses.

These people played a key role in defining the form and substance of policy toward musical institutions and organizations during NEP. Their prejudices and agendas largely determined which reforms were implemented, which groups received funding, and which policies were adopted. In many cases the preferences of these eight people vied with, and were sometimes defeated by, the broader objectives of the Commissariat, factions within the musical community, and the Party and the Komsomol. But the story of the evolution of early state policy toward music as a whole must consider these well-placed individuals a primary focus, for they largely defined the terms under which musical culture was "sovietized." Their continued influence through the twenties also presents a distinct alternative to other fields, such as literature, where the decade witnessed the emergence of a younger cohort of leaders.[11]

Aside from their predominating influence in the administration of musical organizations and institutions, the staff of the state agencies also played a key role in the interfactional relations between groups in the musical community. Musicians holding powerful positions in the state bureaucracy almost invariably also had a post at the Moscow Conservatory or one of the main research institutes or both. In practice, if not in principle, the conservatory establishment and groups like the ASM received significantly more support from the state agencies than did the musical Left. RAPM made a largely valid complaint that the "commanding heights" of musical administration were in the hands of conservative, reactionary forces that supported "unhealthy" influences at the expense of the advocates of genuine cultural change.[12] The alliance between the instruments of Soviet power (the bureaucracy) and the prerevolutionary musical establishment was central to early Soviet musical life and a key target of RAPM's struggle for power and influence.[13]

In the absence of a clear bureaucratic hierarchy and policy guidelines, the staff of Narkompros's semiautonomous agencies formulated policy for musical institutions and organizations on a case-by-case basis. Born of necessity, this piecemeal approach allowed for a nuanced, if eclectic and ideologically muddled, response to the diverse needs of the musical community. While this mode of operation was consistent with the toleration of artistic pluralism that was the foundation of NEP cultural policy, it had both internal and external critics, whose recurring calls for a centralized arts administration and a more coherent arts policy culminated in the founding of Glaviskusstvo (*Glavnoe upravlenie po delam iskusstva*) in 1928. The ad hoc and often contradictory nature of policy-making also reflected the tensions inherent in the Party-state's commitment to accommodating the intelligentsia and the tenuousness of that commitment. The musicians at Narkompros had considerable autonomy on many issues, and proved adept at leveraging claims of music's "exceptionalism," sometimes by collaborating with the Party and other forces outside the Commissariat. But they also found their nominal authority badly compromised when a similar constellation of forces mobilized against them.

The extent of these musicians' influence is revealed in the way the personnel of GUS successfully promoted agendas that favored traditional musical institutions, facilitated contact with the West, and rejected the musical Left, despite the repeated challenges for control of music policy from their colleagues in Glavnauka and the lack of clearly drawn lines of jurisdiction within Narkompros. The efforts to reform the structure of the Moscow Conservatory and the purge of conservatory faculty in 1924 indicate how intervention from the Party could either serve or thwart the interests of the musician-bureaucrats with strong ties to the conservatories. These encounters between the state bureaucracy, the Party, and the conservatories also highlight the importance of political collaboration by musician-bureaucrats and the limited effectiveness of protest against the Party's interventions. Finally, an examination of the widespread frustration with the way that arts policy was formulated and implemented indicates why there was both considerable reluctance and increasing interest in creating a centralized arts administration.

GUS and Glavnauka: Competition for Dominance over Artistic Affairs

The most broadly influential of the Narkompros agencies involved with the administration of musical institutions and organizations was the State Academic Council (GUS). Established in 1919, GUS became an autonomous organ of the Commissariat's Academic Center when the latter was formed in March 1921. A presidium headed by the Marxist historian Mikhail Pokrovskii directed the work of the Council's four sections dedicated to political, technical, pedagogical, and artistic issues. The Council's statute of 1923 described the agency's main duties as the general programmatic and methodological leadership (*rukovodstvo*) of scientific and artistic life, the direction of scientific, technical, and artistic education in the Russian republic, and the development and resolution of all methodological and programmatic questions connected with popular education.[14]

The Council's claim to a leading role in artistic life and education was enhanced by the caliber of its staff. More than any other Narkompros agency, the roster of GUS read as a "who's who" of leading lights in early Soviet intellectual life. In addition to Pokrovskii, many prominent Bolsheviks and respected artists and scholars held appointments at the Council, including Nadezhda Krupskaia, Nikolai Bukharin, Natal'ia Trotskaia (Trotsky's wife), Varvara Iakovleva, the philosopher Vladimir Friche, mathematician Otto Shmidt, poet Valerii Briusov, artist Natan Al'tman, and GAKhN head Pavel

Kogan. Lunacharsky and Kogan headed the artistic section. At Kogan's initiative the section was divided into subsections for music, literature, theater, and graphic arts in September 1923, following a resolution by the Presidium of Narkompros giving GUS more influence over artistic policies.[15]

In keeping with the personnel profile of the Council's other divisions, the staff of the music subsection was made up of highly educated, prominent musicians, each of whom also held administrative posts in other Narkompros agencies or musical institutions. Five were on the faculty of the Moscow Conservatory. This subsection encountered no interference from the scientific-political section of GUS—a Communist stronghold with close ties to the Party's Committee for Agitation and Propaganda (Agitprop) that worked to undermine the conciliatory stance toward the intelligentsia advanced by other Narkompros agencies.[16]

The chair of the subsection, Boleslav Iavorskii, was a prominent theorist with years of experience in popular music education. He had helped organize the Moscow People's Conservatory and served as the director of the People's Conservatory in Kiev. As an outgrowth of the universal claims he made for his theory of modal rhythm, Iavorskii developed a synthetic view of music and learning that focused on integrating art with life. He rejected prevailing images of musicians as virtuosos obsessed with technical accomplishment and as practitioners of an art that was detached from everyday life. Instead, he insisted that professional musicians should receive a thorough grounding in cultural history, music theory, choral singing, and folk music as well as pursuing their specialty. He attached special importance to his method for "listening to music" that was used at all levels of music education—from workers' clubs to schools for music instructors and even at the Moscow Conservatory. In the spring of 1921, Krasin invited Iavorskii to come to Moscow as the point man for music education at Glavprofobr. In addition to his administrative posts at Narkompros, Iavorskii pursued research at the Academy of Artistic Sciences (GAKhN) and taught at the First Musical Technicum, an institution he established at the Moscow Conservatory with a curriculum based on his pedagogical theories.[17]

Iavorskii's former pupil, Nadezhda Briusova, served with her mentor at GUS as well as in the artistic education division of Glavprofobr. Appointed as professor of theory and musical folklore at the Moscow Conservatory in 1921, Briusova served as the assistant rector in charge of academics from 1921 to 1928. In the second part of the decade she was also the dean of the Pedagogical Faculty, where she taught courses designed by Iavorskii on "listening to music" and "the conscious perception of music."[18] She was the only woman to hold an important position related to music at Narkompros. A Party sympathizer and committed activist in the area of popular music education from the prerevolutionary period, Briusova often sided with RAPM and the Komsomol in matters involving administrative and admissions reform at the conservatory, even when this meant opposing Iavorskii.[19] Outside the ranks of RAPM she was the closest thing to an ideologue that the musicians could muster.

The Moscow Conservatory was also represented at GUS by the pianists Aleksandr Gol'denveizer and Konstantin Igumnov, each of whom served as the conservatory's director (Gol'denveizer from 1922 to 1924, and Igumnov from 1924 to 1929) in addition to their teaching responsibilities. Nikolai Miaskovskii and Persimfans head Lev Tseitlin also taught at the conservatory. They were joined at GUS by Arsenii Avraamov and Boris Krasin, both leading figures in the music divisions of Proletkul't during the Civil War. Krasin was the only individual perhaps even more strategically placed than Iavorskii and Briusova. He worked in the administration of the concert organizations, Rosfil and Gosfil, and also pursued research at the ethnography section of the music research institute, GIMN. His primary responsibility, however, was that of head of the music division of Glavnauka. After 1925, he was often accompanied or represented at GUS meetings by his assistant from that agency, N. I. Shuvalov.[20]

The complement to GUS, Glavnauka formed the other half of the Academic Center of Narkompros. Established on February 8, 1921, as the main administrative body for scientific research institutions, including the Academy of Sciences, Glavnauka was reorganized early in 1922 to include the administration of artistic institutions and museums, and divided into four sections: one dedicated to "general" issues, one for museums, and one each for scientific and artistic institutions.[21] With the exception of the conservatories, virtually every musical institution, organization, and association in the Russian republic fell directly under Glavnauka's administrative jurisdiction. The agency's powers included the right to open and liquidate institutions, ratify charters and statutes of institutions and organizations, develop instructional and research programs, conduct scientific expeditions, and convene conferences and congresses.

The art section of Glavnauka nominally had departments for music, the graphic arts, and theater. But unlike the scientific-artistic section of GUS, which had a staff of up to twenty, the entire Glavnauka art section was composed of only four to six people.[22] Given its small staff, the art section met as a single body and not in "subsections," as was the practice at GUS. This meant that its members from other departments, particularly the section's chair, often had significant influence in issues affecting musical institutions.[23]

Glavnauka's direct responsibility for so many musical institutions put the agency in direct competition and administrative overlap with GUS in many areas.[24] Glavnauka's art section repeatedly tried to gain control over artistic policy as a whole and was obsessed with the lack of "bureaucratic rationalism" both within Narkompros and among the institutions in its jurisdiction. The protocols of the art section are peppered with denunciations of "interagency chaos," calls for the "elimination of harmful parallelism," and resolutions to "struggle against bureaucratism."[25]

Along with the "deepening of ideological work" and introduction of "marxist methods of administration" in 1923–24, Glavnauka began seeking more control of all areas of artistic policy.[26] As a first step, the collegium of the art section attempted to change the agency's statute. A resolution dated March 14, 1924, called for amending it to give the art section "general leadership not only over the activities of institutions within the jurisdiction (of Glavnauka), but over the implementation of state policy in the areas of science and art."[27] When the art section submitted its plan for 1924–25 to the collegium, it proposed to hold a series of "methodological conferences" in order to "work out a unified artistic policy for all arts."[28] Its report for the first nine months of 1924 gave full voice to the agency's aspirations and frustrations, and proposed a solution:

> The art section considers it necessary to bring attention to the fact that its work is made extraordinarily difficult by the lack of clarity in its organizational position in connection with the presence of other art sections within Narkompros. The complete or partial liquidation of these sections would create more work for the art section of Glavnauka and broaden its sphere to the boundaries of all the Narkompros glavki. The formal sphere [*kompetentsiia*] of the art section is limited by that of Glavnauka.[29]

The art section's bid for leadership in all matters of artistic policy and the structural reorganization of the Commissariat met with little success. In January 1925 the collegium of Narkompros instructed the section to rework its plan completely, and to clarify the art section's functions in light of the "current situation." The section was to avoid taking on "outside" (*chuzhye*) obligations, and should work more closely with GUS.[30]

Thus, despite Glavnauka's de facto powers and efforts to secure a formal mandate for leadership, GUS wielded the most authority in artistic policy and administration, both in practice and according to Narkompros statutes.

The "general programmatic and methodological leadership of artistic life" accorded GUS in its charter gave it significant influence over institutions and associations technically under the administration of other agencies, particularly Glavnauka and Glavprofobr. The conservatories, musical research institutes, Persimfans, state choirs, and instrument collections all submitted accounts of their activities to the music subsection of GUS for approval and critique. Curriculum reforms, publishing policies, choral, operatic, and concert repertoire, graduate student admissions, and staff appointments were all subject to approval by GUS, even though they were in the primary jurisdiction of another agency. While the former imperial chapel choirs in Moscow and Leningrad were under the administrative jurisdiction of Glavnauka, for example, the music subsection of GUS as well as the censor, Glavrepertkom, influenced the choice of specific works for their repertoire. Similarly, Glavrepertkom and the music division of the State Publishing House, Gosizdat, technically had control over what music was published, but GUS had to approve the publication of all pedagogical materials.

More than any other agency of Narkompros, GUS was best equipped to facilitate interagency cooperation and to supervise the activities of other art sections.[31] The council's plan for 1923–24 described the regulation and normalization of relations with other organs dealing with artistic institutions as the agency's primary task of "supervision" (*nadzor*).[32] In May 1926, the collegium of Narkompros formalized the authority of the GUS scientific-artistic section over the art sections of other central boards, indicating that GUS should assign tasks to the art sections of other *glavki*, which would then report back on their implementation. The Council's plan for 1926–27 called for even closer coordinated work with other agencies.[33]

The potential for such a coordinating role was undermined, however, by ongoing turf wars within the Academic Center. Although Glavnauka's bid for more influence had been rebuffed at the beginning of 1925, later that year it made its own contribution to "parallelism" by setting up a "musical methodological commission" that was to be the "central authority in all areas of policy toward music."[34] Personnel appointments to this committee were extremely contentious, and the committee's membership fluctuated constantly.[35] Since GUS had to approve these appointments, it made sure that at least one and usually two members of its music subsection were on the committee, which was headed by ASM leader Vladimir Derzhanovskii. Glavnauka's music commission did include representatives from RAPM, and it boasted its concern with "Marxist methods of administration." But the content of these methods was never clearly defined, and the commission did little more than sponsor a series of debates and issue policy guidelines.

This meant that GUS remained the most important and influential agency for deciding matters affecting musicians. In its routine business the music subsection of GUS made every effort to promote those groups and activities that conformed with the staff's own vision of what musical life should be. It consistently attempted to improve the quality and vibrancy of concert life, cultivate contact with the West, and perpetuate the legacy of Russia's famous dead composers. In keeping with the culturalist predilections of its staff, the music subsection supported measures that made serious music more accessible to the "broad masses," such as the distribution of free opera tickets through trade unions or concerts in working-class neighborhoods. But it had minimal contact with Glavpolitprosvet and the world of workers' clubs and amateur musicians. Indeed, Briusova described a report on the activities of the Glavpolitprosvet art section in December 1925 as a welcome "first contact."[36] GUS did not even send a representative to the Conference on Musical Enlightenment Work.

Not surprisingly, the music subsection of GUS supported the organizations and institutions that were well represented in its ranks, such as the ASM, Persimfans, and the Moscow Conservatory. GUS consistently endorsed the activities of the ASM both in Moscow and abroad. In March 1925, Derzhanovskii presented a detailed report describing the association's origins, concert work, journal, and participation in the 1924 festival of the International Society for Contemporary Music (ISCM) in Vienna.[37] In an overwhelmingly positive evaluation of the ASM's activities, the music subsection noted the organization's "valuable" work in propagandizing new Russian and Western music, both in the Soviet Union and abroad. It asked that the ASM address the needs of "broader" audiences when planning its concerts and journal, but phrased this as a "desirable" rather than obligatory task.[38] Beliaev reported on the organization's activities again in November, particularly emphasizing its role in recent ISCM festivals in Venice and Prague and the unique nature of its activities in the Soviet Union.[39] This time, the subsection successfully pressured Glavnauka to support the ASM's concert activities with a 1,200 ruble annual subsidy and arranged for the association to have free use of a concert grand piano for its chamber music performances. It also petitioned to have the ASM excused from paying performance taxes.[40]

GUS's interest in cultivating new music and enhancing the international prestige of Soviet music informed other policies as well. Its highly favorable evaluation of the activities of Persimfans in October 1924 called for the conductorless orchestra to include more "contemporary" works by Russian composers in its concert repertoire. Iavorskii even noted that this might keep young, talented composers from emigrating.[41] The music subsection evaluated the composition curriculum of the Moscow and Leningrad conservatories by having students from both institutions perform their work at a subsection meeting. When Konstantin Saradzhev was invited to conduct the Czech Philharmonic in Prague, GUS helped procure the necessary travel documents and insisted that the program include the works of contemporary composers from both Moscow and Leningrad.[42] In 1926, the subsection criticized the concert programs of the Leningrad State Philharmonic for not including enough new Western music or the works of young Moscow and Leningrad composers.[43] GUS's interest in fostering artistic exchange between the Soviet Union and the West even extended to export policies for musical scores. After Derzhanovskii complained about the harmful effects of the ban on taking published Soviet music abroad, the subsection initiated a successful petition to the collegium of Narkompros to have this policy changed.[44]

GUS resisted adopting the politically motivated censorship of religious music endorsed by Glavrepertkom. It approved of the work of the former imperial chapel choirs, and supported their efforts to keep a modicum of religious music in their repertoires. In reviewing plans for memorial concerts honoring Scriabin, Liapunov, and Taneev in 1925, the subsection approved the performance of Taneev's cantatas, *John of Damascus* (*Ioann Damaskin*) and *On the Reading of the Psalm* (*Po prochtenii psalma*), despite the religious content of their texts. Gol'denveizer emphasized that these works were the composer's "greatest artistic achievements," insisting that their performance only served "artistic purposes" and should in no way be construed as religious propaganda.[45]

The musicians at GUS worked especially closely with the State Publishing House, monitoring the quality of the publisher's output in all areas. Given its charge to oversee the production of pedagogical materials, GUS was extraordinarily concerned that etudes and technical exercises receive an appropriate review before publication with GUS's imprimatur.[46] Other decisions reflected a veneration for established hierarchies and conventional assumptions about the distinction between art and entertainment. Instinctively preserving the realm of official recognition for achievement that conformed to traditional standards of artistic excellence, the subsection declined to award Mitrofan Piatnitsky, director of the famous peasant choir, the title of "people's artist" in 1924.[47]

A bias against the musical Left at GUS was more apparent by omission than by any definitive action or stated policy. Between 1923 and 1926, the Proletarian Musicians' association, RAPM, appeared on the music subsection's agenda only once, when Iavorskii reported on the split within the organization in February 1925.[48] Although the subsection's protocols usually included lengthy summaries of such reports, this item merely received a one-line entry on the daily agenda. When Glavnauka organized its "methodological commission" for music in 1925, GUS balked over the inclusion of representatives from RAPM by requesting more information on the nominees' professional qualifications.[49] The Revolutionary Composers' organization, ORK, and the student Prokoll never appeared in the music subsection's protocols.

Standardizing Higher Education and Purging Professors: The Lessons of 1924

While the success with which the musician-bureaucrats at GUS promoted new music, cultivated artistic exchange with the West, upheld publishing standards, and defended religious music reinforces traditional conceptions of cultural policy during NEP, other episodes indicate that the cultural arena was more contested and the behavior of the state agencies' staff more contradictory than these first assessments suggest. As many scholars have noted, 1924 marked a shift in the tenor of intellectual and creative life that was characterized, depending on one's perspective, by further encroachment of the Party's administrative and institutional control, renewed conflict between proponents of the "hard" and "soft" lines on culture, or the emergence of the institutional, ideological, and aesthetic patterns that would reemerge in the thirties as "Stalinism."[50] Among the many factors influencing these changes, certainly one of the most important was Lenin's death in January 1924, which brought the Party leadership struggle out into the open and at least raised the possibility that cultural policy might also change. Two episodes in music higher education—the undertaking of structural reforms at the conservatories and the purge of conservatory faculty—reveal how the intensification of struggles on the third front observable in many areas assumed particular urgency and complexity in the agencies charged with overseeing musical life.

Although the title "Conservatory" suggests an institution of advanced musical education to our twenty-first-century ears, the Moscow Conservatory offered all levels of musical education, from beginning instruction for children in ear training and playing instruments to advanced training in composition and performance at the "university" level. The divisions between various levels of instruction were only approximate, and the tracking of particularly talented pupils into advanced study was done on an individual basis, as there were few formal rules for screening and degree requirements. Prokofiev was admitted to the St. Petersburg Conservatory when he was fourteen, and Shostakovich was only thirteen when he entered Steinberg's composition class in 1919. The informality of this system gave faculty broad discretionary powers and allowed capable students to advance quickly. It also meant that "classes" had little coherence in terms of the maturity and previous training of their participants. In 1921, Reinhold Gliere's composition class, which met as a group instead of for private instruction, consisted of thirty pupils, ranging in age from ten to fifty.[51]

The government's recognition of the conservatories as institutions of higher education (VUZy) in 1918 had significant implications for the institutions' preparatory programs, curriculum, and administration. Although supplemental regulations to the new University Charter acknowledged the particular missions of music education, Narkompros's agenda for higher education clearly involved restructuring the conservatories to conform to universities and other VUZy.[52] In 1922, GUS ratified the first comprehensive plan to rationalize and clarify both the structure and the goals of the conservatories. Designed by Iavorskii, this plan emphasized the diverse objectives of specialized music education and the need for technical expertise to be grounded in a well-rounded artistic education. As an initial step in a process referred to as *tipizatsiia* (literally "typification"), Iavorskii's plan divided the conservatory into three distinct but administratively unified levels: an elementary music school for children ages eight to fourteen, a secondary school (technicum), and a VUZ.[53] The music school was to provide general music education and the foundation necessary for specialization in the more advanced divisions. Graduates of the technicum would be fully qualified orchestral musicians and music teachers, while the VUZ would produce highly-trained composers, performers, conductors, and theorists.

The 1922 plan initiated a confusing series of reforms affecting conservatory curriculum and structure. Between the many proposals prompted by strictly musical concerns (i.e., the need for a musicology program, reform of the voice department, and limiting the study of most orchestral instruments to the technicum) and those pertaining to general Narkompros regulations for VUZy, the conservatories were almost always in a state of administrative, structural, and curricular flux. Negotiations both within the conservatories and between them and the agencies of Narkompros were usually complex and protracted: Matters resolved after long debate were often readdressed a few months later. In the case of *tipizatsiia*, the Moscow Conservatory spent nearly two years redefining and reclassifying its internal divisions, with little interference from Narkompros agencies. But when Narkompros attempted to sever all administrative ties between the school, technicum, and VUZ in order to bring the conservatory into compliance with the Narkompros regulations on VUZy, the conservatory offered stiff resistance. The interactions between the conservatory and Glavprofobr in February 1924 illustrate the complex dynamics at work in the ongoing struggle between the conservatory's particular institutional interests, the goals of certain well-placed individuals, and the broader objectives of Narkompros.

On February 2, 1924, the Glavprofobr methodological commission on artistic education found the structure of the Moscow Conservatory "in contradiction with the basic tendencies of Glavprofobr." Backing a proposal authored by Iavorskii, the commission instructed the conservatory to comply fully with the resolutions adopted by GUS in 1922 and make the conservatory's VUZ, technicum, and school three distinct administrative units. It also insisted that VUZ admissions be conducted according to common Narkompros procedures.[54]

The next day, Briusova, in her capacity as assistant director of the conservatory, fired off a scathing memo to S. Z. Kamenskii, the assistant head of Glavprofobr. Claiming that the commission did not understand the conservatory's reasons for keeping its structure as a unified, three-stage school, Briusova fumed that to conform to the arbitrary demands of a leadership organ would be a serious and senseless setback for the conservatory, which was currently engaged in a tense struggle to raise academic standards and increase representation of proletarian elements in the student body. After threatening to resign from the conservatory administration, Briusova took what she called the more "correct" path, and asked that Glavprofobr review its decision.[55] Her personal appeal was accompanied by a memo from the conservatory's administrative board, which also objected to the demands of the Glavprofobr commission and asked the agency to review the matter once more.[56]

During the next week, support gathered behind efforts by Briusova and the conservatory administration to defend the conservatory's three-step structure. On February 9, the conservatory Party cell and the Komsomol organization sent a resolution to Glavprofobr protesting the "dismemberment" of the conservatory and the incorrect policies of Iavorskii and the music department of Glavprofobr.[57] The presidium of Rabis also supported the conservatory's claim to need a unique structure that deviated from the standardized VUZ model.[58]

On February 13, Briusova and conservatory director Aleksandr Gol'denveizer lobbied for their cause at an expanded meeting of the Glavprofobr collegium presided over by the agency's head, Varvara Iakovleva. Briusova presented a detailed report on the situation in the conservatory, describing the work of younger faculty members and the recently organized Red Professors' Faction in facilitating academic reform and the reeducation (*perevospitanie*) of the students. While the conservatory did combine all levels of musical education, students were clearly assigned to one particular unit. Addressing Glavprofobr's desire to have control over VUZ admissions, Briusova stressed that transfer from the conservatory's technicum to its VUZ required "public tests in the presence of a Glavprofobr representative."[59] By demanding that the conservatory be broken into three distinct administrative units for the sake of "clarity" and uniformity of VUZ structure, Briusova charged, Glavprofobr was overlooking the merits of the current structure and the special needs of musical education. First of all, musicians required many years of training and the availability of large ensembles such as choirs, orchestras, and opera studios. While orchestra musicians did not necessarily need a VUZ degree, composers and conductors needed regular access to large ensembles (from the technicum's resources) in order to practice and hear their work performed. In terms of the conservatory's "social" development, Briusova pointed out that the student groups most sympathetic to the cause of internal reform (i.e., Communists) comprised primarily younger students not yet in the VUZ. To separate the technicum and school away from the VUZ would mean a serious setback for the conservatory's academic reform and social rejuvenation. Finally, separation of the three units did not make administrative or financial sense, as it would greatly increase and complicate both record keeping and expenses.[60] Although it made no mention of specific organizations, Briusova's report clearly reflected the Proletarian Musicians' input by echoing point for point the objections RAPM offered to *tipizatsiia* in an open letter to Glavprofobr assistant head Kamenskii when the agency's plans were first made public.[61]

Faced with such broad-based opposition, the collegium of Glavprofobr adopted a resolution obviously influenced by Briusova's argument. The conservatory was to retain its special structure of three distinct but unified levels, all administratively responsible to one board. The board was to include one member responsible exclusively for the needs of the technicum, another for the needs of the music school. There would be one admissions committee for all three levels, and this committee would follow guidelines set out by Glavprofobr. The lowest level school, however, was to be phased out beginning in the fall.[62] Additional resolutions and instructions passed by the Glavprofobr collegium on March 7 finalized this compromise, although Iakovleva continued to object to the "three in one" structure of the conservatory up to the very end.[63]

Aside from its practical implications for conservatory students and faculty, this chapter in institutional history affords an excellent illustration of the relative weakness of Narkompros when confronted by a united opposition of local Party, trade union, and institutional administrators. The failure of Glavprofobr's efforts to standardize the conservatory structure also highlights the complexities of the personal, political, and institutional loyalties at work in the administration of musical institutions. Nadezhda Briusova, the most influential individual in this process, had been active in various agencies of Narkompros almost from the Commissariat's inception. Yet in this instance at least, she identified more with the conservatory than with her duties as an agent of state authority.[64] Given the strong support within Glavprofobr for *tipizatsiia*, she would have been unable to defend the conservatory's position successfully from the vantage point of a Narkompros bureaucrat. As a member of the very commission that tried to impose general VUZ regulations on the conservatory, she merely would have been an outpowered dissenting voice. Her opposition was effective, in part, because she put on her "other hat" and conducted all of her dealings with the Glavprofobr collegium as the assistant rector of the conservatory. She also displayed little hesitation in challenging Iavorskii, despite her advocacy of his theory and pedagogical methods. Indeed, Briusova undermined Iavorskii's position by rallying Communist students at the conservatory against his reform plan. Rather than acknowledging the broader pressures within Narkompros to rationalize higher education, Communist students identified Iavorskii as the source of a bureaucratic maneuver they felt was designed to weaken their influence at the conservatory.[65]

If the struggle over *tipizatsiia* indicated how an unlikely coalition of musician-bureaucrats and Communist students could successfully leverage claims of exceptionalism for music education, the purge of the conservatories' faculty later that year indicated the limits of the well-placed individual's authority and the ominous potential for Party intervention in cultural life. Among the most important duties assigned to GUS was control over staff appointments at higher educational institutions.[66] Like university professors, conservatory faculty resented GUS's ability to hire, fire, and retire them, claiming the violation of their professional autonomy. Since the conservatory's interests were so well represented at GUS, however, these restrictions initially seemed only minimally offensive. Yet the Council's nominal authority over faculty appointments was circumscribed early on by Party organizations and other agencies within and outside of Narkompros. The procedures and results of staff reductions at the Moscow Conservatory in the summer of 1924 clearly demonstrate the limits of GUS's powers as an administrative body, as well as the extent to which certain decisions ostensibly within its jurisdiction could actually be made elsewhere.

In accordance with the terms of GUS's statute, the teaching staff at the Moscow Conservatory was approved by the scientific-artistic section in the fall of 1923.[67] But in conjunction with the purge of university students initiated after the condemnation of the Trotskyist opposition in the spring of 1924, the Party and Narkompros moved to reevaluate the conservatories' teaching staff.[68] On June 1 the Red Professors' Faction at the Moscow Conservatory adopted a resolution justifying the dismissal of faculty as well as students:

> [We] acknowledge the timeliness and advisability of conducting an academic check [*proverka*] of students at Moscow VUZy and at the Moscow Conservatory in particular. At the same time, the Faction of Red Professors considers it necessary to complete this work by conducting a review of the teaching and scientific-administrative staff. This measure should improve the health of [*ozdorovit'*] the conservatory by liberating it from persons who do not meet the political and productive demands facing the Soviet Republic and the Moscow Conservatory.[69]

In the three weeks that followed, the student Party factions in each department of the conservatory compiled lists of faculty to be dismissed.[70] These lists were forwarded to "preliminary commissions" composed of Briusova and fellow administrators Konstantin Igumnov, Nazarii Raiskii, and Nikolai Sherman. The latter was a Party member who had studied with Iavorskii and graduated from the St. Petersburg Conservatory. The commission also included student representatives from the Party faction in each department, the conservatory Party cell and executive bureau, and a delegate from the local Rabis organization. The preliminary commissions' recommendations were then taken up by the conservatory's instructional council (*uchebnyi sovet*) at two meetings on June 21 and 24.[71] The council included the members of all the preliminary commissions in addition to representatives from the local Party and trade union organizations, Rabis head Slavinskii, and Iavorskii from Glavprofobr. Of the fifty-seven professors and teachers proposed by the student organizations for dismissal, the preliminary commissions and scholastic council recommended the termination or pensioning off of forty-four, the transfer of nine to other departments, and the retention of four.

The proposed dismissals were then taken up at Glavprofobr on July 10, when an "artistic-methodological commission" met to approve the lists drawn up by the conservatory.[72] Iavorskii chaired the meeting, which was also attended by Nikolai Cheliapov (a lawyer who had studied at the Moscow Philharmonic School and was head of the instructional division [*uchebnaia chast'*] of Glavprofobr), Slavinskii, A. P. Baryshnikov, and V. I. Kozlov, as well as the four members of the conservatory administration and Petr Smigla, a violin major representing the Communist students. Party members outnumbered non-Communists six to four. The meeting began with a report from Briusova describing the compilation of the lists. In a motion supported by Raiskii and Igumnov, Iavorskii objected to the dismissals of professors Maria Deisha-Sionitskaia (1859–1932), Vera Petrova-Zvantseva (1876–1944), Solina, Boris Sibor (1880–1961), and Karl Kipp (1865–1925), noting their long years of pedagogical and artistic service. The first three were distinguished voice teachers for whom no specific justification was given for dismissal. Deisha-Sionitskaia had graduated from the St. Petersburg Conservatory in 1881 and completed her training in Vienna and Prague before joining the faculty in 1921. She had worked closely with Iavorskii at the Moscow People's Conservatory. Petrova-Zvantseva, a graduate of the Moscow Conservatory, had been a professor in the voice department since 1916. The student faction requested a pension for Kipp, a respected professor of piano who had recently suffered a severe stroke. The violinist Boris Sibor was accused of neglecting his teaching duties and not giving his students an adequate foundation of technical expertise. After a lengthy discussion focusing particularly on Deisha-Sionitskaia's popularity as a teacher, the commission ratified the dismissal lists minus the five people mentioned above as well as the violinist David Krein (1869–1926).[73]

On July 15 the conservatory dismissals were finally brought before the GUS music subsection, with Iavorskii, Briusova, Miaskovskii, Gol'denveizer, and Smigla in attendance.[74] Briusova noted that the staff reductions had been carried out "according to plan" and ratified by assistant commissar I. I. Khodorovskii, the head of Glavprofobr. Reiterating the main points from the previous meeting, she emphasized that the dismissal lists had been based primarily on student opinion. Although Aleksandr Gol'denveizer was the director of the conservatory he had not participated in any of the preliminary meetings. At this point, however, he voiced an ardent objection to the way in which the whole affair had been conducted. Asserting that an interagency commission should have evaluated the faculty with input from conservatory representatives, he insisted that official procedures dictated that the matter should now go before the plenum of the GUS scientific-artistic section. Briusova brushed his complaints aside with no apparent interference from Iavorskii, who nominally chaired the meeting. Gol'denveizer insisted on his right to object, and abstained from the remaining proceedings. The subsection then voted on the lists, confirming the proposed dismissals of thirty-eight professors and making only two exceptions.[75] Aleksandra Gubert (1850–1937), who had been Briusova's piano teacher, was removed from concert piano instruction but kept on to teach piano accompaniment.[76] Viacheslav Gushchin (1872–1925), whom the student faction claimed was a poor teacher, retained his position teaching trombone and tuba until his death the following year. Of the 141 faculty on payroll in June, only 105 remained after the purge.

Five days later, Gol'denveizer filed a formal complaint about the dismissals with the music subsection of GUS.[77] Insisting that the conservatory and music subsection should only be making preliminary recommendations, he reiterated that these matters should be taken up by the plenum of the scientific-artistic section of GUS. He asserted that this type of mass dismissal would only be warranted by a severe budget crisis, which did not exist at the moment. Nor did he feel that this was an appropriate way to get rid of poor teachers, or even that such teachers were really the targets of the purge. Gol'denveizer was most disturbed by the prominent musicians and teachers who had been candidates for dismissals. Although many cases had been reexamined at the conservatory and the commission that met on June 10, the initial dismissal lists included voice teacher Varvara Zarudnaia-Ivanova (Ippolitov-Ivanov's wife), pianists Elena Bekman-Shcherbina (1882–1951), Petr Strakhov (1875–?), Grigorii Prokof'ev, and Rudol'f Vallashek (1880–1942), the ASM's principal conductor Konstantin Saradzhev, and the "young talents" from the theory department, Sergei Evseev and Aleksandr Shenshin.[78] Gol'denveizer bitterly summarized his assessment of the purge: "Ideological standards are one thing, but if we hold to them we won't have any professors left!"[79]

Gol'denveizer's position was complicated and unenviable. A pillar of the Russian piano school, he had been among those musicians who first supported the new regime, working with the Moscow Soviet, acting as Ippolitov-Ivanov's liaison with various state agencies during the Civil War, and assuming the directorship of the conservatory when Ippolitov-Ivanov resigned in 1922. Earlier in 1924 he had joined Briusova and the conservatory Communists in the struggle over *tipizatsiia*. He now found himself outflanked by his former allies and betrayed by the bureaucratic order he supported. Although he remained on the roster at GUS until the end of the decade, Gol'denveizer turned over his duties as director of the conservatory to Igumnov, who officially claimed the title when a new administrative board was elected in November.

Impassioned as it was, Gol'denveizer's anguish over these events was not unique. Both Boris Krasin and Lev Tseitlin were absent from the July 15 meeting. This meant that only Briusova, Iavorskii, and Miaskovskii actually voted in what was obviously a rubber-stamping of decisions made elsewhere. The next day Miaskovskii wrote to Iavorskii, attempting to resign from his position at GUS. His letter highlights the precarious path that the old musical specialists trod as they attempted to regulate their destiny in the new order, and suggests that the composer's moral compass was badly shaken by his involvement in the proceedings:

> I do not think that I have the qualities necessary to be successful in this role and be genuinely useful. Besides a sufficient reserve of integrity, I also think that a certain minimal amount of intellectual flexibility and the ability to clearly sort out situations, as well as a sufficient reserve of moral firmness and certainty—if not in one's convictions, then at least in one's opinions, at least at a given moment—are required. At [yesterday's] meeting I became convinced that I do not have any of these things. I do not sort out situations and circumstances quickly enough. I possess neither the intellectual nor instinctive shrewdness. . . . I wobble like a weathervane, not from a lack of integrity, but rather from the opposite—it suddenly seems to me that everyone is right, and I don't really know for sure who is actually right enough to entirely convince myself of something. And in conclusion, I really can't make sense of anything and in general do not know anything.[80]

Despite the personal trauma inflicted by the heavy-handed execution of the purges, the staff reductions had a less damaging long-term impact on the conservatory than might have been expected. The majority of dismissals came from the piano and voice departments, both heavily staffed academic units significantly affected by the student purge. This indicates that a concern for balance in the ratio of faculty to students was at least one factor motivating the dismissals. Although political suitability was a stated criterion for dismissal, age, pedagogical reputation, and musicianship instead served as the most significant predictors of job security. Relatively few truly distinguished musical figures appeared on any of the dismissal lists. The most prestigious core of the conservatory's faculty—Miaskovskii and the renowned pianists Samuil Feinberg, Genrikh Neigauz, and Feliks Blumenfel'd—were never in danger. This was also true of the prominent figures involved in the institution's administration such as Gol'denveizer and Igumnov. Virtually all of the big names that did appear on the dismissal lists were either removed along the way or soon reinstated. Nor was the overall reduction in the size of the faculty permanent. A photograph of the faculty in 1927 shows that several victims of 1924 had regained their positions (Fig. 3).[81] When the conservatory celebrated its fiftieth jubilee that year, Aleksandra Gubert received special recognition as the institution's most senior employee.[82] By 1927, teachers and professors numbered 144, slightly more than their pre-purge level of 141.[83]

Clearly there were political and ideological motivations for the purge. Like other academics, the conservatory faculty was largely hostile to the Soviet order and the Party encountered considerable resistance to its efforts to influence the conservatory's affairs. But the dismissals at the conservatory represent an isolated skirmish with relatively minimal long-term impact. As such, they share few parallels with the Party's assault on the Academy of Sciences in 1927–28 and the purge of its members in 1929–30. The staff reductions at the conservatory did not accompany a campaign to subordinate the conservatory to the Party, nor were they followed by an effort to infuse the institution with Communists, as happened at the Academy of Sciences.[84] They preceded a major reform initiative in 1925–26, but, as the next chapter will show, these reforms furthered long-standing agendas of the conservatory faculty more than they advanced the Party's objectives.

The conservatory staff reductions do reveal much about the perceived and actual powers of GUS, the state agency that claimed preeminence among the various forces vying for control of policy in cultural affairs and matters relating to the old intelligentsia. For the Moscow Conservatory, the music subsection of GUS voted on the cases of fifty-seven teachers and professors, approving the dismissal or retirement of thirty-six. But of the remaining twenty-one, only two were "saved" at the meeting on July 15. Six were reevaluated by the artistic-methodological commission on July 10, and the remaining thirteen were transferred to other departments or allowed by the preliminary commission and academic council to keep their posts at the conservatory. Regardless of GUS's theoretical authority over staff appointments, real power in this instance lay with the Party officials and members of the conservatory's administration who participated in every stage of the dismissal process,[85] and with Glavprofobr, which directed the process.

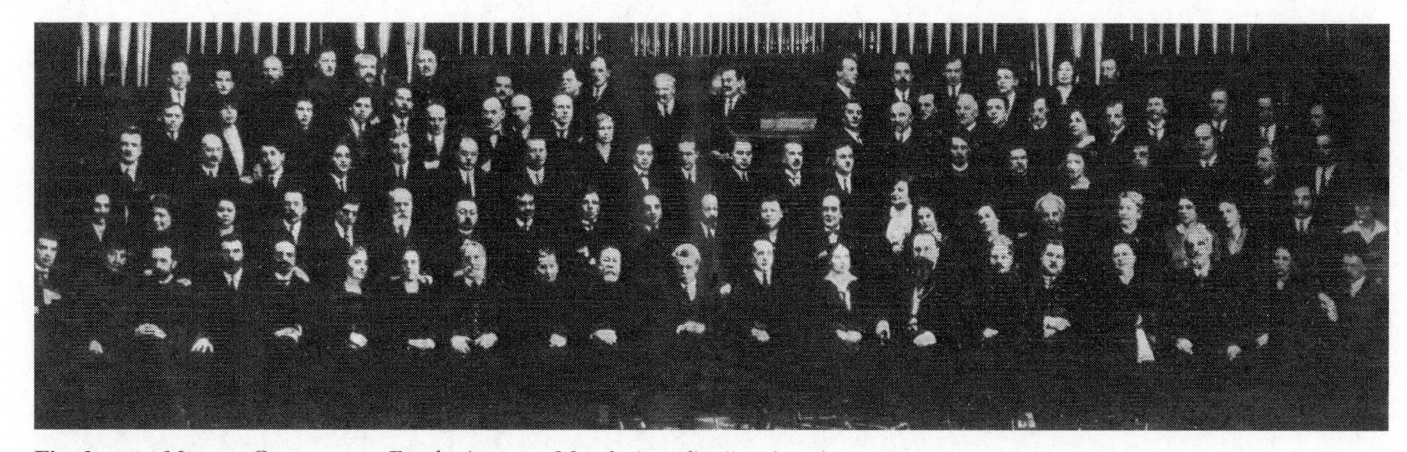

Fig. 3 **The** Moscow Conservatory Faculty in 1927. *Muzyka i revoliutsiia* 4 (1927).
First Row: R. M. Gliere, A. A. Aliavdina, N. Ia. Miaskovskii, A. F. Gedike, F. F. Keneman, M. S. Nemenova-Lunts, E. A. Bekman-Shcherbina, A. A. Brandukov, A. I. Gubert, M. M. Ippolitov-Ivanov, A. B. Gol'denveizer, K. I. Igumnov, N. Ia. Briusova, N. G. Raiskii, K. S. Milashevich, M. K. Konstantinov, M. G. Tsybushchenko, G. P. Gondol'fi, E. I. Vul'f, G. G. Neigauz
Second Row: K. S. Saradzhev, E. V. Kashperova, B. N. Petrova-Zvantseva, S. A. Kozlovskii, V. V. Borisovskii, E. A. Kolchin, N. I. Radtsig, F. F. Ekkert, M. P. Adamov, B. O. Sibor, M. F. Gnesin, A. I. Ostrovskaia, S. V. Rozanov, M. V. Vladimirova, M. N. Khovanskaia, V. P. Bezmenova-Sedel'nikova, A. N. Zagumennaia, M. A. Deisha-Sionitskaia, M. A. Rumer, E. A. Mil'kovich, I. F. Gertovich, ? I. Rentshke
Third Row: I. N. Sokolov, M. V. Ivanov-Boretskii, S. A. Sidiakin, I. I. Dubovskii, S. V. Evseev, I. P. Apekhtin, N. M. Danilin, N. I. Kuvshinikov, N. S. Sherman, V. I. Sadovnikov, S. N. Vasilenko, A. V. Aleksandrov, P. N. Zimin, N. A. Garbuzov, E. A. Mal'tseva, G. P. Liubimov, V. M. Blazhevich, M. I. Tabakov, K. M. Kupinskii
Fourth Row: V. I. Argamakov, O. N. Kartasheva, V. A. Tsukkerman, M. S. Pekelis, I. I. Shishov, A. I. Iampol'skii, L. M. Tseitlin, P. G. Chesnokov, V. A. Ziring, E. Ia. Kaliuzhnaia, E. E. Egorov, V. A. Bagadurov, P. D. Mikulin, V. L. Nardov, V. V. Sokolov, N. M. Novlianskii, E. A. Iuzvitskaia, E. I. Vishniakov, I. I. Kostlian, K. G. Mostras, N. G. Parfenov
Fifth Row: D. A. Rabinovich, A. M. Veprik, N. S. Zhiliaev, N. V. Denisov, V. A. Nikolaev, F. P. Balkanov, I. N. Belkin, B. N. Voskoboinikov, I. I. Nikitinskii, A. S. Shor, G. A. Gek, An. N. Aleksandrov, S. E. Feinberg, E. M. Guznikov, V. V. Nechaev, N. G. Aleksandrova, P. A. Lamm

The dismissal process at the Leningrad Conservatory, which got under way in October, months after the purges in Moscow were complete, found institutional administrators playing an even stronger role and resistance at GUS considerably dissipated. In this and other instances, physical distance from Moscow somewhat diluted or at least delayed conflicts involving the bureaucracy, the Party, and the conservatory. The issue of *tipizatsiia*, for example, was taken up at the Leningrad Conservatory only as part of more comprehensive reforms in 1925–26. A slightly higher percentage of faculty was dismissed from the Leningrad Conservatory than from its sister institution in Moscow (27.8 percent versus 25.5 percent), but many of those "fired" had emigrated or were already dead.[86] As in Moscow, poor teaching and lack of superior musical accomplishment were the main reasons given for dismissals. The conservatory's director, Aleksandr Glazunov, took a very different approach from Gol'denveizer, intervening throughout the proceedings and writing personal assessments of the professional qualifications of each faculty member. Musicians outnumbered Communists on the review boards at the conservatory by four to three, whereas in Moscow, Communist students were heavily represented at the meetings of the academic council. The only truly contentious case in Leningrad involved Marina Barinova (1878–1956), who by all accounts was a gifted, highly respected piano professor and openly anti-Soviet in her politics.[87] When the dismissal lists from Leningrad came before the music subsection of GUS on November 29, Iavorskii successfully moved to overturn Barinova's dismissal.[88] The complete staff of the music subsection was present for this meeting, and it dealt with the dismissals quickly, almost as a matter of normal business. Not even Gol'denveizer objected.

These events testify to the evolving power dynamic between GUS, Glavprofobr, and Party organizations at the conservatory, which was confirmed in the scientific-artistic section's plan for 1924–25. The plan described "continuing work with Glavprofobr on confirming the pedagogical staff at the republic's artistic VUZy" as the section's primary task.[89] The music subsection was to continue work on the structure, admissions requirements, and curriculum of the conservatories, after Briusova reported to the subsection on the "preliminary" discussion of these issues by the Red Professors' Faction and the student executive committee at the Moscow Conservatory.[90] These tensions in the chain of command persisted in the year that followed regarding questions of appointment and verification. In 1926, for example, the GUS music subsection protocol for March 27 includes a cryptic resolution to ask Glavprofobr to confirm the list of Leningrad professors and graduate students as soon as possible.[91] Meanwhile, isolated voices continued to raise concerns about the way political criteria were used to make decisions about musicians. In a manner reminiscent of a common pattern in intra-Party disputes—where the defeated faction suddenly demanded adherence to procedures and open debate—Gol'denveizer remained a staunch champion of procedural norms, calling for more frequent plenary meetings and insisting that "general questions of artistic policy" should be decided after a "mutual exchange of ideas."[92]

The Struggle for an Ideological Mandate and the Creation of a Central Arts Administration

Even when there was a "mutual exchange of ideas," as Gol'denveizer recommended, the problem was that the way "general questions of artistic policy" were hammered out within Narkompros satisfied no one. The overlapping jurisdictions of multiple agencies, the often contradictory agendas of those agencies, and the ongoing tensions between the censor (Glavlit/Glavrepertkom) and other divisions of the Commissariat generated frustration, confusion, and calls for reform from many sources. Critiques of the Commissariat's conciliatory policies toward the old intelligentsia and support for bourgeois culture from the Komsomol and groups like RAPP and RAPM were only one strand of a web of frustrations about the development and implementation of cultural policy. The economic realities of NEP made it difficult for theaters and orchestras to pay their staffs and offer cheap tickets to workers. These same conditions complicated Glavrepertkom's efforts to regulate the kind of music produced at the state's record factory without forcing the factory into bankruptcy. Rabis, the art workers' union, was also a vehement opponent of Narkompros policies and repeatedly lobbied for better wages for its members and more influence in artistic affairs, especially in the theater. Other representatives of the creative intelligentsia, including those on the Narkompros staff, lamented the inconsistencies of arts administration as a sign of the government's lack of interest in nurturing the third front. Over the decade these frustrations combined to create pressure for a unified arts administration, or Glaviskusstvo, that would bring more centralization and coherence in cultural policy.

The issue of creating a central arts administration had been raised by Rabis during the debate over Proletkul't's authority in 1920. At Rabis's initiative, the matter was taken as far as Sovnarkom, which declined to act on it. The resolution on artistic policies cosigned by Narkompros and Rabis was drafted instead, and administration of the arts was distributed among the various agencies of Narkompros.[93] Rabis reopened the issue of centralizing arts administration in October 1922 in the scientific-artistic section of GUS,[94] but when Glavprofobr refused to relinquish control over artistic VUZy, especially the conservatories, the plans were shelved. Instead, Glavprofobr called on GUS to strengthen its ideological leadership of all areas of artistic affairs.[95] The fragmentation of the Narkompros arts sector reflected, at least in part, the Party's ambivalence about the extent to which the state should intervene in artistic life, but throughout the twenties, Rabis and other organizations complained about administrative overlap and the lack of a unified arts policy. The Glaviskusstvo that finally came into being in 1928 was the outcome of a number of unsuccessful plans for a similar agency.

Pressure to form a unified arts administration intensified after 1924. Glavpolitprosvet's journal reported that Lunacharsky had discussed the addition of a new Commissariat at the Presidium of the Central Committee, which approved the formation of a planning commission.[96] The discussion was fueled by a variety of factors, including the intense debates on literary politics leading to the Central Committee's resolution in July 1925. But most concerns stemmed from a widespread frustration over the lack of a unified artistic policy, and the seemingly insoluble bureaucratic morass of jurisdictional overlap, parallelism, and confusion in administration.[97] Again Rabis led the charge, calling for a Marxist foundation to artistic administration and policies, and the establishment of a "link with production." At the Fifth Rabis Congress Lunacharsky proposed the establishment of a unified arts administration and the centralization of Glavrepertkom's work. The Congress supported this motion and also resolved to mandate Rabis approval for economic and administrative posts, eliminate the functional overlap of artistic associations in Narkompros administration, and complete the standardization (*tipizatsiia*) of artistic education.[98] The question of establishing a central board for administering the arts again came before GUS at this time, which as usual lost no time appointing a commission to study the issue.[99]

During these discussions, even Lunacharsky acknowledged that Soviet artistic life suffered from a "lack of sensible leadership."[100] GUS was full of leading specialists, but had no overarching vision regarding policy. Lunacharsky aptly likened it to a "big cogwheel that turns in the air, almost never linking up with anything." The other Narkompros agencies were smaller cogwheels that also spun freely much of the time. When they did link up with each other, it was usually for "the stronger to pull the teeth from the weaker."[101]

Economic policies and realities further complicated efforts to support artistic life, cultivate new forms of artistic expression, and develop the sensibilities of new audiences. Lunacharsky acknowledged that actors earned only about a third as much as they had before World War I, and that graphic artists suffered from the demise of their traditional patrons as well as the high cost and short supply of imported paints.[102] Composers were impoverished, as were conservatory students, whose stipends were pitifully meager. The principle of enterprise cost accounting (*khozraschet*) that was central to NEP required that state institutions show some semblance of economic viability. The repertoire for the state orchestras and theaters thus had to appeal to paying audiences, which consisted primarily of educated people, white collar workers, and students. Performances by foreign luminaries like Otto Klemperer and the classic operatic repertoire sold more tickets than works by unknown Soviet composers and old operas "updated" with revolutionary texts. The free concerts for workers that had blossomed during the Civil War were much more difficult to mount under the stringent conditions of NEP. As Glavrepertkom's representative, Roslavets was appalled by the output of the "Five Years After October" record factory, which consisted primarily of *tsyganshchina* and other "vulgarity."[103] Yet he recognized that strict regulation of this music might put the factory out of business.

For many musicians and other creative intellectuals, these conditions reflected not just the country's poverty but the discrepancy between the state's nominal commitment to cultural revolution and its unwillingness to support artistic life. By 1924, even those hostile to censorship at Narkompros supported the creation of a unified arts policy that entailed more financial support and coherent administration. Iavorskii and Krasin indicated that a unified arts administration (Glaviskusstvo) would help promote the cultural development of the country, and Briusova felt that a Glaviskusstvo would give the arts the priority they deserved and prevent artistic needs from being diluted by other concerns.[104]

But while there was some consensus about the potential benefits of a unified artistic policy, defining the proper role of the censorship organs, Glavlit/Glavrepertkom, was especially problematic. Responsible to both the Party and the State, the censorship agencies nonetheless often charted an independent course. Their primary task was explicitly political—to prohibit the dissemination of literature and art that was openly anti-Soviet. But as David-Fox has shown, Glavlit and especially Glavrepertkom pursued an increasingly broad agenda during the twenties.[105] Although they were technically subordinate to Narkompros, the censorship agencies consistently opposed the Commissariat's soft-line position on accommodation. Glavrepertkom's Vladimir Blium (1877–1941) emerged as one of Lunacharsky's most vehement critics in the debates over funding and repertoire for the academic theaters. At the same time, the hostility of political editors such as Blium and Roslavets to the utilitarian agendas of RAPM and ORK made these groups dedicated opponents of the censorship agencies.

Thus while Glavlit/Glavrepertkom wanted more authority and felt that their vision of ideological control had to prevail over the soft line, many musicians wanted a unified policy to eliminate the censors' arbitrary incursions into artistic affairs. The Leningrad Capella, formerly the Imperial Chapel Choir, found Glavrepertkom's interventions particularly debilitating. Still under the directorship of its prerevolutionary leader, Mikhail Klimov (1881–1937), the choir had modified its repertoire to reflect Soviet conditions. More than three-quarters of the music it performed in 1923 was categorized as "agitational-enlightenment" pieces, folk songs, and secular choral works. GUS and Glavnauka both supported Klimov's efforts to keep some sacred music in the choir's repertoire, particularly music not connected specifically with Russian Orthodoxy.[106] This support stemmed not only from the personal convictions of Krasin, Iavorskii, and Gol'denveizer, but from the Party's basic commitment, affirmed in both the 1920 and 1925 decrees on artistic policy, that the proletariat should have the legacy of the past available to it. Even the militant dogmatists from RAPM agreed that religious music from Western Europe was a crucial part of the artistic legacy, although it denounced Rachmaninoff's *All-Night Vigil* as "opium."[107] But in December 1923, Glavrepertkom forbid the Leningrad Capella to perform even a few Western religious works. Brushing aside the artistic value of the pieces in question, the ban asked rhetorically: "Who needs this demonstration of religious emotion, undoubtedly reaching its highest tension in the works of such composers as Orlando Lasso, Bach, and Beethoven?"[108] Klimov protested, and Lunacharsky had the ban overturned.[109] In the mid-twenties the Leningrad Capella performed Bach's *Mass in B Minor* and *St. Matthew's Passion,* as well as Tchaikovsky's *Liturgy of St. John Chrysostom,* Kastal'skii's *Saving from the Furnace* (*Peshchnoe deistvo*) and even Rachmaninoff's *All-Night Vigil,* but Glavrepertkom continued to censor religious music whenever possible. This created huge headaches for Klimov, who never knew when a particular piece might be banned, how long it would take to get the ban rescinded, and when it might be reimposed. Enormous rehearsal time went toward learning a major work such as Rachmaninoff's *Vigil,* which the choir was ultimately only able to perform once. By 1926, Klimov's complaints to GUS about the vagaries of Glavrepertkom's interventions concluded with a plea for "more clearly developed guiding principles" on which to plan the choir's future performances.[110]

But if Klimov hoped that more unified policies might afford protection from arbitrary censorship, most of the soft-liners at Narkompros resisted setting up a central arts administration because they did not want to give the censorship organs more authority than they already had. In March 1926, the GUS art section presidium rejected the latest proposal from Rabis for a Glaviskusstvo, stating that the issue of political censorship (the provenance of Glavlit/Glavrepertkom) was "problematic for an organ with *artistic* concerns."[111] Rather than create a new agency, GUS proposed that its existing art section be transformed by adding a "sufficient number" of members representing "party thought and ideology."[112]

Before 1927, efforts within Narkompros's Academic Center, notably by Glavnauka, as well as attempts by Rabis to prompt the Commissariat to create a unified arts administration repeatedly came to naught. The existence of such an agency would have necessitated the formulation and implementation of a much more systematic and thorough official arts policy than the compromise resolutions of 1920 and 1925. Given the success of the Narkompros staff in defending the needs and peculiarities of particular institutions and groups within the existing administrative framework, it is hardly surprising that these projects were repeatedly stymied. Other factors were also significant, including the overlap in personnel between different agencies and committees and the reluctance and inability of various agencies to agree on an ideological mode of regulation (censorship) and a way to combine it with arts administration.

At the same time, everyone, including the Narkompros staff, was frustrated with the existing system. Repeated efforts to assert GUS's primacy in artistic policy only exacerbated the struggles among different agencies and within the artistic community as a whole. By mid-decade musicians increasingly asked for clarification of what policy really was and who was in charge of it. The musicians and artists working for Narkompros wanted the government to take art and culture more seriously. Despite their reservations about a more centralized arts administration, they became more supportive of a Glaviskusstvo that would bring this about. Although efforts to create a centralized arts administration repeatedly foundered, there was considerable support for more, rather than less, centralization of artistic affairs at many levels.

In this respect, the complex and conflicted bureaucratic world of arts administration paralleled broader tensions between pluralism and centralization observable in other areas, including the Party's internal struggle to limit dissent while maintaining some tolerance for debate and room for competing proposals to deal with social issues, including the status of women and the challenges of economic diversity. As in other arenas, pressures for more regulation, increased direction, and less debate increased perceptibly in musical life throughout the decade. But as the example of the state agencies indicates and developments at the Moscow Conservatory will show, well-placed representatives of the musical community often proved adept at turning these pressures to their own advantage.

6

"Training Future Cadres"

Modernization and the Limits of Reform at the Moscow Conservatory

Technical exercises, playing well and keeping time, good knowledge of good pieces—those are the main things that should be taught. All the rest doesn't come from skill, but from God.
—Felix Mendelssohn, founder of the Leipzig Conservatory

I am grateful for the fact that he somehow, in his own way, taught me to understand the objective essence of music.
—Viktor Bobrovskii, about Fedor Keneman, his piano teacher at the Moscow Conservatory, 1925–1930

On entering the Moscow Conservatory in the fall of 1921, Vladimir Fere, aspiring pianist, composer, and future Prokoll member, found the school an exhilarating mix of the old world and the new. As was true before the revolution, most students came from educated, relatively affluent backgrounds. But Fere also noted that "among the long velvet blouses and good suits that had not yet lost their elegance, flashed military tunics, workers' shirts, and red kerchiefs" that belonged to "new people"—demobilized soldiers, workers nominated by Party organizations and trade unions, and members of the Komsomol.[1]

How these "new people" made their way among the "former people" (*byvshie liudi*) and members of the non-Communist intelligentsia who made up the majority of the faculty and students is an important dimension of the conservatory's transition to the Soviet period.[2] Making the conservatory a "Soviet institution" meant democratizing access to it, reassessing the social function of the musicians it produced, and undertaking reforms that modernized and professionalized its curriculum and administration.[3] The impetus for many of these changes came from outside the conservatory, reflecting broader efforts to standardize and modernize the educational system as a whole and to meet the unique challenges of the cultural front.

But the implementation of these reforms depended largely on the conservatory's faculty and students, the overwhelming majority of whom were indifferent, if not hostile, to the Bolshevik regime. As in other areas, the need for new cadres of "specialists" drove many reforms in higher music education and made the cooperation of the old "bourgeois" specialists essential. Communists in other educational institutions often relied on sympathetic professors and students to implement reforms. But factors peculiar to the conservatory made the institution's Party officials especially dependent on faculty and students whose "culturalist" predilections overlapped with aspects of the Party's third-front agenda. By leveraging their authority as professors, Party sympathizers, and part-time employees of the relevant agencies of Narkompros, influential faculty members co-opted many reforms and defended the traditional goals and methods of conservatory training.

The curricular and administrative reforms that gained the conservatory official recognition as an institution of higher education (VUZ) for training professional musicians were among the most significant and enduring developments of the twenties. Although Nikolai Rubinstein and the conservatory's other founders worked to provide the school's students with a comprehensive music education, the mission of the conservatory and the social status of its graduates had been contested throughout the prerevolutionary period. Since the conservatory's inception, conflicting images of musicians and their place in society as well as prejudices against an institution that relied heavily on foreign models, methodology, and faculty had underpinned struggles between those who considered the conservatory a school for dilettantes and those who wanted it to be a training ground for professional musicians.[4] With the completion of *tipizatsiia* and the adoption of a new statute (*polozhenie*) for the conservatory in 1926, Rubinstein's vision of the conservatory as a "musical university" became a reality at last. The exclusive commitment to training professional musicians that was implicit and explicit in these reforms resolved ambiguities about the objectives of higher music education that had plagued the conservatory since its inception.

Other aspects of the revolution's impact on the conservatory were more ambiguous. Making the conservatory accessible to people whose socioeconomic position had previously isolated them from "high" musical culture and the lengthy specialized training required for advanced musical study proved to be especially difficult and problematic, while efforts to formulate a new identity for "Soviet" musicians contended with a complex mix of attitudes about musicians and creative intellectuals. Aside from professionalization and the democratization of access to the conservatory, the main concern of reformers in the twenties was instilling musicians with a sense of civic duty. Promoting the conservatory as a training ground for "public-spirited" musicians (*muzykanty-obshchestvenniki*) reflected the utilitarian imperatives of Bolshevism and drew on distinctive Russian traditions that emphasized the moral responsibility of creative intellectuals and the elevating role of "art." But this effort also entailed rejecting, or at least revising, romantic images of musicians as members of an "artistic priesthood" divorced from the real world, and music thus as something only for the "elect."

Given the Party-state's quest to link educational initiatives to economic agendas and the daunting task of "building socialism," artistic VUZy such as the conservatories posed special challenges for reformers. Not only did they lack any obvious connection with "production" in any conventional sense, their purpose of training virtuoso performers and composers for the entertainment of an exploitative elite was politically unacceptable after 1917. But while the lavish elitism of the Bol'shoi Theater's productions motivated radical reformers to suggest that the theater be shut down, no attempt was made to close the conservatories. In many respects the conservatory was a remote enclave, far removed from critical sectors of the economy and overshadowed by other third-front missions. Although personnel matters became politicized at the instigation of the Party in 1924, most curricular and other "educational" issues would be scrutinized internally, with relatively little interference from outside forces such as the Party and Narkompros. Ongoing, intense discussions and reform proposals affecting teaching methods, admissions policies, and the curriculum were the focus of significant energy for conservatory faculty, students, and institutional Party members in the twenties. Many of these debates yielded tangible, significant results, but their impact was far from revolutionary. Traditional conceptions of "talent" and "accomplishment" proved stubbornly persistent to reformist calls (such as those discussed in Chapter 4) to rethink elitist notions of music, musicians, and music-making. The "new people" would leave their mark on this citadel of elite artistic culture, but only if they had "musical ability." Proposals that challenged the assumptions underpinning the perpetuation of the classical musical tradition, such as the movement to provide accordion instruction, received little serious attention. Reformers' calls for cadres of trained music instructors for workers' clubs went largely unanswered, as the status of pedagogues and amateur music-making remained decidedly lower than that of solo pianists and composers. It was clear early on that the conservatory would serve as the vehicle to democratize and perpetuate the old culture rather than provide the training ground for a new one.

Faculty and Factions Within the Moscow Conservatory

As the deprivations of the Civil War began to fade, conservatory life resumed a more normal level of activity in the early twenties. The conservatory's affairs became a matter of concern for virtually every faction of the musical community and finally came to the attention of the Party. Not only was the conservatory the focus of much of Moscow's musical life and the training ground for future musicians; the entire spectrum of the NEP musical scene was represented in the conservatory staff and student body, from the prerevolutionary musical "establishment" to the more Western-oriented members of the ASM and the politically radical Proletarian Musicians, the student "production collective" (Prokoll), and Red Professors' Faction. In the early twenties the conservatory replicated in microcosmic form many of the broader tensions and contradictions of Soviet society, as faculty, students, Party officials, and state agencies jockeyed to reform or protect the institution and determine how it would adjust to Soviet conditions.

The profile of the conservatory's faculty changed rapidly in the early twenties, as new positions were created and replacements were found for vacancies left by émigrés. Although emigration hit the ranks of the piano department particularly hard, a number of professors remained at their posts, ensuring that the prestige associated with the conservatory's prerevolutionary piano program would continue in the Soviet period. Konstantin Igumnov continued a successful career as a pedagogue and versatile performer of the most virtuosic works of the nineteenth- and early-twentieth-century solo piano literature. Like his colleague, Aleksandr Gol'denveizer, who had joined the faculty in 1906, Igumnov took an active part in the administration of the conservatory in the twenties, serving as rector from 1924 to 1929. Famed for training brilliant technicians, Karl Kipp rarely performed in public, but remained much sought after by students eager to learn his "secret" for flawless technique and proud to be known as one of "Kipp's trotters" (*Kippovskie rysaki*).[5] After Iosif Iasser emigrated in 1922, Aleksandr Gedike, who had taught piano since 1909, assumed responsibility for the organ program and became famous for his performances of Bach's organ works.

New appointments in the twenties further enhanced the strength of the piano program. Lunacharsky and Ippolitov-Ivanov recruited Feliks Blumenfel'd (1863–1931), Horowitz's teacher, from the directorship of the Kiev Conservatory in 1922. With him came Genrikh Neigauz (Heinrich Neuhaus, 1888–1964), future director of the conservatory and teacher of Sviatoslav Richter and Emil Gilels. Maria Nemenova-Lunts (1878–1954) and Elena Bekman-Shcherbina, one of the prerevolutionary conservatory's finest graduates (1899) and renowned interpreter of the works of Scriabin, Debussy, and Ravel, both joined the faculty at the end of the Civil War. Samuil Feinberg, who was also famous as a Scriabin specialist and whose compositions presented performers with fiendish technical challenges, assumed a professorship in piano in 1922 that he held for forty years.

In the composition department, Ippolitov-Ivanov and his former student Sergei Vasilenko (1872–1956) provided the continuity with the prerevolutionary period and the traditions of Russian musical classicism that became known as the "academic school" in the twenties. They were joined in 1917 by Georgii Katuar, a mathematician who had studied music privately with K. Klindworth (Klindvort) and later Taneev and Anton Arenskii. In addition to teaching composition, Katuar developed a functional approach to harmony and form based on the work of Hugo Riemann that became the foundation for the first-year theory curriculum. The dean of the composition department, Georgii Konius (Conius, 1862–1933), who had also studied with Taneev and Arenskii, promoted his own theory of metrotectonics, which used graphic representations of musical compositions to depict the symmetry of musical form.[6] The creative orientations of Reinhold Gliere, who came to Moscow from the Kiev Conservatory during the Civil War, and Mikhail Gnesin, who joined the faculty in 1925, relied heavily on Russia's nineteenth-century musical legacy, as well as an interest in traditional Jewish music.

The most prominent addition to the composition department, however, was Nikolai Miaskovskii, who accepted a professorship in 1921. Miaskovskii's formidable erudition, prominence as a symphonist, and interest in new Russian and European music made him tremendously popular with students. He was the mentor of Polovinkin, Mosolov, Shebalin, and other young composers affiliated with the ASM. But as a whole his students were a diverse group, including several Prokoll members as well as the organist Mikhail Starokadomskii and pianist Lev Oborin.[7]

Miaskovskii provided the main hub around which the ASM's activities revolved at the conservatory. Other faculty members, including Feinberg, Pavel Lamm (who taught chamber music and piano ensemble), and the conductors Konstantin Saradzhev and Nikolai Golovanov, also promoted an interest in new music from the West and Russia among their students.[8] Although his compositions bore the stamp of late Russian romanticism, Anatolii Aleksandrov, who joined the faculty in 1923, emphasized new music as well in his harmony classes.[9]

The research institutes (GIMN, GAKhN, and GIII) became important centers for theoretical research and musicology in the twenties, but many scholars at these institutions taught at the conservatory as well. The director of GIMN, Nikolai Garbuzov, was also professor of musical acoustics at the conservatory. Trained both in the natural sciences and music, Garbuzov examined the acoustical bases of harmony and established acoustics as a legitimate branch of Soviet music theory.[10]

Mikhail Ivanov-Boretskii, who also worked at GIMN and GAKhN, began teaching music history at the conservatory in 1922. A lawyer who studied music privately with Rimsky-Korsakov before attending the Florence Conservatory, Ivanov-Boretskii brought tremendous erudition to his courses on music history and criticism. Like Asaf'ev in Leningrad, he emerged as a dominating figure in his field in these years, assuming numerous administrative positions, taking an active part in a number of reform initiatives, organizing a program for "musical science" at the conservatory,[11] and churning out a constant stream of concert reviews and books (in every major European language) as well as scholarly publications.

After completing his studies with Gol'denveizer and Katuar, Sergei Evseev joined the faculty in 1922, teaching theory courses while continuing to give concert-lectures with the ensemble he had organized during the Civil War. Emigration opened up several vacancies in the string department, two of which were filled by pupils of the great Leopold Auer. Lev Tseitlin, former concertmaster for Koussevitzky and founder of Persimfans, became a professor in 1920. Soon thereafter came Abram Iampol'skii (1890–1956), who served as the concertmaster for the conductorless orchestra.

Although some professors were sympathetic to the revolution, there were no Communists on the faculty and very few among the students. The Party's efforts to establish a presence at the conservatory proceeded more incrementally than at other VUZy, necessitated compromise on all sides, and depended heavily on the support and cooperation of sympathetic faculty and students. Party organizations at the conservatory were founded only after a handful of Party nominees came to the conservatory, the majority as students, in the fall of 1922.[12] The newcomers found the conservatory seemingly untouched by the first five years of Soviet power, with a predominantly bourgeois student body and the majority of professors believing that art existed in a realm far removed from politics.[13] Dismayed but undaunted, the group concluded its first meeting on November 7 by singing *The Internationale* and taking down the icons that still hung in every classroom.[14]

From these modest beginnings, the Party's growth at the conservatory was significant but gradual. In 1927 Party and Komsomol members accounted for less than one-tenth of the conservatory's 900 students and 144 faculty.[15] Only four Party members were on the faculty, and all of them taught the recently introduced "social science" courses.[16] None were musicians by training. Throughout NEP, Communists were vastly outnumbered by non-Party faculty and students.

Aside from the existing antipathies and suspicions among musicians toward Bolshevism, which were shared by many intellectuals, two factors slowed the increase of Communists at the conservatory. The first was the undeniable need for musical ability (the "talented individuals" in Lunacharsky's formulation) and preliminary training that undermined efforts to attract politically desirable students. As in other VUZy, preferred admissions were given to workers, peasants, veterans, and nominees of Party and trade union organizations beginning in 1922. But even the Party representative on the admissions committee conceded that few of these candidates had the appropriate musical training.[17] To correct this situation, the Party looked to the *rabfak*, a preparatory department for proletarian students modeled on similar institutions at the universities, and consistently supported and defended its operations.

The second obstacle that slowed the recruitment of Communists into the conservatory was the suspicion and confusion within the Party over the relationship between Communism and the professional study of music. Indeed, the compatibility of Communism with the conservatory was contentious for both sides, and may have been more problematic for Komsomol and Party members than for faculty and students who adopted a pragmatic attitude of passivity to proposed changes. In a later memoir, Mirra Bruk, one of the conservatory's first Komsomol members, recalled how a senior comrade from Moscow University expressed amazement over her dedication to music. To him, studying music seemed a remnant (*perezhitka*) of aristocratic, bourgeois life.[18] Whatever their musical aptitude and interests, many Komsomol members sent to the conservatory in the twenties shared these sentiments, at least initially. Rejecting the traditional image of the conservatory as a "temple for the priests of pure art,"[19] many found it difficult to reconcile professional musicianship with the utilitarian imperatives of building socialism, as suggested in this reported exchange between Komsomol members:

> So you finish the conservatory and join an orchestra, and then you'll spend your whole life piping on your flute. What will become of you? Will you really be a Communist? At a time when the republic needs workers for cooperatives, engineers, agronomists, pilots and social workers? Why don't you, a Komsomol, enter a VUZ that is decisively important to economic construction, rather than studying a luxury such as strumming an instrument for your listening pleasure?[20]

Studying classical music was an embrace of "bourgeois" values and behaviors that threatened to corrupt the revolutionary party even as it struggled to come to terms with the more ideologically threatening circumstances of NEP.[21] Many Communists left, or contemplated leaving, the conservatory.[22] Those who stayed struggled to clarify the place of music in a new Communist way of life by identifying ways for musicians to participate in the task of building socialism. They became tireless champions of "production work" and student practicums that gave musicians firsthand experience with the "new public" they were now supposed to serve.

The Party organization in the conservatory was also weakened by complex factional allegiances and rivalries. Although the Proletarian Musicians' association was originally affiliated with the State Publishing House, it was organized at the initiative of the Moscow Conservatory Party cell.[23] The organization's leaders, Sarra Krylova and Lev Lebedinskii, were both active in the conservatory's Party organization as well. RAPM supported the Party's initiatives on admissions and curriculum reform and initially tried to align its work with the conservatory's Party organization.[24] But the majority of the conservatory's Communists kept their distance from RAPM, especially as the decade progressed. Marian Koval' and Viktor Belyi, both members of the Komsomol, threw their support behind Prokoll, rather than RAPM. Viktor Vinogradov withdrew from RAPM when the Party put him in charge of setting up the music division of the artistic *rabfak*. And at the Conference on Musical Enlightenment Work in 1926, Komsomol member Simon Korev supported resolutions on the mass song that ran counter to RAPM's position.

Given their small numbers, the difficulties of attracting new members, and the obstacles described above, Communists at the conservatory relied heavily on the support and cooperation of non-Party students and especially faculty. These "old specialists" were all professional musicians, trained (sometimes abroad) and active before the revolution. Many had worked in the adult education movement or in musical enlightenment before 1917. An official history of the conservatory's Party organization from the fifties praises Kastal'skii, Gedike, Gliere, Miaskovskii, Feinberg, Neigauz, Krein, Tseitlin, and Iampol'skii for their help in implementing reforms as well as in preserving what the Party considered most valuable about the prerevolutionary conservatory.[25]

As we have seen, other non-Party faculty involved in the institution's administration or employed by Narkompros were also critical in determining the conservatory's fate in these years. Key among them were Aleksandr Gol'denveizer, who succeeded Ippolitov-Ivanov as rector in 1922, and Konstantin

Igumnov, who took over that position from 1924 to 1929.[26] Nazarii Raiskii (1876–1958), a tenor trained at the Warsaw Conservatory, joined the faculty in 1919. As assistant director, he administered the conservatory's finances throughout the twenties, turning to unconventional sources of revenue such as renting out the Large Hall as a movie theater ("The Colossus") between concerts. Nadezhda Briusova remained in the administration until 1928, although her colleagues tried to oust her after her enthusiastic participation in the faculty purges of 1924.[27] As the initial stages of admissions reform and *tipizatsiia* indicate, Lunacharsky's periodic intervention in matters affecting musical education added an important dimension to the often tense relationship between the conservatory and various Narkompros organs, as did the overlap in personnel between the conservatory and the bureaucracy.

The conservatory's Red Professors' Faction provided the Party with important leverage in implementing reforms. Organized in the first weeks of 1924, the Red Professors were not necessarily Party members, but they sought to unite all "revolution-minded" teaching personnel in the effort to restructure the institution's teaching methods and objectives.[28] The Faction's first formal declaration denounced the idea that music exists outside any relationship to a particular social class, the prevalence of an "art for art's sake" mentality, and the traditional attitude toward musicians as artistic "priests" and the conservatory as an institution standing "outside/beyond time and space."[29] The Faction proposed to work closely with student organizations within the conservatory as well as social and artistic agencies such as Glavprofobr, GUS, Rabis, and RAPM, in order to facilitate the political and social education of conservatory students and promote the proletarianization of the student body. The group intended to reform the "ossified routines and scholasticism" of the conservatory's academic program and teaching methods so that the conservatory might produce musicians "possessing a full complement of contemporary knowledge and mastery, tightly connected with and responsive to the needs of the broad masses."[30]

Of the Faction's nine members, only two were Communists: I. K. Mamaev and Nikolai Sherman (1896–?), a graduate of the Petrograd Conservatory and disciple of Iavorskii who was the Party representative on the conservatory's board until 1924. Nadezhda Briusova and Mikhail Ivanov-Boretskii dominated many of the group's discussions and represented the senior faculty, along with Aleksandr Kastal'skii and Lev Tseitlin. Theorist Iosif Dubovskii (1892–1969), pianist Isaak Rabinovich (1897–?), and composer Aleksandr Veprik (1899–1958)—all young, recently appointed teachers—rounded out the group. Other conservatory professors and representatives from student organizations also participated in the group's meetings, as did invited guests from other musical institutions, including Iavorskii. RAPM appointed David Chernomordikov to be its representative to the Faction, but he never attended a meeting.[31]

The Red Professors played a critical role in the many struggles over administration, admissions, curriculum, and teaching methods that occupied conservatory faculty, students, the Party, and state authorities in 1924. The group worked with the Party, the conservatory executive committee, and Rabis to facilitate the installation of Party members on the conservatory board and the purge of students and faculty that summer.[32] In these months it also worked to reform the curriculum of the theory and composition program, and considered Roslavets for a professorship in the composition department.[33] The group's recommendations were taken into account in the final stages of curriculum reform in 1925–26.

The Party funded the faction's bulletin, *Musical Education* (*Muzykal'noe obrazovanie*), which rivaled *Music and Revolution* as the most substantial "thick" music journal of the twenties. Published four to six times annually from 1925 to 1930, *Musical Education* featured a broad range of articles on musical education, performance, and musicology. Its intended audience was "all progressive musicians in the country . . . who see the bringing of musical culture nearer to the broad masses and the creation of 'public-spirited musicians' [*muzykanty-obshchestvenniki*] as the main task of the present."[34] While all could agree in general terms with these objectives, the implementation of such goals remained a source of debate and disagreement among the faculty and its factions.

Defining the Objectives of Communist Musical Education

Before the revolution, the conservatory provided a training ground and working environment for a small number of talented composers and solo performers, while at the same time educating amateur music lovers who desired musical training to make them more "cultured" individuals.[35] Confronting both of these objectives and the pronounced individualism of musical higher education, reformers in the twenties raised key questions about the conservatory's curriculum, admissions policies, and administration: What was the function of musical education in a Communist society? How should the conservatory adapt to the democratic demands of postrevolutionary Russia without compromising the caliber of musicians it produced? What kind of artistic and political training should the "new music education" entail?

The consensus that emerged reflected old and new values and was not uncontested. Along with prerevolutionary disputes about the purpose of the conservatory, reformers in the twenties also inherited contradictory, widely-held perceptions of musicians and their social status. In the decades before 1917, the traditional understanding of musicians as artisans who provided entertainment was challenged by the image of the romantic artist as a uniquely gifted creative individual whose innate genius inspired awe and commanded reverence. The first image, reinforced by Russia's tradition of serf orchestras and theater troupes, meant that music was not considered an appropriate occupation for a person of good education or breeding. The second image, while it accorded considerable prestige to gifted composers or performers, projected talent as a unique, even divinely inspired gift that stood to gain little from standardized structured music schools. The spread of conservatories and the glories of Russian music in the late Imperial period did much to offset these two perceptions. But while star composers and performers were highly esteemed, musicians of more modest reputation were still somewhat suspect. As the son of a Moscow industrialist put it: "they were thought to belong to a different walk of life."[36] Making the professional musician an acceptable, and even desirable, social identity in Soviet Russia involved refocusing these traditional images and reconciling, or at least smoothing over, some of the contradictions between them.

The new order demanded that musicians concern themselves more directly with society and its cultural needs. The conservatory's graduates must be more than masters of their instrument or the art of composition. In his opening address to the Glavprofobr Conference on Artistic Education in April 1925, Lunacharsky insisted that musical higher education could not produce virtuoso performers and composers "as an end in themselves."[37] Communists at the conservatory asserted that rather than training "court composers" and "salon musicians," the conservatory's task was "to give the Soviet cultural front a public-spirited musician with a full professional education."[38] In keeping with the revolution's impetus to democratize access to the arts and the policy directives that emerged from events such as the Conference on Musical Enlightenment Work in 1926, the conservatory in the twenties emphasized the need to produce trained club leaders and choir directors in addition to virtuoso performers and outstanding composers. Both Communists and "bearers of culture" (*kul'turtregery*) insisted that rank-and-file orchestral musicians, choir directors, and music teachers for workers' clubs were needed more than virtuoso pianists, violinists, and singers.[39]

Demands for "cadres" of specialists for the mass musical movement prompted a number of curricular and structural reforms. At Iavorskii's initiative, a pedagogical faculty (*pedfak*) was established in 1921 specifically to train music teachers.[40] Graduates of the *pedfak* were qualified to teach performance and historical-theoretical subjects at musical technicums and to work in general music education programs for adults such as workers' clubs. The need for club instructors was also to be met by graduates of the conservatory's choral program. When the conservatory's postrevolutionary statute was finally approved in 1926, the *pedfak* was made the administrative equal of the performance and composition departments. Furthermore, the training of music teachers for advanced instruction in musical technicums and artistic VUZy, as well as instructors for club work, preschools, and elementary education, was listed as one of the conservatory's three main goals.[41] The resolutions of the 1927 Glavprofobr Conference on Artistic Education integrated pedagogical training more thoroughly into all conservatory academic programs, and required all graduate students to serve as teaching assistants.[42]

But while RAPM and the Party looked to the choral program and the *pedfak* for desperately needed cadres for the workers' club movement, aspects of both programs undercut their intended objectives. The choral program was staffed largely by faculty formerly affiliated with the Moscow Synodal School, including Kastal'skii as well as Nikolai Danilin (1878–1945) and Pavel Chesnokov (1877–1944), a prolific composer of sacred and liturgical music in the twenty years before the revolution. The "model, politically developed club instructors" that the program was supposed to produce were in fact trained by men with decades of experience educating church choir directors (*regenty*).[43]

More complex contradictions surrounded the *pedfak*. The faculty's first dean, pianist Grigorii Prokof'ev, saw the pedagogy program as an opportunity to strengthen the conservatory's role in producing music teachers (most of them female pianists) for the kind of amateur (*liubitel'skii*) "salon" musical activities that the Party, Narkompros, and much of the faculty most wanted to eliminate. As Prokof'ev's replacement, Briusova struggled both to overcome the stigma associated with teaching music as a profession and to orient the pedagogy program to the needs of Soviet popular education programs. Before the revolution, teaching was considered a fall-back option for failed performers and a money-making pastime for bourgeois women. Structural reforms backed by Glavprofobr now gave pedagogy the same priority and status as performance and composition—at least on paper. Students were tracked into a specialty based on admissions tests and auditions when they matriculated. Yet because admission to the more prestigious divisions required demonstrable talent and prior training, the *pedfak* quickly became a haven for students of modest abilities and a stronghold for Komsomol and RAPM members and others whose admission to the conservatory hinged primarily on their nomination by a Party or trade union organization. With their ties to workers' clubs, chorus circles, and general music schools, the *pedfak* students had little in common with those who aspired to compose great symphonies or make a career on the concert stage. The *pedfak* thus had few supporters. Faculty and students in other departments saw it as a "foreign body" at the conservatory and resented the pretensions of its students.[44]

Imperatives to redefine the objectives of musical higher education resonated with many musicians' prerevolutionary commitment to social service. But ambivalence about these new goals was apparent at many levels throughout the twenties, and undoubtedly contributed to the limited success of many reforms. Iavorskii's 1922 reform plan stipulated that the conservatory "should answer the demands of contemporary life, [it] should graduate musical artists necessary and valuable for life, and adapted to practical work." Revealing a continued concern for artistic achievement "for its own sake," however, the "higher achievements in the area of pure artistry" were listed as a central task of the conservatory as an artistic VUZ.[45] Despite a sincere commitment to training musicians for a variety of musical occupations (previously nonexistent or regarded as second-rate) that would better serve the cultural needs of workers and peasants, "star quality" was still highly valued. Artistic excellence was obviously not democratic, and the merits of technical expertise were deeply ingrained in almost everyone's assumptions about what made "good" music composition and performance. Even militant reformers attracted to the mobilizing potential of music fell back on conventional perceptions of music making as an artistic endeavor, and insisted that graduates of the conservatory's pedagogy program should be "highly gifted" and "good performers": "He who is qualified to teach any kind of art must be a master of one's craft [*byt' masterom svoego dela*] since teaching art cannot be founded on some kind of mandatory, generally recognized rules."[46]

Established hierarchies of prestige also proved difficult to revise. Pianists Samuil Feinberg, Grigorii Ginzburg, and Lev Oborin and composers Aleksandr Mosolov and Dmitrii Shostakovich were lauded by all for gaining international recognition at the 1927 Chopin Competition in Warsaw or for having their work featured in ISCM concerts. Whatever their personal politics or artistic credo, the musical community valued these musicians for their "export value," and as evidence that classical music in Russia had survived the loss of Rachmaninoff, Prokofiev, and Koussevitzky.[47]

The traditional status of the composer and scholar above the choir director and orchestra brass player was also perpetuated by the state bureaucracies. Composers, theorists, and musicologists dominated the staff of key Narkompros agencies. Their continued tenure in these positions was ensured and validated in the curriculum reform of 1925–26, which stipulated that musicology and composition students complete their practicums in administrative agencies (GUS, Glavpolitprosvet, Glavprofobr, and the music section of the State Publishing House), while performers and pedagogues were to serve in workers' clubs and orchestras.[48]

Reformers in the twenties perpetuated the nineteenth-century veneration of innate ability, but also affirmed the value and necessity of formal training while emphasizing the redeeming value of public service. The autodidacticism of the Mighty Five was revered as a distinguishing feature of their "nationalism," but it now firmly belonged in the past. The focus was still on genius, though it was recognized that even geniuses needed a structured education. The image of the professional musician that coalesced in these years perpetuated Mendelssohn's assessment of both the importance and the limitations of formal training. In the shifting matrix of social and cultural hierarchies the traditional prejudice against musicians, as well as the uniquely Communist one noted above, subsided as "classical music" became an accepted, even necessary part of Soviet culture. Bobrovskii's appreciation of the "objective" essence of music actually points to the opposite—a regard for an ineffable, subjective, personal musical experience—indicating that the embourgeoisement of the revolution that became writ large in the thirties had been solidly entrenched in some quarters a decade earlier.

The 1925 Conference on Artistic Education and the 1926 Conservatory Statute

The essential contours of Soviet higher music education were formalized at the Conference on Artistic Education in April 1925 and in the ensuing conservatory statute (*polozhenie*) of 1926. Although Glavprofobr convened the conference at least in part to bring artistic education out of the backwaters of neglect and into compliance with Narkompros's general requirements for VUZy, its outcome reflected significant input by faculty from the Moscow Conservatory. Professors from the conservatory accounted for nineteen of the music section's thirty-five members, the remaining slots being claimed by representatives from the Leningrad Conservatory (5), several musical technicums (5), the State Institute of Musical Science (3), GUS (1), and Glavprofobr (2).[49] Reports by Gol'denveizer, Gnesin, Ivanov-Boretskii, and Leonid Nikolaev from the Leningrad Conservatory provided the foundation for resolutions that defined the goals of training performers and composers and the objectives of teaching music history and theory.[50]

Updating the curriculum for composition students was a major concern of the conference. Almost two decades after Nikolai Rimsky-Korsakov's death, his pedagogy still formed the backbone of composition study in Moscow, and was devoutly promoted in Leningrad, where one of Maksimilian Shteinberg's students later recalled that Rimsky-Korsakov's "invisible self was always present in class."[51] Rimsky-Korsakov's method emphasized the thorough, sequential mastery of the principles of harmony, counterpoint and fugue, orchestration, and formal analysis, with "practical composition" beginning only in a student's fourth year of study. The strengths of this program were evident in the impeccable mastery of technique and musical fundamentals displayed by his students, as well as their own successes as composers and teachers. Many of the conference delegates were products of this very system. But with its emphasis on drills and exercises and lack of original composition in the first three years, the Rimsky-Korsakov pedagogy was as rigid as it was rigorous, and faulted by many for its "scholasticism."[52] At the initiative of Vladimir Shcherbachev a new program was adopted that integrated original composition into all phases of the curriculum, beginning in the first year.[53] The other elements of the old system remained essentially unchanged, except for the study of musical form (*oformlenie*), which was expanded to give advanced students exposure to different methodologies, such as Iavorskii's theory of modal rhythm or Konius's metrotectonics.

Pressure for educational reform originating outside the conservatory also had an impact. Criticism of "academicism" and "scholasticism" in the conservatory's curriculum advanced the broader assault on traditional pedagogy backed by Narkompros and the Party's educational specialists, including Krupskaia. Conference resolutions warning against the dangers of "rigid scholasticism" and "moribund abstraction" in the composition program called for the new conservatory curriculum to incorporate aspects of the progressive pedagogy associated with the Dalton Plan, which had been adopted by Narkompros in 1924. Developed by Helen Parkhurst, a disciple of John Dewey, the Dalton Plan promoted practical knowledge and "learning by doing" in an unregimented academic "laboratory."[54] At the conservatory, the "open door" methods of instruction associated with the Dalton plan promised to reform the "autocratic" nature of the student-teacher relationship, while the passive learning associated with lecturing would give way to seminars. Pedagogical courses and student practicums became a central part of the curriculum. Students could choose which classes to attend, and were given the opportunity to hear and evaluate performances of their own work as well as those of their peers.

The political and social science courses that the Party demanded as a "social minimum" for higher educational institutions did not challenge the expertise of faculty or the integrity of disciplinary fields at the conservatory in the same way they did at the universities.[55] Still, professors at the conservatory objected to "overburdening" students with courses on political economy, the foundations of Leninism, and historical materialism.[56] The Party disregarded these concerns, but also failed in its effort to develop a "Marxist world view" among students in the composition department.[57] Courses in art and music history grounded "on a sociological foundation" replaced fencing and church singing, but were taught by people like Ivanov-Boretskii, who was far from a Marxist. Since Party members were in particularly short supply at the conservatory, Communist students such as Viktor Belyi and D. Rabinovich were enlisted to teach the mandatory political courses.[58]

Many Narkompros initiatives, like the promotion of the Dalton Plan, overlapped with the agendas of reformers within the conservatory. Emphasis on "scientific" approaches to musicology, music theory, and music history reflected the influence of Ivanov-Boretskii in particular as well as the politically driven abandonment of "idealist" and "subjective" approaches to art history and aesthetics in other areas of artistic education. Similarly, resolutions calling for students of music history to hear live performances of the works under scrutiny and to learn about folk music as well as the classical tradition were consistent both with the principles of the Dalton Plan and the prerevolutionary convictions of reformers such as Briusova, Iavorskii, and Ivanov-Boretskii.[59]

But along with the buzzwords and catch phrases associated with and mandated by extra-musical agendas, members of the music section promoted their own vision of a conservatory curriculum that would produce highly qualified, well-rounded professional musicians. After cursory statements on the mission of the *pedfak* and the need to coordinate the conservatory's work with the political enlightenment programs sponsored by Glavpolitprosvet, the most detailed resolutions dealt with the conservatory's traditional mission of training performers and composers. Resolutions on the performance curriculum asserted that "highly qualified performers" should work for the musical enlightenment and education of the broad masses, but stipulated that training "artists and masters (virtuosos)" was also the program's task.[60]

The conservatory's statute of 1926 incorporated the resolutions described above and strengthened the institution's image as a VUZ.[61] After years of constant internal reorganization, the conservatory's structure took on a more or less stable configuration of three basic faculties: composition/musicology, performance, and pedagogy. Degree programs varied from three years for brass and double bass players, four years for woodwind, harp, and voice students, and five years for composers, musicologists, conductors, pianists, violinists, and cellists. The struggle over *tipizatsiia* was resolved by removing the children's music school from the conservatory's administration. In accordance with the agreement reached between the conservatory and Glavprofobr in 1924, the VUZ and technicum retained their separate identities under a common administrative board.[62]

The reforms of 1925–26 integrated the conservatory into the Soviet educational system, secured its status as a VUZ, and overcame the traces of "dilettantism" that remained from the prerevolutionary period. The new statute clearly stated that the conservatory's purpose was to train "professional artists," and listed composers, scholars, and solo performers before "technicum teachers, and instructors for club work, preschool, and general music education." The new curriculum reflected an extraordinary concern for distinctions between different levels of artistic accomplishment and technical expertise. Performance programs included tracks for "virtuoso," "chamber," and "orchestral" musicians, while examinations after the third year of study provided a mechanism to offer a technicum degree to students who failed to measure up to the standards necessary for VUZ graduation.[63] In order to graduate, *pedfak* students were required to complete a report on their pedagogical work or a thesis on their theoretical research, while performers were required to put on a full recital and composers had to submit an original large-scale work such as a symphony or part of an opera.[64]

Making music education more "modern" and professional also meant expanding the conservatory's programs to include musicology and graduate programs. In the case of musicology, the conservatory won out against a concerted bid by the State Academy of Artistic Sciences (GAKhN) for the right to train "musical scientists."[65] The establishment of a structured graduate program (*aspirantura*) replaced the prerevolutionary system of informal apprenticeship of advanced students to a professor.[66] Under the new statute, conservatory graduates received the title of "artist-musician" (*khudozhnik-muzykant*) in the area of their expertise (composition, performance, or pedagogy). These were updated versions of prerevolutionary appellations, intended to accord musicians a professional status comparable to doctors or engineers.[67]

Overall, the 1925–26 reforms are striking for their limited agenda and modest impact on the substance of conservatory training. Although the conservatory's purpose was reevaluated and significant measures taken to broaden the social function of the musicians it trained, the reforms did little more than update teaching methods and course content. The curricular core of music education remained virtually untouched and all but unchallenged.[68] In 1925, as thirty years earlier, training at the Moscow Conservatory served first and foremost to impart the technical expertise and theoretical knowledge necessary to master the riches of the classical musical legacy. In large part this orientation reflected the preferences of the students and faculty, who summarily dismissed genuinely radical proposals for reform.

As a staple of traditional musical education, the piano continued to enjoy a central place in the curriculum, even though the Proletarian Musicians campaigned (with limited success) to decrease new admissions to a department traditionally associated with "salon musicians" and virtuoso performers. The crisis in public support and financial resources for the Bol'shoi Theater notwithstanding, the conservatory devoted considerable energy and funds to training musicians for the operatic stage.[69] Beginning in 1923 Mikhail Ivanov-Boretskii offered courses on the history of opera, and throughout the twenties the conservatory sponsored operatic productions to provide students with practical experience. The first complete production was mounted in 1926 and featured Rimsky-Korsakov's *The Tsar's Bride.*

Some efforts to apply egalitarian and "revolutionary" ideals to traditional modes of performance and composition did find their way into the conservatory during NEP. The activities of the student Prokoll in this area were noteworthy, and Persimfans founder Lev Tseitlin used "conductorless" principles when rehearsing advanced orchestral students. But these were informal, spontaneous endeavors lacking any official institutional support. The curriculum remained inherently conservative, reflecting a commitment to perpetuating the legacy of the past both by producing skilled composers and performers and by making this heritage more accessible to previously disadvantaged groups. When Roslavets proposed scuttling the core of the Rimsky-Korsakov system in favor of a pedagogy that would give preference to "practice over theory" and cultivate a student's original style by helping him "overcome" the influence of earlier composers, he was attacked by a formidable alliance of non-Party specialists (Konius and Iavorskii) and Communists (Vinogradov and Lebedinskii).[70] As a result, Roslavets's candidacy for a faculty position was dead in the water.

Admissions Policies

Although admission to the prerevolutionary conservatory was not restricted by social position, ethnicity, or gender, the economic resources needed to prepare for and fund conservatory studies meant that advanced musical education belonged almost exclusively to the privileged classes. The retention of admissions policies based on talent and preparatory training meant that few candidates who were socially or politically desirable from the Party's perspective actually entered the conservatory during the Civil War and the beginning of NEP. The first Communist students, who enrolled in the fall of 1922, were struck by the "traditional" outlook pervading the conservatory atmosphere and the skeptical, haughty attitude of the students from previously "protected" classes.[71]

In many respects, then, the difficulty of defining the purpose of professional music education paled in comparison with the challenge of broadening access to the conservatory and changing the social profile of its student body. The "cultural front" needed qualified specialists. But almost everyone at the conservatory agreed that musical aptitude as well as some preparatory training were crucial prerequisites not only for virtuoso performers, but also for elementary music teachers and choir and club directors. During NEP the Party pursued two strategies, both of which were resisted fairly effectively by the faculty, to bring more workers and peasants into the conservatory and to reduce the numbers of the untalented and politically or socially undesirable from the student body.

The first strategy was to cut existing numbers of students by means of examination (*proverka*). Initial efforts of this sort yielded modest results. At the insistence of the Party, and with what Krylova described as a "gigantic effort," the conservatory administration examined all current pupils in the fall of 1922, with the stated objective of weeding out "weak" and "eternal" students.[72] This *proverka* marked the initial steps toward *tipizatsiia*. Only sixty of the institution's 925 students were dismissed, but the remainder were assigned to one of the conservatory's three levels, with fifty-nine admitted to the VUZ, 578 to the technicum, and 228 to the school.[73]

A much more thoroughgoing *proverka* was conducted in the summer of 1924 as part of the general purge of VUZ students following one of Trotsky's setbacks in the Party leadership struggle. Initiated by the Red Professors' Faction, the student *proverka* was a prelude to purging the conservatory staff.[74] As was true in the universities and other VUZy, the purge at the conservatory had many often contradictory objectives that reflected the frequently conflicting concerns of the institution, the Party, and Narkompros.[75] While the Party wanted to expel students who were "alien" in terms of their politics or social origins, Narkompros supported dismissals for poor academic performance and for such innocuous misdeeds as skipping classes. In the conservatory's quarterly report to GUS that June, Briusova addressed these objectives by portraying the purge primarily as an effort to raise academic standards that mainly affected the technicum and school, rather than the more "academically valuable" VUZ.[76] Routing out oppositionists and Trotsky's supporters might have been a major goal of the Party leadership, but this objective seems to have been turned on its head at the conservatory. The Red Professors' Faction moved to invite Trotsky to address the students on "art and contemporary life" at the same meeting it initiated the purge. (At the next meeting Mamaev reported that he had been unsuccessful in making arrangements with the triumvirate's vanquished rival, and the Faction moved to postpone the appearance until the fall. By December, the group's attentions had turned to Bukharin, who they hoped would publish an article in *Musical Education.*)[77]

While Narkompros hoped to use the purge to raise academic standards, it also provided RAPM and Party organizations within the conservatory with a golden opportunity in their ongoing quest to reduce "swollen" (*razbukhshikh*) departments overburdened with "socially alien" elements and cultivate recruitment to the more "socially useful" pedagogical and choral departments.[78] Training pianists had been a main focus for the conservatory since its inception. Indeed, pianists made up nearly 50 percent of the student body in 1910. RAPM boasted that this statistic had been reduced by 17 percent in 1923–24.[79] But as in the case of *tipizatsiia*, militants met stiff opposition from Iavorskii on the issue of limiting admissions to the piano program. At his initiative Glavprofobr approved admission for twenty-four pianists in the fall of 1923, even though the conservatory board and admissions committee had agreed to accept only twelve.[80] But pianists and voice students were particularly hard hit by the 1924 purge, which eliminated more than half of the existing piano majors and almost 40 percent of voice students.[81]

Whatever the broader objectives of the student purge, in individual terms its impact was often idiosyncratic, arbitrary, and quickly reversed. Both ASM protégé Aleksandr Mosolov and Prokoll darling Aleksandr Davidenko were among those dismissed in the initial *proverka*. With the support of patronage networks within and beyond the conservatory, however, they were able to continue their studies. For Davidenko, who had been expelled for skipping class, lobbying by Kastal'skii and Gliere was sufficient to gain him reinstatement.[82] Mosolov also had a poor attendance record and had failed to graduate on schedule. Like Davidenko, he turned to Gliere, who vouched for the young composer's satisfactory progress and creative potential. Gliere's affidavit supplemented Mosolov's own petition for reinstatement emphasizing the innocence of his actions (his own illness and Gliere's absence from Moscow had kept him from completing his studies the previous year), his commitment to serve Soviet society, and his voluntary service in the Red Army against Denikin. These documents received sympathetic reinforcement from Boris Krasin, who successfully reopened the case, allowing Mosolov to graduate in May 1925.[83]

The most obvious consequence of the purge was a significant, if temporary, reduction in the number of students at the conservatory. The *proverka* initially reduced the size of the student body by 40 percent, bringing the conservatory's total enrollment down to 517, a much larger cut than the 25 percent reductions at other Moscow VUZy.[84] By the time the dust settled, however, at least eighty students had been reinstated.[85] In an attempt to mitigate what it regarded as excessive purging for nonacademic reasons, Glavprofobr allowed students who had been dismissed on nebulously defined "general principles" to resume their studies in the fall. The agency also authorized students who had been in their final year of study to take exams "externally," without attending classes. The new class admitted to the conservatory in the fall brought the total number of students back to nearly 700. Despite the best efforts of the conservatory Communists, the fall admissions campaign was much less effective in advancing the cause of "proletarianization" or "bolshevization" at the conservatory than at other VUZy. Only 17 percent of the conservatory's 100 new admittees were workers or peasants, while 31 percent of the incoming students at Leningrad University were from the working class.[86] Nearly half of the students admitted to VUZy in Leningrad were Komsomol and Party members, whereas these groups accounted for only 21 percent of the conservatory's incoming class.[87]

Given the difficulties of finding qualified candidates of desirable social origins and political sympathies, Communists at the conservatory looked to a special "workers' faculty" program (*rabfak*) as a second method of "rejuvenating" the conservatory student body. The original idea for a musical *rabfak* belonged to Efim Vilkovir, who presented his plans to the RAPM membership in 1923.[88] In one of the most utopian proposals to emerge from the debates on music education, Vilkovir suggested that training genuinely "proletarian" musicians would involve an overhaul of the very foundations of music education.[89]

Echoing commonly heard complaints, Vilkovir maintained that detached isolation (*zamknutost'*) and bourgeois, "ultra-individualistic tendencies" made conservatories and music schools completely incapable of bringing music to the masses. To remedy this, he called for the establishment of musical workers' faculties, modeled on those in universities, that would produce the public-spirited musicians so needed on the cultural front. Vilkovir saw the musical *rabfak* as a means of recruiting students from a proletarian background, actively involving teachers in educating the broad masses, and developing new teaching methods. He also saw the musical *rabfak* as an opportunity to overcome two of the most difficult presumptions affecting recruitment to musical higher education—the necessity of demonstrable "talent" and the need to begin musical training in childhood. Vilkovir maintained these obstacles were nothing more than prejudice, insisting that any able-bodied adult (age sixteen to twenty-two) with a "strong desire" to study music could be prepared for admissions to the conservatory in three to four years. Like Iavorskii, Briusova, and Lebedinskii, he pointed out that traditional tests for "talent" favored those from privileged social backgrounds by focusing almost exclusively on physical dexterity and pitch memory, both of which were more often developed through training rather than present as native "gifts."[90] He insisted that new pedagogical techniques take this into account and rely on scientific principles rather than "foggy, mystical conceptions" of inspiration, talent, and genius.[91]

When the conservatory Party cell began to implement this proposal, pragmatism, conservatism, indifference, and financial constraints soon watered down much of its radicalism. The musical department of the Unified Artistic Rabfak opened on October 23, 1923, under the auspices of the Advanced Artistic and Theatrical Studio (VKhUTEMAS). Ceremonies held in the conservatory's small concert hall featured speeches given by Lev Lebedinskii, representing the conservatory Party cell, and Aleksei Sergeev, who was still affiliated with RAPM. Briusova and a local Party official also addressed an audience consisting of mainly *rabfak* students from other institutions. Only two professors helped the Communist students organize the new program and no representative from Iavorskii's division of Glavprofobr was present.[92]

The musical *rabfak* offered programs in pedagogy, theory, and performance designed to qualify students as instructors for workers' clubs or for conservatory matriculation in three to four years. Enrollment was limited to workers and peasants with at least a three-year term of service (*stazh*) in production immediately prior to admission. Applicants had to be nominated by a Party, trade union, or other Soviet organization, and had to display "general musical qualities" (*dannye*), including a good ear, accurate memory, and well-developed sense of rhythm. Although the *rabfak* was supposed to provide people with little or no formal training with a jump start in learning to play an instrument, *rabfak* organizers quickly concluded that young adults who had spent years doing heavy labor and factory work encountered great difficulty acquiring competence on the violin and piano. Within three years requirements had been increased: Applicants for these specialties were required to be able to read music and have existing proficiency on their instrument, such as the ability to play Bach two-part inventions.[93]

Although its operations grew steadily through the decade, the *rabfak* was plagued by a range of problems. Applications increased more than threefold in its first five years of operation, from twenty-eight in 1923 to ninety-six in 1927. From an initial cohort of twenty-five students, the *rabfak* grew to include 102 students in 1927, with 60 percent of them Party or Komsomol members.[94] In theory, students were provided with stipends, housing, an instrument, and textbooks, but chronic financial difficulties and scarce material resources made these promises difficult to keep. In 1923 the musical *rabfak* received only 1,800 rubles of the 9,500 it requested from the conservatory and Narkompros.[95] It had only one piano and four teachers. A number of the more reform-minded faculty members at the conservatory and their graduate students were eventually enlisted to teach, and by 1926, the *rabfak* had access to fourteen pianos.[96] But students often lurked in the halls of the conservatory from dawn to dusk in search of an open practice room, and in 1925 the *rabfak* had yet to secure an annual subsidy from Glavprofobr.[97]

The difficulties of bringing proletarian elements into the conservatory and the contradictory nature of many Narkompros policies are evident in the evolution of admissions policies for graduates of the music *rabfak* to the conservatory, which followed a divergent trajectory from *rabfaki* at other VUZy. In the first part of the decade, *rabfak* graduates were granted automatic entry, without examination, into other VUZy. Given Lunacharsky's dispensation to the conservatory to retain admissions policies based on ability and training, a Glavprofobr regulation from 1921 gave *rabfak* graduates, workers, Civil War veterans, and individuals nominated by trade unions and Party organizations preferred status for admission to the conservatory, but still required them to meet minimum requirements in musical preparation and ability.[98] These standards, which were developed by Kastal'skii and Ivanov-Boretskii at the request of the Red Professors' Faction, included a good sense of pitch and rhythm and proficiency on an instrument.[99]

In 1926, major changes were made in the Narkompros policies affecting recruitment to higher education. As part of a national effort to raise academic standards and the quality of VUZ graduates, admissions examinations were instituted for all VUZ applicants, including *rabfak* graduates, who had previously been granted automatic VUZ admission.[100] In contrast, the conservatory's new statute of 1926 included four dense pages describing its tough new admissions tests, but stipulated that *rabfak* graduates be exempt from taking them.[101]

The *rabfak* proved to be completely ineffective as a means of proletarianizing the conservatory. Indeed, "proletarian elements" still made up less than 13 percent of conservatory students in 1928–29.[102] Several factors compromised the *rabfak*'s success in enhancing proletarian recruitment to the conservatory. Perhaps the most serious problem was finding students committed to making music their livelihood. Many came to the *rabfak* because they "just liked music" or wanted the opportunity to live in Moscow.[103] Although intended to help "proletarian youth master musical education and culture," the seriousness of the *rabfak*'s curriculum discouraged many who saw music making as an entertaining pastime. Students disliked the "arithmetic" that dominated the compulsory classes in theory, harmony, and counterpoint, and balked at the prospect of spending four years at the *rabfak* followed by more study at the conservatory. The rate of attrition was high: only sixteen of the twenty-five students who entered in 1923 continued to the second course.[104] At the end of NEP, only two *rabfak* students had advanced to the conservatory's VUZ.[105]

The peculiarities of music education came into sharpest relief in the area of admissions. It was simply unavoidable that some musical background and ability were necessary for conservatory admission, and this made the recruitment of "socially desirable" students a difficult and slow process. The 1925 Glavprofobr Conference on Artistic Education cited the "flow (*priliv*) into the VUZy of a new student body, answering the basic task of proletarianizing higher education" as one of the three main tasks facing reformers.[106] The musical *rabfak* was supposed to provide up to 50 percent of first-year VUZ students, but in 1926, students from a worker or peasant background accounted for just 12 percent of the 850 students at the conservatory overall, most of whom were in the technicum rather than the VUZ. Indeed, the numbers of "proletarian elements" at the conservatory had actually declined slightly (from 15.3 percent) since 1924, while the ranks of those identified as "toiling intelligentsia" had swollen from 36 percent in 1924 to 60 percent in 1926.[107] The original director of the musical *rabfak* noted with frustration that the proletarianization of the conservatory was proceeding at a "different" pace from other VUZy,[108] a dispirited understatement given Narkompros's statistics indicating that proletarian and peasant elements composed 51 percent of all VUZ students in the Russian Republic in 1927–28.[109]

Student Activism, Communists, and Conservatory Affairs

If admissions policies presented reformers with difficult quandaries, so did the issue of student activism and the role of the Party in conservatory affairs. Giving students a more active role in the administration and daily life of higher education was a key goal of Narkompros in the twenties. As early as 1921, Glavprofobr made provisions to have student representatives sit as advisers on VUZ subject commissions.[110] Through mechanisms designed by Narkompros as well as Party and professional organizations, students were first involved in economic issues, then curriculum, and later the daily issues of academic life. With Party encouragement, many students surpassed Narkompros in their demands for more radical educational reform. As Sheila Fitzpatrick has noted, the Komsomol successfully aspired to play an independent role in national politics in this period, and emerged as Narkompros's most vocal and consistent opponent.[111]

At the conservatory, Communist students frequently clashed with an older generation of administrators and teachers over admissions policies and curriculum. Although RAPM, Prokoll, and the Komsomol had a devoted supporter in Briusova, she was often at odds with their impatience and militancy. Like Lunacharsky, Briusova believed deeply in the ultimate success of a gradualist approach to cultural change. For both of them the power of education and inclusion was more appropriate and potent than that of purge and exclusion.

The staff dismissals of June 1924 marked the high point of Communist students' involvement in educational reform during NEP. When presenting the candidates for dismissal to the music section of GUS, Briusova emphasized that the opinions of the student factions and pupils of each department were the basis for compiling the initial list.[112] Given that the student purge had just reduced the student body by 40 percent, it seems no coincidence that this list included exactly 40.4 percent of the 141 professors and teachers. No specific reason was given for thirteen of the thirty-six who were actually dismissed, but these teachers all came from the piano and voice departments. In other departments, "poor teaching" was the main reason people were let go. Six teachers were dismissed because their subjects (e.g., philosophy) were no longer taught. In only one case does it seem that ideology and political unsuitability played a decisive role. The pianist Grigorii Prokof'ev was accused of teaching only the children of merchants and the intelligentsia, producing the dreaded "salon musicians." Third-year students in the *pedfak* had boycotted

Prokof'ev's classes in 1923–24, insisting that his teaching was "useless" and even "dangerous."[113] It is interesting to note that among those professors proposed for dismissal by the students and Party were some who were quite active in the *rabfak*, including voice professor Maria Deisha-Sionitskaia, theorist Sergei Evseev, and violinists Boris Sibor and Konstantin Mostras.

Through their professional organization's executive bureau (*ispolbiuro*), students gained representation on virtually every internal body of the conservatory. Formed in 1922 at the same time as the Party cell and the Komsomol, the executive bureau was initially constituted of Party members: Lev Lebedinskii, V. Ozol, and V. Revich. In 1923 two non-Communists joined and the bureau had representatives on all examination, admissions, curriculum, and administrative committees. The bureau also formed committees dealing with the more practical aspects of student life, including stipends, housing, practicums, and production work. In 1924, Narkompros enhanced the bureau's powers by assigning its "academic section" (*ak sektsiia*) the task of helping Glavprofobr and other Soviet academic organs to reorganize and improve academic affairs in a given department.[114]

Student practicums and "production" work were an integral part of the effort to train socially useful musicians endorsed both by the Party and Narkompros. Practicums took a variety of forms, including work in state agencies or with workers' clubs and performance ensembles, as well as teaching at the *rabfak* and Sunday Workers' Conservatory. In response to student complaints about their "separation" (*otryv*) from the masses, and in conjunction with a broader campaign to make higher education more responsive to the needs of industry, GUS approved proposals from the Red Professors' Faction and student executive bureau to strengthen the ties of artistic VUZy with the working class in 1924–25.[115] Production practicums in workers' clubs and factories would help the conservatory produce qualified musicians capable of "carrying culture and necessary, healthy ideology to the masses" by creating art that was both close and accessible to them.[116] Beginning in December 1924, students from all conservatory departments participated in concerts, lectures, and choral instruction at seven workers' clubs and one Red Army facility selected by the regional Party organization.

Although a commission of students and faculty and the conservatory's Komsomol organization co-coordinated student practicums with the regional Party organization, the same dynamics emerged in these activities that haunted activists in the music circles and in the club movement at large. Virtually all students used explanatory introductions and program notes to enhance the "accessibility" of musical performances, which usually concluded with a round of mass singing.[117] But the choice of music depended on the ideological preferences of the students. Prokoll embraced these practicums as an ideal means to test out their compositions, while RAPM and other Komsomol activists advocated using programs of accessible examples from the nineteenth-century repertoire and the well-known songs of the revolutionary movement. But "nonaligned" students failed to heed the moralizing didacticism of the committed reformers, and filled their practicum programs with *tsyganshchina* on revolutionary themes.[118]

To many reform-minded students, Narkompros policies and the conservatory curriculum often seemed insufficiently concerned or even at odds with the goal of significantly enhancing the musical life of the working class. In 1926, a group of conservatory Komsomol members challenged Narkompros concert policies and the ideology of the Commissariat's head, Lunacharsky, in an open letter published in RAPM's journal, *Music and October*.[119] Referring to a recent article by Lunacharsky in *Pravda*,[120] the students decried his designation of the conservatory's composers, Miaskovskii, Anatolii Aleksandrov, and Shebalin, as "ours," insisting that despite its high technical quality, the music of these composers reflected the ideology of the degenerate bourgeoisie. The students called for the state to support the composers of "agitational" music, and those already writing for a working-class audience (specifically Kastal'skii, Lebedinskii, and Lazarev of RAPM, and Davidenko and Shekhter from the conservatory's Prokoll), rather than these "formalists."

In his answer, Lunacharsky defended his reference to the conservatory composers as "ours" because they lived and worked in the Soviet Union, and cautioned the youth against the inaccurate use of concepts like formalism, which was more appropriate for literature than for music. "Agit music" served an important function, but did not necessarily have any artistic value. Composers of this music were, for the most part, young, and needed to complete their training before they could be compared to "masters" like Miaskovskii. As for Davidenko and Shekhter, Lunacharsky pointed out that concerts of their works would never yield the profits of those featuring the compositions of Prokofiev and Miaskovskii. In conclusion, Lunacharsky admonished the students to study these masters rather than disdain them. Only through assimilating the mastery of living inheritors of the bourgeois musical heritage would the foundations of the music of the future be revealed. The penalty for breaking with this heritage would be severe: "In view of the colossal organicity of music, in view of the fact that music as a whole is built on age-old traditions, breaking away from these traditions will lead to barbarism and an abrupt downfall."[121]

Different Perspectives on the Conservatory's Sixtieth Jubilee

As the Moscow Conservatory marked its sixtieth jubilee at the end of 1926, reformers of all stripes expressed satisfaction that the conservatory had become a full-fledged modern VUZ offering a well-rounded professional education. Beyond this shared sense of accomplishment, however, many tensions remained unresolved. On the one hand, the activities of Prokoll, the integration of folk music into the curriculum, and the institution of separate tracks for soloists and ensemble musicians suggested that the conservatory had made its activities more relevant to new demands. Yet Communists still faulted the conservatory for trying to distance itself from the issues that engulfed the energies of other activists on the musical front, such as the debates on revolutionary and proletarian music and the popularity of *Little Bricks*. Although a few professors and students had taken an active part in the accordion campaign, Viktor Vinogradov pointed out that the conservatory had yet to sponsor a debate or public discussion on the topic.[122]

Faculty insisted that the charges leveled against their institution were misguided or inappropriate. Both Igumnov and Evseev maintained that the conservatory had not only endorsed but embraced its "new tasks" and was doing its best to fulfill them.[123] The difficulties in realizing these goals stemmed from the government's lack of support and the widespread "indifference" to musical affairs. More money and better cooperation with the agencies involved in musical enlightenment were needed to train and mobilize the "army of highly-qualified pedagogues and instructors" that the *pedfak* was producing for the battle against "homemade dilettantism" in the workers' clubs.

Only months after the new conservatory statute was ratified, concerns about lingering strains of individualism and students' interest in "playing for themselves" prompted Glavprofobr to remind the conservatory that it must satisfy the needs of the state by producing more teachers and fewer performers, only allowing the truly talented to pursue training as soloists.[124] The Party continued to worry about the number of students pursuing degrees in piano and voice, and Briusova lamented that there were still hordes of pianists and singers in the technicums.[125]

Questions concerning cadres and proletarianization were especially thorny. Given the complexities of social identity during NEP and the extreme importance that Bolshevik ideology attached to class origin, anxieties and uncertainties about the social origins of conservatory students ran deep.[126] But factors peculiar to the conservatory also made these concerns more muted than in other institutional contexts. That the conservatory lagged so far behind other institutions of higher education in the recruitment of proletarian students was clearly cause for concern for the Party. And the "army" of "highly-qualified cadres" that the conservatory trained during NEP was in fact only a battalion, which did more to perpetuate and resupply the orchestras of the capitals' concert halls and the conservatory's own teaching staff than it did to raise the caliber of instruction and repertoire at workers' clubs. But given the considerable overlap between the agenda of the conservatory Communists and that of the old "specialists," as well as the difficulties of attracting Communist students to the conservatory, attitude was more important in these years than social origin or political affiliation.[127] Prokoll's interest in reaching a broad audience and questioning traditional hierarchies and routines mattered much more than the class background of its members. Out of place and vastly outnumbered, Communists at the conservatory yielded to reform-minded faculty, who shared a general commitment to preserving the conservatory as a training ground for professional musicians and a repository for the riches of the musical legacy. Well-placed individuals like Ivanov-Boretskii, Igumnov, and Briusova thus managed to co-opt, or at least guide, large portions of the reform agenda. Although some felt that the conservatory must become even more of a "university" by attaching itself more directly to life outside its walls, there was a remarkably broad consensus among faculty, Narkompros agencies, RAPM, and the institution's Communists that the conservatory must remain a protector of the musical legacy and traditions of the past.

The hesitant pace and limited nature of reform at the conservatory would fuel the fires of radicalism during the years of the Great Break. But to a large extent, the sovietization of the conservatory was accomplished during NEP at the hands of prerevolutionary professionals committed both to old-fashioned *kul'turtregerstvo* and traditional conceptions of artistic talent and excellence.

7

The Music of 1927

Commemorating the Tenth Anniversary of the Revolution and the Centennial of Beethoven's Death

Our state and musical society should use the Beethoven festivities to set our young composers on the right path and lay the foundation of a healthy and beautiful musical culture. In our circumstances this foundation can only be Beethoven—the greatest leader of revolutionary art.

—Narkompros Beethoven Committee, 1927

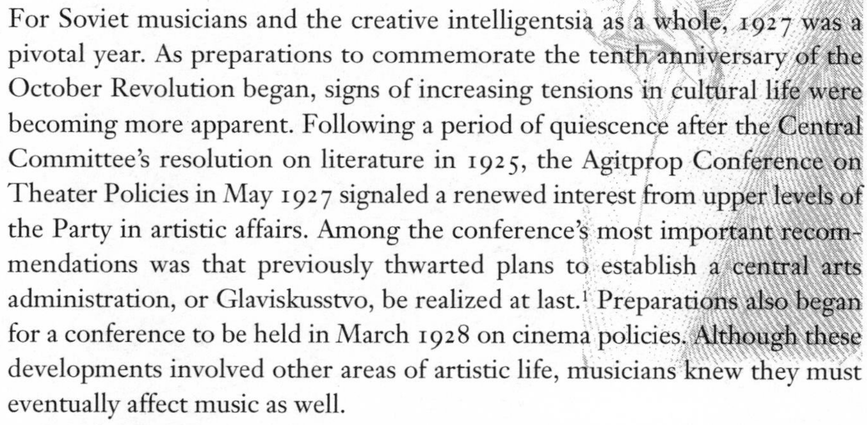

For Soviet musicians and the creative intelligentsia as a whole, 1927 was a pivotal year. As preparations to commemorate the tenth anniversary of the October Revolution began, signs of increasing tensions in cultural life were becoming more apparent. Following a period of quiescence after the Central Committee's resolution on literature in 1925, the Agitprop Conference on Theater Policies in May 1927 signaled a renewed interest from upper levels of the Party in artistic affairs. Among the conference's most important recommendations was that previously thwarted plans to establish a central arts administration, or Glaviskusstvo, be realized at last.[1] Preparations also began for a conference to be held in March 1928 on cinema policies. Although these developments involved other areas of artistic life, musicians knew they must eventually affect music as well.

But despite an increasing sense of urgency about the politics of cultural life, the Soviet musical community's attention in the first half of 1927 was largely focused on the legacy of a giant of Western art music, Ludwig van Beethoven. As we have seen, Beethoven's music was associated with the spirit of the revolution from the first days of Soviet power. The triumphant finale of the Ninth Symphony and the heroism and pathos of the Third and Fifth Symphonies made them staples in musical celebrations and concerts during the Civil War. The debut concert of the Moscow Soviet's conductorless orchestra, Persimfans, featured an all-Beethoven program, consisting of the *Coriolan* Overture, the Violin Concerto, and the Third Symphony.

March 1927 marked the centennial of the German composer's death. Commemorative concert series, lecture cycles, anthologies on his life and works, and even a biographical play[2] indicated Beethoven's central place in Soviet musical life.[3] The Moscow Conservatory published a facsimile edition of a recently discovered sketchbook.[4] Distinguished foreigners, including Artur Schnabel (who received permission to bring his own Bechstein piano with him) and Otto Klemperer, were invited to participate in the festivities.[5] A delegation of Soviet musicians prepared to attend the celebrations in Vienna. Beethoven's significance for Soviet musical culture was underscored by the formation of a special Narkompros committee charged with coordinating and supervising the events of the centennial.

Scarcely had the dust subsided after the Beethoven centennial than the tenth anniversary of the revolution prompted a no less impressive flurry of concerts and publishing. Journals ran lengthy lead articles on topics such as "October and Music," the conservatories and philharmonics published retrospectives of the past decade, and composers finished symphonies and oratorios dedicated to "October." In their critical assessments of the state of Soviet music and their evaluations of particular commemorative pieces, musicians from all sectors of the aesthetic and political spectrum weighed in on the impact of October 1917 on musical culture. Having just completed a concert season devoted to both the Beethoven centennial and its own fifth anniversary, Persimfans also assumed a leading role in commemorating the revolution. Although concert programs for the revolution's anniversary included many classics from the Russian and European repertoire (and almost invariably *The Internationale*), the pieces that drew the most attention (and controversy) were those by Soviet composers written specifically for the anniversary.

For many the coincidence of the tenth anniversary of the revolution and the Beethoven centennial strengthened an already-established resonance between the composer's life and work and the Soviet revolutionary agenda. In part, embracing and appropriating Beethoven as a revolutionary in 1927 was a logical evolution of Russians' historic attitude toward the German composer, described by Boris Schwarz as "unique, admiring and possessive."[6] But this embrace had profound consequences for musical aesthetics in the Soviet Union. At a time when multiple visions of what the revolution meant for Russian musical culture still competed for backing and dominance, enthusiasm for Beethoven as an integral part of the Soviet musical legacy overlapped otherwise deep-seated aesthetic and political divisions. As the executor of a stylistic revolution within the boundaries of traditional forms, Beethoven was critical to the evolving foundation of what would be identified as socialist realism for music in the thirties. Yet this was not obvious at the time. The politics of the Beethoven centennial and the musical commemorations of the tenth anniversary of the revolution indicate that musicians interpreted the revolution's impact on their art from disparate perspectives. The two jubilees also highlighted the creative and organizational weaknesses of the musical Left, even as official support for the pluralist cultural policies of NEP declined.

Creating Beethoven the Revolutionary

The official tone for the Beethoven centennial was set by the Narkompros Beethoven committee. Formed in the fall of 1926, it was headed by Lunacharsky and included representatives from key musical organizations, institutions, and Narkompros agencies.[7] In its summons to the musical community for participation in the festivities, the committee left no doubt as to its estimation of Beethoven's significance: As a "superlative genius [*genial'neishego*] musician-thinker, and revolutionary,"[8] Beethoven gave musical voice to the aspirations of the masses. The committee's leaders, Lunacharsky and Pavel Novitskii, proclaimed that Beethoven's music was an appeal for brotherly unity and that the basic characteristics of his work were linked closely to the aspirations of Soviet socialist culture.[9]

Throughout the centennial activities Lunacharsky and Novitskii promoted an image of Beethoven and his music that strongly identified the composer with the Soviet revolutionary agenda. Refuting "futurists and hooligan opponents of the classics," Lunacharsky insisted that Beethoven's music was closer to socialist art and proletarian culture than most contemporary music.[10] Like Danton and Robespierre, Beethoven belonged to the "democratic intelligentsia" of the eighteenth century.[11] To Lunacharsky, Beethoven's music expressed the aspirations of the French Revolution, the restless striving of a new consciousness and confidence in the triumph of reason. Echoing an argument advanced earlier by Oswald Spengler, and endorsed by RAPM, Lunacharsky asserted that after Beethoven bourgeois art began to decay, hiding its ideological emptiness in luxurious, virtuoso forms. As a result, much of contemporary music was accessible only to small circles of aesthetic connoisseurs.[12]

Pavel Novitskii was even more explicit in promoting Beethoven as a genius of indomitable will and courage, the embodiment of revolutionary ideals and values.[13] Novitskii identified "titanism" as the primary characteristic of the composer and his work. In defying convention and tradition Beethoven was never weak. His work expressed the pathos of his epoch and the liberated individual's struggle for free expression that was at its core.[14] Furthermore, according to Novitskii, the historical boundaries of the bourgeois revolution did not limit Beethoven's connection with the future because Beethoven's individualism never turned into the dead end of subjectivity and pessimism. Despite physical hardships and deafness, Beethoven never lost courage or succumbed to despair. While the bourgeois world would commemorate Beethoven's place in the museum of music history, for the proletariat he was the still vibrant cornerstone of revolutionary musical culture.[15]

In their assessments of Beethoven, musicologists supported these views, fleshing out the image of the heroic musical revolutionary. Leningrad modernists Boris Asaf'ev and Semen Ginzburg emphasized the difficulties and tragedies of Beethoven's personal life—exploitation by his alcoholic father, loneliness and disappointments in romantic love, and, above all, his struggle against progressive deafness—to draw a more intimate portrait of the composer and his social milieu.[16] In his popular biography, Evgenii Braudo employed a sociological approach to clarify the social prerequisites (*predposyl'ki*) of Beethoven's music.[17] Braudo lamented the paucity of sources on Beethoven's political beliefs, but a lack of concrete information did not keep him from attributing revolutionary values and sympathies to the composer.[18] Indeed, Braudo asserted that Beethoven was a "warrior" whose belief in creativity, freedom, and social equality was inseparable from the revolutionary ideas brewing in France.[19]

These depictions of Beethoven as a revolutionary, with their recurring emphasis on his timeless popularity and his music's expression of revolutionary passion, courage, and brotherhood, involved more than an enthusiastic effort to make the centennial of a long-dead German composer relevant to current Soviet conditions.[20] Championing the legacy of a musician whose artistic merits were acknowledged by all and in whose oeuvre the aspirations of both the revolutionary hero and the commoner could so easily be identified was an important step in securing the cornerstones of what would become socialist realism in music ten years hence. Activists such as Nadezhda Briusova felt that Beethoven's music was clearly "socialist" in content. It was heroic, full of pathos, never despairing. By expressing a strong, active will and the feeling of the collective, it was "closer" to the Soviet revolution than most contemporary music.[21] In terms of harmonic language and the use of established forms it represented the pinnacle of musical development for its time. Yet formal mastery and complexity served as vehicles for conveying musical content, never becoming ends in themselves.

Aside from the amended title of the Third Symphony (*Eroica*), little evidence survived to indicate that Beethoven's sympathies with the agenda of the French Revolution consisted of more than a general commitment to Enlightenment ideals of individual freedom and brotherhood. Yet the image of Beethoven as a political revolutionary gained considerable currency. In his "biographical sketch" of Beethoven, the senior musicologist at the Moscow Conservatory drew a direct comparison between the composer's commitment to liberty and the "cry of the Third Estate."[22] For those eager to embrace Beethoven as the musical patron saint of the Soviet proletariat's revolution, even the composer's nationality was subject to reinterpretation. Braudo confidently asserted that Beethoven preferred the "Russian pronunciation" of his last name, i.e., with the accent on the second syllable.[23] The Narkompros committee called for making the Soviet Union Beethoven's "second motherland,"[24] even while its representatives mocked spokesmen from bourgeois countries who claimed Beethoven as "theirs."[25] The preeminent Beethoven scholar at GAKhN insisted that, after Germany, no other country besides the Soviet Union had embraced Beethoven with more passion and so completely made him "their own."[26]

Even those committed more to Russian musical nationalism than to the cause of proletarian culture identified Slavic and eastern European affinities in Beethoven's music. Glazunov applauded his deft use of Hungarian themes in *The Ruins of Athens* (Op. 113) and *König Stephan* (Op. 117) as well as his "masterful" incorporation of Russian folk songs in certain piano variations and string quartets. Beethoven might be a "German genius," but Glazunov maintained that the trio of the Ninth Symphony's scherzo could be the work of a "pure-blooded Russian composer."[27]

Central to Beethoven's appeal as a universal symbol of revolutionary heroism and freedom was the supposed accessibility of his music to everyone. Musicians across the aesthetic and political spectrum felt that Beethoven's music spoke not just to a small circle of mandarins, but to the masses. Yet only part of the composer's oeuvre in fact met that claim, and the concert and recital programs of the Soviet centennial clearly reflect this. With the exceptions of the Ninth Symphony and *Missa Solemnis*, they consist almost exclusively of compositions from Beethoven's "middle period" (1802–16). The dissonances and violent rhythms of the late string quartets (Opp. 127, 130, 131, and 135), piano sonatas (Opp. 106, 109, 110, and 111), and the *Grosse Fugue* (Op. 133) made late Beethoven "difficult" even for sophisticated musical palates, although scholars did acknowledge the virtues of these final works and the importance of this period in the composer's life.[28] The main concert series of the Soviet celebrations thus featured the symphonies, especially the third, fifth, and ninth; the Violin Concerto (Op. 61); the Fourth Piano Concerto (Op. 58) and the Fifth Piano Concerto (Op. 73, "The Emperor"); the music to Goethe's *Egmont* (Op. 84); and the *Coriolan* Overture (Op. 62), the latter two with both literary antecedents and historical-political themes.[29]

Although audiences for many events were undoubtedly far from the idealized masses envisioned in official rhetoric, the centennial organizers did make efforts to involve a broad section of the populace in the centennial. Tickets for all concerts organized by the Narkompros Committee for the official Beethoven Week (May 27–June 2) were distributed free to factory committees, Komsomol cells, and musical technicums. In addition to the main concert organizations, workers' clubs and even domra orchestras prepared commemorative programs.[30]

But for all of the revolutionary rhetoric and efforts to bring Beethoven to the masses, many activities spoke to the preferences of more traditional musical publics. For experts and refined audiences—those for whom Beethoven was already somewhat "old-fashioned"[31]—the ASM presented a recital series focusing on the evolution of the piano sonata from Beethoven to contemporary Russian composers. Featuring the German pianist Friedrich Brürer, these recitals included the *Diabelli* Variations (Op. 120) and the Piano Sonata in A-flat (Op. 110). They also featured representative works of the German Romantics, as well as Liszt and Chopin, and the modern Russian school, namely sonatas by Stravinsky and Sergei Protopopov, as well as Scriabin's Ninth Sonata (Op. 68) and Prokofiev's Third Sonata (Op. 28).[32]

The major research institutes also observed the centennial with scholarly reports and publications geared toward specialists rather than popular audiences. In Leningrad, the music history department of GIII marked both its seventh anniversary and the Beethoven centennial with the presentation of three reports on Beethoven and his milieu.[33] In Moscow, the music division of GAKhN undertook a much more extensive project, beginning preparations for a volume dedicated to Beethoven in the 1925–26 academic year.[34] On March 26 the academy hosted a special Beethoven evening featuring a performance of the composer's rarely heard *Bundeslied* (Op. 122) as well as reports on Beethoven's influences on Saint-Simon, his significance to contemporary music, and his final days.

RAPM in the Shadows

Although it included advocates of many aesthetic perspectives, the Narkompros Beethoven committee issued official pronouncements echoing the agenda of the Proletarian Musicians' organization to a striking degree. Since its inception, RAPM had identified Beethoven's music as a healthy foundation for the proletarian music of the future. The committee's slogans—"Through Beethoven to proletarian music!" and "Through Beethoven to mastery of all of the musical legacy!"—were perfectly consistent with the Proletarian Musicians' stance on the German composer.[35] Besides Lunacharsky and Novitskii, RAPM leader Lev Lebedinskii was the only member of the official Beethoven committee to speak on the committee's behalf during the "Beethoven Week" festivities.[36] Like RAPM, the committee's declared objective was to assure Beethoven's position as a pillar of Soviet musical culture. The centennial would naturally feature extensive performances of Beethoven's music, but these activities were second in importance to the primary task: "Our state and musical society should use the Beethoven festivities to set our young composers on the right path and lay the foundation of a healthy and beautiful musical culture. In our circumstances this foundation can only be Beethoven—the greatest leader of revolutionary art."[37]

Lunacharsky's support of RAPM's stance on Beethoven clearly played an important role in defining the committee's purpose. In a major article written for the centennial, the Commissar directly endorsed RAPM's veneration of Beethoven and largely concurred with the Proletarian Musicians' perspective on the musical past. Recapitulating views on Beethoven and musical culture first set out in 1921,[38] Lunacharsky maintained that the proletariat had destroyed the base of the old culture when it overthrew the bourgeoisie. It would create its own, new culture, but first it must master the artistic legacy of the past. In music, "revolutionary modernism" required a critical, creative approach to the past as a formal school for artists of the future.[39]

RAPM obviously hoped that the Beethoven centennial, which marked at least the partial convergence of its agendas with other preferences in the musical community, would enhance its status and influence in musical affairs. It took the initiative in founding a Soviet Beethoven society, exulted over the official declarations of the Beethoven committee, and made a point of noting that the "decadents" affiliated with the ASM had been too swept away by Prokofiev's return to work on the official celebration.[40] RAPM was not, however, able to capitalize on Lunacharsky's conditional or coincidental patronage, and remained sidelined from struggles in other areas of the cultural front.

By the spring of 1927, the militant leadership of the proletarian literary organization, RAPP, had become more outspoken and effective in its criticism of official policy toward the arts in general and literature in particular. RAPP's repeated attacks on Voronskii, Trotsky's erstwhile supporter and champion of the literary "fellow travelers," brought about his dismissal as editor of *Red*

Virgin Soil—a feat facilitated by the downward spiral of Trotsky's political fortunes. In May, the Party's Agitprop committee addressed complaints lodged by RAPP and other radicals about the high level of funding for the former Imperial theaters and Narkompros's toleration of the artistic and political conservatism of these institutions. Although Agitprop did not dictate a change in official policy, it recommended a number of administrative and financial adjustments, including the establishment of a central arts administration at Narkompros.[41] For the next two years, Narkompros's policies of conciliation toward and accommodation of the old intelligentsia came increasingly under fire from RAPP, the Komsomol, and other militant groups, and were eventually eroded by the convergence of these demands with Stalin's political and economic agendas.

But this shift in the balance of forces found RAPM still struggling to gain influence. While RAPP was increasingly able to lobby the political soundness of its position with Party leaders, RAPM had difficulty sustaining much more modest endeavors. A Beethoven society was established, but it became an honor roll for the musical establishment and only one RAPM member was admitted.[42] The Proletarian Musicians had no journal in 1927, and relied on a monthly subsidy of eighty rubles to fund their modest operations, which were run from a private apartment.[43] Since RAPM had no composers in its ranks in 1927, its own assessment of the decade in music focused on the expansion of music activities in workers' clubs, reforms in music education, and development of musicology rather than any music written since the revolution.[44]

The limits of RAPM's influence were apparent in the controversy over the composition of the Soviet delegation sent to the Beethoven centennial in Vienna. Narkompros had decided to send a delegation to the Viennese festivities in the spring of 1926, even before the Soviet Beethoven committee was established. At that time, the music-methodological commission of Glavnauka nominated a contingent of six established composers, theorists, and musicologists: Aleksandr Glazunov, Nikolai Miaskovskii, Boleslav Iavorskii, Boris Asaf'ev, Dmitrii Melkikh, and Mikhail Ivanov-Boretskii. RAPM members protested their exclusion directly to Lunacharsky, insisting that as Beethoven's staunchest advocates and as key organizers of the Soviet celebrations they deserved to have a representative on the Viennese delegation. In a direct attack on the ASM members (Asaf'ev, Miaskovskii, and Melkikh), they questioned why Beethoven's "enemies"—those who treated him as a museum piece and praised music that "doesn't express an idea"—enjoyed special (*sugubyi*) patronage. Not only did they control the key posts in various commissions, *glavki*, and institutions, these people also were allowed to travel abroad at the government's expense. Surely the delegation's composition should be modified to reflect more completely the spectrum of Soviet musical culture![45] The complaint initiated a prolonged fight over the composition of the delegation that ended only on March 22, 1927, less than a week before the festivities began in Vienna.[46] As a result, the Soviet delegation arrived late, missing the opening ceremonies in which they were scheduled to participate. RAPM was able to send a representative, the honor naturally falling to Lebedinskii. Olga Kameneva, Iavorskii, and Ivanov-Boretskii rounded out the Soviet contingent, which was much scaled down from its original formulation.[47]

Revolutionary Music-Making: The Conductorless Orchestra in 1927

A vital contribution to both the Beethoven centennial and the commemorative concerts for the tenth anniversary of the revolution was made by the Moscow Soviet's conductorless orchestra, Persimfans. Founded in 1922 under the leadership of Lev Tseitlin, a professor of violin at the Moscow Conservatory, Persimfans occupied a unique place among the various factions and organizations within the musical community. Advocates of proletarian culture lauded the group's commitment to collectivism in musical performance and success in promoting classical music among workers and soldiers. At the same time, the orchestra's technical achievements and popularity with more traditional audiences won it the respect of such "experts" as Otto Klemperer and Sergei Prokofiev.

One of the most striking examples of revolutionary experimentation in the twenties, the conductorless orchestra presented an intriguing alternative to the basic structural and creative principles of the modern symphonic orchestra.[48] By rehearsing and performing without a conductor, Persimfans sought to overcome the "tyranny" of a single individual and thereby empower the orchestra as a whole. Musicians bore responsibility not only for the correct technical execution of their individual parts, but for tempo, nuance, and interpretation as well. In what one scholar describes as a "utopia in miniature,"[49] each member developed an appreciation for a musical composition as an organic whole. Without the visual image of a conductor's interpretive directions, performers and audiences alike experienced the music more directly, focusing more completely on the auditory element of musical performance.[50]

On a more practical level, the formation of Persimfans represented a significant gesture of support for Soviet power from an important component of the creative intelligentsia.[51] A group of nine faculty members from the

Moscow Conservatory made up the orchestra's core, which was supplemented with musicians from the orchestra of the Bol'shoi Theater. Conservatory students also participated, including twelve violinists from the studios of professors Tseitlin, Konstantin Mostras, and Abram Iampol'skii. Despite the many difficulties encountered by the orchestra, Persimfans' membership fluctuated little over the years. And the difficulties were considerable and persistent: the orchestra struggled constantly to fund its operations, receiving its first significant subsidy (10,000 rubles from Sovnarkom) only in 1925. In the winter of 1923 it rehearsed and performed in an unheated hall. It could rarely pay its members, who volunteered their time for rehearsals and performances while working or studying full-time elsewhere. In his reports and petitions to Narkompros, Tseitlin repeatedly cited problems securing rehearsal space, music—especially foreign scores—and even instruments for the orchestra.[52]

Material difficulties notwithstanding, Tseitlin and the group's primary spokesman, Arnol'd Tsukker, worked consistently to uphold the orchestra's commitment to excellence in performing both the classics of the symphonic repertoire and contemporary music from Russia and the West. Programs initially relied heavily on Beethoven overtures and symphonies, but the orchestra soon moved on to more difficult modern scores of Debussy, Richard Strauss, Scriabin, and even Prokofiev and Stravinsky.[53] After repeated promptings from Narkompros, the ensemble began to perform new works by Soviet composers in the 1926–27 season.[54]

In many respects Persimfans was the most effective musical *kul'turtreger* of the twenties. The orchestra performed not only in the main concert halls of Moscow, but in factories, working-class neighborhoods, army garrisons, and, after 1926, for radio broadcast across the country. Tseitlin and Tsukker developed effective techniques for introducing working-class audiences to classical music. Simple oral presentations on a composer's social background and the pieces being performed reinforced information provided in printed program notes.[55] For audiences experiencing classical music for the first time, pieces were often performed twice to fix them more securely in the memory of the listener. Despite the organization's recurring financial difficulties, both individual and season ticket prices were kept low in order to make concerts affordable to people of limited financial means. Enterprise and regional Party organizations also received ticket blocks for free distribution.

The social background of the audience determined how a given concert was presented, but Persimfans performed the same repertoire for workers and soldiers as it did for the more musically literate public that patronized the conservatory or the Hall of Columns. Tseitlin and Tsukker vehemently rejected suggestions that the orchestra simplify its offerings for "underprivileged" audiences, insisting that the orchestra's commitment to propagandizing the best of classic and contemporary music was particularly appropriate for these groups.[56] The "new public" would not become cultured on spoon feedings of "musical semolina porridge" (*muzykal'naia mannaia kashka*). Indeed, audience surveys indicated that workers appreciated the "lively rhythms" and unique harmonies of Prokofiev more than did listeners "raised on Tchaikovsky."[57]

Appropriately for this "child of the revolution," as it was often called,[58] Persimfans celebrated its own fifth anniversary in 1927. The jubilee concert at the conservatory on February 14 reflected the preferences of the orchestra's working-class audiences by featuring Prokofiev's *Scythian Suite* (Op. 20) and Scriabin's *Le poeme de l'extase* (Op. 54).[59] In the musical press, critics and representatives from workers' organizations and factories waxed eloquent about the artistic merits and services of the group.[60] Lunacharsky conferred the title of "Honored [*zasluzhennyi*] Collective of the Republic" on the orchestra, marking the first instance in which the Soviet state recognized the artistic achievements of a group rather than an individual.

Persimfans's status as one of the country's most active concert organizations as well as its commitment to bringing musical culture to the masses ensured that it would have a conspicuous role in both the Beethoven centennial and the musical commemorations of the tenth anniversary of the revolution. Certainly no other musical organization was so intimately and conspicuously involved with both events. The orchestra, which had launched its career with an all-Beethoven program in 1922, made the nine symphonies the centerpiece of its 1926–27 concert series. The final concert was introduced by Lunacharsky and played to a packed house at the Moscow Conservatory on March 14. Soloists from the Bol'shoi Theater and the State Capella joined Tseitlin's group for a rousing performance of the Ninth Symphony. The orchestra also presented two all-Beethoven concerts to working-class youth at the Kukhmisterov Club (Figs. 4 and 5).[61]

The conductorless orchestra further solidified Beethoven's image as the patron saint of revolutionary music by giving him a prominent place in its concerts for the tenth anniversary of the revolution. In concluding its musical tribute to the October Revolution with the Fifth Symphony, Persimfans essentially fused the two jubilees and set the tone for other musical commemorations of "October." These commemorative concerts provided a unique opportunity for musicians to assess the impact of the revolution on their art.

Fig. 4 Persimfans Concert in the Large Hall of the Moscow Conservatory. Note how the ensemble's unusual seating arrangement accommodates the solo pianist. *Persimfans* 6 (1928–29): 6.

Musical Culture and the Revolution: The Ten-Year Appraisal

In many respects musical life ten years after the revolution seemed healthier than at any time since before the beginning of World War I. The year leading up to the tenth anniversary of 1917 was remarkable for the diversity and international scope of the concerts in the nation's capitals. Such distinguished foreigners as Alban Berg and Darius Milhaud visited the Soviet Union to oversee performances of their music. In January 1927, Prokofiev made his first postrevolutionary visit to his native land for performances with Persimfans and the Leningrad Philharmonic. Modernist associations in Leningrad sponsored concerts featuring works by Hindemith, Berg, Krenek, and Honegger, as well as new compositions by young Soviet composers, including Joseph Schillinger, Leonid Polovinkin, and Dmitrii Shostakovich. The Leningrad Capella's highly successful performances of Stravinsky's *Les Noces* (*Svadebka*)

Fig. 5 Persimfans Concert at the Aschenbrenner Military School, Moscow. The conductorless orchestra performs for an audience of Red Army soldiers and white-collar workers in a converted riding hall. *Persimfans* 2 (1927–28): 4.

and Bach's *St. Matthew Passion* demonstrated both the ideological toleration characteristic of NEP and the wealth of artistic expertise available in the young Soviet state.

It even seemed possible that the demands of the "new musical consumer" and the perpetuation of the concert traditions of Western art music might not be completely incompatible with one another. By 1927, Persimfans was not alone in cultivating the sensibilities and appreciation for classical music among previously disadvantaged audiences. Both the ASM and the Leningrad Philharmonic had abandoned (albeit by directive from Narkompros) their exclusive concentration on the traditional concert-going public. The ASM now offered special "accessible" (*obshchedostupnye*) programs, accepting engagements at workers' clubs.[62] In Leningrad, the philharmonic boasted an increasingly higher percentage of workers, students, Komsomol members, and soldiers among its patrons.[63]

From the vantage point of later events, this vitality and diversity appear as testimony to the viability and health of NEP musical culture. Yet consideration of other aspects of Soviet musical life indicates that 1927 was more than a stunning blossoming of pluralism before the regimentation that followed. The tenth anniversary of the revolution prompted an outpouring of commemorative works. A number of young composers eager to capture and convey the spirit of the revolution in music wrote symphonic works dedicated to "October." Virtually all of these pieces had a mixed reception in 1927 and none secured a lasting place in the symphonic repertoire. But the structure, conventions, and harmonic language of these works reflected and defined how musicians understood the revolution in musical terms. In the fall of 1927, these works served as the starting point for searching appraisals of the "state of the field" in the musical press.

Besides Beethoven's Fifth Symphony, the Persimfans concerts of November 21 and 28 featured *The Internationale* and two pieces by the young Leningrad composer, Joseph Schillinger. If the inclusion of Beethoven on this commemorative program was natural and even expected, the choice of Schillinger's work was a bold gesture guaranteed to provoke controversy. A student of Jazeps Vitols and Nikolai Cherepnin, Schillinger began his career as a composer and conductor in the same year the Bolsheviks came to power. His musical portrayals of the revolutionary epoch, the Sonata-Rhapsody for Piano (Op. 17) and Symphonic Rhapsody (Op. 19), both employed innovative thematic and formal techniques in a daring effort to capture the essence of the October Revolution.

To depict the full scope of the revolutionary era, the Symphonic Rhapsody used fourteen revolutionary and popular songs interwoven with two original themes. Although the rhapsody divided roughly into three sections—the first evoking the beginning of the revolutionary period, the second portraying everyday life during NEP, and the third suggesting the period of "peaceful construction"—its form was free-flowing and (as the name rhapsody would imply) not typical of conventional symphonic structure. The composer described the form as "cinematic," explaining the rapid shifts in thematic material as homage to the art form that many felt best expressed the spirit of the age.[64] Even the performance styles and various ensembles required for the piece broke with convention. The rhapsody featured not only a conventional symphony orchestra, but also a smaller chamber ensemble, a military band, solo piano, a jazz band, and a noise orchestra.

A sympathetic critic speculated that the rhapsody would spark yet another round in the ongoing debate over musical form and content. Acknowledging the piece's kaleidoscopic use of revolutionary folklore, this observer praised Schillinger for taking a daring step forward in the search for new means of artistic expression. He also anticipated that the work would receive a wide range of critical responses, not all of them positive.[65]

Schillinger's *Rhapsody* did provoke a storm of protest, although few critiques responded to the call for sophisticated theoretical discussions of the relationship between form and content. The piece was denounced for its chaotic organization, or lack thereof, for its "potpourri effect," and for its "cold, mechanical" execution. Kabalevsky and others charged that it "lowered and vulgarized the idea of October."[66] But among the many negative reviews one criticism always preceded and formed the foundation for all others—namely Schillinger's use of "street songs" such as *Alesha-sha* and *Chicken* as well as popular dance tunes including jazz and fox-trots. Particularly for RAPM and ORK, this was simply not appropriate thematic material for a piece commemorating the spirit of the revolution. Simon Korev described the audience as "a bit shocked and disappointed" to hear vulgar street songs interwoven with such hallowed relics of the revolutionary struggle as *You Fell Victim* and *Boldly, Comrades, in Step*.[67] Kabalevsky asked sarcastically why Schillinger had neglected to include *Little Bricks*,[68] and ORK was incensed by the ASM's decision to include the rhapsody in the upcoming International Festival of Contemporary Music in Siena.[69]

Much more successful with critics of all persuasions was Shostakovich's Second Symphony, *To October* (*Oktiabriu*), which was commissioned by the state publishing house and premiered under Nikolai Malko's baton in Leningrad on November 5. Although called a symphony, the piece was short, consisting of one movement with a concluding chorus set to text by the Komsomol poet Aleksandr Bezymenskii. Like Schillinger's rhapsody, it featured a tremendous variety of thematic material, yet had no main theme. Indeed, throughout the piece no subject was heard more than once. One reviewer noted that the sick eroticism, mysticism, and overrefinement of the contemporary West were foreign to Shostakovich's music.[70] Yet the composer clearly used modernist techniques such as polytonality and polyrhythm to evoke the revolutionary milieu. No trace of romanticism or lyricism competed with the driving, angular rhythms and aggressive dissonance that defined the piece's style.[71]

Ivanov-Boretskii had high praise for Shostakovich's talent, which had already been noticed in his First Symphony, presented as his graduation exercise the previous year. Reviewers in ORK's journal hailed the young composer as a "true child of our revolution," a "first swallow of spring."[72] The symphony might warrant designation as a genuinely Soviet tribute to the revolution, a welcome alternative to the "academicized" mass songs and countless programmatic pieces having "nothing in common with the revolution besides a title or text."[73]

While Shostakovich earned critical acclaim by using modernist musical language to frame Bezymenskii's unambiguously revolutionary text, Nikolai Roslavets retreated from his most radical style in his tribute to the revolution, a cantata titled *October*. Like Shostakovich's symphony, Roslavets's *October* was included in the program for the ASM's commemorative concert on December 4. A four-bar "epigraph" of unison horns opened the piece and linked its settings of five poems by the proletarian poets Vladimir Kirillov, Vasilii Aleksandrovskii, and Sergei Obradovich. As Roslavets was the most flamboyant and controversial of the modernist composers, it surprised no one that the cantata drew its share of vicious criticism from his opponents in RAPM.[74] But more than one critic commended him for abandoning his usual "constructivist principles" in favor of a style more accessible to a broad audience.[75] Simon Korev noted with approval that the brash, uncompromising critic of "populism" and other "pseudo-revolutionary" tendencies had overcome the artificial and cerebral characteristics of his earlier work. Korev felt that *October* was genuinely popular and festive without being pompous or pretentious.[76]

In addition to Roslavets's cantata and Shostakovich's symphony, two other pieces rounded out the program for the ASM's concert dedicated to the tenth anniversary of the revolution. First, *Prologue*, by Leonid Polovinkin, had been commissioned by the ASM for a commemorative concert that never materialized in 1926. Receiving its premiere at last in 1927, the piece elicited little positive attention from either modernists or the musical Left. Both groups found its emotional romanticism conveyed through conventional instrumentation and the use of sonata form outmoded and inappropriate to the task at hand.[77]

Finally, a suite from the projected ballet *Steel* by Aleksandr Mosolov met a more mixed response. Mosolov also used traditional forms, including sonata, toccata, and fugue. But his treatment of the orchestra and harmonic language aroused more interest than in the case of Polovinkin. The first piece in the suite, *Zavod* (which became famous in the West as *Steel Factory* or *The Iron Foundry*), epitomized musical "constructivism." Often compared to Honegger's *Pacific 231*, a percussive tour de force that evokes an accelerating steam train, *Steel Factory* used ostinato rhythms and brief timbral and melodic "blocks" to imitate the movement and sounds of a modern factory. Although the ballet was never performed, and in fact most of the score was lost, *Steel Factory* became an international hit, playing to audiences at the International Contemporary Music festival in Liège in 1930 and in Hollywood in 1932.[78]

Two aspects of Mosolov's suite were typical of other commemorative pieces as well. Not only were none of them symphonies in any conventional sense of the term, but, like *Steel Factory*, most of them in some way paid homage to the aural world of modern industrial life.[79] For example, Mosolov evoked the din of the steel factory by dragging a stick across a sheet of corrugated metal. In Shostakovich's symphony a factory whistle announced the final chorus. The fourth section of Roslavets's cantata used the percussion section to portray a train crossing the Russian plain.

The homage to industrial noise was a single point of consensus, but these works also reveal how contradictory and vague the expectations for "revolutionary music" were in 1927. Modernism, and even constructivism, could be commendable in the case of Shostakovich or Mosolov, while Schillinger's use of jazz, noise orchestras, and popular song exposed him to charges of eclecticism and cheapening the spirit of the revolution. Mosolov's and Polovinkin's attempts to infuse classical forms with new harmonic or melodic content met with radically different critical responses. Perhaps because identifying acceptable "content" was so difficult, most composers relied on revolutionary texts to ensure that their piece's content would be unmistakably clear.

A final commemorative piece, *October's Path* (*Put' Oktiabria*), Prokoll's collectively composed oratorio, also made extensive use of text, but differed from the other works in many respects. Using poetry by Mayakovsky, Gorky, Blok, and others, *October's Path* was a montage of twenty-seven songs, choruses, and rhythmic declamations that related the history of the revolution from 1905 to Lenin's death. The oratorio was intended to be suitable for amateur performance and called for piano, trumpet, percussion, accordion, and optional organ accompaniment of a choir and soloists. It presented a fascinating blend of old and new, exemplifying Prokoll's commitment to writing music that incorporated tradition as well as innovative trends from contemporary artistic life. Among the new features were devices borrowed from living newspapers and mass festivals such as placards and slides, which enhanced the narrative of the piece and challenged the generic conventions of the oratorio as a purely vocal and instrumental form. Extensive use of rhythmic declamations as well as vocal and instrumental sound effects like whistling and foot stomping reflected the increased use of melodeclamation in the musical theater, and the technique of *sprechstimme* in the music of Berg and Schoenberg.[80] Among the old devices was the use of traditional forms, including the fugue in Davidenko's chorus, *The Street Is in Turmoil* (*Ulitsa Volnuetsia*), one of the oratorio's few enduring selections that secured a modest niche in the Soviet repertoire.

More than any of the other commemorative pieces, *October's Path* blurred the boundaries between high and popular art: This was music that workers should not just hear, but perform. The ultimate popular instrument, the accordion, was used not simply "for effect" but was a vital part of the musical fabric. Texts by avant-garde poets were interspersed with more popular forms such as a variation of the folk song *Down on Mother Volga* and the old revolutionary song *Boldly, Comrades, in Step*, which served as background for Shekhter's rhythmic declamation *The Capture of the Winter Palace* (*Vziatie Zimnego*).

Unlike the other commemorative pieces, however, *October's Path* received scant attention, since it was first performed several weeks after the anniversary of the revolution, and then not in its entirety. Under Davidenko's direction, the combined choirs of four workers' clubs gave a "social demonstration" of most of the oratorio in the recital hall of the Moscow Conservatory on December 18, but the placards, light effects, percussion, and accordion were lacking.[81] And although Prokoll had started to work on the piece early in the year, the fall found them still debating which selections to include and how those numbers should be changed.[82] In November, when the oratorio was still not ready for publication, a "troika" consisting of Davidenko, Shekhter, and Chemberdzhi was appointed to finish it.[83] Prokoll's ethos of egalitarianism and collectivism resonated strongly with other currents in the social and political discourse of the twenties, but the clumsiness and inefficiencies of "collective composition" had made it impossible for Prokoll to get its piece ready in time.

This paradox and the ambiguities raised in other commemorative works did not go unnoticed. Rather, they pointed to the contradictory and uneven nature of change in other areas of musical life. After ten years of Soviet power, musicians and critics of all political stripes found it difficult to reconnoiter adequately the state of the musical front and were even more hard pressed to prescribe a course of action for the upcoming decade.

Yet in many areas even limited successes gave some cause for optimism. At least one critic noted that the country's young compositional talent had not met the tenth anniversary passively. Mosolov, Schillinger, and Roslavets had written their musical tributes to October even though the Party's Central Executive Committee (TsIK) had refused to give Lunacharsky money to fund a national competition. To Nikolai Malkov, these works signaled that composers had begun to forge a new relationship with society. Abandoning the previously "sacred nature" of their profession, and freed from the patronage network of the old social structure, they had started to become the public-spirited musicians so idealized by conservatory reformers.[84]

In terms of *kul'turtregerstvo*—bringing musical culture to the masses—much had been accomplished that would have seemed fantastic ten years ago. The revolution had brought symphonies to workers' clubs, textile factories, and military schools and a "Club for Lovers of Beethoven's Music" to a provincial village.[85] Gains had even been made in the area of technology. Already, radio had expanded the possibilities for the dissemination of music to remote corners of the countryside. Robert Pel'she, the head of the art division of Glavpolitprosvet, lauded Lev Termen's electric "Termenvox," and Arsenii Avraamov's "universal tone system" as first steps toward a technological revolution in the musical world.[86]

The progress of the accordion campaign also gave reformers some cause to celebrate. The 1927 competitions far outstripped their predecessors in popularity. More than 30,000 entrants participated in 2,500 preliminary contests, with sixty finalists competing in the final round at the Hall of Columns.[87] Activists boasted that eighteen months of work promoting the instrument and developing its repertoire and training had brought about significant changes. They proudly noted that the *baian*, a chromatic button accordion, was surpassing the more primitive diatonic "two row" accordion in popularity, and reported that classical, revolutionary, and "genuine" folk music had made significant headway in displacing "pseudo folk" and light genre music.[88]

But reporters declined to provide exact statistics on the shift in repertoire, which probably reflects an overly optimistic interpretation of minimal changes. Certainly the promotion of the accordion as a means of spreading musical literacy was only marginally successful. Although 65 percent of the finalists were described as "musically literate," only a fraction of the contestants could read music. It was also apparent that although the Komsomol and RAPM saw the promotion of accordion playing as a means to develop cultural sophistication and political awareness, many people had flocked to the newly formed accordion circles and courses just because they wanted to relax and have fun.[89] Lunacharsky's opening speech for the final competition skillfully conveyed the pragmatic compromise behind the pro-accordion campaign. Acknowledging the instrument's flaws and the opposition to the Komsomol's promotion of it, the Commissar insisted that realism demanded a positive approach to the accordion for now. Until resources sufficed to bring the piano and symphony to the countryside, Lunacharsky concluded, the accordion was the best musical means available to organize and influence the mass audience.[90]

While the accordion competitions revealed the tensions between reformers' agendas and the difficulties of changing popular preferences, the critical response to the "October" pieces suggests that many felt that the revolution in musical culture was still in its formative stages. None of the gains cited above were unqualified. Regardless of their success in capturing the spirit of October in music, the works of Roslavets and Shostakovich were known only to a handful of people. The mass audience had no access to their music, which was not widely distributed on phonograph records or by radio.[91] Furthermore, critics commended the symphonic tributes to October as "first efforts." Serious composers had begun to grapple with the challenge of realizing a revolution in large-scale symphonic music, but no one considered the problem solved. Truly Soviet music was still in the (distant) future, its basic qualities much debated and only nebulously defined.

As with the coming of the messiah, no one could predict when or in what form this music would appear, but everyone felt sure they would recognize it when it did. In general terms, they could even agree as to its necessary characteristics, despite their divergent biases. Across the aesthetic and political spectrum critics equated the spirit of the revolution with large-scale works. To convey revolutionary pathos music required "*monumental'nost'*," the realization of a deep-seated longing for great, monumental art.[92] ORK expected that revolutionary music would be "strong-willed, dynamic, and easily comprehended."[93] Similarly, Roslavets foresaw "bold, clear rhythms" and "simple, natural expressions of melodic line."[94]

But beyond this most superficial level, consensus disintegrated. While Roslavets envisioned revolutionary music emerging from "radical, internal, organic restructuring," the Revolutionary Composers' organization insisted it would come only from the masses' mastery of classic forms.[95] For all of the rhetoric about Beethoven serving as the foundation on which young composers should build revolutionary music, none of the commemorative pieces showed any reference to the great German. In their work on *October's Path*, members of Prokoll repeatedly stumbled over their own limitations and inexperience as well as the challenge of writing high quality music that was accessible to amateur performers. They adopted the "montage" structure of linked individual pieces after their efforts to use more complex symphonic forms failed.[96] The unresolved questions about the folk song and "musical populism" raised the previous year at the Glavpolitprosvet Conference on Musical Enlightenment Work also remained very much in evidence. Korev denounced as "socially dangerous" Ippolitov-Ivanov's *Hymn to Labor* (*Gimn Trudu*), which featured traditional peasant work songs.[97] Roslavets and Schillinger called for the removal of agit-composers "speculating on the revolution" by using primitive material such as folk songs for their artistically inferior musical propaganda.[98] At the same time, Pel'she and Asaf'ev maintained that Russian music had always reflected an emotional, personal attachment to nature and the countryside. Without succumbing to the "poison of sentimental populism," folk songs reflecting Russians' love of nature must be incorporated into the music of the future, along with music inspired by the urban environment of the industrial proletariat.[99]

To many, confusion and disagreement over how to define and cultivate revolutionary music were symptomatic of music's relative backwardness vis-à-vis the other arts. Regardless of the political perspective of the critic, appraisals of the decade inevitably noted that music "had always lagged behind" or that its particular characteristics made it slower to respond to the revolution than the more "advanced" areas of cinema, theater, or literature.[100] Even as determined and optimistic a *kul'turtreger* as Briusova could only describe the decade as "difficult but not unfruitful."[101]

Frustrations over limited success in meeting the demands and cultivating the musical tastes of the new consumer, combined with the difficulty of defining a creative agenda for the development of truly Soviet music, fueled growing interest from many quarters to see these issues taken up by central authority. In the twilight of NEP culture, RAPM was not alone in calling for intervention from the center in musical affairs. On behalf of Persimfans, Arnol'd Tsukker called for an "authoritative social conference" to uncover and liquidate unhealthy elements lingering in the area of musical work.[102] In the LASM's journal, Orest Tsekhnovitser pointed to the recent Party conference on theater and the upcoming meeting on cinema, insisting that music must be next.[103]

Though remarkable and oft-noted, the vibrancy and diversity of concert life were not the most significant or telling aspects of musical culture in 1927. Other developments were far more portentous for the future of Soviet music, namely, the virtually unqualified embrace and enshrinement of Beethoven's oeuvre as the model for revolutionary music, the confusion and dissension among musicians over what kind of music best conveyed the spirit of the revolution in the present, and the growing conviction among many musicians that as the Party began to deal with the third front, music's backwardness would finally come to an end.

8

Cultural Revolution

Before the 7th Sonata (1932) I had written nothing for a long time. The Rapmovtsy beat me out of working condition.
—Anatolii Aleksandrov

Obviously RAPM's right to leadership will come not in the form of a mandate from Narkompros or the presidium of Vseroskomdram. It will become a leading and leadership organization only with broad initiative and creative work.
—Levon Avtom'ian, secretary of the Vseroskomdram composers' section, December 1931

The crisis on the cultural front began in the countryside in the winter of 1927–28. Despite good harvests, peasants' grain sales to the state were down, jeopardizing the success of the ambitious industrialization program that had just been approved at the Fifteenth Party Congress. In the first weeks of 1928 Stalin ordered local authorities to revive methods shelved since the Civil War and requisition the grain by force. For the next year, debates over agrarian policy split the Kremlin leadership, with Bukharin, Aleksei Rykov, and Mikhail Tomsky assuming the role of rightists who opposed Stalin's use of force and favored the continuation of NEP, while Stalin and his supporters insisted that the grain crisis reflected the sharpening of class struggle and the resurgence of socialism's enemies. When charges of conspiracy and industrial sabotage against a group of engineers and mining specialists from the Shakhty district of the Donbass were announced in March, the political crisis converged with the mounting discontent with Narkompros's policies. The "great turning point" (*velikii perelom*) in official policy on the cultural front had begun.[1]

Stalin's claim that the Shakhty affair signaled a revival of class struggle and the need to take aggressive measures to establish "proletarian hegemony" in all areas resonated strongly with many Party activists, workers, and proletarian organizations in the arts who had long resented the privileged status of the old specialists and the ideological compromises demanded by NEP. These groups also endorsed the program adopted at the July Plenum of the Central Committee, which ordered the massive recruitment of Communists and workers to higher education. The old specialists were to be replaced with a new Communist intelligentsia whose political loyalty, social origins, and practical skills were beyond reproach.[2] Although the primary objective of *vydvizhenie*—the rapid education and promotion of Party members and working-class youth—was to train engineers and other industrial specialists, a demand for new cadres would also figure prominently in the cultural arena.

As opposition to both Stalin's promotion of "class war" in the countryside and the attack on the bourgeois specialists congealed around the Politburo Right, RAPP capitalized on long-standing claims to speak for proletarian interests and its repeated efforts to provoke Party intervention in the cultural sphere. In May, a resolution by the Central Committee's Agitprop department indicated how the issues raised by the Shakhty affair would affect the arts. Implicitly faulting Narkompros for its conciliatory policies toward the old intelligentsia and its promotion of bourgeois culture, the resolution called for increased proletarian control of literary and artistic organizations and for the art section of the Communist Academy to strengthen its influence in these organizations and the government organs involved in artistic affairs.[3] In December, the Central Committee's resolution instructing publishing houses to show preference to proletarian writers solidified the Party's sponsorship of the proletarian literary movement and implied support for other proletarian arts organizations.

There was thus considerable initiative for cultural revolution "from above." Because debates among the Party leadership over the implementation of *vydvizhenie* and the First Five-Year Plan involved educational and social policies staunchly defended by supporters of "NEP culture," a link was quickly established between "rightism" on policies toward the peasants and moderation toward old technical and cultural specialists.[4] But militant groups in the arts such as RAPP and RAPM needed little encouragement from above to abandon the preferential treatment of the old intelligentsia that characterized NEP. This was just what they had always wanted and they embraced "class war" with a fervor that often surpassed the ambitions of higher authorities.[5]

The Cultural Revolution was a period of extremes in which the assault on bourgeois culture and its practitioners was just one element in a turbulent, unpredictable landscape of confrontation. The unleashing of militant artistic groups and the often deadly campaigns against "class enemies" such as kulaks, speculators, and priests were part of the attack on Russian "backwardness" and tradition. This attack was exemplified by campaigns for universal schooling and acts such as blowing up churches and burning icons. The period from 1928 to 1931 witnessed diverse outbursts of revolutionary utopianism and iconoclasm, from visionary town planning to programs for the "withering away" of the law and the school.[6] But the vehement assertion of Bolshevik agendas, some of them contradictory, necessitated the final suppression of many of the utopian currents that had flourished in the postrevolutionary decade. Science fiction, "God building," and many forms of egalitarianism succumbed to the obliterating fury of ideological zeal.[7]

Although the main tenets of this model of cultural revolution are commonly invoked, even in textbooks, to elucidate the complex links between cultural developments and the swiftly evolving political imperatives of the First Five-Year Plan,[8] much recent scholarship emphasizes the longer-term processes and forces at work in the evolution of Soviet culture.[9] Indeed, Michael David-Fox maintains that identifying the Cultural Revolution as a unique and discrete episode deflects attention away from the Bolsheviks' broader and more long-standing agendas in the cultural arena.[10] Certainly the developments of these years must be seen in the context of long-term processes, including the Bolsheviks' quest for cultural control and domination of the intelligentsia, as well as their commitment to enlightenment, education, and moral improvement as essential components of cultural transformation. But as I have argued elsewhere, the concept of a chronologically bounded Cultural Revolution remains useful to understanding both the turbulence of the First Five-Year Plan as well as what came before and after.[11] Viewing these years from the vantage point of musical life also offers a valuable countermodel to much-studied developments in other areas such as literature.

As was true in other fields, the chaotic atmosphere of repressive anarchy and "proletarian hegemony" unleashed by the turn in official policy wrought a fair amount of havoc in the musical community. Among the early casualties was Persimfans, whose institutional autonomy and involvement with foreign musicians proved too much for the xenophobia and anticommercialism of the period as well as the state's ever-stronger penchant for control.[12] The conservatories reeled in the face of determined efforts to proletarianize the student body, purge the musical legacy of decadent influences, and make music education address the needs of the First Five-Year Plan. Grades and exams were eliminated. Students were organized into "brigades" that spent most of the year touring collective farms and industrial sites. Portraits of the famous composers of the past were removed from the recital hall of the Moscow Conservatory, leaving only Beethoven and Musorgsky as the officially recognized forefathers of proletarian music. In 1931 the "conservative" inflection of the institution's name became unbearable, and it was renamed the "Feliks Kon Higher Music School" in honor of the current head of the Narkompros arts administration.

Most of the "excesses" of this period would later be blamed on RAPM, which eagerly wielded what authority it could claim on behalf of proletarian hegemony.[13] At the conservatories, especially in Moscow, and in music publishing, RAPM's influence was indeed considerable. But other bizarre and extraordinary developments during this period did stem from the totalizing ambitions of the Party's radicals and the merging of social and economic agendas with cultural struggles.[14] This was especially true in the final year of the Cultural Revolution, when utilitarian programs overrode all others. The state's demand that artistic energies be channeled exclusively toward fulfilling the objectives of the Five-Year Plan actually subverted radical creative agendas and undermined RAPM's quest for dominance.

For all of its extremism, the Cultural Revolution in music was more radical in form than in content. Contrary to its own aspirations and self-representation, and decades of scholarly assumption, RAPM never exercised a hegemonic role. Despite the group's best efforts it never developed a viable creative platform or a mass following. Nor is there any evidence that it enjoyed the same kind of personal support that Stalin offered to RAPP. The old specialists came under fire in music just as they did in other areas but they played an important and often winning role in many of the period's most critical encounters. As the first decade of Soviet rule at the conservatories suggested, expertise and ability were to prove more essential than ideology or social origin.

Rightism at the Moscow Conservatory

Trouble was brewing at the Moscow Conservatory even before the announcement of the Shakhty affair. It was instigated not by RAPM or politicians, but by conservatory faculty eager to reverse one of the postrevolutionary reforms they found most objectionable. What the Komsomol described as an "attack" on the *pedfak* began in January 1928 when Gol'denveizer suggested that the conservatory could save money by eliminating the *pedfak* as an independent unit and incorporating parts of its program into the performance and composition faculties. Under his leadership, the initiative to eliminate the *pedfak* gathered momentum behind a range of charges. Although Gol'denveizer's group billed its proposal as a cost-saving administrative measure, inspectors from Rabkrin found that concerns about the objectives and quality of the program were far more significant. At the plenary session of the GUS scientific-artistic section, where the issue was debated in February, Gol'denveizer testified that the pedagogy students were poorly prepared for conservatory study and showed little musical aptitude.[15] Many faculty felt that the system of tracking students into the pedagogy major in their first year contributed to the low quality of the program.[16] Furthermore, the investigation had revealed deficiencies and student dissatisfaction with parts of the curriculum, namely, the courses on modal rhythm and "listening to music." Gol'denveizer and Ivanov-Boretskii claimed that the students lacked adequate expertise on their own instruments, and complained that they were isolated from "living work" in this area (a charge difficult to believe given the emphasis on "practice" at the First Technicum). The conservatory's director, Konstantin Igumnov, insisted that the teachers using Iavorskii's method taught their subjects poorly.[17]

Responding to these charges, Lunacharsky and representatives from Glavpolitprosvet and Rabis defended the *pedfak* with all of the reasons the program had been established in the first place. Lunacharsky insisted that the country needed professional music teachers and the conservatory was the place to train them. The head of the art section of Glavpolitprosvet, Robert Pel'she, noted that the growth of clubs meant there was an increased need for music teachers who were trained, gifted "organizers [and] conveyers of musical culture to the masses."[18] Rabis leader Iuvenal Slavinskii demanded that the situation be evaluated not in terms of economics, but from an "ideological" position.[19] Others agreed that the anti-Soviet atmosphere at the conservatory and the poor caliber of students majoring in pedagogy were more significant than the proposal's emphasis on economics implied. Student representatives at the meeting admitted that there were deficiencies in the quality of students and instruction at their institution, but they felt both were improving, and opposed the liquidation of the faculty. Nadezhda Briusova echoed these sentiments.[20] The only member of the regular conservatory faculty to speak in support of the *pedfak* was Mikhail Gnesin.[21] Interestingly, both Iavorskii, whose program and teaching methods were under attack, and Lebedinskii, whose organization had strong support in the *pedfak*, remained quiet throughout the discussion.

In the end, Lunacharsky ushered a resolution through the plenum that supported the preservation of the *pedfak*. Another commission was appointed to investigate the complaints about the program, and the faculty's future was unclear for several months. In the summer the matter came before the Little Sovnarkom, a subgroup of the Council of People's Commissars (Malyi Sovnarkom), which also ruled in favor of preserving the *pedfak*. The existence of the pedagogy program seemed secure, but members of the Komsomol still complained that most students had not supported the *pedfak* in its hour of need, and warned that a new attack on the courses in modal rhythm and "listening to music" was gathering momentum.[22]

As the general political climate shifted, the campaign against the *pedfak* became the focal point of an array of criticisms about the conservatory raised by the Komsomol and supported by RAPM. Gol'denveizer and the assistant rector, Nazarii Raiskii, were identified as the core of a group of "reactionary" professors intent on stifling the further Sovietization of the conservatory. The Komsomol maintained that under the influence of these reactionaries the conservatory continued to produce virtuoso performers and composers who lacked both a sense of social responsibility and the skills necessary to meet the musical needs of workers and peasants. The professors in question also undermined efforts to increase the flow of proletarian students into the conservatory by refusing to support the *rabfak* and trying to eliminate or reduce funding for the *pedfak*.[23] Rightists within the conservatory's Party organization supported the reactionary professors by sponsoring a policy of "civil peace" within the conservatory rather than confrontation and class struggle with harmful ideological influences.[24] There were more specific grievances as well. RAPM protested that professors and musicians from the Bol'shoi Theater violated pedagogical norms and Narkompros regulations by performing as soloists in "student" concerts.[25] They also complained that the music history curriculum was not being taught by the seminar method approved in 1925.[26] The conservatory's Komsomol organization was incensed by the Party cell's accommodation of the professors and outraged that Nikolai Golovanov, whom the Komsomol had just hounded out of the Bol'shoi Theater on trumped-up charges of anti-Semitism and discrimination against the "proletarian" bass-baritone Aleksandr Baturin, was now conducting highly publicized concerts at the conservatory.[27] The Komsomol also tried to make modal rhythm the foundation of the first-year music theory program, rather than the composite "classic" European method (a synthesis of Reiman, Gevaert, and Prout) developed by Katuar.[28]

In the final months of 1928 a series of articles appeared in the musical press and newspapers denouncing these conditions and describing an atmosphere of "civil war" at the conservatory.[29] A commission headed by Nikolai Cheliapov[30] began to investigate these charges early in 1929.[31]

A number of steps soon were taken to address the complaints registered by RAPM and the Komsomol.[32] Despite the objections of the conservatory Party organization, which supported the candidacy of Ippolitov-Ivanov, Boleslav

Pshibyshevskii, a Communist with little musical training, became the conservatory's director on June 13.[33] In an effort to accelerate the recruitment of proletarian elements, proposals were drafted to move the music division of the Unified Artistic *rabfak* to the conservatory, expand the activities of the Sunday Workers' Conservatory, and reorganize the *pedfak*'s programs. Although even faculty members who staunchly supported RAPM argued that the government's lack of financial and material support (in the form of stipends and dormitories) was largely to blame for the slow pace of proletarianization in artistic education,[34] more political measures were also enacted. Conservatory students, especially those in graduate programs, were reexamined for social and political suitability, and many of them were expelled. Reactionary professors were sent on extended "vacations" or intimidated from exerting further influence on those students who remained. Students from a working-class or peasant background made up 36 percent of the incoming class for 1929–30.[35]

The dynamics underlying these developments clearly echo broader pressures to proletarianize the student body of higher education overall, the distrust of "specialists," and the attack on right-wing tendencies within the Party. Events at the conservatory also reflect the frustration felt in many quarters with the compromises of NEP and indicate that contradictions would persist even during this episode of officially sanctioned class struggle. Many of the Komsomol's complaints about the conservatory were based on sound observation, but few would be solved to its satisfaction. The leaders of the conservatory Party organization had colluded with the reactionary professors in a number of areas, and many of these rightists would remain at their posts even after the defeat of rightism in Moscow in the summer of 1929. The conservatory had produced some fine musicians since the advent of Soviet rule, but few were the socially engaged *muzykanty-obshchestvenniki* that reformers so desired. The conservatory was now launched on the path to "proletarianization" but RAPM, Pshibyshevskii, and the Komsomol would find that "proletarian" students displayed as little proficiency in "political literacy" and interest in "production work" as their temporarily disgraced white-collar colleagues. Meanwhile the conflict that began at the conservatory soon moved to other arenas.

RAPM's Campaign for Hegemony on the Musical Front

Given RAPP's command of literary affairs in this period and its interventions in other areas such as philosophy and the theater, literature has been the model for scholarly interpretations of the Cultural Revolution in the arts. Led by a zealous cohort of polemicists, RAPP had a number of literary works to its credit and a well-developed base of support. It exemplifies the pressure "from below" that is integral to the paradigm of Cultural Revolution. Yet the fortunes of RAPM present a striking contrast to those of RAPP, indicating the complexities and paradoxes of cultural debates during the First Five-Year Plan.

As the Cultural Revolution gained momentum in other quarters, RAPM struggled to consolidate its position, scrambling to ride the Proletarian Writers' coattails whenever possible. RAPM's report to Party and government organizations in June 1928 emphasized how undersupported its operations were by comparison with RAPP, which had a "considerable apparatus."[36] Lebedinskii's group looked to the newly-created Glaviskusstvo for backing, but was often disappointed. Indeed, until February 1930, Glaviskusstvo's policies were remarkably preservationist. Even as it praised RAPM for its focus on the proletariat and efforts to understand music in terms of its class content and social significance, the agency criticized the association's hostility toward modern music and its overemphasis on the classical legacy.[37] RAPM did receive an office, funding for two full-time staff members, and a journal, *Proletarian Musician* (*Proletarskii muzykant*). But Glaviskusstvo failed to give RAPM exclusive preference among musical organizations, and at least initially declined to punish the association's enemies. Given its organizational ties to Narkompros and the fact that its first head, Aleksei Sviderskii, was an ousted rightist from the Commissariat of Agriculture, Glaviskusstvo labored from its inception under the stigma of being on the cultural Right.[38] In 1928–29 it regarded all musical groups as "equal," including the AMA, whose production plan and requests for paper were approved for the 1928–29 fiscal year.[39]

Nor did other musical groups gracefully acquiesce to RAPM's authority. The first year of the Cultural Revolution was marked by contest and struggle that left the musical scene polarized. The ASM reorganized itself as the All-Russian Society of Contemporary Music (VOSM) in July 1928.[40] Its journal, *Contemporary Music*, ceased publication in 1929, but the group found a new leader in the theater critic and censor (political editor) Vladimir Blium, a Party member who had initially supported RAPM and *Musical Virgin Soil* and vociferously opposed Lunacharsky on censorship issues.[41] The ASM/VOSM led an embattled existence until it was dissolved, along with RAPM, in April 1932. But its very survival and Blium's willingness to challenge RAPM's policies on modern music and the light genre—repeatedly and publicly—suggest that RAPM's official support remained shaky even in the organization's heyday.

Tensions between organizations on the Left initially increased. When RAPM began to put out its own journal again, ORK challenged its claims to leadership in musical affairs in what RAPM characterized as a "gas attack."[42] ORK faulted the Proletarian Musicians for emphasizing ideology at the expense of creativity, insisting that even RAPM's talk of the "first sprouts" of proletarian music was premature.[43] Opposition to RAPM's authority continued at a discussion of the association's activities held at the Communist Academy on March 29, 1929. RAPM's leaders clearly expected a show of support for their program, but instead faced criticism from many quarters. Representatives of Narkompros, the Party cell at the Moscow Conservatory, and the Academy's Institute of Literature and Art joined Shul'gin and Sergeev in reproaching RAPM for its disregard of agitational music, its simplistic assessment of the musical legacy (Boris Krasin pointed out that Lenin had loved Tchaikovsky's *Barcarolle*), and its claim to speak for the working class without engaging in wide-scale work with the masses.[44]

Members of Prokoll were torn over where to place their loyalties. In 1926 they had considered joining the ASM, and some Prokoll members, notably Kabalevsky, belonged to both the ASM and RAPM. Prokoll also maintained friendly contacts with Shul'gin and ORK, and many Prokoll members published their work with the agitational music section of the State Publishing House. Davidenko had always insisted that the group maintain its independence. But as most of the original Prokoll members graduated in 1929 or 1930 they joined RAPM.[45] Davidenko became one of the association's leaders and edited its mass journal, *For Proletarian Music* (*Za proletarskuiu muzyku*). The addition of Prokoll members strengthened RAPM's ranks and changed its profile considerably. Davidenko, Marian Koval', Boris Shekhter, Nikolai Chemberdzhi, and Viktor Belyi were all professionally trained composers—albeit with newly bestowed credentials. In 1929 RAPM could finally anticipate the composition of proletarian music from within its ranks.

But even as RAPM sought to consolidate its position as the leader of the Cultural Revolution in music, challenges to its authority continued to appear. In March 1929, workers' correspondents (*rabkory*) at *The Workers Newspaper* (*Rabochaia gazeta*) and *Screen* (*Ekran*) joined Communist rightists at the Moscow Conservatory to found a new organization called Music to the Masses (*Muzyka-massam*).[46] Music to the Masses billed itself as a mass organization committed to popularizing music and fostering amateur music-making (*samodeiatel'nost'*). Its organizers understood cultural revolution in music to mean democratizing access to musical activities, encouraging workers and peasants to learn to play an instrument or sing, and providing popular musical literature to these groups. The organization's platform made no reference to using music for overtly political ends.[47]

Not surprisingly, then, RAPM had stormy relations with the new organization from the beginning.[48] RAPM tried to define itself as the new group's senior partner and the ideological leader of Music to the Masses' efforts to develop a broad movement amidst the working class.[49] Although its claims about membership numbers proved to be greatly exaggerated (far fewer than the 15,000 reported early in 1930), Music to the Masses immediately involved many times more members than RAPM. The new group thwarted RAPM's initial efforts to co-opt it and balked hard at more heavy-handed tactics, which included putting Dmitrii Gachev, a RAPM member, on the board in March 1930.

Throughout the twenties RAPM and other groups had lobbied for a clearly defined official policy on music. As the Cultural Revolution gathered momentum, RAPM naturally applauded an initiative from Glaviskusstvo to formulate (at last) a coherent state policy on music. The All-Russian Music Conference, which met in Leningrad June 16–20, 1929, appeared to answer calls from across the political spectrum for clarification of official policy in the musical sphere.[50] With the participation of delegates from Narkompros, the Party, the Komsomol, trade unions, and virtually every major musical institution and organization, the conference was to address the broad range of issues that made up the "musical front." This included factional relations within the musical community, the musical theater, concert policies, musical life in the national republics, music education, and, above all, mass musical enlightenment work. The state theaters, concert organization (*Sofil*), state choirs, and conservatories all put on performances in conjunction with the conference. Similarly, the Leningrad and Moscow trade union associations organized musical olympiads and musical "holidays" in working-class neighborhoods.

But in preparing for the conference, the central authorities worked to regulate the "spontaneous" lobbying of RAPM and other radical groups. Two days before the conference began, the Central Committee's Agitprop department held a special meeting in Moscow to "unify party and social opinion."[51] The meeting and ensuing discussion revealed the main tensions and concerns of Communist activists in musical affairs and the ambiguity of RAPM's position. Although this was the first official discussion of musical policy since the 1926 Conference on Musical Enlightenment Work, neither the Party nor the state felt it necessary to send their top officials. Agitprop's deputy head, Platon Kerzhentsev, and the deputy head of Glaviskusstvo, Lev Obolenskii, presented drafts of resolutions to be adopted at the upcoming conference. Party members representing RAPM, ORK, Music to the Masses, and a number of musical institutions, as well as the Komsomol and trade unions, then discussed the resolutions and keynote speeches. The meeting's organizers reined in RAPM's attacks on the modernists and ORK,[52] while a representative from the Moscow Conservatory cautioned that the Party's policy must not be identified as that of any one group, even though RAPM's policy was "close to us."[53] Yet Pshibyshevskii pointed out that the similarity between the resolutions and RAPM's position was obvious to everyone.[54] Others called on the Central Committee to support RAPM and quit criticizing them.[55] But no one complained that the primary purpose of the Agitprop meeting was to orchestrate events for the conference. Indeed, many participants lobbied for even more definite direction "from above." They protested that the resolutions were too vague—that they still did not present a coherent Party line on music and musical affairs.[56]

The resolutions refrained from explicitly evaluating different musical groups, which many argued would make implementing cultural revolution in music more difficult.[57] They emphasized the centrality of the mass song, without addressing the argument between RAPM and ORK over its structure. They did not offer practical solutions to the perceived danger of kulaks who sang anti-Soviet *chastushki* or church choir directors who controlled the repertoire for village choral circles.[58] Some delegates criticized the Party for not taking musical affairs seriously, even now. They noted that the campaign to "proletarianize" music education could not succeed without support for working-class students in the form of stipends, instruments, and dormitories.[59] A representative from Tula described how the local Party organization made light of one activist's work on the administration of the local music school and refused to give another time off to sing in a workers' choral circle.[60]

Vagueness notwithstanding, in both their preliminary and final forms the conference resolutions supported the agenda set out in RAPM's platform,[61] thus affirming RAPM's claims to leadership and dominance in musical affairs without giving them an explicit, formal mandate. But the conference failed to solve the most stubborn, and only partially acknowledged, paradox of RAPM's approach to cultural transformation in music and musical life; namely, that the nonrepresentational qualities of music cut in two directions. Activists claimed that the abstract nature of musical creativity was responsible for music's "backwardness" vis-à-vis the other arts. From this perspective, the difficulties of defining, much less regulating, the ideological content of nonrepresentational artistic expression, combined with the need for both aptitude and lengthy study in training composers and performers, largely explained why music had not been conquered (*zavoevana*) by the proletariat. Yet at the same time, Obolenskii and the ideologues of RAPM maintained that music's nonrepresentational qualities made it accessible to all. Everyone, they maintained, regardless of education or social background, was "naturally" drawn to music.[62]

These debates reveal that one of the most urgent issues on the cultural front as a whole—the need for control of the "commanding heights" by qualified specialists committed to building socialism—was particularly intractable in the area of music.[63] For all of the zeal with which RAPM assaulted formalism and its representatives, whatever truly radical ambitions the organization had were curbed early on by authorities who ensured that the musical specialists would not suffer the fate of bourgeois engineers.

The conference organizers admitted that the Proletarian Musicians were not yet ready to take the place of established musicians. Obolenskii affirmed RAPM's own admission that proletarian musicians existed only as "sprouts."[64] Former members of Prokoll showed promise, but were also young and inexperienced. Like the composers affiliated with ORK, they had yet to meet the challenge of writing pieces that would be accessible to audiences with little exposure to classical music without sacrificing compositional technique and sophistication. This meant that the talent and skill of music's bourgeois specialists must not be sacrificed unnecessarily. Like the old technical intelligentsia, which was a primary target of class war, conservatory professors and members of the ASM possessed invaluable expertise.[65] The reactionary influences of these people must be curbed, but the proletarian state needed their services. Echoing Gol'denveizer's warning about purging the conservatory faculty in 1924, Kerzhentsev insisted that "we cannot afford to lose all of them!"[66] The attack on the old elite was thus more guarded in music than in literature, a fact RAPM steadfastly refused to acknowledge.[67] Despite repeated injunctions to "win over" the "fellow travelers" and adopt a more inclusive perspective on the musical legacy, RAPM never tempered its critique of "reactionary" and "decadent" influences and their representatives.[68]

Like the Party's "literary debates" of 1923–24 and more recent conferences on theater and film, the All-Russian Music Conference dedicated considerable attention to theoretical issues and policies affecting artistic professionals. But even more time was devoted to issues first broached at the 1926 Conference on Musical Enlightenment Work. Conference organizers and delegates emphasized the growing need for music and music teachers geared toward the needs of workers and peasants. Although it had been on the periphery of RAPM's activities, music enlightenment work had grown impressively in scope since the mid-twenties. As of April 1928, more than 30,000 music circles had been organized in Russian villages.[69] In the cities workers turned to more than 4,500 clubs and circles for musical training and entertainment.[70] The formation and initial popularity of Music to the Masses indicated the popular thirst for music. But activists in this area faced two significant obstacles: a dearth of suitable repertoire and a severe shortage of appropriately trained instructors. Efforts to solve these two problems were at the heart of the Cultural Revolution in music.

The conference attempted to establish proletarian hegemony and resolve the problem of cadres in a manner consistent with measures taken in other areas. Proletarian elements were to assume control of the "commanding heights" by fiat and aggressive quota policies. The cultural front needed competent, talented composers and performers; therefore, the conservatories must train musicians who were proletarian in terms of social origin as well as outlook. Cultural revolution also demanded huge numbers of another type of musician—the teacher-leader of amateur music-making who would be deployed in the cities and villages across the country. Reformers in this area faced obvious and intractable difficulties due to the need for demonstrable talent and the many years of study in training a musician. No amount of "shock work" and storming could train a composer, violinist, or pianist in five years, much less four. And even preparing qualified teachers for amateur music groups would take more than the few months or weeks allowed by the "campaigns" of the Cultural Revolution.

For all the difficulties reformers faced at the conservatories and other institutions of music education, however, the question of cadres was in many respects more tractable than the more fundamental question of repertoire. After many years of theorizing and discussion, RAPM was now called upon to ante up on proletarian music and the mass song. But writing music that was politically correct and "selling it" to the masses remained as daunting a task during the Cultural Revolution as it had been during NEP. Observers of all political and aesthetic persuasions agreed that the divide between popular and high culture loomed especially large in music. During the Cultural Revolution RAPM made a number of sincere, albeit crude and unsuccessful, efforts to smooth over this gap. They attempted to use the "best of the classics" to leaven the first flowering of genuine proletarian musical creativity, and tried to overhaul the repertoire used in amateur mass musical work, replacing the agitational literature written by ORK with selections from the classics and their own compositions. They launched, at last, a frontal assault on the composers of light genre music and their compositions. And, most importantly, they struggled to write mass songs that would realize Lenin's oft-repeated summons for an art form with roots "deeply implanted in the very thick of the laboring masses."[71]

Despite RAPM's clearly stated desires for a monopoly in musical affairs, the ASM/VOSM survived the All-Russian Music Conference. Their members were to be evaluated on an individual basis, and RAPM was enjoined to "try to win them over."[72] But RAPM's longtime competitor on the Left capitulated to its rival in short order. After losing its journal and experiencing an administrative shake-up at the State Publishing House, the Revolutionary Composers dissolved their organization in October. In a public declaration Shul'gin and Sergeev recanted the main tenets of ORK's guiding principles, acknowledged that RAPM's ideological position was correct in every respect, and asked to be readmitted to the association. Two of ORK's best composers, Klementii Korchmarev and Dmitrii Vasil'ev-Buglai (also one of the original defectors), submitted similar statements.[73] The penitents' petitions were accepted, and the core of ORK became members of RAPM (Fig. 6).[74] As a seasoned and accomplished composer, Vasil'ev-Buglai was soon (re)embraced.[75] But whereas RAPM fully accepted and welcomed the leadership of Prokoll, Sergeev and Shul'gin virtually vanished from the musical scene.

The end of the first phase of the Cultural Revolution, marked by the defeat of the Right Opposition in the Politburo and the resignation of Lunacharsky, Sviderskii, and other supporters of NEP from Narkompros,[76] found the forces of the musical Left consolidated under RAPM's leadership. Lunacharsky's replacement by Andrei Bubnov, the former head of Agitprop, signaled the further erosion of the boundaries between the realm of the Party and that of the state on the third front, as well as the elision of political and cultural agendas.[77] Yet even as the Proletarian Musicians savored their victory, political challenges and creative dilemmas compromised their efforts to establish their hegemony.

The Attack on the Light Genre and the Campaign for the Mass Song

RAPM's broad program for cultural revolution overlapped with the agendas of other groups interested in education, scholarship, criticism, the new mass media of radio and film, the operatic and dramatic theaters, and publishing policies. In many of these areas, however, the mobilizing efforts of the Komsomol and trade unions overshadowed and even superseded RAPM's efforts. After the All-Russian Music Conference, RAPM did attempt to broaden its

Fig. 6 The Leadership of RAPM, October 1929. *Proletarskii muzykant* 6 (1929): 38.
Back Row: A. Davidenko, A. Groman-Solovtsov, S. Korev, N. Vygodskii, B. Shteinpress
Middle Row: Iu. Keldysh, L. Lebedinskii, S. Krylova, L. Kaltat
Front Row: M. Koval', D. Rabinovich, V. Belyi, D. Gachev

influence and build up a mass following. Its Leningrad division became more active and delegates were dispatched to several regional centers to develop affiliate organizations. In 1930 RAPM began to publish a "mass" journal, *For Proletarian Music*, which was cheaper, had a larger print run, and featured shorter articles than *Proletarian Musician.* But the Proletarian Musicians were spread too thin from the start. Their persecution of the modernists and domination of publishing after 1930 were remarkable and impressive. Yet their activities in the field of "popular" music reveal the main tensions confronting the group and the paradoxes underpinning their ideology and actions in other areas. Although RAPM's critique of urban popular music would influence the popular songs of the thirties, its efforts to reform popular music during the Cultural Revolution failed to muster even modest, much less mass popular, support. RAPM's campaign to eradicate the degenerate, bourgeois music of the past and then replace it with new, healthy proletarian mass songs revealed the main tensions confronting the group and the paradoxes underpinning its efforts in other areas.

In the charged atmosphere of the Great Break, RAPM elaborated and intensified the critique of light genre music formulated by the musical Left in the twenties. Identifying a range of harmful effects this music had on those who sang, listened to, and danced to it, RAPM became even more specific in condemning the musical elements of *tsyganshchina* style. Objections to sentimental chromaticism now expanded to include a denunciation of stylistic traits that "fogged the consciousness," such as excessive syncopation, monotonous rhythms, and melodic units that began and ended on the same tone. Naturally, *Little Bricks* was said to exemplify these dangerous characteristics. RAPM ideologues maintained that because the song was built on just one rhythmic pattern (two pick-up notes and an eighth-note triplet) and its basic melodic unit used only three ascending step-wise notes that then returned, also by steps, to the starting tone, *Little Bricks* stifled a person's aspirations: "[It] dulls the will, discourages striving and development, and brings everything back to the starting point."[78] They felt that the suspensions, melodic chromaticism, and "heart-rending" skips by minor sixths and sevenths, which characterized the *tsyganshchina* style, conveyed decadent dissoluteness and lack of will.[79] Lebedinskii asserted that Aleksandr Vertinsky, whose prerevolutionary hits such as *Cocaine Lady* (*Kokainetka*), *Lily White Negro* (*Lilovyi negro*), and *The Long Road* (*Dorogoi dlinnoiu*) remained popular, used cadences commonly found in religious choral music to intensify the "anguished" mix of religion, eroticism, and death that characterized his songs.[80] Nadezhda Briusova claimed that the tawdry sentimentality of the words in songs like *Cut-Glass Tumblers* was emphasized by "sharp" (*rezkii*) tones that "irritated," but remained unresolved, or that an undertone of (sexual) "teasing" was created by the "unexpected" appearance of new tones in the melody of *Tambourine's Jingle* (*Bubna Zvon*) and *All That Was* (*Vse chto bylo*).

RAPM activists also insisted that workers and Komsomol members under the influence of the light genre had less enthusiasm for "social work." *Tsyganshchina* and fox-trots provided diversion and entertainment for workers, but "blunted" their militant, revolutionary aspirations: "*Khaltura* demagnetizes the worker's will, fogs his consciousness, and leads him away from the ranks of the active fighters for socialism. It pulls him back to the old *byt*."[81] RAPM also attributed more specific harmful consequences to the light genre and its proponents. For instance, in 1930 a "hackwork" leader took over the musical stage ("estrada") circle at a large Moscow factory. Soon thereafter, one young circle member performed an anti-Semitic *chastushka* in public and all of the other members quit their political activities. One even withdrew from the Komsomol and the Party. The stage circle was dissolved and the leader fired.[82]

Heartened by recent denunciations of jazz by Gorky and Lunacharsky, RAPM's prudish critique of popular dances also intensified.[83] As with the critique of gypsy music, RAPM blamed excessive syncopation and repetitive melodic and rhythmic elements for the debilitating influences of tangos and fox-trots. RAPM members claimed that the tango's simple, smooth movements cast a hypnotic spell evoking repressed desire and even death, while the fox-trot, characterized as "mechanical" and "lifeless," was equally dangerous—a dance of slaves from the "slave culture of capitalism." Lebedinskii was alarmed to witness the jerky, "unnatural" motions and "trancelike" state of an impromptu fox-trotter at a Komsomol club in 1930.[84] The American-European origins of the tango and fox-trot made them all the more susceptible to RAPM's charge that this music was a "narcotic," the masked weapon of the capitalist wrecker.

RAPM's criticism of fox-trots, tangos, and most gypsy music centered on the "mood" that this music conveyed, whether it inspired unproletarian, unrevolutionary feelings of hopelessness and ennui or erotic arousal. But the Proletarian Musicians found "pseudo-revolutionary" music even more insidious, and reserved particular opprobrium for pieces such as Iulii Khait's *Ever Higher* and *The Young Successors* (*Smena*), as well as songs by Valentin Kruchinin and the Pokrass brothers. They felt that the "bold" and "revolutionary" lyrics of these songs were undermined by music that was "trite," "hackneyed," and reminiscent of a "cheap little chansonette." In an effort to prove this, one RAPM activist set the melody of *Ever Higher* in a duet with a music hall song to expose the similarities in structure and style of the two pieces (Example 12).[85] But although the melodic structure of *Ever Higher* made it possible to pair Khait's song with the chansonette, the simple accompaniment of the latter deprives *Ever Higher* of its chromaticized cadence and throws off the phrasing by a measure. The "duet" altered the mood of *Ever Higher* beyond recognition and "proved" little about Khait's piece as a whole.

RAPM's use of images of corporal corruption (from sex to narcotics) to denounce the light genre certainly corroborates Eric Naiman's analysis of how anxieties about the legitimacy of Bolshevik rule and the future of the revolution were projected into discourse about the body, sex, and communicable disease during NEP. Naiman has suggested that in other arenas the "Gothic anxieties haunting Soviet ideology began to evaporate" with the advent of the First Five-Year Plan and the return of ideological purity and militancy.[86] Yet while RAPM had always focused on what it identified as the "contaminating" influences of *tsyganshchina* and fox-trots, its critique of this music in the twenties had been relatively staid. The shocking, explicit

Example 12 R. G., *Shliapa paradi*. Russian text by N. Kh. Epikur. Set as a duet with the melody of *Ever Higher* (*Vse vyshe*) (see also example 4b). V. Vinogradov, *Sud nad muzykal'noi khalturoi*. Moscow: Gosudarstvennoe muzykal'noe izdatel'stvo, 1931.

metaphors that Naiman associates with the ideological uncertainties of NEP appear in RAPM's discourse only after 1929, suggesting that the environment of the Great Break exacerbated rather than resolved the Proletarian Musicians' ideological dilemmas and insecurities.

RAPM's attack on the light genre sharpened its conflicts with the modernists, who often included jazz motifs or fox-trots in their serious compositions to characterize the bustle or decadence of modern life. Shostakovich was particularly zealous in his appropriation of popular urban styles. Meierhold's use of jazz and modernist pieces (by Prokof'ev, Stravinsky, and Hindemith, among others) as incidental music in his theatrical productions made him a favorite object of RAPM's ire. Vladimir Blium's defense of the light genre, based on an insistence that without text music was nothing more than pure mathematical relationships, exacerbated RAPM's conflict with the ASM/VOSM.[87]

At the grassroots level, RAPM used practical, didactic strategies to expose the perceived evils of the light genre. In addition to articles published in its journals, it made direct efforts to win the leaders of workers' music circles and "socially active" workers over to the cause. RAPM members made oral presentations and organized demonstrations of "good" and "bad" music for amateur music organizations. After June 1930, they promoted agitational "trials" of "hackwork," scripting "backward" workers, hooligans, and hackwork composers as the defenders of *The Young Successors* and *Tahiti Trot* (Boris Fomin's version of Vincent Youman's *Tea for Two*). Politically conscious workers and music specialists who supported the Sixteenth Party Congress's position on cultural enlightenment work, on the other hand, extolled the merits of Davidenko's *Today We Are All Sailors* (*Vse my segodnia matrosy*) and Boris Shekhter's *Relay Race* (*Estafeta*).[88]

As the Cultural Revolution unfolded, RAPM encountered some support of its campaign against the light genre, as well as concerted resistance. The widespread and long-lingering suspicion of monetary profit and hatred of commercialism that underpinned a range of cultural developments in this period certainly worked to RAPM's advantage in its persecution of the "Nepman-hackwork-composers," for whom song writing had been a lucrative business.[89] The elimination of private enterprise and the state's consolidation of control over the publishing industry facilitated its campaign against the light genre. It also applauded the dissolution of the AMA and the sentencing of its leader, Anatolii Pereselentsev, to four years of hard time for corruption early in 1930. A purge and administrative shake-up of Glaviskusstvo in February of that year set the agency on a more militant course at last. "Hidden friends" of the light genre and other "reactionaries" and "wreckers" lost their positions in the bureaucracy. This included Roslavets, who was drummed out of his positions at Glavrepertkom and Glaviskusstvo.[90]

But even with these changes RAPM was not entirely successful in dominating strategically positioned musical institutions and administrative agencies. In February 1930 it failed in its bid for control of the composers' section of Vseroskomdram (the All-Russian Society of Composers and Dramatists), an association formed from the merging of two authors' associations, MODPIK (the Moscow Society of Dramatic Writers and Composers) and the Union of Dramatists. Despite RAPM's strong-arm tactics at the elections for the unified section's provisional board, Vladimir Messman (1898–1972), a band director, champion of light music, and previous secretary of MODPIK, retained that position in the new administration, which was headed by Reinhold Gliere.[91] The authors' associations offered collective support to their members, especially in the negotiation and collection of royalties. Although many musicians belonged to Rabis, the art workers' union, at this point they had no organization comparable to FOSP, the writers' union organized in 1925 that included "fellow travelers" as well as members of RAPP and other literary factions. From its inception, the composers' section of Vseroskomdram would serve as a nascent union for the musicians and as an alternative organizational center from which to combat RAPM's influence.

The difficulty of consolidating political control over musical institutions reflected a more problematic condition undermining RAPM's chances for success. The music the Proletarian Musicians opposed was genuinely popular and widespread—a profoundly troubling condition that they explained in terms of the pervasive influences of degenerate, bourgeois culture and (until recently) capitalist economic relations. Most of their strategy for eradicating musical "hackwork" assumed that this music's evils became evident with careful, directed listening. But even the carefully selected testimonials from music circle members and activists in *Proletarian Musician* and *For Proletarian Music* indicate that the scales did not fall from people's eyes quite so easily.[92] RAPM leaders faced an uphill struggle to win over the very leaders of clubs and amateur music groups on whom they depended to deliver and instill the message. Throughout the Cultural Revolution RAPM's staunchest activists continued to assail not just the ordinary worker's attachment to *Little Bricks*, but repeated instances in which Komsomol members and Party officials sang, paraded to, or danced to gypsy music, fox-trots, or worse, seeing nothing ideologically dangerous about doing so.[93] While Lebedinskii and others steadfastly insisted that proletarian victory over NEP music was just around the corner, others acknowledged that the struggle against the light genre was only the first stage of a prolonged campaign to improve the cultural life of Russia's toiling masses.[94]

The challenges that haunted the Left's earlier efforts to write music for the revolution also remained. Educational campaigns and administrative efforts to eradicate the light genre would only be successful if RAPM could provide palatable and attractive substitutes for the music it criticized. In place of *tsyganshchina* and fox-trots RAPM offered "revolutionary, proletarian music," songs from the international revolutionary movement and the prerevolutionary underground, and selections from the nineteenth-century classical repertoire. Virtually all of the compositions RAPM promoted as "its own" were written by the former leaders of Prokoll: Davidenko, Belyi, Koval', Chemberdzhi, and Shekhter. The ORK veteran Vasil'ev-Buglai joined this *kuchka* as a more or less genuine "proletarian composer."[95]

Most importantly, RAPM embraced the mass song as the cornerstone of proletarian music and devoted considerable energy to its propagation.[96] It insisted that all members work on composing mass songs, and demanded that "fellow travelers" also write them as a step in their "reeducation." Embedded within RAPM's ideology and practice, however, were intractable obstacles that undermined its efforts to compose proletarian mass songs.

RAPM's rejection of most genuinely popular musical idioms, including virtually all popular urban styles, left it with a narrow range of ideologically acceptable musical material. It continued to affirm that traditional folk songs had "great artistic value" and defended Davidenko's use of folk song idioms in his most successful pieces, such as *Budennyi's Cavalry* and *They Wanted to Vanquish Us* (*Nas pobit' pobit' khoteli*). But RAPM activists insisted that folk songs themselves were not appropriate for the consciousness of the contemporary worker or collective farmer.[97] In 1930 the only piece that Lebedinskii felt truly warranted designation as a proletarian mass song was Belyi's *Workers of the World* (*Proletarii vsekh stran*).[98] The Left's aversion to lyricism, already evident in Prokoll's debates in the twenties, also hardened. Like the militants affiliated with the *Litfront* faction within RAPP, RAPM composers tried to banish all traces of individual emotions, which they called "psychologism," from their work. They felt that personal emotions diverted attention away from social themes and the tasks of politically influencing the masses.[99] While the vocal music RAPM criticized treated a broad range of human experiences and emotions, its own songs focused on a discrete set of themes: the travails and exploits of the revolutionary period, Lenin's leadership, the historic destiny of Soviet youth, the transformation of the countryside, and the glory of the armed forces, especially the air force.

Eschewing lyricism, especially its romantic variant, RAPM composers wanted to write music that was "bold" and "infused with brave emotion." They made generous use of fanfares and predictable uplifting modulations from a minor verse to a major refrain. But their equation of "bold" with march tempos and dotted rhythms yielded work that was much less distinctive than the *tsyganshchina* they abhorred.[100] The restrictions they placed on musical material inevitably produced stilted, cookie-cutter *agitki* much like ORK's pieces that they had so despised.

RAPM's music was also too "hard" to gain popularity. The group wanted to write "music for millions," yet it never produced simple, accessible tunes that could catch on quickly. The pieces of the former Prokoll members did get less complicated in these years, but remained too difficult for their intended audience. Many of the group's mass songs were not terribly easy to sing, and the piano or accordion accompaniments were often moderately difficult as well.

RAPM steadfastly refused to "write down" to their audience. Indeed, it remained hostile to the very notion of accessibility. Instead, the group's ideologues advanced an argument often made about modern music, insisting that an audience's "resistance" to new music was a measure of its validity and eventual durability. They did not want to meet the masses on their current level, but wanted their songs "to change and enrich the masses' psyche."[101] Although they underwent constant soul-searching to identify the musical language that would deserve the designation "proletarian," their ideology convinced them that the form and content of this new music would have clear debts to the "best" of the nineteenth-century legacy. Indeed, at some level, with the exception of Davidenko and Vasil'ev-Buglai, they rejected indigenous "popular" musical culture altogether. Instead they worked to create a new kind of "classical" music that would be embraced by the masses once they had been delivered from the corrupting influences of bourgeois mentalities and had their own cultural level raised with rudimentary music lessons,[102] instruction on how to appreciate opera,[103] and exposure to Beethoven, Brahms, Mendelssohn, and Musorgsky.[104]

Expertise and Accessibility: The Limits of Proletarian Hegemony and Modernism

RAPM's efforts to reform popular music foundered on its inability to produce catchy, compelling songs that were accessible and popular. At some level, the group's composers recognized their limits, always cautioning that their music still represented just the first "sprouts" of proletarian music, and that "contradictions and weaknesses" remained.[105] But ideology also informed their choice of genre. They focused overwhelmingly on short vocal pieces because they thought these forms best served the needs of the mass audience.[106]

A shortage of expertise and talent also doomed RAPM's struggle for hegemony within the professional musical community. RAPM's concerns about the ideological implications of instrumental music and "major forms," such as symphonies and operas, had figured prominently in the debates over formalism in the twenties. But as the discussions of the commemorative pieces for 1927 indicated, there was a widespread consensus that the revolutionary age demanded music that was magnificent and monumental. Despite all of RAPM's talk about such art, however, its members' own efforts to create large-scale works were few in number and evaluated less than favorably even by RAPM critics.

After *October's Path* was finally finished, Davidenko's group arranged an accompaniment for orchestra. This new version was performed a few times in January 1929, but met a lukewarm response even in potentially sympathetic quarters. RAPM's Iurii Keldysh applauded Prokoll's effort to create a new form for revolutionary content, but felt the oratorio lacked coherence.[107] Other critics agreed that the piece was stylistically too disparate and betrayed the "immaturity" of its composers, even though Prokoll members were contemporaries of Shostakovich and Mosolov. Aleksandr Veprik noted that the orchestration was done "without mastery," in such a way that the accompaniment drowned out the singers.[108]

After the collective failure of *October's Path*, Davidenko worked for nearly two years on his first major work, an opera about the Civil War titled *The Year 1919* (*1919 god*, also known as *Pod"em vagona*). When just one of the opera's acts was finally performed in November 1931 at a factory club, RAPM critics applauded this "first significant attempt" to write large-scale proletarian music and devoted an entire issue of both *Proletarian Musician* and *For Proletarian Music* to the piece. Yet Keldysh and Lebedinskii also found serious technical flaws in the work's music and criticized Davidenko's portrayal of the masses during the Civil War.[109] Other composers scoffed at the technical shortcomings of the opera, and suggested that the group's preference for short songs reflected a lack of expertise with the techniques of orchestration.[110]

Issues of expertise and accessibility were thus decisive factors in RAPM's failure to establish credibility among professional musicians and its efforts to reach a mass audience. A brief look at two works by Shostakovich in these years indicates how accessibility, technique, and efforts to combine popular and elite cultural forms were equally central to the reception of music written outside RAPM's orbit, further demonstrating the limits of RAPM's influence.

While RAPM's composers never overcame their lack of technique, Shostakovich, on the other hand, had an abundance of technical ability, but found that accessibility was an obstacle for his work. The Cultural Revolution coincided with the peak of his most daring youthful creativity. In these years he produced the Third Symphony (*To the First of May*), his first opera, two ballets, and several scores for the theater and film. His opera *The Nose* (*Nos*) and the ballet *The Golden Age* (*Zolotoi vek*) were both highly original, fiendishly difficult works that challenged generic traditions and the expectations of performers and audiences. RAPM responded negatively to both works, and after 1936 both were denounced for their formalism. But RAPM's hostility had little effect on the reception of either work during the Cultural Revolution.

The Nose, based on Gogol's grotesque short story about a bureaucrat's struggle to recover his missing nose, had been scheduled for production at the Leningrad Malyi Theater in the 1928–29 season, but was in rehearsal for nearly a year and a half.[111] In the age of *Wozzek* and *Der ferne Klang*, *The Nose* was still an unusual work, employing the montage technique of successive "frames" and a raft of unorthodox vocal and instrumental effects. Excerpts of the opera were performed for the delegates to the All-Russian Music Conference in 1929. In the discussion that ensued, RAPM praised Shostakovich's talent and skill, but criticized the opera for being overly complicated, remote from contemporary concerns, and preoccupied with naturalistic imitations of physiological processes such as sneezing and nose blowing.[112] But this critique did not prevent the production from going forward. *The Nose* finally had its premiere in January 1930, and received fourteen performances over the next six months and two the following season.

Shostakovich's first ballet, *The Golden Age*, related the fortunes of a Soviet soccer team's tour to capitalist "Faschland" and the efforts of a Western variety dancer, "Diva," to seduce the captain of the team.[113] The ballet incorporated gymnastics, fox-trot, a tap dance, and elements of contemporary urban life such as parades and olympiads—devices used in the political reviews put on by the Blue Blouse theater troupes. A parody of the capitalist West, *The Golden Age* was part detective story, part variety show. The ballet blurred the line between high and popular culture in provocative ways, evoking the music hall and the parade in an art form that set its standards by Tchaikovsky and Glazunov. RAPM particularly objected to Shostakovich's setting of Vincent Youman's fox-trot, *Tea for Two* (*Tahiti Trot*), which provided the entr'acte to the third act, and was also performed as an independent number in symphonic concerts.[114] Yet the ballet's premiere on October 26, 1930, was a "great and noisy success."[115] *The Golden Age* was given nineteen performances in Leningrad that season and also played in Kiev and Odessa.

For both *The Nose* and *The Golden Age*, accessibility and technical difficulty were far more problematic than RAPM's hostility. The performers of both works complained at the time of the excessive demands placed on them, or confessed later that they did not really understand or appreciate the music. Bewildered by the complexity of Shostakovich's scores and confused by the encroachment of popular culture in quintessentially elitist forms, audiences were hard pressed to make sense of the grotesque parody of *The Nose* or the slapstick satire of *The Golden Age.* The film director Grigorii Kozintsev later recalled his first impressions of *The Nose:*

> Gogol's grotesque raged around us; what were we to understand as farce, what as prophecy? The incredible orchestral combinations, texts seemingly unthinkable to sing ("And what makes your hands stink?" sung Major Kovalyov) . . . the unhabitual rhythms (the mad accelerando when the Nose is being beaten up at the police station and the chorus shrieks: "Take that, take that, and that!"); the incorporating of the apparently anti-poetic, anti-musical, vulgar, but what was in reality the intonation and parody of real life—all this was an assault on conventionality.[116]

The "uncompromising avant-garde aesthetic"[117] of *The Nose* failed to revolutionize the operatic stage just as Belyi's *Workers of the World* failed to revolutionize popular song. Belyi foundered due to insufficient talent and skill, while in this instance at least, Shostakovich was undone by an excess of technical facility and daring innovation. But while the inaccessibility of these stage works thwarted their success, Shostakovich's ability and mastery earned him respect in all quarters of the musical community. Authority based on skill and peer recognition of ability and accomplishment would prove essential in the decisive struggles on the musical front.

Moderation at the Peak of Radicalism: Specialists and the Quest for a Marxist Musicology

One of the most significant of these struggles focused on the search for a theoretical approach to music that could be identified as Marxist. The revolution had provided a powerful impetus to theoretical research in music. Beginning in the studios of Proletkul't during the Civil War, musicians found numerous avenues through which to pursue research into the formal, acoustical, and theoretical dimensions of musical creativity. Debates over formalism, atonality, ultrachromaticism, and the implications of the revolution for music fueled a diverse array of theoretical inquiry at the research institutes GIMN, GAKhN, and GIII. While the foundations for Asaf'ev's work on form, Konius's metrotectonic analysis, Garbuzov's explorations of acoustics, various "sociological" approaches, and Iavorskii's theory of modal rhythm had all been laid before 1917, the need to come to terms with Marxism in the cultural realm affected all of these research agendas in some fashion. In 1930, a peculiar confluence of circumstances brought Iavorskii's research into the forefront of an effort to identify a Marxist musical science.

Iavorskii's theory of modal rhythm aroused enthusiasm in this period for many of the reasons that Nikolai Marr's Japhetic theory came to dominate the field of linguistics. At a time when many intellectuals felt an increasing need to develop a coherent Marxist theory of culture, Marr promoted a linguistic theory that foresaw linguistic unification—the evolution of one common language that would be spoken in a classless society. This unified language would emerge from the repeated "hybridization" of the tongues of people brought together by common economic need.[118] Iavorskii's theory of modal rhythm, which explained all musical development in terms of the instability of the tritone, was comparably grandiose, but had more scholarly integrity than Marr's linguistics. Yet while Marr's Japhetic theory gained a prominence and official backing during the Cultural Revolution that it maintained for twenty years, Iavorskii's ideas received only limited endorsement for reasons that illustrate the limits of radicalism and the persistence of moderation in the musical realm.

Like Marr's linguistics, universal claims made Iavorskii's theory of modal rhythm both compelling and contentious. Iavorskii considered music a natural phenomenon—a form of expression and communication with demonstrable auditory principles and many commonalities with speech. "Intonations," the inflection of sounds, gave meaning to speech as well as music. Like Ferdinand de Saussure, he understood language as a system of signs in which there was no intrinsic link between the signifier and signified, and insisted that the study of music not be limited to its written form. Hence his emphasis on "learning by listening" in his pedagogy and his scholarly work. While other theoretical approaches to music focused on formal or harmonic analysis, Iavorskii maintained that the principles of musical structure and meaning were revealed in the relationships between musical tones as they unfold in time. These relationships were defined by principles of "tonal gravitation" that determined the regular changes between different forms of stability and instability, or the establishment and disruption of equilibrium in musical speech.[119]

The complexity and constant evolution of these ideas made them difficult to popularize. Iavorskii was also reluctant to publish his work, which prevented him from promoting it more aggressively in the twenties.[120] But the "dialectical" nature of tonal gravitation and Iavorskii's emphasis on the "natural" principles that guided it attracted those interested in identifying an appropriately materialist foundation for Marxist musicology. The fact that Iavorskii's scholarly work informed a pedagogical method (*slushanie muzyki*) that was widely used in workers' clubs as well as at the *pedfak* and First Musical Technicum made modal rhythm seem more accessible to those in training and more applicable to everyday life than traditional theories. Most importantly, for those hoping to identify and regulate the content of artistic expression, considering music as a form of communication analogous to speech opened up the possibility that music meant something, offering a method for evaluating its content.

Support for Iavorskii's theories varied according to political and professional affiliation. The most enthusiastic champions of modal rhythm were Komsomol members and young faculty at the conservatory, whose zeal had intensified in the wake of the attack on the *pedfak*. Given their opposition to Iavorskii over *tipizatsiia* and admissions, the Proletarian Musicians' relationship with Iavorskii was marked more by hostility than by goodwill. Their support for modal rhythm in this period was lukewarm and quickly dissipated. Yet Iavorskii was respected in academic circles. He influenced Asaf'ev's thinking on mode and formal development, and was admired by the young Shostakovich. But the professional musical community rejected modal rhythm's broad and essentially unprovable claims, as well as its challenge to the legitimacy of other approaches. These contrasting evaluations set the stage for an official conference on modal rhythm that exemplified the complexities of the Cultural Revolution in music.

In the face of increasing clamor from Iavorskii's young supporters in the Komsomol and on the conservatory faculty, Narkompros agreed to hold a conference to determine the extent to which modal rhythm adhered to the principles of dialectical materialism and could serve as a point of departure for Marxist musical science. Iavorskii's longtime supporter, Lunacharsky, convened the All-Union Conference on the Theory of Modal Rhythm on February 5, 1930, in the recital hall of the Moscow Conservatory. Iavorskii's supporters hoped that the conference would certify the Marxist credentials of modal rhythm and thus give them more ammunition with which to shake up the curriculum at the conservatory. But instead of a pep rally exalting the Marxist virtues of modal rhythm, the conference served as a forum for a two-pronged attack on Iavorskii's ideas from the heart of the musical establishment.

Iavorskii's first critic was the music historian Mikhail Ivanov-Boretskii. In 1928 Ivanov-Boretskii had opposed the *pedfak* and helped ensure that "classic" approaches to musical form and harmony remained at the core of the theory curriculum. Now he used his erudition and fluency with Marxist jargon to undermine claims about modal rhythm's applicability to all music and its compatibility with dialectical materialism.[121] Ivanov-Boretskii identified precursors of Iavorskii's basic premise—that the tritone is the major source of musical instability—in theories of music dating to the late eighteenth and early nineteenth centuries. The originality of Iavorskii's theory lay not in this idea but in his elaboration of it. Ivanov-Boretskii pointed out that modal rhythm had been formulated in an effort to understand the musical language of impressionism. Since impressionism reflected and validated the worldview of the bourgeoisie in its period of decline and fall, he asserted that modal rhythm could in no way be considered Marxist. It had simply become "overgrown" with Marxist phraseology in the last few years.[122] Citing the constantly evolving nature of Iavorskii's work and the few published elaborations of it, Ivanov-Boretskii insisted that the theory needed more time to develop, as well as a thorough methodological evaluation by the Communist Academy.

A more partisan critique was presented by Nikolai Garbuzov, who sought support for his own work on the acoustical bases of harmony.[123] Garbuzov claimed that Iavorskii overlooked the purely physical characteristics of musical sounds and reiterated his earlier assertion that "the basic thesis of modal rhythm opposes the givens of acoustics."[124] Rejecting Iavorskii's concept of the "gravitation of tones" as an imprecise and misleading metaphor, Garbuzov instead maintained that an "acoustical affinity" determined the relationship between tones that was analogous to the affinity between chemical elements. Garbuzov claimed that through "pure" experimentation with overtones one could discover the natural combination of tones that lie at the base of modal structures.[125]

Modal rhythm's most vocal champions included Iavorskii's former pupil Arnol'd Al'shvang (1898–1960) and Lev Kulakovskii (1897–?), both recently hired as teachers of music history and folklore at the conservatory. Nadezhda Briusova and several other proponents of Iavorskii's pedagogical methods were unable to deliver their speeches due to the long-windedness of the main speakers. Iavorskii's own presentation and response to his critics lasted nearly five hours and left everyone confused. The most effective defender of modal rhythm was Lunacharsky. Although he was no longer the head of Narkompros, Lunacharsky's comments carried the authoritative weight of technical expertise. He rebutted the major objections raised against modal rhythm by Garbuzov and Ivanov-Boretskii, identified the most valuable aspects of Iavorskii's theory, and indicated its weaknesses. His speech shaped and explained the resolutions adopted at the conference's end.

Lunacharsky acknowledged that Marxist phraseology had only recently been applied to modal rhythm, but asserted that the theory itself was inherently dialectical and had "found in Marxism its natural ally."[126] He drew explicit comparisons to Marr's linguistic theories, which were also difficult to understand and predated the revolution, but which had become more intelligible "under the influence" of dialectical materialism.[127] He claimed that Garbuzov's uncritical application of physical-acoustical principles to music kept him from appreciating the unique merits of modal rhythm. Where others saw exaggerated claims, Lunacharsky found Iavorskii's method valuable because it could explain all types of musical forms. Because it emphasized perception it turned the analyst's attention away from strictly physical phenomena and toward psychological factors. Since these factors (in Lunacharsky's approach to Marxism) were subordinated to social elements, Iavorskii had found the potential for revealing and understanding the social meaning of music.[128] Here was the great potential of modal rhythm.

Lunacharsky maintained that even without philosophical, theoretical proof, millions of listeners felt that music did have content—that its purely musical structure had some kind of deep meaning "relating to life itself."[129] But until now, no one had attempted to find social meaning in the purely musical sphere. To be sure, not all music was programmatic, but even the most "pure" constructions (those following only purely musical logic) had a living, spiritual, psychological-social content. Modal rhythm had the potential to reveal and identify that content.

Lunacharsky asserted that Iavorskii had revealed the "law" governing the movement of sounds. This law was found not only in acoustics, but also in the place that acoustic phenomena, as they are perceived by the ear, form our sensation and depiction of the objective world in our musical thinking. Lunacharsky confirmed the claims made more polemically, and less convincingly, by Al'shvang and Kulakovskii; namely, that Iavorskii's theory provided music—which did not express social content in concrete, logical sounds—

with a materialist foundation. Modal rhythm also opened up the possibility of scientifically researching those particular qualities of musical thought, ideas, and style that make a given construction the reflection of social reality.[130]

The conference resolutions recognized the importance of modal rhythm and affirmed that it offered *one* approach both to a purely materialist and dialectical theory of music and to Marxist methods of researching music history. But the resolutions did not privilege modal rhythm over other theories in musical science and pedagogy, since it lacked complete scientific exposition and adequate textbooks. The resolutions called for continued research and exposition of the theory and approved its expanded use in music education at all levels.

Given the uncompromising atmosphere of the Cultural Revolution, the course and outcome of the modal rhythm conference are striking in a number of respects. The conference resolutions are astonishingly moderate. In acknowledging modal rhythm's weaknesses as well as strengths and in refraining from giving it unqualified preference over other theories, these resolutions mirror the tone and substance of the Party's earlier decrees on artistic policy in 1920 and 1925 that defended the cultural legacy of the past and declined to give a mandate to militant proponents of proletarian culture.

This echoing of earlier, conservative policy statements was clearly at odds with the aggressive assertion of proletarian hegemony, which was at its peak in 1930. As such, it points to the fairly moderate nature of the Cultural Revolution in music and to the assertive and influential role of the prerevolutionary intelligentsia in the upheaval. The proletarianization of the conservatories and the campaign against light genre music represent the pressure "from below" that is central to Fitzpatrick's interpretive paradigm of the Cultural Revolution. But the modal rhythm conference indicates that some of the battles with the most significant long-term impact on Soviet music were dominated neither by zealous, if dubiously competent, proletarian elements nor by a master script written by Party authorities. The men who were most influential came from "the middle," or even more accurately, "the past."[131] As indicated by RAPM's quandaries about writing large-scale works, ability and competency were indispensable to success on the musical front. Iavorskii's professional and chronological peers shaped the form and outcome of the debate on modal rhythm because no one else had the technical expertise to participate fully in the discussion. Ivanov-Boretskii's contribution was especially important. An accomplished professional and veteran of many debates over the Sovietization of musical life, he could easily use the language of materialism and Marxism to identify modal rhythm's shortcomings in these areas without completely discrediting Iavorskii's work. He thus prevented the radicals (soon to be denounced for their "vulgar sociology") from monopolizing an analytical approach to music that he found valuable but unjustified in its claims to universality.[132]

The "excesses" of the Cultural Revolution at the conservatories and in the concert halls soon would be tamed and reversed, resulting in little lasting effect. But for the most part, the resolutions of the modal rhythm conference would stick. In the thirties Iavorskii's approach to musical analysis would become an important component of Soviet musicology and music theory. Although modal rhythm would not be adopted wholesale, Iavorskii's method, particularly his conceptions of intonation (*intonatsiia*) and mode, would gain widespread acceptance in the ideas of others, especially Asaf'ev, as the conceptual underpinnings of socialist realism in music.[133]

The Sixteenth Party Congress and After

RAPM's position and influence soon became even more tenuous than the persistent disagreement about the "difficulty" of the mass song and the outcome of the modal rhythm conference suggest. In the summer of 1930, the resolutions of the Sixteenth Party Congress, held from June 26 to July 13, thrust the Cultural Revolution in a more practical direction by summoning it into more direct service of the social and economic tasks of the First Five-Year Plan. Activists from the entire spectrum of the cultural front were instructed to "fill all cultural-enlightenment work with socialist content."[134] This demand made RAPM's task even more difficult, because music now had to be a completely utilitarian vehicle for promoting political and economic campaigns. The increased emphasis on fulfilling the Five-Year Plan meant that the range of acceptable topics for RAPM composers became even more narrow—they were enjoined to write only about industrialization, collectivization, socialist competition, and so forth. Keeping up with the ever-changing political climate presented daunting challenges captured succinctly by the head of music publishing, who complained that "we don't know in February what the slogans will be in May, and therefore we can't get the May Day compositions ready in time."[135] During this final phase of the Cultural Revolution, from June 1930 to the summer of 1931, RAPM's fortunes were clearly in decline as the organization scrambled to address directives from above that were often totally at odds with its long-stated goals of purging both elite and popular music of the degenerate legacy of the past and democratizing access to music and musical institutions.

Although its chief ideologues, who were not composers, held tight to the doctrine of "resistance" plus Beethoven and Musorgsky, RAPM never achieved complete consensus on this agenda even within the organization, and even at the peak of the Cultural Revolution. Participants in a discussion about the proletarian mass song at the Communist Academy in October 1930 still advanced ORK's position that the mass song must be easily understood.[136] Others countered the RAPM position that genuinely popular songs such as *We Will Go to Battle Boldly*, which had perfectly acceptable texts, were indeed "corrupted" by politically suspect melodies.

More ominous signs of official dissatisfaction with RAPM's work soon surfaced. In January 1931 a staged denunciation of the VOSM and its leader, Vladimir Blium, held at the Communist Academy, became as much a referendum on RAPM as an attack on the modernists. One academy member faulted RAPM for remaining a group of "professionals," rather than a mass organization, and noted that RAPM had far more declarations and theoretical battles to its credit than actual music.[137] Another branded RAPM's ideology a "left deviation," insisting that the group needed a more inclusive, sophisticated stance on the musical legacy and a more conciliatory policy toward the "fellow travelers."[138] In his concluding remarks, Lebedinskii plumbed new rhetorical depths, rebutting these charges while acknowledging that RAPM remained small and not entirely effective. To become the equivalent of RAPP for music, he pleaded, RAPM needed help from the Party, the working class, and RAPP itself.[139]

Criticism of RAPM's work found more formal articulation in the resolutions to the organization's first and only All-Russian Conference, which was held in March 1931, a scant three months before Stalin signaled the end of official sponsorship for the Cultural Revolution by calling for better relations with the intelligentsia and denouncing the radical theorizing of Communist intellectuals.[140] While they ostensibly endorsed RAPM's agenda and programs, the conference resolutions in fact reiterated and elaborated on the organization's weaknesses raised at the debate with the VOSM.[141] The resolutions also reflected the confusion that resulted from the elision of the authorities' caution regarding old specialists and their efforts to mobilize everyone behind the goals of the First Five-Year Plan. Neither the resolutions nor RAPM members acknowledged that the tasks assigned to RAPM were at best incoherent and at worst blatantly contradictory: how was the group supposed to be both the leader of a mass movement of musical propaganda *and* "win over" the "fellow travelers"?

Emboldened by the widening chinks in RAPM's armor and the encouragement implicit in Stalin's rehabilitation of the bourgeois specialists, leaders of the musical community began to mobilize against the radical theorists and establish alternative organizational centers. Expertise and authority among one's peers began to have more currency than a particular ideology and rhetoric. In August a group of nine "fellow travelers" declared their intent to work closely with RAPM to help build socialism. Led by Miaskovskii and Vissarion Shebalin, "the nine" promised not only to "master Marxist-Leninist methodology" and mass songs, but to embrace the "primary task" of work on symphonies and operas.[142] No one really considered this gesture sincere, but the emphasis on major forms pointed to RAPM's most glaring deficiency. A few weeks later, Shostakovich issued his own "declaration of a composer's responsibility," lamenting the demise of purely instrumental music and the "catastrophic" situation on the musical front. Repudiating composers' flight (including his own) to "applied" (*prikladnaia*) work for theater and film, Shostakovich announced his own intent "to return to the symphony," thus implicitly rejecting RAPM's aesthetic and the stifling effects of subordinating art to utilitarian agendas.[143]

In the fall of 1931, the composers' section of Vseroskomdram, which now had nearly 400 members, became the center for an increasingly effective challenge to RAPM. Mikhail Gnesin, previously one of RAPM's few supporters at the conservatory and one of the first composers to write music on a Soviet theme, now emerged as its fierce critic. In October, Gnesin, Shebalin, and other representatives of the composers' section successfully drove a wedge between RAPM and its more powerful ally, RAPP, by conferring with the RAPP leaders who dominated the secretariat of Vseroskomdram and insisting that RAPM representatives not attend. Shebalin, who had just professed his intent to "join forces with RAPM," denounced the organization's influence at the conservatory and in publishing, and accused Davidenko and Belyi of "kulakism" because they hired undergraduates to orchestrate their work. RAPM published 6,500 annotated copies of the meeting's stenogram decrying this "slander," but to little effect.[144] In an effort to relieve the "impoverishment" of musical life wrought by RAPM and the First Five-Year Plan, Vseroskomdram put on several concerts of instrumental music at the Bol'shoi Theater, where RAPM's influence was minimal.

A plenary session of the Vseroskomdram council in December marked the eclipse of RAPM and the coalescence of support for a creative association not dominated by any one faction. Shostakovich and Gnesin led a deftly orchestrated denunciation of RAPM's creative shortcomings and overemphasis on Beethoven and Musorgsky, while representatives of RAPP laundered an exhaustive list of the Proletarian Musicians' ideological deficiencies, their refusal to undertake self-criticism "like good Bolsheviks," and, once again, their failure to produce music: "In literature, and film the arguments are about works. . . . *The Rout*, *Birth of a Hero*, *Bruski* . . . [and the films] *Alone*, *Road to Life*, and *The Golden Hills*. And in music? Mostly about resolutions. Even after the last two years there aren't major, genuine musical compositions, but only debates."[145]

There was, in the end, no music for the Cultural Revolution. RAPM failed in its campaign to cleanse popular culture from its degenerate, petit-bourgeois past because it offered nothing appealing to replace what it condemned. More importantly, its members lacked the ability and expertise to compete with other musicians in the arena of large-scale works. Under the banner of proletarian hegemony RAPM effectively silenced many composers, but it had nothing with which to fill the resulting void. Armed only with ideological zeal that masked traditional aesthetic preferences, RAPM could not prevail in the decisive battles on the musical front. For the Proletarian Musicians, the tactic of "class war" had little support from above and was ineffective on the ground. Given the nonrepresentational nature of musical expression and the difficulties of evaluating musical content in ideological terms, it was the technical expertise and authority among their peers possessed by music's senior specialists and rising stars that mattered most.

EPILOGUE

With the ebbing of the Cultural Revolution the basic features of Soviet musical culture emerged, and it became clear that the musical community had an important role in defining them. As in other areas, bourgeois specialists, many of them trained in the prerevolutionary period, resumed positions of leadership and influence in musical life. The issues that had most concerned musicians in the first decade after the revolution continued to inform developments in the thirties, although broader patterns of political and social consolidation transformed many of them.

In the early weeks of 1932, the Party sent Stanislav Shatskii (1878–1934) to become the director of the Felix Kon Higher Music School. An admirer of Tolstoy's educational theories and a long-time champion of progressive education at Narkompros, Shatskii had studied voice at the Moscow Conservatory at the turn of the century. Under his leadership a large measure of normalcy returned to the conservatory's affairs, beginning with the restoration of the institution's name in October 1932.

Besides restoring order to academic life and returning the portraits of Tchaikovsky, Bach, and Chopin to the recital hall, Shatskii helped establish a Central Special Music School at the conservatory to provide general education and specialized music training for gifted children. The primary impetus for this reincarnation of the preparatory division was Tolstoy's former chess partner, Aleksandr Gol'denveizer, now back in his former position as assistant director. When Juri Jelagin took the arduous entrance exams for the violin program in 1934 he felt that the conservatory had fully recaptured the superior standards that had made it famous before the Great Break.[1] The *pedfak* had already been disbanded, and the elimination of the *rabfak* the following year solidified the conservatory's focus on artistic excellence and the reversal of the innovations that had most challenged that focus in the twenties. Soviet rule had confirmed and strengthened the mission of the "musical university" founded by the Rubinstein brothers nearly seventy years before.

On April 23, 1932, the Central Committee issued a resolution criticizing the sectarianism of RAPP and RAPM and denouncing the factionalism that had plagued artistic life since the revolution, dominating it in the last four years. The Decree on the Reformation of Literary and Artistic Organizations liquidated all independent arts organizations and summoned writers and artists who supported the cause of building Soviet socialism to form creative unions that included a Communist faction. Like other creative intellectuals, musicians greeted the resolution as a liberation from the tyranny of a strident, intolerant minority without fully appreciating that along with support and security the creative unions also would provide unique mechanisms for the control and regulation of artistic expression.

Although the thirties often have been seen as a time of "regimentation" and of increased political intervention in musical life,[2] new research suggests that many of the dynamics that governed musical life in the twenties remained in force after the Cultural Revolution. Caroline Brooke's findings from the archives of the Composers' Union and the state's administrative organs show that the bureaucratic confusion and overlap that was the hallmark of policy formation in the twenties persisted throughout the thirties, even as the network of administrative organs expanded. She also asserts that "there was no coherent Party line" on many musical issues, and assigns musicians "a significant role in defining the boundaries within which they lived and worked."[3] The thirties were a time of increased supervision and bureaucratization, but these processes also facilitated the further entrenchment and increased importance of the social circles and patronage networks that had been so crucial in the twenties. When Alexander Mosolov was sentenced to the camps for "anti-Soviet propaganda" in 1937, his mentors, Reinhold Gliere and Nikolai Miaskovskii, successfully appealed the decision, just as they had overturned Mosolov's expulsion from the conservatory in 1924.[4] As respected members of the musical elite, well-placed individuals such as Miaskovskii, Gliere, and Gol'denveizer remained central to the process by which policies affecting music and musicians were developed and implemented.

Clearly the abstract nature of musical creativity continued to play an important role in the relationship between musicians and the regime, whose representatives found it difficult to censor that which they could not understand or assign meaning to. The regime's most traumatic intervention in musical affairs, the denunciation of Shostakovich in 1936, involved an opera whose libretto and subject matter substantiated claims about the decadence of the music. For the most part, mastery of an abstract art gave musicians room to operate, distancing them from outside scrutiny and positioning them as the only qualified arbiters of acceptability.

The ineffable qualities of instrumental music also meant that the authorities continued to regard music as a less than critical ideological arena. This was seen in the management of musical institutions, the functioning of the regulatory apparatus, and the body count that remains one of the primary yardsticks by which the ravages of Stalinism are measured. The conservatory obviously was not a prestigious appointment for the terminally ill Shatskii, whose educational theories now bore the stigma of "rightism."[5] The Party parked him there while it waited for him to die, reinforcing its now well-established assertion of music's secondary or even tertiary importance. After Shatskii's death in 1934, Genrikh Neigauz, the versatile and distinguished pianist, took over. The conservatory resumed its anomalous status as being the only institution of higher learning in the Soviet Union not administered by a Party member.[6] That same year, Maxim Gorky presided over the adoption of socialist realism as the official aesthetic at the carefully orchestrated and widely publicized inaugural congress of the Writers' Union. The Composers' Union, in contrast, functioned as a loose affiliation of city and republican organizations until the eve of World War II. Its first congress convened only in 1948 in response to the furor of the reinvigorated, xenophobic campaign against formalism and "cosmopolitanism." There were casualties among musicians during the great purges, including the composers Nikolai Zhiliaev and Mikhail Kvadri, who were too closely associated with Marshal Tukhachevksy, the leader of the Red Army, as well as RAPM veteran Dmitrii Gachev, who had ties to Bulgarian Communists.[7] But while the purges devastated the ranks of the nation's leading poets and writers, none of the most prominent composers perished in the terror, and repressed musicians numbered in the dozens, rather than the hundreds or thousands.[8] Conservative aesthetics significantly modified many careers, but most of the individuals affiliated with the ASM and the groups on the musical Left moved on to relatively successful futures.

A notable exception was Nikolai Roslavets, whose fate exemplifies the irony of the artistic avant-garde that was swept away by the revolutionary maelstrom they had hoped to guide. In 1930, Roslavets left Moscow to take a position as music director of the Uzbek Musical Theater in Tashkent and wrote a ballet dedicated "to the struggle for independence of the cotton industry of the USSR."[9] In this piece and the few that followed, he abandoned his synthetic chord technique, turning to meager commissions for medleys of popular mass songs to make ends meet.[10] Unlike Asaf'ev, who suffered few long-term ill effects from his ASM association, or the younger Shostakovich, who found ways to both subvert and uphold the musical dimensions of socialist realism, Roslavets never recovered from the setbacks of the Cultural Revolution. He was admitted to the Composers' Union only in 1940, after a stroke had left him unable to speak and perhaps spared him from planned repression.[11] For decades after his death in 1944 Soviet writers castigated him with a viciousness otherwise reserved for émigrés such as Sabaneev and Lourié, and his works remained unpublished and unperformed.

Just as the abstract nature of music continued to influence the way officials evaluated music's political significance, so did musicians' ongoing efforts to realize certain professional and creative objectives figure prominently in the development of their professional organization. The Composers' Union did serve as a mechanism of regulation and control, but it also enabled musicians to enhance their status in Soviet society and gave them a measure of agency in the system that regulated the production and consumption of music. Kiril Tomoff's groundbreaking dissertation on the All-Union Composers' Union charts the development of a fully professional organization run by highly qualified composers and musicologists.[12] As such, this organization nurtured and monitored the creative work of its members, giving musicians access to the housing, instruments, and other material resources they needed. Musicians thus secured a significant role in the administration of musical life and consolidated their identity as professionals. The Union's closed screening sessions where members could hear their new work performed and discussed by colleagues were designed to help young composers master their craft. They also provided an ideal forum for musicians to monitor their own creativity,[13] bringing to bear claims made repeatedly in the twenties that music had to be evaluated by those with the appropriate expertise. Like the other creative unions, the Composers' Union filled the gap created by the state's forced retreat from cultural affairs during the Cultural Revolution and the Party's unwillingness or inability to assume complete responsibility for cultural policy.[14] The resources and privileges the Union bestowed on its members rewarded musicians for serving the Soviet state and society with their art.

The qualities of the music produced in the thirties illustrate the significance of this book's perspective on musical life in the twenties. The state supported musicians through the Composers' Union, but in return musicians were expected to make significant and positive contributions to Soviet society. This meant that debates about the "meaning" of Soviet music persisted, and concerns about the popular appeal of various styles and pieces remained central to those debates. Thus, modernism survived both RAPM's persecution and the liquidation of the ASM, only to be tamed out of the same kind of concern over Western influences, accessibility, and the prudishness that RAPM had articulated in the twenties, now reinforced by the traditional aesthetics of many musicians and the broader cultural conservatism of Stalinism.[15]

The divide between popular and elite music that so preoccupied reformers in the twenties persisted into the thirties, but was legitimized by the renegotiation and reassertion of traditional cultural hierarchies. In June 1931 Stalin introduced differential wages, marking the official end of the Bolsheviks' commitment to egalitarianism in the workplace. This was one of the first steps of what has been called the Great Retreat, a tactical withdrawal from the more contentious and divisive elements of the revolutionary agenda that laid the foundations for the perplexing hierarchies of privilege and status that would define Stalinist society.[16] The neoconservatism of the Great Retreat accorded respect and privileges to experts, and condoned the aspirations of upwardly mobile workers for a "cultured" lifestyle.[17] An appreciation for classical music characterized this lifestyle, as did the cultivation of table manners and the ability to dance to "Soviet jazz."

Stalinist society was increasingly hierarchical, but a new, integrative social identity also emerged in the thirties, giving people a sense of pride and participation in the building of Soviet socialism even if they personally suffered from the deprivations and coerciveness of the regime's policies. Articulating and supporting this new sense of commonality was a mass culture, controlled by the state, that nonetheless "spoke the language of most people."[18] Mass songs exemplifying the traits identified at the 1926 conference (clear, singable melodies; bold, uplifting rhythms; and so forth) became a mainstay of this mass culture. The puritanical component of the musical Left's critique of light music contributed to the sanitizing of the genre, which avoided many of the melodic conventions and sensualized topics of *tsyganshchina*. But the mass songs of the thirties also incorporated elements of the *tsyganshchina* tradition, as well as influences from Jewish folk music, the Russian folk song, and other urban genres. Unlike their predecessors in the twenties, which had focused almost exclusively on the revolution, the mass songs of the thirties dealt with a broad range of human experience and were closely associated with film, the cornerstone of Stalinist mass culture. Although the personal and the political received a carefully optimistic treatment that was often widely divergent from the realities of Soviet life, millions of Russians embraced the catchy tunes and compelling strains of songs such as Isaac Dunaevsky's *Song of the Motherland* (*Pesnia o rodine*) immortalized by Liubov Orlova in the 1937 film *Circus*. The fact that the most successful mass song composers came from the ranks of the light genre musicians so detested by RAPM reflected the limits of reformist efforts to mold popular taste, as well as the importance to Stalinist culture of genuine popular appeal.[19] The tension between the Great Retreat's embrace of hierarchy and the reification of a unified Soviet society meant that the kings of the mass song such as Dunaevsky and Iulii Khait received the same privileges and Composers' Union membership accorded to Prokofiev and Shostakovich.

Stalinist musical culture had emerged from a collaborative process informed by the interests and preferences of bureaucrats, politicians, and musicians, as well as audiences and consumers. This study has charted the formative stages of that process, suggesting that the twenties were far more than an ill-fated experiment or a prelude to artistic regimentation. The essential dynamics of musicians' relationship with Soviet power were defined in the first years after the revolution, and were influenced by prerevolutionary concerns about musical language, the social status of musicians, the authority of creative intellectuals, and the cultural predilections of educated elites.

Music for the revolution was the product of the unique political and social context of Stalinism that emerged in the thirties and prevailed through the agonies of World War II and the sacrifices of postwar reconstruction. The revolution's music was not heard in the twenties—not in the blare of Avraamov's factory whistles, not in the anguished juxtaposition of French revolutionary songs and an Orthodox funeral hymn in Miaskovskii's Sixth Symphony, and not in the commemorative pieces of 1927. But the debates and developments of the twenties conditioned the ground for the appearance of music in the next decade that would fulfill the aspirations of composers and the expectations of audiences, as well as the often brutal demands of the Soviet regime. When the music for the revolution was heard—in the determined optimism of Dunaevsky's mass songs, the tragic heroism of Shostakovich's *Leningrad Symphony*, and the majestic strains of the new national anthem—so was the legacy of the struggles of the twenties.

NOTES

Introduction

1. Maxim Gorky, *Days with Lenin* (New York, 1932), 52.

2. The coercive and censorial aspects of Soviet culture dominated the attention of previous generations of Western scholars and figure prominently in post-Soviet Russian scholarship. Examples of the former, which focus on literature, include Max Eastman's polemical *Artists in Uniform: A Study of Literature and Bureaucratism* (New York, 1972 [1934]), as well as more balanced assessments such as Edward J. Brown, *Russian Literature Since the Revolution* (Cambridge, 1982 [1963]); Max Hayward and Leopold Lebedz, eds., *Literature and Revolution in Soviet Russia, 1917–1962* (Oxford, 1963); Ronald Hingley, *Russian Writers and Soviet Society, 1917–1978* (New York, 1979). Using newly accessible archival sources, recent Russian scholarship also charts the ruinous effects of the Soviet regime on artistic freedom and expression. See Arlen Blium, *Za kulisami "Ministerstva pravdy": Tainaia istoriia sovetskoi tsenzury, 1917–1929* (St. Petersburg, 1994); Arlen Blium, *Sovetskaia tsenzura v epokhu total'nogo terrora, 1929–1953* (St. Petersburg, 2000); T. M. Goriaeva, ed., *Istoriia sovetskoi politicheskoi tsenzury. Dokumenty i kommentarii* (Moscow, 1997); A. N. Artizov and O. N. Naumov, eds., *Vlast' i khudozhestvennaia intelligentsiia. Dokumenty TsK RKP(b)-VKP(b), VChK-OGPU-NKVD o kul'turnoi politike. 1917–1953 gg.* (Moscow, 1999). For germane studies devoted to music, see Leonid Maksimenkov, *Sumbur vmesto muzyki. Stalinskaia kul'turnaia revoliutsiia, 1936–1938* (Moscow, 1997); A. Bogdanova, *Muzyka i vlast' (poststalinskii period)* (Moscow, 1995).

3. Juri Jelagin, *Taming of the Arts*, trans. Nicholas Wreden (New York, 1951). Western studies of Soviet music echo the interpretive framework alluded to above. Musical life has been defined by a perverse combination of patronage for the musical elite and periodic, arbitrary censorship, as well as the promotion of socialist realism, the official aesthetic whose codes were developed for literature and then crudely adapted to music. Representative scholarship includes Andrei Olkhovsky, *Music under the Soviets: The Agony of an Art* (Westport, 1975 [1955]) and Richard Anthony Leonard, *A History of Russian Music* (Westport, 1977 [1957]). Even the finest scholarship on Soviet music assumes that socialist realism was imposed not only "from above" but also "from outside" and then adapted to music. Boris Schwarz's encyclopedic *Music and Musical Life in Soviet Russia, 1917–1981* (Bloomington, 1983 [1972]) remains the best general source. See also Stanley Dale Krebs, *Soviet Composers and the Development of Soviet Music* (New York, 1970); Francis Maes, *A History of Russian Music: From Kamarinskaya to Babi Yar*, trans. Arnold J. Pomerans and Erica Pomerans (Berkeley and Los Angeles, 2002). For more nuanced musicological assessments of the relationship between musicians and the Soviet state, see Richard Taruskin, *Defining Russia Musically: Historical and Hermeneutical Essays* (Princeton, 1997), especially 81–98, 468–544; Levon Hakobian, *Music of the Soviet Age, 1917–1987* (Stockholm, 1998).

4. On the synthesis of elite and popular forms in the evolution of Soviet culture, see Jeffrey Brooks, *Thank You, Comrade Stalin! Soviet Public Culture from Revolution to Cold War* (Princeton,

2000); Catriona Kelly and David Shepherd, eds., *Constructing Russian Culture in the Age of Revolution: 1881–1940* (Oxford, 1998); Richard Stites, *Russian Popular Culture: Entertainment and Society Since 1900* (Cambridge, 1992). On jazz, see S. Frederick Starr, *Red and Hot: The Fate of Jazz in the Soviet Union* (New York, 1983).

5. Denise Youngblood, *Movies for the Masses: Popular Cinema and Soviet Society in the 1920s* (Cambridge, 1992); Youngblood, *Soviet Cinema in the Silent Era, 1918–1935* (Ann Arbor, 1985); Lynn Mally, *Revolutionary Acts: Amateur Theater and the Soviet State* (Ithaca, 2000); Hugh D. Hudson, *Blueprints and Blood: The Stalinization of Soviet Architecture, 1917–1937* (Princeton, 1994); Peter Konecny, *Builders and Deserters: Students, State, and Community in Leningrad, 1917–1941* (Montreal, 1999); Lisa A. Kirschenbaum, *Small Comrades: Revolutionizing Childhood in Soviet Russia, 1917–1932* (New York, 2000); Anne E. Gorsuch, *Youth in Revolutionary Russia: Enthusiasts, Bohemians, Delinquents* (Bloomington, 2000); William B. Husband, *"Godless Communists": Atheism and Society in Soviet Russia, 1917–1932* (DeKalb, 2000); Daniel Peris, *Storming the Heavens: The Soviet League of the Militant Godless* (Ithaca, 1998); Glennys Young, *Power and the Sacred in Revolutionary Russia: Religious Activists in the Village* (University Park, Pa., 1997).

6. An emerging body of scholarship on Stalinist culture suggests how complex interactions between party and state officials, artists, scholars, and audiences informed cultural production. See Thomas Lahusen, *How Life Writes the Book: Real Socialism and Socialist Realism in Stalin's Russia* (Ithaca, 1997); Sheila Fitzpatrick, *The Cultural Front: Power and Culture in Revolutionary Russia* (Ithaca, 1992); Boris Groys, *The Total Art of Stalinism: Avant-Garde, Aesthetic Dictatorship, and Beyond* (Princeton, 1992); Hans Günther, ed., *The Culture of the Stalin Period* (New York, 1990); Victoria E. Bonnell, *Iconography of Power: Soviet Political Posters under Lenin and Stalin* (Berkeley and Los Angeles, 1997); Evgeny Steiner, *Stories for Little Comrades: Revolutionary Artists and the Making of Early Soviet Children's Books*, trans. Jane Ann Miller (Seattle, 1999); Karen Petrone, *Life Has Become More Joyous, Comrades: Celebrations in the Time of Stalin* (Bloomington, 2000); Brian Kassoff, "The Knowledge Front: Politics, Ideology, and Economics in the Soviet Book Publishing Industry, 1925–1935" (Ph.D. diss., University of California, Berkeley, 2000); David Brandenburger, "The 'Short Course' to Modernity: Stalinist History Textbooks, Mass Culture, and the Formation of Russian Popular Identity, 1934–1956" (Ph.D. diss., Harvard University, 1999).

A number of recent doctoral dissertations address these issues for musical life in the Stalinist period. See Kiril Tomoff, "Creative Union: The Professional Organization of Soviet Composers, 1939–1953" (Ph.D. diss., University of Chicago, 2001); Robin C. LaPasha, "From Chastushki to Tchaikovsky: Amateur Activity and the Production of Popular Culture in the Soviet 1930s" (Ph.D. diss., Duke University, 2001); Caroline Brooke, "The Development of Soviet Music Policy, 1932–1941" (Ph.D. diss., Cambridge University, 1999); Susannah Lockwood Smith, "Soviet Arts Policy, Folk Music, and National Identity: The Piatnitskii State Russian Folk Choir, 1927–1945" (Ph. D. diss., University of Minnesota, 1997).

7. Acknowledging the "huge martyrology" of Soviet arts and letters, Levon Hakobian maintains that the abstract qualities of music actually gave it a privileged position among the arts. See Hakobian, *Music of the Soviet Age*, 12.

8. The complexities and implications of the intelligentsia's quest for authority in the Soviet cultural matrix are articulated in Katerina Clark, *Petersburg: Crucible of Cultural Revolution* (Cambridge, 1995).

9. In an extreme take on more commonly held views, Richard Taruskin asserts that in fact "there simply was no avant-garde in Russian music" before the revolution. Taruskin, *Defining Russia Musically*, 86.

10. Kelly and Shepherd, *Constructing Russian Culture*, 128–29; Robert Rothstein, "Death of the Folk Song?" in *Cultures in Flux: Lower-Class Values, Practices, and Resistance in Late Imperial Russia*, ed. Stephen P. Frank and Mark D. Steinberg (Princeton, 1994), 108–20.

11. The staying power of this group makes musicians a striking exception to the pattern of a generational shift in authority in other areas of creative endeavor such as literature. See Katerina Clark, "The 'Quiet Revolution' in Soviet Intellectual Life," in *Russia in the Era of NEP: Explo-*

rations in Soviet Society and Culture, ed. Shelia Fitzpatrick, Alexander Rabinowitch, and Richard Stites (Bloomington, 1991), 210–30.

12. On the various strands of culturalism, see E. Anthony Swift, *Popular Theater and Society in Tsarist Russia* (Berkeley and Los Angeles, 2002), especially 4–7, 42–46; Jeffrey Brooks, *When Russia Learned to Read: Literacy and Popular Literature, 1861–1917* (Princeton, 1985), 318–33; Joan Neuberger, *Hooliganism: Crime, Culture, and Power in St. Petersburg, 1900–1914* (Berkeley and Los Angeles, 1993), 139, 253–54. Similar "liberal" perspectives also figured prominently in other national contexts. See, for example, Paul Fussell, *The Great War in Modern Memory* (Oxford, 1975).

13. Stephen P. Frank, "Confronting the Domestic Other: Rural Popular Culture and Its Enemies in Fin-De-Siècle Russia," in *Cultures in Flux*, ed. Frank and Steinberg, 96–99.

14. Stites, *Russian Popular Culture*, 12, 20.

15. On the breadth and diversity of the Bolsheviks' cultural agenda, see William G. Rosenberg, ed., *Bolshevik Visions: First Phase of the Cultural Revolution in Soviet Russia* (Ann Arbor, 1990 [1984]); Abbott Gleason, Peter Kenez, and Richard Stites, eds., *Bolshevik Culture: Experiment and Order in the Russian Revolution* (Bloomington, 1985). On the utopian dimensions of the revolution, see Richard Stites, *Revolutionary Dreams: Utopian Vision and Experimental Life in the Russian Revolution* (Oxford, 1989).

16. Detlef Gojowy, *Neue sowjetische Musik der 20er Jahre* (Laaber, 1980); Larry Sitsky, *Music of the Repressed Russian Avant-Garde, 1900–1929* (Westport, 1994); David Haas, *Leningrad's Modernists: Studies in Composition and Musical Thought, 1917–1932* (New York, 1998); Peter Deane Roberts, *Modernism in Russian Piano Music: Skriabin, Prokofiev, and Their Russian Contemporaries*, vols. 1–2 (Bloomington, 1993). Soviet music histories also portrayed this period in terms of factional strife, condemning both the elitist and Western orientation of the modernists and the crude Marxist aesthetics of the proletarian musicians. See *Istoriia russkoi sovetskoi muzyki*, vol. 1 (Moscow, 1956), 35–39; *Istoriia muzyki narodov SSSR*, vol. 1, ed. Iurii Keldysh (Moscow, 1970), 134–40; Liudmila Poliakova, *Soviet Music*, trans. Xenia Danko (Moscow, n.d.), 9–10. A recently published text for conservatory students suggests this interpretive paradigm retains some credibility, at least in some quarters. See Mikhail Tarakanov, ed., *Istoriia sovremennoi otechestvennoi muzyki*, vol. 1 (Moscow, 1995), 25–42.

17. For an unjaundiced view of the creative efforts of these musicians, see Neil Edmunds, *The Soviet Proletarian Music Movement* (Bern, 2000).

18. Maes, *History of Russian Music*, 241.

Chapter 1

1. Faubion Bowers, *Scriabin: A Biography of the Russian Composer, 1871–1915*, vol. 2 (Palo Alto, 1969), 265–66.

2. Feodor Chaliapin, *Pages from My Life*, ed. Katharine Wright, trans. H. M. Buck (New York, 1927), 307. Chaliapin offers additional detail on the incident in his second autobiographical volume, *Man and Mask*, trans. Phillis Megroz (New York, 1932), 239–40.

3. Nikolai Malko, *A Certain Art* (New York, 1966), 136.

4. A classic account that does this is William Henry Chamberlin, *The Russian Revolution 1917–1921*, vol. 1 (Princeton, 1987 [1935]), 313. For a more recent example, see Orlando Figes, *A People's Tragedy: The Russian Revolution 1891–1924* (New York, 1996), 484.

5. *Istoriia russkoi sovetskoi muzyki*, 15; Iurii Keldysh, *Sto let Moskovskoi konservatorii* (Moscow, 1966), 97–98.

6. For a partial list of émigrés, see Schwarz, *Music and Musical Life*, 20. For an overview of the "musical emigration," see Maes, *History of Russian Music*, 271–97.

7. Sergei Prokof'ev, *Materialy, dokumenty, vospominaniia*, ed. S. I. Shlifstein (Moscow, 1961), 161. Quoted in Harlow Robinson, *Sergei Prokofiev: A Biography* (New York, 1987), 137.

8. Iurii Got'e, *Time of Troubles, The Diary of Iurii Vladimirovich Got'e: Moscow, July 8, 1917 to July 23, 1922*, ed. and trans. Terence Emmons (Princeton, 1988), 87, 91, 114, 115.

9. Sheila Fitzpatrick, *The Commissariat of Enlightenment: Soviet Organization of Education and the Arts Under Lunacharsky, October 1917–1921* (Cambridge, 1970), 112–16. For the theaters, see Richard G. Thorpe, "The Management of Culture in Revolutionary Russia: The Imperial Theaters and the State, 1897–1928" (Ph.D. diss., Princeton University, 1991), 77–118.

10. James C. McClelland, "The Professoriate in the Russian Civil War," in *Party, State, and Society in the Russian Civil War: Explorations in Social History*, ed. Diane P. Koenker, William G. Rosenberg, and Ronald Grigor Suny (Bloomington, 1989), 243–44.

11. Gosudarstvennyi istoricheskii arkhiv Leningradskoi oblasti (now the Tsentral'nyi gosudarstvennyi istoricheskii arkhiv Sankt Peterburga), f. 361, op. 11, d. 361, l. a28. Quoted in *Iz istorii sovetskogo muzykal'nogo obrazovaniia. Sbornik materialov i dokumentov*, ed. L. A. Barenboim et al. (Leningrad, 1969), 209.

12. N. A. Mironova, *Moskovskaia konservatoriia. Istoki* (Moscow, 1995), 17.

13. Decree reprinted in *Muzykal'naia zhizn' Moskvy v pervye gody posle Oktiabria*, ed. Svetlana Romanova Stepanova (Moscow, 1972), 80.

14. On the ambiguous outcomes of the All-Russian Conference on the Reform of Higher Education in July 1918, see McClelland, "The Professoriate in the Russian Civil War," 254–58; Fitzpatrick, *Commissariat of Enlightenment*, 73–75.

15. "Otvet narodnogo komissara po prosveshcheniiu A. V. Lunacharskogo na voprosy delegatsii konservatorii, 29 Iiulia, 1918g.," reprinted in Barenboim et al., *Iz istorii sovetskogo muzykal'nogo obrazovaniia*, 218–23.

16. McClelland, "The Professoriate in the Russian Civil War," 256–58; Fitzpatrick, *Commissariat of Enlightenment*, 77.

17. Decree dated September 23, 1918, reprinted in Barenboim et al., *Iz istorii sovetskogo muzykal'nogo obrazovaniia*, 31.

18. Fitzpatrick, *Commissariat of Enlightenment*, 9–10; Michael David-Fox, *Revolution of the Mind: Higher Learning Among the Bolsheviks* (Ithaca, 1997), 74.

19. Isaac Deutscher, introduction to *Revolutionary Silhouettes* by Anatoly Lunacharsky, ed. and trans. Michael Glenny (New York, 1968), 18; Carmen Claudin-Urondo, *Lenin and the Cultural Revolution* (Atlantic Highlands, 1977), 7–33; Stites, *Revolutionary Dreams*, 77. For a discussion of the ways that Lunacharsky's and Lenin's perspectives on education differed in emphasis, see Larry E. Holmes, *The Kremlin and the School House: Reforming Education in Soviet Russia, 1917–1931* (Bloomington, 1991), 4–5.

20. Fitzpatrick, *Commissariat of Enlightenment*, 119–23.

21. For Soviet criticisms of Lourié, see *Istoriia muzyka narodov SSSR*, vol. 1 (Moscow, 1970), 207; *Istoriia russkoi sovetskoi muzyki*, 30; V. Bogdanov-Berzovskii, ed., *V pervye gody sovetskogo muzykal'nogo stroitel'stva* (Leningrad, 1959), 67, 80. For an example of how official opinion softened considerably in the late Soviet period, see I. V. Nest'ev, "Iz istorii russkogo muzykal'nogo avangarda," *Sovetskaia muzyka* 1 (1991): 75–87. For Western assessments, see Sitsky, *Music of the Repressed*, 87–110; Detlef Gojowy, *Arthur Lourié und der russische Futurismus* (Laaber, 1993).

22. Arthur Lourié, *Sergei Koussevitzky and His Epoch* (New York, 1931), 74. For Blok's famous disquisitions on the musical essence of revolution, see Alexander Blok, *The Spirit of Music*, trans. I. Frieman (Westport, 1973 [1946]), 7–19, 68–70; Blok, *Sobranie sochinenii v vos'mi tomakh*, vol. 6, ed. V. N. Orlov, A. A. Surkov, and K. I. Chukovskii (Moscow, 1962), 9–20, 360–63.

23. Leonid Sabaneev, "Three Russian Composers in Paris," *Musical Times* (1927): 882. Like many of the reform projects envisioned by radical intellectuals in this period, Lourié's Musical Universities existed only on paper. See "Osnovnoe polozhenie o gosudarstvennom muzykal'nom universitete. Oktiabr' 1919g.," in *Iz istorii sovetskogo muzykal'nogo obrazovaniia*, ed. Barenboim et al., 39; Edmunds, *Soviet Proletarian Music Movement*, 55–56.

24. On the composer's sartorial habits, see B. Kats and R. Timenchik, *Anna Akhmatova i muzyka: Issledovatel'skie ocherki* (Leningrad, 1989), 32.

25. Sheila Fitzpatrick found at least forty-two departments, subdepartments, committees, subsections, and commissions affiliated with Narkompros at the end of 1918. See Fitzpatrick, *Commissariat of Enlightenment*, 22–23. According to a Rabkrin report on Muzo in October 1920, the section was established on June 1, 1918. Gosudarstvennyi arkhiv Rossiiskoi Federatsii (henceforth "GARF") f. 2306, op. 25, d. 292, l. 10b. This date probably refers to the beginning of the agency's tenure in Moscow, since Muzo's internal report for 1918–19 gives January 1918 as the date of its organization in Petrograd. GARF f. 2306, op. 25, d. 39, l. 1. See also O. Lamm, "Pervye gody raboty Gosudarstvennogo muzykal'nogo izdatel'stva. Dela i liudi," in *Sovetskaia muzyka. Kul'tura, istoriia, traditsii, sovremennost'*, ed. D. G. Daragan (Moscow, 1980), 190.

26. GARF f. 2306, op. 25, d. 353, l. 46. S. R. Stepanova estimates Muzo's staff, including "various instrumental collectives and workshops," in 1920 to be 798, but does not provide the source of her information. See Stepanova, *Muzykal'naia zhizn' Moskvy*, 16.

27. "Polozhenie o muzykal'nom otdele Narodnogo Komissariata po Prosveshcheniiu," in *Iz istorii sovetskogo muzykal'nogo obrazovaniia*, ed. Barenboim et al., 33–34. Reprinted from *Zhizn' iskusstva*, November 22, 1918.

28. Muzo's activities are described in *Kalendar'-spravochnik Muzykal'nogo otdela Narodnogo komissariata po prosveshcheniiu na 1919-i god* (Petrograd and Moscow, 1919); *Sbornik dekretov, postanovlenii i rasporiazhenii po muzykal'nomu otdelu Narkomprosa* (Petrograd, 1919).

29. GARF f. 2306, op. 25, d. 39, l. 1.

30. Lamm, "Pervye gody raboty," 192–93.

31. McClelland, "The Professoriate in the Russian Civil War," 245. For an overview of prerevolutionary developments in musicology and theory, see Ellon D. Carpenter, "Russian Music Theory: A Conspectus," in *Russian Theoretical Thought in Music*, ed. Gordon McQuere (Ann Arbor, 1983), 33–41.

32. Sergei Taneev, *Podvizhnoi kontrapunkt strogogo pis'ma* (Moscow, 1909); Boleslav Iavorskii, *Stroenie muzykal'noi rechi* (Moscow, 1908).

33. Taneev died in 1915. Society members Mikhail Ivanov-Boretskii, Aleksandr Grechaninov, and Emil Rozenov all worked in Muzo. GARF f. 2306, op. 25, d. 292, l. 4.

34. D. Ivanov-Boretskii, "Deiatel'nost' Ak Muzo Narkomprosa—nachal'naia stranitsa sovetskogo muzykoznaniia (iz arkhiva M. V. Ivanova-Boretskogo)," in *Iz proshlogo sovetskoi muzykal'noi kul'tury*, vol. 2, ed. T. N. Livanova (Moscow, 1976), 264.

35. They included several members of the prerevolutionary Society of Lovers of Natural Science, Anthropology, and Ethnography: Nikolai Ianchuk, V. A. Fedorov, Aleksandr Grechaninov, Aleksandr Kastal'skii, Viacheslav Paskhalov, Ivan Tezarovskii, and Iulii Engel'. See Ivanov-Boretskii, "Deiatel'nost' Ak Muzo Narkomprosa," 275.

36. For an overview of theoretical research at GIMN, see Carpenter, "Russian Music Theory," 42–46; T. N. Livanova, "Iz proshlogo sovetskoi muzykal'noi nauki (GIMN v Moskvu)," in Livanova, *Iz proshlogo sovetskoi muzykal'noi kul'tury*, vol. 1, 267–335.

37. Briusova's lecture notes and instructions (dated 1919) for teaching popular audiences how to listen to and understand music (*slushanie muzyki*) are in GARF f. 2306, op. 25, d. 177, ll. 1–90b.

38. In January 1919 the choral studios in Moscow had 1058 participants. See "Otchet o deiatel'nosti Moskovskogo proletkul'ta za 1919 g.," in *Muzykal'naia zhizn' Moskvy*, ed. Stepanova, 288.

39. H. G. Wells was struck by the dire straits of scientists and intellectuals, and by the government's (meager) efforts to support them. See Wells, *Russia in the Shadows* (Westport, 1973 [1921]), 48–52.

40. Under the four-tiered "class-based" ration system implemented in October 1918, employees of Narkompros received category 2 rations. Intended for white-collar employees and those engaged in light manual labor, this "academic" ration was much more generous than that for members of the intelligentsia (category 3) and the bourgeoisie (category 4). Mary McAuley discusses the practical and ideological ramifications of the rationing system in "Bread Without the Bourgeoisie," in *Party, State, and Society*, ed. Koenker et al., 158–79.

41. GARF f. 2306, op. 25, d. 353, l. 57–57ob. See also Fitzpatrick, *Commissariat of Enlightenment*, 82.

42. Mally, *Culture of the Future*, 111.

43. Wells, *Russia in the Shadows*, 47.

44. A. Borovskii, "Vospominaniia (1915–1920)," in *Vospominaniia o Moskovskoi konservatorii*, ed. E. N. Alekseeva et al. (Moscow, 1966), 211.

45. Smith, "Soviet Arts Policy, Folk Music, and National Identity," 25.

46. For example, see the reminiscences of E. V. Koposova-Derzhanovskaia, "Pamiati druga," in Nikolai Miaskovskii, *N. Ia. Miaskovskii. Sobranie materialov v dvukh tomakh*, vol. 1, ed. S. I. Shlifshtein (Moscow, 1964), 219. Even the "academic" ration was so spartan that people almost starved if it was their only source of food. In the winter of 1919, authorities at Narkompros and the Moscow Conservatory sent agents out to the provinces for provisions. See Fitzpatrick, *Commissariat of Enlightenment*, 163; Alekseeva et al., *Vospominaniia o Moskovskoi konservatorii*, 546.

47. See his letter to I. M. Diomidov (May 31, 1920) in *M. M. Ippolitov-Ivanov. Pis'ma, stat'i, vospominaniia*, ed. N. N. Sokolov (Moscow, 1986), 182.

48. Sheila Fitzpatrick, "Ascribing Class: The Construction of Social Identity in Soviet Russia," *Journal of Modern History* 65 (1993): 745–70; Fitzpatrick, "The Problem of Class Identity in NEP Society," in *Russia in the Era of NEP*, ed. Fitzpatrick et al., 12–13. Christopher Read emphasizes how the Bolsheviks' obsession with class struggle underpinned punitive policies toward the intelligentsia. See Read, *Culture and Power in Revolutionary Russia: The Intelligentsia and the Transition from Tsarism to Communism* (London, 1990), 53.

49. There were incidents in which musicians openly challenged or defied Bolshevik authority. Soon after the October Revolution Aleksander Ziloti refused to hand over the keys to the Imperial box at the Mariinskii theater and was briefly incarcerated. Koussevitzky publicly denounced the Bolsheviks as "the harshest, most despotic and violent regime that has ever reigned over us." Yet despite the confiscation of his land, bank accounts, and publishing house, he served as an advisor to Lourié and briefly directed the State Orchestra. See Fitzpatrick, *Commissariat of Enlightenment*, 118; Thorpe, "The Management of Culture," 111–12; Lourié, *Sergei Koussevitzky*, 160–61.

50. GARF f. 2306, op. 25, d. 140, l. 85.

51. A certificate included in his personnel file for 1918 verifies that his "category 2" status included the rights to remain in his present domicile (which he shared with seven other people) and to be exempt from having his furniture, linens, clothing, and musical instruments requisitioned. (The latter were to be inventoried by the "appropriate" organization.) See GARF f. 2306, op. 44, d. 127, ll. 1, 4, 9, 11. While visiting in 1927, Prokofiev marveled at Derzhanovskii's ability to retain the apartment and some semblance of his prerevolutionary lifestyle. See Oleg Prokofiev, ed. and trans., *Sergei Prokofiev: Soviet Diary 1927 and Other Writings* (London, 1991), 26–27.

52. GARF f. 2307, op. 9, d. 256, l. 94.

53. Chaliapin, *Man and Mask*, 277.

54. Clark, *Petersburg*, 124. On the cultural iconoclasm and mass celebrations of the civil war years, see Stites, *Revolutionary Dreams;* James von Geldern, *Bolshevik Festivals, 1917–1920* (Berkeley and Los Angeles, 1993).

55. Brooks, *When Russia Learned to Read*, 319–20; Stites, *Revolutionary Dreams*, 88; Clark, *Petersburg*, 138–39.

56. The most influential advocate of this interpretation in the Soviet period was V. V. Gorbunov. See his "Bor'ba V. I. Lenina s separatistskimi ustremleniiami Proletkul'ta," *Voprosy istorii KPSS* 1 (1958): 29–40; "Kritika V. I. Leninym teorii Proletkul'ta ob otnoshenii k kul'turnomu naslediiu," *Voprosy istorii KPSS* 5 (1968): 83–93; *V. I. Lenin i Proletkul't* (Moscow, 1974). Western scholars following this approach include Edward J. Brown, *The Proletarian Episode in Russian Literature, 1928–1932* (New York, 1953); Herman Ermolaev, *Soviet Literary Theories, 1917–1934: The Genesis of Socialist Realism* (Berkeley and Los Angeles, 1963); Zinovia Sochor, *Revolution and Culture: The Bogdanov-Lenin Controversy* (Ithaca, 1988). Alternative perspectives are provided by

Gabriele Gorzka, *A. Bogdanov und der russische Proletkul't* (Frankfurt, 1980); L. A. Pinegina, *Sovetskii rabochii klass i khudozhestvennaia kul'tura, 1917–1932* (Moscow, 1984). For a nuanced and perceptive study, see Mally, *Culture of the Future.*

57. Maes, *History of Russian Music,* 238–39; Schwarz, *Music and Musical Life,* 20–21; *Istoriia russkoi-sovetskoi muzyki,* 16–17.

58. These included Nikolai Garbuzov, Petr Renchitskii, Petr Zimin, and N. V. Petrov, who worked in Proletkul't research sections as well as at Muzo. See P. N. Zimin, "Nauchnaia i tekhnicheskaia rabota Muzykal'nogo otdela Moskovskogo proletkul'ta (ca. April, 1921)," in *Muzykal'naia zhizn' Moskvy,* ed. Stepanova, 292–94.

59. Lynn Mally, "Intellectuals in the Proletkul't: Problems of Authority and Expertise," in *Party, State, and Society,* ed. Koenker et al., 296–311.

60. Mally, *Culture of the Future,* 122–23. Besides "revolutionary romanticism," Mally also identifies avant-garde efforts to break completely with the cultural forms of the past and education in Russia's prerevolutionary cultural heritage as the three broad approaches that informed Proletkul't programs.

61. D. L. Lokshin, *D. S. Vasil'ev-Buglai* (Moscow, 1958), 6–7.

62. Mally, *Culture of the Future,* 141.

63. "*Na tëmnykh mogilakh, / Iz shchebnia Bylogo, / Iz smekha i slëz iznurënnykh serdets,— / My, gordye, stroim, my, gordye, stroim, / My stroim Rabochii Dvorets!*" First verse of *Rabochii dvorets,* in *Antologiia sovetskoi pesni. 1917–1957,* vol. 1 ed. Viktor Belyi (Moscow, 1957), 73.

64. *Protokoly pervoi vserossiiskoi konferentsii proletarskykh kul'turno-prosvetitel'nykh organizatsii, 15–20 Sept. 1918* (Moscow, 1918), 125–28. Excerpt from Kirillov's report published in Rosenberg, *Bolshevik Visions,* 455.

65. Nicolas Slonimsky, "The Changing Style of Soviet Music," *Journal of the American Musicological Society* 3 (1950): 236.

66. Zimin, "Nauchnaia i tekhnicheskaia rabota Muzykal'nogo otdela," 292–94.

67. Arsenii Avraamov, "Simfoniia gudkov," *Khudozhnik i zritel'* 1 (1924): 50.

68. For a detailed description of the Baku symphony of factory whistles and Avraamov's organizational plans and instructions for making a *magistral',* see Avraamov, "Simfoniia gudkov," *Gorn* 9 (1923): 109–16. Rene Fuelop-Miller also describes this event in *The Mind and Face of Bolshevism* (New York, 1962 [1926]), 183–84. See also "Simfoniia gudkov," *Pravda,* November 14, 1923, 5; Vladimir Tolstoy, Irina Bibikova, and Catherine Cook, eds., *Street Art of the Revolution: Festivals and Celebrations in Russia, 1918–33* (New York, 1990), 146–47.

69. From the German *kulturträger,* meaning "spreader of culture" or "civilizer."

70. GARF f. 2306, op. 25, d. 39, l. 1; Nest'ev, "Iz istorii russkogo muzykal'nogo avangarda," 80.

71. Mark von Hagen, *Soldiers in the Proletarian Dictatorship: The Red Army and the Soviet Socialist State, 1917–1930* (Ithaca, 1990), 94, 153. Similar concerns informed the "entertainment or enlightenment debate" over the form and purpose of cinema. See Youngblood, *Movies for the Masses,* 35–49.

72. A. D. Kastal'skii, "K voprosu ob organizatsii muzykal'nykh zaniatii v Tsentral'noi studii Moskovskogo proletkul'ta" (1918?), excerpts published in *Muzykal'naia zhizn' Moskvy,* ed. Stepanova, 283–84; N. Ia. Briusova, *Zadachi narodnogo muzykal'nogo obrazovaniia. Doklad prochitanyi na konferentsii kul't.-pros. proletarskykh organizatsii* (Moscow, 1919), 6, 14.

73. Kastal'skii, "K voprosu ob organizatsii muzykal'nykh zaniatii," 284.

74. P. Rumiantsev, "O Sergee Vasil'eviche Evseeve," in *Vospominaniia o Moskovskoi konservatorii,* ed. Alekseeva et al., 489.

75. Grigorii Liubimov, "Narodnye orkestry i ikh znachenie v muzykal'nom prosveshchenii mass," *Gorn* 2–3 (1919): 99–105; Stepanova, *Muzykal'naia zhizn' Moskvy,* 286.

76. Briusova, *Zadachi narodnogo muzykal'nogo obrazovaniia,* 7, 10.

77. Liubimov, "Narodnye orkestry," *Gorn* 2–3 (1919): 104.

78. N. Roslavets, "Iz otcheta o rabote Lekstionno-repertuarno-izdatel'skoi sektsii i Kontsertnogo podotdela Muzykal'nogo otdela Moskovskogo proletkul'ta (July, 1920),"

Gosudarstvennyi arkhiv Moskovskoi oblasti (GAMO), f. 889, op. 1, ed. khr. 19, l. 44–56. Published in Stepanova, *Muzykal'naia zhizn' Moskvy*, 289–92. See especially 291.

79. Nest'ev, "Iz istorii russkogo muzykal'nogo avangarda," 80.

80. A. V. Lunacharskii, "Narodnye kontserty gosudarstvennogo orkestra," *Petrogradskaia pravda*, September 27, 1918, 2. Reprinted in A. V. Lunacharskii, *V mire muzyki. Stat'i i rechi* (Moscow, 1958), 261–62.

81. Rumiantsev, "O Sergee Vasil'eviche Evseeve," in *Vospominaniia o Moskovskoi konservatorii*, ed. Alekseeva et al., 489.

82. E. Bronfin, *Muzykal'naia kul'tura Petrograda pervogo poslerevoliutsionnogo piatiletiia, 1917–1922* (Leningrad, 1984), 68–69.

83. S. Migai, "Kontserty dlia naroda," *Sovetskaia muzyka* 11 (1957): 29–33. Reprinted in Rosenberg, *Bolshevik Visions*, 459–63. See especially 460.

84. GARF f. 2306, op. 25, d. 140, ll. 34–34ob.

85. Liubimov, "Narodnye orkestry," *Gorn* 2–3 (1919): 101.

86. *Protokoly pervoi vserossiiskoi konferentsii proletarskykh kul'turno-prosvetitel'nykh organizatsii*, 125–28. Excerpts from Krasin's report published in Rosenberg, *Bolshevik Visions*, 453–54; and Stepanova, *Muzykal'naia zhizn' Moskvy*, 284–85.

87. A. Preobrazhenskii, "A. D. Kastal'skii (materialy k biografii)," in *A. D. Kastal'skii. Stat'i, vospominaniia, materialy*, ed. D. V. Zhitomirskii (Moscow, 1960), 41.

88. Kastal'skii, "K voprosu ob organizatsii muzykal'nykh zaniatii," 283.

89. Mally, *Culture of the Future*, 123.

90. On revolutionary theater and mass festivals, see von Geldern, *Bolshevik Festivals;* Clark, *Petersburg*, especially 74–139; Stites, *Revolutionary Dreams*, 78–100; Mally, *Revolutionary Acts;* Tolstoy et al., *Street Art of the Revolution*, 11–120.

91. Elizabeth Wilson, *Shostakovich: A Life Remembered* (Princeton, 1994), 22.

92. Of the 2083 musical works published by the State Music Publisher as of February 1922, only 323 were new pieces. The rest were reprints. See Lamm, "Pervye gody raboty," 201–2.

93. For example, Beethoven's music was featured in fourteen of the twenty-four concerts sponsored by Muzo Narkompros between December 15, 1920, and January 15, 1921. One program was dedicated to French composers, and the remainder to the Russian "Five," Glinka, and Tchaikovsky. See GARF f. 2306, op. 25, d. 140, ll. 79–80. The tremendous popularity of Beethoven's music in the revolutionary and Civil War period is discussed in detail in I. V. Nest'ev, "Muzyka Betkhovena v sovetskoi Rossii," in *Betkhoven. Sbornik statei*, vol. 2, ed. N. L. Fishman (Moscow, 1972), 239–50.

94. Bronfin, *Muzykal'naia kul'tura Petrograda*, 45, 49; Stites, *Revolutionary Dreams*, 85; Stepanova, *Muzykal'naia zhizn' Moskvy*, 121.

95. Orlando Figes and Boris Kollonitsky, *Interpreting the Russian Revolution: The Language and Symbols of 1917* (New Haven, 1999).

96. Ibid., 39–40.

97. Ibid., 188.

98. Ibid., 40.

99. Kastal'skii's score is in 4/4 and marked "torzhestvenno." See Simen Dreiden, *Muzyka—revoliutsiia*, 3d ed. (Moscow, 1981), 148.

100. Dreiden, *Muzyka—revoliutsii*, 145–46; Stites, *Revolutionary Dreams*, 87–88.

101. "*Ty zvoidi, solntse krasnoe*," "*Kak u sokola, kak u iasnogo*," and "*Iskhodila mladeshen'ka*." See Stepanova, *Muzykal'naia zhizn' Moskvy*, 105.

102. Leonid Sabaneev, *Muzyka posle Oktiabria* (Moscow, 1926), 26, 33.

103. Stepanova, *Muzykal'naia zhizn' Moskvy*, 183.

104. Fitzpatrick, *The Cultural Front*, 2–6.

105. On the universities, see Sheila Fitzpatrick, *Education and Social Mobility in the Soviet Union, 1921–1934* (Cambridge, 1979), 63–67; McClelland, "The Professoriate in the Russian Civil War," 261–62; Read, *Culture and Power*, 179–83; David-Fox, *Revolution of the Mind*, 51–54.

106. Ippolitov-Ivanov did resign his post later that fall, and was replaced by his former student Aleksandr Gol'denveizer.

107. On the Academy of Sciences, see Loren Graham, *The Soviet Academy of Sciences and the Communist Party, 1927–1932* (Princeton, 1967); Kendall E. Bailes, *Science and Russian Culture in an Age of Revolutions* (Bloomington, 1990), 148–59; Vera Tolz, *Russian Academicians and the Revolution: Combining Professionalism and Politics* (New York, 1997).

108. Fitzpatrick, *Commissariat of Enlightenment*, 188–209; Read, *Culture and Power*, 142–58; Mally, *Culture of the Future*, 193–213. The implications of these reforms are examined in Chapter 5.

109. "O Proletkul'takh," *Pravda*, December 1, 1920. Reprinted in V. I. Lenin, *Lenin o literature i iskusstve*, ed. N. Kriutkov (Moscow, 1986), 408–10.

110. Mally, *Culture of the Future*, xxii–xxiii.

111. GARF f. 2306, op. 25, d. 140, l. 30.

112. Mally, *Culture of the Future*, 196; Read, *Culture and Power*, 144–45; David-Fox, *Revolution of the Mind*, 43–44.

113. GARF f. 2306, op. 25, d. 140, l. 51.

114. Nest'ev, "Iz istorii russkogo muzykal'nogo avangarda," 83; Gojowy, *Neue sowjetische Musik*, 99–100.

115. Rabis was also called "Vserabis," from *Vserossiiskii soiuz rabotnikov iskusstv* (All-Russian Union of Art Workers).

116. Fitzpatrick, *Commissariat of Enlightenment*, 167–68.

117. "Tezisy ob osnovakh politiki v oblasti iskusstva," *Vestnik rabotnikov iskusstv* 2–3 (1920): 65–66.

118. For the Rabkrin report on Muzo Narkompros, see GARF f. 2306, op. 25, d. 292, ll. 1–60b.

119. Ibid., l. 20b.

120. "Tezisy ob osnovakh politiki," *Vestnik rabotnikov iskusstv* 2–3 (1920): 65; GARF f. 2306, op. 25, d. 292, l. 1.

121. GARF f. 2306, op. 25, d. 292, l. 10b.

122. Krasin assumed his post on January 25, 1921. See GARF f. 2306, op. 25, d. 365, l. 4.

123. His brother was Leonid Krasin, another of Bogdanov's associates from the prewar period, who would become a famous Soviet diplomat and architect of the Soviet Union's first international trade policies.

124. For a summary of Krasin's career, see K., "B. B. Krasin," *Sovetskaia muzyka* 7 (1936): 106–7; RGALI f. 2004, op. 1, d. 23, ll. 1–3.

125. Arthur Lourié, "The Russian School," *Musical Quarterly* 18 (1932): 524. Quoted in Sitsky, *Music of the Repressed*, 105.

Chapter 2

1. Schwarz, *Music and Musical Life*, 60–87; Gojowy, *Neue sowjetische Musik*, 5–42; Haas, *Leningrad's Modernists*, 10–18, 30–51; Sitsky, *Music of the Repressed*, 1–7.

2. The "Termenvox," which produced an eerie, ethereal sound in response to the gentle arm motions of the performer, attracted Lenin's interest and was later used by American rock bands (The Beach Boys' *Good Vibrations*) and for spooky sound effects in American science fiction and noir movies. See Albert Glinsky, *Theremin: Ether Music and Espionage* (Urbana, 2000); Stephen Montague, "Rediscovering Leon Theremin," *Tempo* 177 (1991): 18–23; and the documentary film *Theremin: An Electronic Odyssey*, directed by Steven M. Martin (MGM Home Entertainment, 1995).

3. I refer to these groups as the "musical Left" because of their position outside the musical establishment and their radical political and creative agenda. Although this is an appropriation of the label the modernists sometimes applied to themselves, I feel the term "the Left" more accurately describes the ideological orientation of RAPM, ORK, and Prokoll.

4. *Istoriia russkoi sovetskoi muzyki*, 35–39; *Istoriia muzyki narodov SSSR*, 134–40; Poliakova, *Soviet Music*, 9–10; A. I. Shaverdian, ed., *Puti razvitiia sovetskoi muzyki. Kratkii obzor* (Moscow, 1948), 27–46.

5. Gojowy, *Neue sowjetische Musik,* 5–26; Schwarz, *Music and Musical Life,* 49–60; Sitsky, *Music of the Repressed;* Carpenter, "Russian Music Theory," 50–51.

6. This involved partial rehabilitations of modernist composers, musical institutions, and organizations from the twenties, as well as certain types of popular song. See Inna Barsova, "Aleksandr Mosolov: dvadtsatye gody," *Sovetskaia muzyka* 12 (1976): 77–87; Mikhail Druskin, "Iz khroniki muzykal'noi zhizni Leningrada 20-kh godov," *Sovetskaia muzyka* 9 (1974): 113–22; Druskin, *Issledovaniia: vospominaniia* (Leningrad, 1977); Inna Barsova, ed., *A. V. Mosolov: Stat' i i vospominaniia,* comp. Nina Meshko, (Moscow, 1986); Vladimir Shcherbachev, *V. V. Shcherbachev. Stat'i, materialy, pis'ma,* ed. A. Kriutkov, comp. R. Slonimskaia (Leningrad, 1985); Marina Lobanova, "L'eredita di N. A. Roslavec nel campo della teoria musicale," *Musica / Realta* 4 (1983): 41–65. Three important volumes edited by T. N. Livanova appeared under the title *Iz proshlogo sovetskoi muzykal'noi kul'tury* (Moscow, 1975–82). Robert Rothstein documented the return to official favor of a particular popular song from the twenties in "The Quiet Rehabilitation of the Brick Factory: Early Soviet Music and Its Critics," *Slavic Review* 29 (1980): 373–88. Soviet scholars also began to examine the varied spectrum of musical life in the immediate postrevolutionary period. See Stepanova, *Muzykal'naia zhizn' Moskvy;* Bronfin, *Muzykal'naia kul'tura Petrograda.*

7. For an early summons to extend *glasnost'* to the music of the early Soviet period, see Daniel Zhitomirskii, "O proshlom bez prikras," *Sovetskaia muzyka* 2 (1988): 96–105.

8. Sitsky, *Music of the Repressed;* Haas, *Leningrad's Modernists;* Roberts, *Modernism in Russian Piano Music;* Marina Lobanova, *Nikolaj Andreevič Roslavec und die Kultur seiner Zeit* (Frankfurt, 1997); Anna Ferenc, "Reclaiming Roslavets: The Troubled Life of a Russian Modernist," *Tempo* 182 (1992): 6–9; Andreas Wehrmeyer, *Studien zum russischen Musikdenken um 1920* (Frankfurt, 1991); Gerard McBurney, "The Resurrection of Roslavets," *Tempo* 173 (1990): 7–9. These works build on Detlef Gojowy's pioneering study of the twenties, *Neue sowjetische Musik der 20er Jahre.* Numerous recording companies have made the work of the Russian modernists available, including Olympia, Chant du Monde, Wergo, and Russian Disc.

9. Richard Taruskin, review of *Modernism in Russian Piano Music: Skriabin, Prokofiev, and Their Russian Contemporaries,* by Peter Deane Roberts, *Slavic Review* 53 (1994): 866.

10. Fitzpatrick's conception of the "soft line" emerged as part of a debate over whether the evils of the Soviet system were inherent in Lenin's revolution or primarily attributable to Stalin's rule. See Sheila Fitzpatrick, "The Soft Line on Culture and Its Enemies," *Slavic Review* 33 (1974): 267–87. See also Fitzpatrick, *The Cultural Front,* 91–114; James McClelland, "Utopianism versus Revolutionary Heroism in Bolshevik Policy: The Proletarian Culture Debate," *Slavic Review* 39 (1980): 403–25; A. Kemp-Welch, "New Economic Policy in Culture and Its Enemies," *Journal of Contemporary History* 13 (1978): 449–65; Kemp-Welch, *Stalin and the Literary Intelligentsia, 1928–1939* (New York, 1991), 21–35.

11. On the centrality of this issue in the early Soviet period, see Kendall E. Bailes, *Technology and Society under Lenin and Stalin: Origins of the Soviet Technical Intelligentsia, 1917–1941* (Princeton, 1978); Fitzpatrick, *Education and Social Mobility;* Fitzpatrick, *The Cultural Front,* 1–15; Loren Graham, *Science in Russia and the Soviet Union: A Short History* (Cambridge, 1993); Graham, *The Academy of Sciences and the Communist Party.*

12. For a fascinating analysis of the ways that ideological and political anxieties about the NEP order were articulated in discourse focusing on corporal corruption, see Eric Naiman, *Sex in Public: The Incarnation of Early Soviet Ideology* (Princeton, 1997).

13. Read, *Culture and Power;* Michael S. Fox, "Glavlit, Censorship, and the Problem of Party Policy in Cultural Affairs, 1922–1928," *Soviet Studies* 44 (1992): 1045–68; Steven Richmond, "'The Conditions of the Contemporary': The Censors and Censoring of Soviet Theater, 1923–1927," *Russian History* 27 (2000): 1–56; A. V. Blium, *Za kulisami "Ministerstva Pravdy";* M. V. Zelenov, "Glavlit i istoricheskaia nauka v 20–30-e gody," *Voprosy istorii* 3 (1997): 21–35. The bureaucratic and institutional dimensions of the NEP order are examined in Chapter 5.

14. David-Fox, *Revolution of the Mind.*

15. In the case of Shostakovich, attention to the effect of official criticism on his work has been heightened by a controversy over the composer's own attitudes toward the regime. See Solomon Volkov, *Testimony: The Memoirs of Dmitrii Shostakovich as Related to and Edited by Solomon Volkov*, trans. Antonina W. Boius (New York, 1979); Laurel Fay, "Shostakovich versus Volkov: Whose Testimony?" *Russian Review* 39 (1980): 484–93; Ian MacDonald, *The New Shostakovich* (London, 1990); I. D. Glikman, ed., *Pis'ma k drugu: Dmitrii Shostakovich—Isaaku Glikmanu* (Moscow, 1993); Taruskin, *Defining Russia Musically*, 486–510; Allan Ho and Dmitry Feofanov, *Shostakovich Reconsidered* (London, 1998). Other important studies of Shostakovich include Laurel Fay, *Shostakovich: A Life* (Oxford, 2000); Rosamund Bartlett, ed., *Shostakovich in Context* (Oxford, 2000); David Fanning, ed., *Shostakovich Studies* (Cambridge, 1995); Wilson, *Shostakovich*; Christopher Norris, ed., *Shostakovich: The Man and His Music* (London, 1982); Dmitrii Sollertinsky and Liudmilla Sollertinsky, *Pages from the Life of Dmitrii Shostakovich*, trans. Graham Hobbs and Charles Midgley (New York, 1980). Shostakovich's primary Russian-Soviet biographer is Sofiia Khentova. See her *Shostakovich, zhizn' i tvorchestvo*, vols. 1–2 (Leningrad, 1985); *Udivitel'nyi Shostakovich* (St. Petersburg, 1993); *Shostakovich v Moskve* (Moscow, 1986); *D. D. Shostakovich v gody Velikoi Otechestvennoi voiny* (Leningrad, 1979); and *Molodye gody Shostakovicha* (Leningrad, 1975).

16. For an excellent discussion of the complexities of literary politics, see David Shepherd and Peter Kenez, "'Revolutionary' Models for High Literature: Resisting Poetics," in *Russian Cultural Studies: An Introduction*, ed. Catriona Kelly and David Shepherd (Oxford, 1998), 29–30.

17. Michael David-Fox, "What Is Cultural Revolution?" *Russian Review* 58 (April 1999): 182; David-Fox, "*Mentalité* or Cultural System? A Reply to Sheila Fitzpatrick," *Russian Review* 58 (April 1999): 210. For related perspectives on the dynamics of the Cultural Revolution, see Clark, "The Quiet Revolution"; Stefan Plaggenborg, *Revolutionskultur. Menschenbilder und kulturelle Praxis in Sowjetrussland zwischen Oktoberrevolution und Stalinismus* (Cologne, 1996); David Joravsky, "Cultural Revolution and the Fortress Mentality," in *Bolshevik Culture: Experiment and Order in the Russian Revolution*, ed. Gleason et al., 93–109.

18. Douglas R. Weiner identified similar patterns at work among naturalists and the field of nature protection. See Weiner, *Models of Nature: Ecology, Conservation, and Cultural Revolution in Soviet Russia* (Bloomington, 1988). For an exploration of this dynamic in other fields of creative endeavor, see Youngblood, *Movies for the Masses;* Clark, *Petersburg*.

19. Barbara Walker, "*Kruzhok* Culture: The Meaning of Patronage in the Early Soviet Literary World," *Contemporary European History* 11 (2002): 107–8.

20. On their influence in these institutions, see Chapters 5 and 6.

21. As Christopher Norris has noted, an uninterrupted line of aestheticians and philosophers from Eduard Hanslick to Stravinsky have insisted on music's autonomy. See Norris, ed., *Music and the Politics of Culture* (New York, 1989), 7. Inspired by the work of Theodor Adorno and Walter Benjamin, and borrowing from the methodologies of literary criticism, the sociology of art, and cultural studies, a "new musicology" has emerged in the last fifteen years that proposes various methods for identifying the social function of music and the ways in which music articulates particular values and ideas. See Richard Leppert and Susan McClary, eds., *Music and Society: The Politics of Composition, Performance, and Reception* (Cambridge, 1987); John Shepherd, *Music as Social Text* (Cambridge, 1991); Rose Subotnik, *Developing Variations: Style and Ideology in Western Music* (Minneapolis, 1991).

22. GARF f. 2306, op. 25, d. 140, ll. 11, 40; Stepanova, *Muzykal'naia zhizn' Moskvy*, 44–45; Lobanova, *Roslavec*, 40, 44.

23. These "concert-exhibits" were first held in the hall of Mezhdunarodnaia kniga at Kuznetskii most, No. 12. The exhibitions featured books and music published by the State Publishing House and the German publishers Breitkopf & Hertel, Peters, Litolf, and M. P. Beliav, among others. See *Vospominaniia o Moskovskoi konservatorii*, ed. Alekseeva et al., 553.

24. The November date is given by ASM head Derzhanovskii in a report to the State Academic Council (GUS) in March 1925. See GARF f. 298, op. 1, d. 128, l. 61. Protocols from the

music section of GAKhN indicate that the ASM already existed and was asking for an affiliation with the arts institute in the fall of 1922. See RGALI f. 941, op. 5, d. 2, l. 2. See also Koposova-Derzhanovskaia, "Pamiati druga," 221.

Founding members (in addition to Derzhanovskii and Sabaneev) were Viktor Beliaev (musicologist), Pavel Lamm (critic, Musorgsky scholar), Konstantin Saradzhev (conductor), Anatolii Aleksandrov (composer), Nikolai Miaskovskii (composer), and Samuel Feinberg (pianist/composer). See Gojowy, *Neue sowjetische Musik*, 25; Fred K. Prieberg, *Musik in der Sowjetunion* (Cologne, 1965), 55.

25. Taruskin, *Defining Russia Musically*, 87–93. Taruskin maintains that the "authentic" avant-garde of the twenties was not the ASM at all, but rather its opponents in RAPM. Ibid., 92. Although this perspective gives due weight to RAPM's countercultural stance, militant rhetoric, and eagerness to act on its program, it overlooks the diversity of the Left as a whole and the extent to which polemical hyperbole masked conservatism and veneration of tradition.

26. Taruskin also emphasizes that Shostakovich had affinities both with the "elite modernists" from which he was descended and the "revolutionary scepticism" of RAPM. See Taruskin, *Defining Russia Musically*, 93–94; Fitzpatrick, "The Lady Macbeth Affair: Shostakovich and the Soviet Puritans," in *The Cultural Front*, 183–215.

27. For an excellent summary of the distinguishing characteristics of modernism in music and the arts, and the various connotations of "avant-garde" music, see Georgina Born, *Rationalizing Culture: IRCAM, Boulez, and the Institutionalization of the Musical Avant-Garde* (Berkeley and Los Angeles, 1995), 40–50.

28. Hakobian, *Music of the Soviet Age*, 42, 46;

29. Vissarion Shebalin, *Literaturnoe nasledie: vospominaniia, perepiska, stat'i, vystupleniia* (Moscow, 1975), 20–21.

30. Leonid Sabaneev, "Sovremennaia muzyka," *Muzykal'naia kul'tura* 1 (1924): 9.

31. Sergei Prokof'ev, "Pis'mo v redaktsiiu," *K novym beregam muzykal'nogo iskusstva* 2 (1923): 15–17; "Khronika," *K novym beregam muzykal'nogo iskusstva* 2 (1923): 57.

32. Nikolai Roslavets, "'Lunnyi P'ero' A. Shenberga," *K novym beregam muzykal'nogo iskusstva* 3 (1923): 28–34.

33. *Teatral'naia Moskva* 2 (1926–27), 211. The activities of Lamm's circle and the personalities of its members are described by O. Lamm in "Druz'ia Pavla Aleksandrovicha Lamma i uchastniki muzykal'nykh vecherov v ego dome (20-e gody XX veka)," in *Iz proshlogo sovetskoi muzykal'noi kul'tury*, vol. 1, ed. Livanova, 72–102.

34. Barbara Walker characterizes these relationships as an essential part of the "*Kruzhok* (circle) culture" that the literary intelligentsia carried over from the prerevolutionary period. See Walker, "*Kruzhok* Culture," 109–13.

35. Other regular participants were Aleksandr Shenshin (1880–1944), who taught theory, Dmitrii Melkikh (1885–1943), who worked in the conservatory's library, and Vissarion Shebalin (1902–63), who joined the faculty in 1928.

36. The piano "quartet" for these performances usually included Lamm, Miaskovskii, Sergei Popov, and Shebalin. Lamm had perfected his skills as a transcriptionist during World War I, which, thanks to his German heritage, he spent in detention in the Urals. Prokofiev, *Soviet Diary 1927*, 126–27.

37. Haas, *Leningrad's Modernists*, 13, 17.

38. Shcherbachev's pupils Khristofer Kushnarev (1890–1960) and Petr Riazanov (1899–1942) were regular guests at Vogt's, as were Dmitrii Shostakovich, Vladimir Deshevov, and Nikolai Malko. For analysis of Asaf'ev's and Shcherbachev's place in the Leningrad musical community, as well as the general characteristics of the "Leningrad school" of modernist composition, see Haas, *Leningrad's Modernists*.

39. The former were Asaf'ev, Shcherbachev, critic Viacheslav Karatygin, and Andrei Rimskii-Korsakov (son of Nikolai Rimsky-Korsakov). Maksimilian Shteinberg and Aleksandr Ossovskii, both from the conservatory composition department, and A. Pashchenko from the Philharmonic

represented the traditionalists. Details of the LASM's organizational crisis and early personnel changes may be found in V. Bogdanov-Berezovskii, "Leningradskaia Assotsiatsiia Sovremennoi Muzyki," *Novaia muzyka* 1 (1927): 37–41. See also Haas, *Leningrad's Modernists*, 17.

40. Iurii Karnovich was president, Iulia Veisberg was vice president, and N. P. Malkov served as secretary. E. V. Bortkevich and Joseph Schillinger headed the artistic council with the assistance of "member-experts" A. M. Zhitomirskii, L. V. Nikolaev, Ossovskii, and Shteinberg.

41. Iu. Vainkop, "Kruzhok Novoi Muzyki," *Novaia muzyka* 1 (1927): 42.

42. An insider's perspective on the history of the New Music Circle and the LASM may be found in Druskin's memoirs, excerpted in "Iz khroniki muzykal'noi zhizni Leningrada 20-kh godov," 113–22; and published in full as Druskin, *Issledovaniia: vospominaniia*.

43. The New Music Circle was chaired by Asaf'ev, although the responsibility for organizing concerts and recitals fell primarily to the group's secretary, Mikhail Druskin, a pianist and graduate student at the institute. Other members of the Circle's board were V. A. Dranishnikov (assistant head), Semion Ginzburg, and Vladimir Deshevov. Iu. Vainkop became secretary when Druskin moved to LASM. The organizational history and repertoire of the New Music Circle are outlined in Vainkop, "Kruzhok Novoi Muzyki," 42–47.

44. Haas, *Leningrad's Modernists*, 18.

45. Programs for the ASM's concerts from 1923 to 1926 are found in *Sovremennaia muzyka* 15–16 (1926): 166–75. The 1927–28 season is described in *Sovremennaia muzyka* 31 (1928): 178–82.

46. GARF f. 298, op. 1, d. 128, ll. 64ob., 195–195ob., 197ob.; N. Malkov, "Assotsiatsiia sovremennoi muzyki," *Zhizn' iskusstva* 3 (1926): 14; Malkov, "V assots. sov. muz.," *Sovremennaia muzyka* 11 (1925): 29.

47. Lamm, "Druz'ia Pavla Aleksandrovicha," 78. Prokofiev's diary reveals how various groups scrambled over each other for his attentions during his 1927 tour. See Prokofiev, *Soviet Diary 1927*, 20–27. See also Vladimir Fere, "Nash uchitel' Nikolai Iakovlevich Miaskovskii," in *Vospominaniia o Moskovskoi konservatorii*, ed. Alekseeva et al., 430–31.

48. Besides Shebalin, the "Moscow Six" included Lev Oborin, Starokadomskii, Iurii Nikol'skii, Misha Cheremukhin, and Mikhail Kvadri. See Wilson, *Shostakovich*, 38.

49. Sitsky, *Music of the Repressed*, 177–78.

50. See Vladimir Derzhanovskii, "Assotsiatsiia Sovremennoi Muzyki," *Sovremennaia muzyka* 23 (1927): 3–4; L. Sabaneev, "Vystavka v 'knige,'" *Pravda*, November 14, 1923, 5.

51. See Evg. Braudo, "Itogi sezona," *Pravda*, June 20, 1925, 8.

52. See N. Zhiliaev, "Sergei Prokofiev," *K novym beregam* 1 (1923): 18.

53. E. M., "Poslednee slovo otzhivaiushchei kul'tury," *Muzyka i revoliutsiia* 9 (1927): 3–4; L. Shul'gin, "Sovremennoe muzykal'noe tvorchestvo i predposylki nashei tvorcheskoi raboty," *Muzykal'naia nov'* 4 (1924): 15; L. Kaltat, "O podlinno-burzhuaznoi ideologii gr. Roslavtsa," *Muzykal'noe obrazovanie* 3–4 (1927): 38.

54. E. M., "Poslednee slovo otzhivaiushchei kul'tury," *Muzyka i revoliutsiia* 9 (1927): 3–4; L. Kaltat, "O podlinno-burzhuaznoi ideologii gr. Roslavtsa," *Muzykal'noe obrazovanie* 3–4 (1927): 38.

55. "'Industrializm' i 'narodnichestvo,'" *Muzyka i revoliutsiia* 3 (1928): 8.

56. E. M., "Poslednee slovo otzhivaiushchei kul'tury," *Muzyka i revoliutsiia* 9 (1927): 3.

57. Islamei, "Moe osoboe mnenie o 'novoi' muzyki," *Zhizn' iskusstva* 30 (1924): 14; Sergei Bugoslavskii, "Massovaia muzyka," *Zhizn' iskusstva* 39 (1926): 8; M. –M., "Zaumnaia muzyka," *Zhizn' iskusstva* 10 (1925): 21.

58. Sergei Bugoslavskii, "Massovaia muzyka," *Zhizn' iskusstva* 39 (1926): 8.

59. "'Levyi' flang sovremennoi muzyki," *Muzyka i revoliutsiia* 1 (1927): 5; Sergei Bugoslavskii, "Bloknot muzykanta," *Zhizn' iskusstva* 6 (1925): 11.

60. V. Beliaev, "A. V. Mosolov," *Sovremennaia muzyka* 13–14 (1926): 81–88.

61. "'Levyi' flang sovremennoi muzyki," *Muzyka i revoliutsiia* 1 (1927): 4; S. Gres, "LASM," *Zhizn' iskusstva* 21 (1927): 17.

62. Iu. Vainkop, "Novaia muzyka i rabochie auditorii," *Novaia muzyka* 2 (1927–28): 47.

63. Orest Tsekhnovitser, "Novaia muzyka i proletariat," *Novaia muzyka* 2 (1927–28): 15. As quoted by Slonimsky in "The Changing Style of Soviet Music," 237; and Schwarz, *Music and Musical Life*, 53.

64. William Weber, "Wagner, Wagnerism, and Musical Idealism," in *Wagnerism in European Culture and Politics*, ed. David Large and William Weber (Ithaca, 1984), 34.

65. For a richly textured exploration of these developments in France, see James H. Johnson, *Listening in Paris: A Cultural History* (Berkeley and Los Angeles, 1995).

66. Weber, "Wagner," 37–38, 50.

67. Henry Raynor, *Music and Society Since 1815* (New York, 1976), 149.

68. Charles Rosen, *Arnold Schoenberg* (New York, 1975), 65–66.

69. Weber, "Wagner," 70.

70. Derzhanovskii, "Assotsiatsiia Sovremennoi Muzyki," *Sovremennaia muzyka* 23 (1927): 3.

71. Weber, "Wagner," 65.

72. A recent text for Russian conservatory students still faults the ASM for having "misunderstood the huge significance of the connection between music and living society" and ignoring the interests of the "mass audience." See Tarakanov, *Istoriia sovremennoi otechestvennoi muzyki*, 34–35.

73. L. Sabaneev, "Vystavka v 'Knige,'" *Pravda*, November 14, 1923, 5; "Assotsiatsiia sovremennoi muzyki," *Biulleten' GAKhN* 1 (1925): 48.

74. L. Sabaneev, "Pro domo sua," *Sovremennaia muzyka* 6 (1924): 153.

75. *Persimfans* 2 (1927–28): 7.

76. Vas. Alekseev, "Kontsert iz proizvedenii N. A. Roslavtsa," *Muzykal'naia nov'* 6–7 (1924): 27.

77. GARF f. 298, op. 1, d. 128, l. 59.

78. Both Soviet and Western scholarship often identify these men as critical proponents and advocates of musical modernism. See Haas, *Leningrad's Modernists*, 10–18; Schwarz, *Music and Musical Life*, 51, 54; *Istoriia russkoi sovetskoi muzyki*, 36.

79. Schwarz, *Music and Musical Life*, 36. In the decade after Asaf'ev's death, five volumes of his writings were published. See Boris Asaf'ev, *Izbrannye trudy*, 5 vols. (Moscow, 1952–57). His principal biographer, Elena Orlova, published *B. V. Asaf'ev: put' issledovatelia i publitsista* (Leningrad, 1964). She also contributed to several publications commemorating the centennial of Asaf'ev's birth in 1984. See Andrei Kriukov, *Materialy k biografii B. Asaf'ev* (Leningrad, 1981); Elena Orlova and Andrei Kriukov, *Akademik Boris Vladimirovich Asaf'ev: Monografia* (Leningrad, 1984); Iurii Keldysh, ed., *B. V. Asaf'ev i sovetskaia muzykal'naia kul'tura: materialy Vsesoiuznoi nauchno-teoreticheskoi konferentsii* (Moscow, 1986); U. Gen-Ur, ed., *Aktual'nye voprosy muzykal'nogo obrazovaniia na sovremennom etape i nasledie B. V. Asaf'ev* (Petrozavodsk, 1984).

80. *De Musica* (1926–28) and *Muzykoznanie* (1929).

81. Kriukov, *Materialy*, 15–17; Schwarz, *Music and Musical Life*, 10.

82. See "Simfonism V. Shcherbacheva," *Sovremennaia muzyka* 15–16 (1926): 118–24; "Pacific 231," *Sovremennaia muzyka* 13–14 (1926): 69–73; "Kshenek i Berg, kak opernye kompozitory," *Sovremennaia muzyka* 17–18 (1926): 181–88.

83. Boris Asaf'ev, *Kniga o Stravinskom* (Leningrad, 1929); Asaf'ev, *Muzykal'naia forma kak protsess* (Moscow, 1930).

84. The neologisms usually involve abstractions of familiar nouns. Thus "tone" becomes "tonation," and "symphony" "symphonism." The precise meaning of these new terms remains unclear. See Gordon D. McQuere, "Boris Asafiev and *Musical Form as Process*," in *Russian Theoretical Thought in Music*, 223. On Asaf'ev's form-as-process, see Haas, *Leningrad's Modernists*, 53–80.

85. Haas, *Leningrad's Modernists*, 54.

86. "Krizis lichnogo tvorchestva," *Sovremennaia muzyka* 4 (1924): 100.

87. "Kompozitory pospeshite!" *Sovremennaia muzyka* 6 (1924): 148–49. See also "Zadachi i metody sovremennoi muzykal'noi kritiki," *Muzykal'naia kul'tura* 1 (1924): 20–36. Asaf'ev's

summons to take music "to the streets" ran counter to the general trend identified by Clark in which the intelligentsia abandoned their Civil War efforts to take their art to public spaces and returned to their own highbrow cultural institutions. See Clark, *Petersburg*, 143–61, especially 146–48, 161.

88. Igor Glebov, "Bytovaia muzyka posle Oktiabria," *Novaia muzyka* 2 (1928): 17–32; Glebov, "Motsart i sovremennost'," *Sovremennaia muzyka* 25 (1927): 55–59; Glebov, "Shubert i sovremennost'," *Sovremennaia muzyka* 26 (1927): 76–82.

89. Igor Glebov, "A. D. Kastal'skii," *Muzyka i revoliutsiia* 1 (1927): 9.

90. Ibid., 235.

91. Nikolai Roslavets, "O sebe i svoem tvorchestve," *Sovremennaia muzyka* 2 (1924): 134–35.

92. Reviews of *Three Compositions for Piano* (1914) and *Grustnye peisazhi* (settings of Verlaine for piano and voice, 1913), *Muzyka* 195 (1914): 542–44. Reprinted in Miaskovskii, *N. Ia. Miaskovskii. Sobranie materialov v dvukh tomakh*, vol. 2, 199–201.

93. Unpublished autobiographical sketch by Roslavets (ca. 1933). Quoted in Lobanova, *Roslavec*, 40.

94. Request to regional Party committee, January 3, 1921. RGALI f. 2659, ed. khr. 94, l. 1. Quoted in Lobanova, *Roslavec*, 45.

95. Glavrepertkom was established in February 1923. Roslavets joined its staff in May. See his personnel file in GARF f. 2306, op. 53, d. 260, l. 1. Anna Ferenc indicates that he had earlier worked for the Commissariat of Internal Affairs, and found a pass from the Moscow *Cheka* that gave Roslavets access to all buildings under its jurisdiction in the composer's personal papers in RGALI, f. 2659, ed. khr. 89, ll. 37–38. See Ferenc, "Investigating Russian Musical Modernism: Nikolai Roslavets and His New System of Tone Organization," Ph.D. diss. (University of Michigan, 1993), 11.

96. Fox, "Glavlit," 1060.

97. Ibid., 1057; Richmond, "The Conditions of the Contemporary," 26.

98. Fox, "Glavlit," 1060.

99. See Chapter 3.

100. Lobanova, *Roslavec*, 61–62.

101. The best study of Voronskii and his place in Soviet literature remains Robert A. Maguire, *Red Virgin Soil: Soviet Literature in the 1920s* (Evanston, 2000 [1968]).

102. See Arsenii Avraamov, "Klin klinom," *Muzykal'naia kul'tura* 1 (1924): 42–44; Giorgii Konius, "Metrotektonicheskoe razreshenie problemu muzykal'noi formy," *Muzykal'naia kul'tura* 1 (1924) 1: 36–41; Iu., "K voprosu ob atonal'noi muzyki," *Muzykal'naia kul'tura* 3 (1924): 261–64; A. Abaza, "Muzyka i tekhnika," *Muzykal'naia kul'tura* 3 (1924): 189–200.

103. "Nashi zadachi," *Muzykal'naia kul'tura* 1 (1924): 3–4.

104. Ibid., 3.

105. Dialektikus, "O reaktsionnom i progressivnom v muzyke," *Muzykal'naia kul'tura* 1 (1924): 48–49.

106. Roslavets, "O sebe i svoem tvorchestve," 138. Besides using an explicitly Marxist platform to defend his music, Roslavets also promoted himself as a revolutionary musician with an impeccable social background. In an autobiographical sketch published in *Sovremennaia muzyka* he recast his social origins, claiming to be the son of poor peasants rather than a scribe-carpenter. He also concealed his first marriage (to the daughter of Moscow notable and arts patron, Aleksei Langovoi), and portrayed himself as an autodidact, which, while partially true, failed to acknowledge the impact of his early tuition and performances with a *klezmer* in his native region of Chernigov. See Roslavets, "O sebe i svoem tvorchestve," 132. Lobanova examines the discrepancies in various sources dealing with the composer's biography in *Roslavec*, 25–30.

107. Born, *Rationalizing Culture*, 44.

108. For a concise overview of Roslavets's method in English, see Sitsky, *Music of the Repressed*, 39–55. See also Lobanova, *Roslavec*, 176–88. Roslavets asserted that the synthetic chords

were to be more than "color," also assuming some of the functions traditionally served by tonality. See Roslavets, "O sebe i svoem tvorchestve," 134–35.

109. Roslavets, "O sebe i svoem tvorchestve," 136.

110. "Khorovaia rabota v soiuze tekstil'shchikov," *Muzyka i revoliutsiia* 1 (1926): 37; Sergei Bugoslavskii, "Avtorskii kontsert Roslavtsa," *Izvestiia*, February 15, 1926, 6; L. Kaltat, "O podlinno-burzhuaznoi ideologii gr. Roslavtsa," *Muzykal'noe obrazovanie* 3–4 (1927): 34–35. Sitsky, *Music of the Repressed*, 40; For a more charitable assessment, see Lobanova, *Roslavec*, 176–88.

111. For one of the most impassioned, polemical critiques of his music and politics, see Kaltat, "O podlinno-burzhuaznoi ideologii," 32–42.

112. Clark, *Petersburg;* Boris Groys, "The Birth of Socialist Realism from the Spirit of the Avant-garde," in *The Culture of the Stalin Period*, ed. Hans Günther (New York, 1990), 122–47.

Chapter 3

1. Klara Zetkin, *My Recollections of Lenin* (Moscow, 1956), 19.

2. *Istoriia russkoi sovetskoi muzyki*, 39; *Istoriia muzyki narodov SSSR*, 135–36; Schwarz, *Music and Musical Life*, 55; Tarakanov, *Istoriia sovremennoi otechestvennoi muzyki*, 30–33; Krebs, *Soviet Composers*, 49–50; McQuere, *Russian Theoretical Thought in Music*, 50; Sitsky, *Music of the Repressed*, 6.

3. Sheila Fitzpatrick shows how RAPM's puritanical, anti-Western, antimodernist stance unified its activities in "The Lady Macbeth Affair: Shostakovich and the Soviet Puritans," 183–215. For a reassessment of RAPM's dominance and the paradigm of "Cultural Revolution," see Amy Nelson, "The Struggle for Proletarian Music: RAPM and the Cultural Revolution," *Slavic Review* 59 (2000): 101–32. See also Neil Edmunds, "Music and Politics: The Case of the Russian Association of Proletarian Musicians," *Slavonic and East European Review* 78 (2000): 66–89; Taruskin, *Defining Russia Musically*, 92.

4. Seeking to redress the partisan bias of previous accounts, Neil Edmunds offers a detailed and impartial view of these three groups in *The Soviet Proletarian Music Movement*. While Edmunds makes much valuable material about these musicians accessible for the first time, his goal is simply "to explain their ideas and discuss their activities" (13). The commitment to evenhandedness robs his study of an analytical framework that could provide an alternative to the old interpretive paradigm.

Aside from Edmunds's study, scholarly literature on ORK is almost nonexistent. The group is mentioned briefly in Schwarz, *Music and Musical Life*, 56; Gojowy, *Neue sowjetische Musik*, 15; and in Soviet texts such as *Istoriia russkoi sovetskoi muzyki*, 39; Arnol'd Sokhor, *Russkaia sovetskaia pesnia* (Leningrad, 1959), 109–14.

The activities of Prokoll are better documented. There is a fairly rich body of memoir literature by former members and many reviews of the group's music in Russian. Some records of Prokoll's meetings are in the fond of Sergei Riauzov at the Glinka Museum (fond 447), and have been examined by Valentina Zarudko in "Istoriia muzyki. Iz proshlogo sovetskoi muzykal'noi kul'tury," in *Moskovskii muzykoved*, vol. 1, ed. M. E. Tarakanov (1990), 5–19. For scholarship in English, see Neil Edmunds, "Alexander Davidenko and Prokoll," *Tempo* 182 (1992): 1–5; Schwarz, *Music and Musical Life*, 56–57.

5. In different periods the organization went under the name of APM and VAPM, but is best known as RAPM.

6. "Assotsiatsiia proletarskykh muzykantov," *Pravda*, August 26, 1923, 5. The idea to form the association emerged among "Communist musicians" in March. The Party organization at the Moscow Conservatory also supported the project. See P. Smigla, "Iz vospominanii o Moskovskoi konservatorii dvadtsatykh godov," in *Vospominaniia o Moskovskoi konservatorii*, ed. Alekseeva et al., 226.

7. A. Sergeev, "Assotsiatsiia proletarskykh muzykantov," *Muzykal'naia nov'* 1 (1923): 27. The other founding members were Lev Lebedinskii (1904–92), Sarra Krylova (1894–?), Sergei Chemodanov (1888–1942), and Efim Vilkovir (1888–1963).

8. "Assotsiatsiia proletarskykh muzykantov," *Pravda*, August 26, 1923, 5. The vagueness of RAPM's initial program was noticed by higher authorities and later acknowledged by RAPM itself. See G. B., "Muzykal'naia nov'," *Pravda*, February 25, 1924, 6; L. Lebedinskii, "Assotsiatsiia proletarskykh muzykantov," *Oktiabr'* 12 (1925): 145.

9. A. Sergeev, "Muzykal'nyi tupik," *Muzykal'naia nov'* 1 (1923): 8. The reference to "new shores" was, of course, a jab at the ASM, as well as an evocation of one of Belinsky's most characteristic images.

10. "Nashi zadachi," *Muzykal'naia nov'* 1 (1923): 6.

11. *Pervyi sbornik revoliutsionnykh pesen. 10 pesen, garmonizovannykh A. D. Ch.* (St. Petersburg, 1906).

12. "1924," *Muzykal'naia nov'* 12 (1924): 2; "Teatr i muzyka," *Pravda*, February 7, 1925, 6; Sergei Bugoslavskii, "Proletarskie muzykanty," *Zhizn' iskusstva* 15 (1925): 8; Lev Lebedinskii, *8 let bor'by za proletarskuiu muzyku* (Moscow, 1930), 28–30.

13. The others were Vasilii Alekseev (1884–1946), Efim Vilkovir, V. Klemens (?–?), and K. Postavnichev (?–?). *Muzykal'naia nov'* 12 (1924): 26.

14. RAPM's first platform appeared in the final issue of *Muzykal'naia nov'* (1924: 24–25). Two revisions (in 1926 and 1929) elaborated and retuned the organization's basic positions without eliminating their more problematic contradictions. See *Muzyka i Oktiabr'* 1 (1926): 22–24; supplement to *Proletarskii muzykant* 1 (1929): 3–12.

15. "Ideologicheskaia platforma Vserossiiskoi assotsiatsii proletarskykh muzykantov," *Muzyka i Oktiabr'* 1 (1926): 22.

16. Sh. "Kompozitor-Komsomolets," *Muzykal'naia nov'* 8 (1924): 21; Wilson, *Shostakovich*, 334.

17. Dmitrii Gachev (1902–45), Klavdia Golovskaia (1895–1948), Anatolii Solovstov (Groman-Solovtsov, 1898–1965), Lev Kaltat (1900–1946), Iurii Keldysh (1907–95), Sarra Krylova, M. M. Lazarev (?–?), Lev Lebedinskii, and Boris Shteinpress (1908–86).

18. Gachev, Solovtsov, and Shteinpress were also students of Ivanov-Boretskii.

19. The association admitted "Communist-musicians," and "persons of a certain class inclination" who worked among the proletarian masses as composers, performers, and pedagogues. A. Sergeev, "Assotsiatsiia proletarskykh muzykantov," *Muzykal'naia nov'* 1 (1923): 28.

20. "Assotsiatsiia proletarskykh muzykantov," *Muzykal'naia nov'* 11 (1924): 3; "Otchet RAPMa," supplement to *Proletarskii muzykant* 1 (1929): 14.

21. The group's senior member, David Chernomordikov, was 54 in 1923. At 19, Lev Lebedinskii was the youngest. Although their presence was always strongly felt, Communists never again dominated the organization. At the outset of the Cultural Revolution they made up exactly one third of RAPM's membership. "Otchet RAPMa," supplement to *Proletarskii muzykant* 1 (1929): 14.

22. Lebedinskii wrote a few vocal pieces but soon redirected his energies to musicology and criticism.

23. K., "M. Lazarev," *Muzyka i Oktiabr'* 4–5 (1926): 12.

24. A. Kastal'skii, "O vechere narodnostei v Bol'sh. teatr," *Muzykal'naia nov'* 2 (1923): 25–26. For RAPM's explanation of Kastal'skii's affiliation, see L. Kaltat, "O podlinno-burzhuaznoi ideologii gr. Roslavtsa," *Muzykal'noe obrazovanie* 3–4 (1927): 40.

25. For a detailed discussion of Kastal'skii's work with RAPM, see Edmunds, *Proletarian Music Movement*, 164–79.

26. Dmitrii Aleksandrov (1898–?), Nikolai Kudriavtsev (1893–?), and Sergei Tesh (1899–?).

27. Liubimov's work with Proletkul't is discussed in Chapter 1. His championing of the "Liubimov domra" became especially politicized during the Cultural Revolution in conjunction with his efforts to put the instrument into mass production.

28. E. Br., "10-letie gos. ak. ansamblia narodnoi pesni," *Pravda*, January 30, 1925, 8.

29. The group's full name was the "Organization of Revolutionary Composers and Musical Activists" (*Ob"edinenie revoliutsionnykh kompozitorov i muzykal'nykh deiatelei*).

30. "Proletarskaia revoliutsiia i sovremennaia muzyka," *Muzyka i revoliutsiia* 2 (1926): 7.

31. M., "Ob'edinenie revoliutsionnykh kompozitorov," *Muzyka i revoliutsiia* 1 (1926): 39; M., "Ob'edinenie revoliutsionnykh kompozitorov," *Muzyka i revoliutsiia* 5–6 (1927): 20–21.

32. "Ob'edinenie revoliutsionnykh kompozitorov," *Muzyka i revoliutsiia* 1 (1926): 39.

33. Elena Shul'gina, comp., *L. V. Shul'gin. Stat'i, vospominaniia* (Moscow, 1977), 16.

34. The organization's initiative group consisted of Shul'gin, Sergeev, Vilkovir, Dmitrii Vasil'ev-Buglai (1888–1956), Vladimir Dasmanov (1896–?), V. Klemens (?–?), S. V. Kliachko (?–?), Klimentii Korchmarev (1899–1958), Mikhail Krasev (1897–1954), Georgii Polianovskii (1894–?), and Nikolai Dem'ianov (1899–1960). See photo in *Muzyka i revoliutsiia* 5–6 (1927): 21.

35. "Sovremennoe muzykal'noe tvorchestvo i predposylki nashei tvorcheskoi raboty," *Muzykal'naia nov'* 4 (1924): 16.

36. M. Ivanov-Boretskii, "Agitatsionno-prosvetitel'naia muzykal'naia literatura," *Muzykal'naia nov'* 8 (1924): 27. Lunacharsky's assessment of the *agitki* softened with time. Later in 1926 he acknowledged that the task of "revolutionary" composers was difficult, and maintained that many did "healthy, necessary" work. See A. V. Lunacharskii, *V mire muzyki. Stat'i i rechi* (Moscow, 1971), 186–87; Lunacharskii, "Oktiabr' i muzyka," *Muzyka i revoliutsiia* 11 (1926): 5–6.

37. Vladimir Frumkin, "Tekhnologiia ubezhdeniia: zametki o politicheskoi pesne," *Obozrenie* 6 (1983): 24. Although Frumkin identifies these songs as coming from composers in "production collectives," it seems clear that they were written by members of ORK.

38. E. M., "Mikhail Krasev," *Muzyka i revoliutsiia* 1 (1928): 14–15.

39. The State Academic Council (GUS) objected to the low quality and large number of Krasev's compositions. GARF f. 298, op. 1, d. 129, l. 158ob. For RAPM's critique, see Iurii Keldysh, "Problema proletarskogo muzykal'nogo tvorchestva i poputnichestvo," *Proletarskii muzykant* 1 (1929): 19.

40. For a detailed discussion of Krasev's work, see Edmunds, *Soviet Proletarian Music Movement*, 197–208.

41. Vasil'ev-Buglai's civil war activities are discussed in Chapter 1. For a detailed examination of his work in the 1920s, see Edmunds, *Soviet Proletarian Music Movement*, 179–96.

42. Workers' positive response to this piece is described by Sergei Bugoslavskii, "Bloknot muzykanta," *Zhizn' iskusstva* 25 (1924): 16. For an in-depth discussion of Vasil'ev-Buglai's music, see Edmunds, *Soviet Proletarian Music Movement*, 179–97.

43. *Tsentral'nyi dom iskusstva v derevne im. V. D. Polenova.* In the thirties this institution was renamed the *Vsesoiuznyi dom narodnogo tvorchestva im. N. K. Krupskoi.*

44. Quote referring to RAPM from Sitsky, *Music of the Repressed*, 6; see also Stites, *Russian Popular Culture*, 46; Schwarz, *Music and Musical Life*, 54.

45. B. Shekhter, "Gody tvorcheskogo obshcheniia," in *Aleksandr Davidenko. Vospominaniia. Stat'i. Materialy*, comp. Martynov, 45.

46. Vl. Fere, "Moskovskaia konservatoriia v 20-e gody," *Sovetskaia muzyka* 11 (1958): 23.

47. Sergei Riauzov, "Vospominaniia o 'Prokolle,'" *Sovetskaia muzyka* 7 (1949): 54.

48. Excerpt from the group's statute published in "Proizvodstvennyi kollektiv studentov MGK," *Muzyka i revoliutsiia* 1 (1926): 40. The complete text is found in Zarudko, "Istoriia muzyki," 8–9.

49. L. A. Ginzburg et al., eds., *Moskovskaia konservatoriia, 1866–1966* (Moscow, 1966), 319.

50. Prokoll had twenty-two members in 1927. Its secretary recorded a total of twenty-seven participants during the organization's existence. See V. B., "Prokoll," in Moskovskaia gosudarstvennaia konservatoriia, *K desiatiletiiu Oktiabria, 1917–1927. Sbornik statei* (Moscow, 1927), 34; Riauzov, "Vospominaniia," 54.

51. L. Lebedinskii, "A. Davidenko. Materialy dlia tvorcheskoi biografii," *Sovetskaia muzyka* 4 (1935): 26.

52. L. Levinson, "V pamiat' druzhby," in *Aleksandr Davidenko*, comp. Martynov, 96–98.

53. M. Koval', "O sebe i o svoei muzyke," *Sovremennaia muzyka* 32 (1929): 12.

54. Daniel Zhitomirskii, "O Davidenko i Prokolle," in *Aleksandr Davidenko*, comp. Martynov, 78–79.

55. M. Koval', "Riadom s Aleksandrom Davidenko," in *Aleksandr Davidenko*, comp. Martynov, 74–75.

56. A list of forty-one pieces published by Prokoll members as of November 1927 includes only one instrumental work, a piano sonata by Shekhter. See Moskovskaia gosudarstvennaia konservatoriia, *K desiatiletiiu Oktiabria*, 34–35.

57. See Chapters 7 and 8.

58. Zhitomirskii, "O Davidenko i Prokolle," 80.

59. Neil Edmunds provides an in-depth examination of Prokoll's music, focusing in particular on the work of Davidenko, Shekhter, Koval, and Belyi. See Edmunds, *Soviet Proletarian Music Movement*, 211–88.

60. Sokhor, *Russkaia sovetskaia pesnia*, 134.

61. Fere, "Nash uchitel' Nikolai Iakovlevich Miaskovskii," 430.

62. *Sovremennaia muzyka* 16–17 (1926): 170, 174; *Sovremennaia muzyka* 31 (1928): 178, 181.

63. V. Belyi, "Levaia fraza muzykal'noi reaktsii," *Muzykal'noe obrazovanie* 1 (1928): 43–47; Marion Koval', "Propaganda dzhaz-banda," *Muzyka i revoliutsiia* 5–6 (1927): 49.

64. "Proizvodstvennyi kollektiv studentov MGK," *Muzyka i revoliutsiia* 1 (1926): 40.

65. See Chapter 5.

66. Roslavets initially banned Lebedinskii's scathing assessment of Sabaneev, Roslavets, and *Muzykal'naia kul'tura*, which appeared in a significantly edited version as "Beglym ognem," in *Muzykal'naia nov'* 8 (1924): 13–17. Roslavets then attempted to control the polemics by setting out "four rules" for debate in *Muzykal'naia kul'tura* 2 (1924): 135–37. RAPM rejected these "Trotskyist" ground rules, and theoretical exchanges between the two groups virtually ceased. The conflict was later characterized as "the plow (folk song) versus the tractor (Roslavets' New Tone System)" by Arsenii Avraamov. See his "Ia protestuiu," *Zhizn' iskusstva* 22 (1927): 15.

67. Roslavets's protest to Rabis head Iuvenal Slavinskii (dated December 28, 1924) is reprinted in "Organizator zvukov," *Muzykal'naia gazeta* 6 (1990): 4; and in Lobanova, *Roslaveč*, 60–63. On RAPM's response to the reorganization, see L. Lebedinskii, "Reorganizatsiia Muzsektora Giz'a," *Muzykal'naia nov'* 12 (1924): 3–6.

68. The final version of the resolution was written by Bukharin and published as "O politike partii v oblasti khudozhestvennoi literatury," *Pravda*, July 1, 1925, 6. On the literary debate, see Maguire, *Red Virgin Soil*, 148–87; Brown, *The Proletarian Episode*, 35–45.

69. Lebedinskii, *8 let bor'by za proletarskuiu muzyku*, 28–30.

70. Gojowy, *Neue sowjetische Musik*, 31.

71. M. Grinberg [Sokol'skii], "Dmitrii Shostakovich," *Muzyka i revoliutsiia* 11 (1927): 16–20; Grinberg, "Sergei Prokof'ev," *Muzyka i revoliutsiia* 2 (1927): 15–17.

72. "Proletarskaia revoliutsiia i sovremennaia muzyka," *Muzyka i revoliutsiia* 2 (1926): 3–10; "Nekotorye voprosy muzykal'noi revoliutsii," *Muzyka i revoliutsiia* 4 (1926): 3–13; "'Levyi flang' sovremennoi muzyki," *Muzyka i revoliutsiia* 1 (1927): 3–7; E. M., "'Poslednee slovo' otzhivaiushchei kul'tury," *Muzyka i revoliutsiia* 9 (1927): 3–6.

Chapter 4

1. G. Soboleva, *Russkii-sovetskii romans* (Moscow, 1985), 18.

2. On the history and characteristics of the gypsy romance in this period, see Soboleva, *Russkii-sovetskii romans*, 3–44; Gerald Stanton Smith, *Songs to Seven Strings: Russian Guitar Poetry and Soviet Mass Song* (Bloomington, 1984), 60–64; Rothstein, "The Quiet Rehabilitation of the Brick Factory," 375–76; Rothstein, "Popular Song in the NEP Era," in *Russia in the Era of NEP*, ed. Fitzpatrick et al., 271–73; Stites, *Russian Popular Culture*, 12–15.

3. On the variety of tangos and other Western dances popular with Soviet youth in this period, see Gorsuch, *Youth in Revolutionary Russia*, 120–25.

4. Starr, *Red and Hot*, 54–66.

5. M. F. Leonova, *Dmitrii Pokrass* (Moscow, 1981), 36.

6. M. I. Zil'berbrandt, "Pesnia na estrade," in *Russkaia sovetskaia estrada 1917–1929 gg. Ocherki istorii*, ed. E. Uvarova (Moscow, 1976), 209–10.

7. Pioneering detail of the fame and fortunes of *Little Bricks* and its significance in Soviet popular musical culture is presented by Rothstein in "The Quiet Rehabilitation of the Brick Factory," 373–78.

8. In addition to Rothstein, "The Quiet Rehabilitation of the Brick Factory," 381–82, see Iurii Sokolov, *Russian Folklore*, trans. Catherine Ruth Smith (New York, 1950), 627–29; Sokhor, *Russkaia sovetskaia pesnia*, 98–99; Zil'berbrandt, "Pesnia na estrade," 236–37. A recording of the song may be found on the companion cassette to James von Geldern and Richard Stites, eds., *Mass Culture in Soviet Russia: Tales, Poems, Songs, Movies, Plays, and Folklore, 1917–1953* (Bloomington, 1995). See *Mass Culture in Soviet Russia*, 69–70, for Russian and English versions of the text. For contemporary accounts of the widespread popularity of *Little Bricks*, see A. Groman, "O muzyke dlia derevni," *Muzyka i Oktiabr'* 1 (1926): 7; P. Bosh, "O chem poet molodaia derevnia," *Zhizn' iskusstva* 15 (1926): 14. For a review of the film, see "Kirpichiki," *Izvestiia*, January 17, 1926, 5.

9. On the cruel romance and underworld songs, see Rothstein, "Popular Song in the NEP Era," 278–88; Stites, *Russian Popular Culture*, 48; Smith, *Songs to Seven Strings*, 64–70.

10. "Murka. Blatnye i ulichnye pesni" Compact Disc. United Service Limited.

11. Fedor Malov, "Chastushka v tsyfrakh," *Sovetskoe iskusstvo* 1 (1927): 44–45; Iu. M. Sokolov, "Chastushka," *Sovetskoe iskusstvo* 1 (1925): 32–36; L. Subbotin, "Agropropaganda cherez iskusstvo," *Sovetskoe iskusstvo* 2 (1925): 40–44; Sokolov, *Russian Folklore*, 632–47; Rothstein, "Popular Song in the NEP Era," 277–78; von Geldern and Stites, *Mass Culture in Soviet Russia*, 15–16.

12. "Nashi zadachi," *Muzykal'naia nov'* 1 (1923): 5; Nikolai Shuvalov, "Muzykal'noe prosveshchenie prezhde i teper'," *Muzykal'naia nov'* 1 (1923): 23; "Proletarskaia revoliutsiia i sovremennaia muzyka," *Muzyka i revoliutsiia* 2 (1926): 3–4; "Muzyka i revoliutsiia," *Muzyka i revoliutsiia* 1 (1926): 3–4.

13. S. Korev, "Pervyi kamen'," *Sovetskoe iskusstvo* 4 (1926): 36; S. Bugoslavskii, "K itogam muzykal'nogo sezona," *Sovetskoe iskusstvo* 2 (1925): 77; N. Briusova, "Muzykal'noe prosveshchenie i obrazovanie za gody revoliutsii," *Muzyka i revoliutsiia* 1 (1926): 29; Shuvalov, "Muzykal'noe prosveshchenie," *Muzykal'naia nov'* 1 (1923): 23.

14. "Muzyka i revoliutsiia," *Muzyka i revoliutsiia* 1 (1926): 5; Shuvalov, "Muzykal'noe prosveshchenie," *Muzykal'naia nov'* 1 (1923) 24; Groman, "O muzyke dlia derevni," *Muzyka i Oktiabr'* 1 (1926): 7.

15. Grigorii Liubimov, "Muzykal'naia ruda," *Muzyka i Oktiabr'* 1 (1926): 7; L. Shul'gin, "Massovaia pesnia," *Muzyka i revoliutsiia* 2 (1926): 19; E. V., "K itogam I-oi konferentsii po muzykal'noi politprosvetitel'noi rabote," *Muzyka i revoliutsiia* 4 (1926): 14; E. V., "Soveshchaniia pri Glavpolitprosvete po voprosu o sozdanii muzyki dlia mass," *Muzyka i revoliutsiia* 2 (1926): 39.

16. Ra-Be, "Rabkory o muzyke," *Muzykal'naia nov'* 11 (1924): 14.

17. "Nekotorye voprosy muzykal'noi revoliutsii," *Muzyka i revoliutsiia* 4 (1926): 13; L. Lebedinskii, "K voprosu o proletarskoi muzyke," *Muzyka i Oktiabr'* 2 (1926): 1; A. Groman, "O muzyke dlia derevni," *Muzyka i Oktiabr'* 1 (1926): 7; Sarra Krylova, "Po povudu stat'i tov. Paskhalova," *Muzyka i Oktiabr'* 2 (1926): 8.

18. N. Shuvalov, "O muzykal'nom nasledstve, o 'kursakh' i izdatel'stve," *Muzykal'naia nov'* 2 (1923): 11.

19. M. Koval', "Pesni ulitsi," *Muzyka i Oktiabr'* 3 (1926): 21.

20. N. Vygodskii, "Izuchaite muzykal'nyi byt!" *Muzykal'noe obrazovanie* 1–2 (1926): 51–52.

21. N. Shuvalov, "Muzykal'noe prosveshchenie," *Muzykal'naia nov'* 1 (1923): 24. RAPM's perception of the light genre bears interesting parallels with the nineteenth-century intelligentsia's denunciation of the penny novel (*kopeika*) as a "poison." See Brooks, *When Russia Learned to Read*, 331.

22. Shul'gin, "Massovaia pesnia," *Muzyka i revoliutsiia* 2 (1926): 19.

23. Sergei Bugoslavskii, "Vasil'ev-Buglai," *Muzykal'naia nov'* 2 (1923): 23.

24. GTsMMK f. 446, ed. khr. 776, l. 1–4. The collection was published as *Pesni katorgi i ssylki* (Moscow, 1930). In the fall of 1931, Davidenko and Belyi (who were now members of

RAPM), Krylova, and Lebedinskii were invited to sing these songs for Nadezhda Krupskaia and Lenin's sister. S. Krylova, "Poezdka v Gor'kii," in *Aleksandr Davidenko*, comp. Martynov, 117.

25. L. V. Shul'gin, "U istokov sovetskoi pesni," in *L. V. Shul'gin*, comp. Shul'gina (Moscow, 1977), 26.

26. Examples include: *My krasnye soldaty*, *Rasstrel kommunarov* (melody either *My mirno stoiali pred zimnom dvortsom* or *My sami kopali mogilu svoiu*), and *Tam vdali za rekoi* (melody *Lish tol'ko v Siberii zaimetsia zaria*).

27. N. Shuvalov, "O muzykal'nom nasledstve," *Muzykal'naia nov'* 2 (1924): 11; N. Briusova, "Na bor'bu s muzykal'nym durmanom," in *Dovesti do kontsa bor'bu s NEPmanskoi muzyki* (Moscow, 1931), 17–18.

28. E. M., "Paralleli," *Muzyka i revoliutsiia* 3 (1926): 3–5. RAPM's objections to these dances were not isolated or without precedent. Campaigns against jazz were common in the West in this period, and both the tango and fox-trot had generated considerable outcry and public debate when they first came to Russia before World War I. See Starr, *Red and Hot*, 34–36, 86; Yurii Tsivian, "The Tango in Russia," *Experiment* 2 (1996): 307–35; Chris Gilman, "The Fox-Trot and the New Economic Policy: A Case Study in 'Thingification' and Cultural Imports," *Experiment* 2 (1996): 443–75.

29. The musical Left's explanation for the popularity of light genre music echoed the concerns of nineteenth-century educated Russians who blamed the success of popular commercial literature on a lack of "good" alternatives and external forces such as publishers' greed and the market dynamics of capitalism. See Brooks, *When Russia Learned to Read*, 321–22. The intelligentsia's hostility to commercial influences on culture is also examined at length in Swift, *Popular Theater and Society;* and Clark, *Petersburg*. For a broader discussion of the development and critiques of commercial culture in the late Imperial period, see Kelly and Shepherd, *Constructing Russian Culture*, 106–55.

30. The musical Left's confrontation with the "backwardness" of musical *byt* paralleled and extended campaigns by the Komsomol to eradicate objectionable behavior such as drinking, dancing, and swearing (hooliganism) and inculcate appropriate "Communist" mores. Objections to musical "hackwork" and fox-trots from RAPM and ORK thus supported the larger effort to stamp out the hooliganism among youth, and were comparably unsuccessful. See Peter Gooderham, "The Komsomol and Worker Youth: The Inculcation of 'Communist Values' in Leningrad during NEP," *Soviet Studies* 34 (1982): 506–28; Gorsuch, *Youth in Revolutionary Russia*, 116–25.

31. The varied, often contradictory uses of the word "culture" in revolutionary Russia among intellectuals and revolutionaries has warranted extensive discussion. See Mally, *Culture of the Future*, xvi–xvii; Sheila Fitzpatrick, "Introduction: On Power and Culture," in *The Cultural Front*, 1–15; Peter Kenez, "Introduction: The Bolsheviks and the Intelligentsia," in *Party, State, and Society in the Russian Civil War*, ed. Koenker et al., 241; Abbott Gleason, "Introduction," *Bolshevik Culture*, vii–ix; Rosenberg, *Bolshevik Visions*, 17–24.

32. S. Krylova, "Assotsiatsiia proletarskykh muzykantov," *Muzykal'naia nov'* 2 (1923): 17.

33. S. Chemodanov, "O Betkhoven i sovremennosti," *Muzykal'naia nov'* 2 (1923): 14–16; "Ideologicheskaia platforma Vserossiiskoi assotsiatsii proletarskykh muzykantov," *Muzykal'naia nov'* 12 (1924): 24; "Ideologicheskaia platforma Vserossiiskoi assotsiatsii proletarskykh muzykantov," supplement to *Proletarskii muzykant* 1 (1929): 5–6; "Proletarskaia muzyka i sovremennaia muzyka," *Muzyka i revoliutsiia* 2 (1926): 8.

34. L. Shul'gin, "K postanovke voprosa o slushanii muzyki v kruzhkakh," *Muzyka i revoliutsiia* 1 (1926): 22.

35. "Industrializm i 'narodnichestvo' v muzyke," *Muzyka i revoliutsiia* 3 (1928): 8–9.

36. "Proletarskaia muzyka i sovremennaia muzyka," *Muzyka i revoliutsiia* 2 (1926): 8; N. Shuvalov, "Muzykal'noe prosveshchenie," *Muzykal'naia nov'* 1 (1923): 23.

37. Vasil'ev-Buglai's *Kon' i khoziain* and *Tserkovnaia sluzhba* and Kastal'skii's *Troika* are identified as ideologically appropriate and of acceptable artistic quality to warrant the designation "proletarian music" in "V tsentral'nom dome rabotnikov iskusstv," *Muzykal'naia nov'* 11 (1924): 24. Lazarev's *Bei molotom* is praised in "M. Lazarev," *Muzyka i Oktiabr'* 4–5 (1926): 12.

38. A. Tsenovskii, "Sbornik 'Krasnyi Oktiabr',''" *Muzykal'naia nov'* 10 (1924): 30; L. Lebedinskii, "Reorganizatsiia Muzsektora Giz'a," *Muzykal'naia nov'* 12 (1924): 3; Lebedinskii, "A. Davidenko," *Sovetskaia muzyka* 4 (1935): 29–30; Sergei Rauzov, "Vospominaniia o 'Prokolle,'" *Sovetskaia muzyka* 7 (1949): 54–55.

39. "Nekotorye voprosy muzykal'noi revoliutsii," *Muzyka i revoliutsiia* 4 (1926): 13.

40. L. Shul'gin, "Dostizheniia revoliutsionnoi muzyki," *Sovetskoe iskusstvo* 1 (1925): 91–92; L. Lebedinskii, "Assotsiatsiia proletarskykh muzykantov," *Oktiabr'* 12 (1925): 143–44; M. Koval', "O sebe i o svoei muzyke," *Sovremennaia muzyka* 32 (1929): 12; Zhitomirskii, "O Davidenko i Prokolle," 78–79.

41. A. S., "Tovarishch D. Vasil'ev-Buglai," *Muzykal'naia nov'* 2 (1923): 22.

42. Sergei Bugoslavskii, "Vasil'ev-Buglai," *Muzykal'naia nov'* 2 (1923): 23.

43. L. Shul'gin, "Sovremennoe muzykal'noe tvorchestvo i predposylki nashei tvorcheskoi raboty," *Muzykal'naia nov'* 4 (1924): 4.

44. Bugoslavskii, "Vasil'ev-Buglai," *Muzykal'naia nov'* 2 (1923): 23. The Left's suspicions of instrumental music parallel those of reformers during the French Revolution, but were not as fully elaborated. See Johnson, *Listening in Paris*, 135–36.

45. "Chistoi muzyki Kreml' ne liubit." D. V. Buglai, "Klub im. Sverdlova VTsIK," *Muzykal'naia nov'* 1 (1923): 34.

46. L. Shul'gin, "Massovaia pesnia," *Muzyka i revoliutsiia* 2 (1926): 18; S. Krylova, "Assotsiatsiia proletarskykh muzykantov," *Muzykal'naia nov'* 2 (1923): 18. As songs of protest or laments over the hardships of life, these songs were also precursors of revolutionary songs and were promoted by the revolutionary movement. See Suzanne Ament, "Russian Revolutionary Songs of 1905 and 1917: Symbols and Messengers of Protest and Change" (M.A. thesis, Georgetown University, 1984), 14, 40–41.

47. Scholars have emphasized RAPM's hostility to the folk song. But even during the Cultural Revolution they considered the peasant folk song an artistic treasure that warranted preservation, even if it was not acceptable as the foundation for proletarian music. See L. Lebedinsky, "Nash massovoi muzykal'noi byt," *Proletarskii muzykant* 9–10 (1930): 9; L. Kaltat, "O podlinno-burzhuaznoi ideologii gr. Roslavtsa," *Muzykal'noe obrazovanie* 3–4 (1927): 41.

48. A. S., "Tovarishch D. Vasil'ev-Buglai," *Muzykal'naia nov'* 2 (1923): 23.

49. Grigorii Liubimov, "Muzykal'naia ruda," *Muzyka i Oktiabr'* 1 (1926): 6–7.

50. N. Vygodskii, "Izuchaite muzykal'nyi byt!" *Muzykal'noe obrazovanie* 1–2 (1926): 51–52.

51. L. Shul'gin, "Agitotdel Muzsektora Giz'a," *Muzykal'naia nov'* 10 (1924): 8; L. Lebedinskii, "K voprosu o proletarskoi muzyki," *Muzyka i Oktiabr'* 2 (1926): 1. Activists in the twenties were not the first to express these concerns. Observers had lamented the "corruption" and "decline" of the folk song in Russia since the 1870s. See Rothstein, "Death of the Folk Song?" 108.

52. L. Kaltat, "K voprosu o klubno-muzykal'noi rabote," *Muzyka i Oktiabr'* 4–5 (1926): 24–25.

53. Conservatives within the church hierarchy objected to this line of inquiry, insisting that church chant was unsullied by popular influences. See Daniel Zhitomirskii, ed., *A. D. Kastal'skii. Stat'i, vospominaniia i materialy* (Moscow, 1960), 31.

54. A. Kastal'skii, "Pervye shagi," *Muzykal'naia nov'* 11 (1924): 8–10; Kastal'skii, "Posleduiushchie shagi," *Muzykal'naia nov'* 12 (1924): 9–10.

55. See Chapter 3, examples 4a and 5a.

56. For an overview of the club movement in this period, see John Hatch, "The Formation of Working Class Cultural Institutions during NEP: The Workers' Club Movement in Moscow, 1921–1923," *Carl Beck Papers in Russian and East European Studies* 806 (1990); Hatch, "Hangouts and Hangovers: State, Class, and Culture in Moscow's Workers' Club Movement, 1925–28," *Russian Review* 53 (1994): 97–117; Vance Kepley Jr., "Cinema and Everyday Life: Soviet Worker Clubs of the 1920s," in *Resisting Images: Essays on Cinema and History*, ed. Robert Sklar and Charles Musser (Philadelphia, 1990), 108–25.

57. On the place of the clubs in developing socialist culture, see Leon Trotsky, "Leninism and Workers Clubs," in *Problems of Everyday Life and Other Writings on Culture and Science* (New York, 1973), 288–319.

58. John Hatch, "The Politics of Mass Culture: Workers, Communists, and Proletkul't in the Development of Workers' Clubs, 1921–25," *Russian History / Histoire Russe* 13 (1986): 119. Many of the Left's activists, including Vasil'ev-Buglai and Grigorii Liubimov, were veterans of Proletkul't and had been active in the prerevolutionary workers' education-enlightenment movement.

59. Sergei Bugoslavskii, "Metodika muzykal'noi raboty v klube," *Prizyv* 1 (1925): 52.

60. S. Krylova, "Muzyka v rabochem klube," *Prizyv* 7 (1924): 35.

61. Ts. Ratskaia, "Khorkruzhki," *Muzykal'naia nov'* 11 (1924): 6–7.

62. Theater and cinema groups had the largest followings. See Hatch, "Hangouts and Hangovers," 107–13; Diane P. Koenker, "Class Consciousness in a Socialist Society: Workers in the Printing Trades during NEP," in *Russia in the Era of NEP*, ed. Fitzpatrick et al., 49–51; Mally, *Revolutionary Acts;* and Kepley, "Cinema and Everyday Life."

63. Georgii Polianovskii, "Khorovaia i muzykal'naia rabota v soiuze Shveinikov," *Muzyka i revoliutsiia* 2 (1926): 31; N. Dem'ianov, "Novaia ustanovka klubno-khorovoi raboty," *Muzyka i revoliutsiia* 4 (1927): 9.

64. Ivan Lipaev, "Tserkovniki ili obshchestvenniki," *Muzykal'naia nov'* 11 (1924): 7; S. Krylova, "Muzyka v rabochem klube," *Prizyv* 7 (1924): 34; V. Furman, "Kontserty v rabochykh klubakh," *Muzyka i revoliutsiia* 3 (1926): 29.

65. S. Abakumov, "V Moskovskoi Gos. Konservatorii. Khorovoi otdel," *Muzykal'naia nov'* 12 (1924): 28.

66. Rybinskii, "Kursy dlia klubnykh rukovoditelei," *Pravda*, January 16, 1924, 7; "Khorovaia rabota v soiuze tekstil'shchikov," *Muzyka i revoliutsiia* 1 (1926): 36; N. Dem'ianov, "Muzykal'naia samodeiatel'naia rabota i professional'noe muzykal'noe iskusstvo," *Muzyka i revoliutsiia* 4 (1929): 11; V. A. Dasmanov, "Derevenskie instrumental'nye kruzhki," *Muzyka i revoliutsiia* 4 (1929): 14.

67. R., "V Moskovskoi Gos. Konservatorii. Pedagogicheskii otdel," *Muzykal'naia nov'* 10 (1924): 26.

68. S. Bugoslavskii, "Metodika muzykal'noi raboty v klube," *Prizyv* 1 (1925): 53.

69. N. Dem'ianov, "Formy i metody raboty khor-kruzhka," *Muzykal'naia nov'* 5 (1924): 14; Ts. Ratskaia, "Muzykal'naia rabota v khorkruzhkakh," *Muzykal'naia nov'* 10 (1924): 11–12; K. Kastal'skii, "Pervye shagi," *Muzykal'naia nov'* 11 (1924): 8–10; Kastal'skii, "Posleduiushchie shagi," *Muzykal'naia nov'* 12 (1924): 9–10; S. Bugoslavskii, "Metodika muzykal'noi raboty v klube," *Prizyv* 1 (1925): 52–56; I. Dubovskii, "Besedy po muzykal'noi gramoti," *Muzyka i Oktiabr'* 2 (1926): 11–15.

70. M. Pekelis, "O slushanii muzyke," *Muzyka i Oktiabr'* 1 (1926): 11–15. Iavorskii developed this method in the prerevolutionary period and used it in choral singing classes at the People's Conservatory founded after the 1905 Revolution. In the twenties Nadezhda Briusova become an ardent proponent of the method, which provided the curricular backbone for the Krasnaia Presnia School of Musical Instructors. See A. D., "Muzykal'naia shkola instruktorov imeni Krasnoi Presni," *Muzyka i revoliutsiia* 1 (1926): 41. A summary of Briusova's lectures on "listening to music" is in GARF f. 2306, op. 25, d. 77, ll. 1–2.

71. L. Shul'gin, "K postanovke voprosa o slushanii muzyki v kruzhkakh," *Muzyka i revoliutsiia* 1 (1926): 19–22; Gr. Avlov, "V bor'be za pesniu," *Zhizn' iskusstva* 5 (1927): 7.

72. L. Shul'gin, "K postanovke voprosa o slushanii muzyki v kruzhkakh," *Muzyka i revoliutsiia* 1 (1926): 21.

73. G. Polianovskii, "Khorovaia i muzykal'naia rabota v soiuze Shveinikov," *Muzyka i revoliutsiia* 2 (1926): 31.

74. G. Polianovskii, "Vecher-pokaz khudozhestvennykh klubnykh kruzhkov Moskovskikh profsoiuzov dlia delegatov VII Vsesoiuznogo s"ezda profsoiuzov," *Muzyka i revoliutsiia* 1 (1927): 25.

75. N. Dem'ianov, "Muzykal'naia samodeiatel'naia rabota i professional'noe muzykal'noe iskusstvo," *Muzyka i revoliutsiia* 4 (1929): 12; S. Krylova, "Muzyka v rabochem klube," *Prizyv* 7 (1924): 38.

76. L. Shul'gin, "K postanovke voprosa o slushanii muzyki v kruzhkakh," *Muzyka i revoliutsiia* 1 (1926): 21; "Razgovor v rabochem klube," *Muzyka i revoliutsiia* 1 (1926): 22–23; L. Kaltat, "K voprosu o klubno-muzykal'noi rabote," *Muzyka i Oktiabr'* 4–5 (1926): 24.

77. Sosnovskii, "Garmoshka," *Rabochaia gazeta* 203 (1924); Vas. Alekseev, "Nezasluzhenno prenebregaemyi, poleznyi dlia tselei vospitaniia instrument," *Muzykal'naia nov'* 9 (1924): 18–19; N. Vasil'ev, "O garmoshke," *Muzykal'naia nov'* 12 (1924): 7; V. Paskhalov, "Muzykal'nye ressursy garmoshki," *Muzyka i Oktiabr* 2 (1926): 7; S. Krylova, "Po povudu stat'i tov. Paskhalova," *Muzyka i Oktiabr'* 2 (1926): 8–9.

78. S. Bugoslavskii, "Vnimanie garmonike," *Izvestiia*, July 14, 1926, 5. Zharov also promoted the accordion's association with revolutionary musical creativity in *The Red Accordion*, a widely distributed collection of political *chastushki*. See A. Zharov, *Krasnaia garmoshka*, 2d ed. (Moscow, 1925).

79. Sosnovskii, "Garmoshka," *Rabochaia gazeta* 203 (1924); G. Bolychevtsev, "Chem zhivet derevnia v oblasti muzyki," *Muzyka i Oktiabr'* 3 (1926): 3, 16; Islamei, "Zadachi massovoi muzykal'noi raboty," *Zhizn' iskusstva* 34 (1926): 4.

80. "Teatr—Muzyka—Kino," *Izvestiia*, September 30, 1926, 5; "Konkurs na luchshego garmonista," *Izvestiia*, October 19, 1926, 5; I. I. Zemtsovskii and V. P. Il'in, "Muzykal'naia samodeiatel'nost'," in *Muzykal'naia kul'tura Leningrada za 50 let*, ed. V. M. Bogdanov-Berezovskii (Leningrad, 1967), 470–71.

81. Vasil'ev, "O garmoshke," *Muzykal'naia nov'* 12 (1924): 7; Illar. Skladnev, "Muzykal'naia rabota Rabkluba Troitskogo Sol'zavoda," *Muzyka i Oktiabr'* 2 (1926): 22. Two 1920s films demonized the accordion's influence on working-class and peasant culture: Pudovkin's *Mother* and Preobrazhenskaia's *Peasant Women of Riazan'*.

82. Dem'ian Bednyi, "Garmon' ili delo ot bezdel'ia," *Izvestiia*, December 19, 1926, 5.

83. Paskhalov, "Muzykal'nye ressursy," *Muzyka i Oktiabr'* 2 (1926): 7.

84. G. Polianovskii, "Konkurs garmonistov," *Muzyka i revoliutsiia* 1 (1927): 26–27.

85. L. Gurevich, "Na vernom puti," *Muzyka i revoliutsiia* 5–6 (1928): 11; "Muzyka sil'na v bytu," *Zhizn' iskusstva* 43 (1926): 1.

86. S. Krylova, "Po povudu stat'i tov. Paskhalova," *Muzyka i Oktiabr'* 2 (1926): 8; L. Lebedinskii, "K voprosu o proletarskoi muzyki," *Muzyka i Oktiabr'* 2 (1926): 2; Illar. Skladnev, "Muzykal'naia rabota Rabkluba," *Muzyka i Oktiabr'* 2 (1926): 22; M. and Sh., "Kul'tivirovat' ili izzhivat' garmoniku?" *Muzyka i revoliutsiia* 4 (1927): 14; L. Lebedinskii, "Garmonika i ee znachenie," *Na literaturnom postu* 14 (1927): 45.

87. L. Kaltat, "K voprosu o klubno-muzykal'noi rabote," *Muzyka i Oktiabr'* 4–5 (1926): 24. On the debates surrounding the objectives of *samodeiatel'nyi* theater groups in this period, see Mally, *Revolutionary Acts*, 47–57, 78–108. See also Clark, *Petersburg*, 146.

88. L. Kaltat, "Klub imeni t. Stalina pri Sekretariate TsKVP(b)," *Muzyka i Oktiabr'* 2 (1926): 20. Activists sometimes claimed that audiences' musical sensibilities were more sophisticated than the musicianship of the choral circles. See N. Dem'ianov, "Novaia ustanovka klubno-khorovoi raboty," *Muzyka i revoliutsiia* 4 (1927): 9.

89. N. Dem'ianov, "Semeinye vechera v rabochykh klubakh," *Muzyka i revoliutsiia* 3 (1926): 10.

90. N. D., "O muzykal'no-khorovoi kruzhkovoi rabote v klubakh Mosraikoma VSRM," *Muzyka i revoliutsiia* 1 (1926): 39; G. Polianovskii, "Khorovaia rabota v soiuze Shveinikov," *Muzyka i revoliutsiia* 2 (1926): 31–32; N. Dem'ianov, "Semeinye vechera," *Muzyka i revoliutsiia* 3 (1926): 10–12; "Rabota muzykal'nykh kruzhkov v soiuze Stroitelei," *Muzyka i revoliutsiia* 4 (1926): 24. The "classic" category included choral settings of pieces by Bach, Haydn, Mozart, Beethoven, and Schubert, many choral works by nineteenth-century Russian composers, and a number of pieces for smaller ensembles (duets and trios) by Dargomyzhsky, Tchaikovsky, Rachmaninov, and Rimsky-Korsakov.

91. N. Dem'ianov, "Semeinye vechera," *Muzyka i revoliutsiia* 3 (1926): 10.

92. "Khorovaia rabota v soiuze tekstil'shchikov," *Muzyka i revoliutsiia* 1 (1926): 37.

93. N. Dem'ianov, "Semeinye vechera," *Muzyka i revoliutsiia* 3 (1926): 10.

94. Ibid. The exact origins of the concept of the mass song are unclear. In Germany, socialist political songs were called *Massenlieder* (mass songs), but were also known as workers' songs (*Arbeiterlieder*). See Vernon Lidtke, *The Alternative Culture: Socialist Labor in Imperial Germany* (New York, 1985), 103. In the course of 1925 the term came into common usage in many quarters. See Sokhor, *Russkaia sovetskaia pesnia*, 113.

95. "Khorovaia rabota v soiuze tekstil'shchikov," *Muzyka i revoliutsiia* 1 (1926): 37; "O massovykh pesniakh," *Muzyka i revoliutsiia* 2 (1926): 33. Shul'gin had acknowledged the difficulties of competing with light genre music and the "uneven" quality of the *agitotdel's* output in 1924. See Shul'gin, "Agitotdel Muzsektora," *Muzykal'naia nov'* 10 (1924): 7.

96. In December 1925, officials at Glavprofobrazovanie blamed the lack of popular enthusiasm for *agitki* on poor quality. Guidelines regulating repertoire for conservatory student recitals published in 1926 reiterated these concerns, noting that the most popular revolutionary music heard at funerals was the old underground hymn *You Fell Victim* and funeral marches by Beethoven and Chopin. See "O repertuare muzykal'no-professional'nykh uchebnykh zavedenii," *Muzykal'noe obrazovanie* 5–6 (1926): 54; GARF f. 298, op. 1, d. 128, ll. 194–94ob.

97. S. Bugoslavskii, "K itogam muzykal'nogo sezona," *Sovetskoe iskusstvo* 2 (1925): 75; N. Shuvalov, "Muzykal'noe prosveshchenie," *Muzykal'naia nov'* 1 (1924): 24.

98. Sheila Fitzpatrick discusses the formation of Glavpolitprosvet in *Commissariat of Enlightenment*, 175–86. The evolution and delineation of Glavpolitprosvet's role vis-à-vis the Agitprop section of the Central Committee is described by Peter Kenez in *Birth of the Propaganda State: Soviet Methods of Mass Mobilization, 1917–1928* (Cambridge, 1985), 123–27, and from a different perspective by Michael David-Fox in *Revolution of the Mind*, 64–70.

99. R. Pel'she, "Nashi osnovnye blizhaishie zadachi," *Sovetskoe iskusstvo* 2 (1925): 4.

100. E. V., "Soveshchaniia pri Glavpolitprosvete po voprosu o sozdanii muzyki dlia mass," *Muzyka i revoliutsiia* 2 (1926): 39–40.

101. S. K-va, "K predstoiashchei konferentsii po massovoi muzykal'noi rabote," *Sovetskoe iskusstvo* 2 (1926): 56–57; B. "Muzykal'naia konferentsiia," *Izvestiia*, March 21, 1926, 6.

102. "Resoliutsiia i konferentsii po muzykal'noi politprosvetrabote," *Sovetskoe iskusstvo* 6 (1926): 75–78. The resolutions are also found in "Konferentsiia," *Muzyka i Oktiabr'* 3 (1926): 10–12; "S"ezdy, konferentsii, soveshchaniia," *Muzyka i revoliutsiia* 4 (1926): 30–31.

103. "Resoliutsiia i konferentsii po muzykal'noi politprosvetrabote," *Sovetskoe iskusstvo* 6 (1926): 77–78; L. Lebedinskii, "K voprosu o proletarskoi muzyki," *Muzyka i Oktiabr'* 2 (1926): 2–3.

104. One conference participant noted that *Little Bricks*, which had a recent print run of 61,000 copies, fit Shul'gin's definition of a mass song. See "Konferentsiia," *Muzyka i Oktiabria* 3 (1926): 11.

105. Ibid.; "K voprosu o proletarskoi muzyke," *Muzyka i Oktiabr'* 2 (1926): 1.

106. L. Shul'gin, "Massovaia pesnia," *Muzyka i revoliutsiia* 2 (1926): 18–19.

107. As always, the problems with changing musical culture seemed particularly intractable in comparison with developments in literature. Anatolii Groman contrasted the problems of musical enlightenment work with the successes of the proletarian literature movement. He noted that RAPP's success was due to the fact that it had "raised the cultural level of the proletariat." RAPP had thousands of members, plus 200 to 300 worker-correspondents. "The masses read and study literature. And therefore 'proletarian literature' is being created." "Konferentsiia," *Muzyka i Oktiabr'* 3 (1926): 11.

108. Ibid.

109. The parameters of the debate over "musical populism" were set out by Korev in "Pervyi kamen'," *Sovetskoe iskusstvo* 4 (1926): 35–37. Roslavets had long scorned the notion that the folk song was suitable material for the music of the future. See Dialektikus, "O reakstionnom i progressivnom v muzyke," *Muzyka i kul'tura* 1 (1924): 45–46; N. Roslavets, "O psevdo-proletarskoi

muzyki," in *Na putiakh iskusstva. sbornik statei,* ed. V. M. Bliumenfeld, V. F. Pletnev, and N. F. Chuzhak (Moscow, 1926), 180–92. Korev headed the committee that drafted the resolutions, which also included Roslavets and representatives from RAPM and ORK.

110. Starr, *Red and Hot,* 72.

Chapter 5

1. A. Lunacharskii, "Khudozhestvennaia politika Sovetskogo gosudarstva," *Khudozhnik i zritel'* 1 (1924): 3–4. Also published in *Zhizn' iskusstva* 9 (1924): 1–2, and 10 (1924): 1–2.

2. The motivations and plans for this restructuring are discussed by Sheila Fitzpatrick in *Commissariat of Enlightenment,* 162–209, and from a much different perspective in Read, *Culture and Power,* 142–85. On the political implications and ideological contradictions underpinning administrative and institutional changes in the early twenties, see David-Fox, *Revolution of the Mind,* 48–64. See also T. Iu. Krasovitskaia and A. P. Nenarokov, "Protokoly Kollegii Narkomprosa RSFSR kak istoricheskii istochnik," in *Sovetskaia kul'tura. 70 let razvitiia,* ed. B. B. Piotrovskii (Moscow, 1987), 353–62. For a broad analysis of the early Soviet bureaucracies, see Don K. Rowney, *Transition to Technocracy: The Structural Origins of the Soviet Administrative State* (Ithaca, 1989).

3. Read, *Culture and Power,* 162.

4. The term is Sheila Fitzpatrick's. For her interpretation of Narkompros's weaknesses vis-à-vis VSNKh and other organs of state power, see Fitzpatrick, *Education and Social Mobility,* 11.

5. On the Politburo's restrictions on Lunacharsky's authority as head of Narkompros, see David-Fox, *Revolution of the Mind,* 74; Fitzpatrick, *Commissariat of Enlightenment,* 190.

6. Glavprofobr established a "methodological commission" to develop plans on restructuring the conservatories in 1924. See GARF f. 1565, op. 1, d. 86, l. 3. In October 1925, Glavnauka organized a similar committee to formulate the agency's basic ideological positions and regulate the activities of the research institutes and performance groups under its jurisdiction. See GARF f. 2307, op. 10, d. 35, l. 130; S., "V Muzo Glavnauki," *Muzyka i Oktiabr'* 4–5 (1926): 25. Michael David-Fox describes Narkompros as a "divided" institution, whose own agencies often worked at cross purposes to each other and the censorship bodies (Glavlit and Glavrepertkom) and Agitprop. See David-Fox, *Revolution of the Mind,* 74–75.

7. N. Shuvalov, "Muzykal'noe prosveshchenie," *Muzykal'naia nov'* 2 (1923): 24; L. Lebedinskii, "Voprosy khudozhestvennogo obrazovaniia," *Muzykal'naia nov'* 6–7 (1924): 9; GARF f. 2307, op. 10, d. 60, l. 17ob.; GARF f. 2307, op. 10, d. 35, ll. 139–42; GARF f. 2307, op. 9, d. 263, l. 25ob.

8. On the broader contradictions of Bolshevik efforts to use the state bureaucracy to build socialism, see Moshe Lewin, *Lenin's Last Struggle* (New York, 1968), 117–28.

9. In this respect their aspirations closely paralleled those of other specialists and the intellectual leadership from the Academy of Sciences. See Fitzpatrick, *Education and Social Mobility,* 84–85.

10. Briusova and Tseitlin did join by the onset of World War II.

11. Clark, "The Quiet Revolution," 222–24.

12. A. Sergeev, "Potustoronnye," *Muzykal'naia nov'* 5 (1924): 8–9.

13. "Itogi konferentsii," *Muzyka i Oktiabr'* 3 (1926): 1; "Otchet RAPMa," supplement to *Proletarskii muzykant* 1 (1929): 16–18.

14. GARF f. 298, op. 1, d. 1, ll. 14–15.

15. GARF f. 298, op. 1, d. 115, l. 66.

16. On the activities of the scientific-political section, see David-Fox, *Revolution of the Mind,* 74–75.

17. For an introduction to Iavorskii's ideas in English, see Gordon D. McQuere, "The Theories of Boleslav Yavorsky," in *Russian Theoretical Thought in Music,* ed. McQuere, 109–65. For

discussions of his pedagogical and administrative work in the twenties, see Amy Nelson, "Assigning Meaning to Musical Speech: The Theories of Boleslav Yavorsky in the Cultural Revolution," in *Intersections and Transposition: Russian Music, Literature, and Society*, ed. Andrew Baruch Wachtel (Evanston, 1998), 253–73; N. Ia. Briusova, "Boleslav Leopol'dovich Iavorskii," in B. L. Iavorskii, *Vospominaniia, stat'i i pis'ma*, vol. 1, ed. I. S. Rabinovich and D. S. Shostakovich (Moscow, 1964), 207–13; L. A. Averbukh, "Iavorskii v pervom Moskovskom Gosudarstvennom muzykal'nom tekhnikum," in B. Iavorskii, *Stat'i, vospominaniia, perepiska*, vol. 1, 2d ed., ed. I. S. Rabinovich and D. S. Shostakovich (Moscow, 1972), 133–48.

18. On Briusova's pedagogical work and contribution to Soviet music education, see N. N. Minor, *N. Ia. Briusova i ee shkola muzykal'nogo obrazovaniia* (Saratov, 1994).

19. Briusova applied for Party membership in the twenties, but was rejected, despite enthusiastic references from Lebedinskii and Krylova. In 1930 she turned to Krupskaia, who (tactfully) declined to sponsor her candidacy. RGALI f. 2009, op. 1, d. 9, ll. 1–3; RGALI f. 2009, op. 1, d. 35, ll. 1–2. Eventually she was admitted, and served as the assistant secretary of the conservatory's Party organization during World War II.

20. Shuvalov was appointed early in 1924. GARF f. 2307, op. 9, d. 262, l. 5.

21. A director (*zaveduiushchii*) headed the agency and presided over a collegium consisting of the chairs and assistant chairs of the four main sections. In 1923, a separate division of Glavnauka was organized for the relevant institutes in Leningrad. N. P. Eroshkin, *Vysshie organy gosudarstvennoi vlasti i organy tsentral'nogo upravleniia RSFSR (1927–1967gg.)* (Moscow, 1971), 458; *Biulleten' glavnogo upravleniia nauchnikh, khudozhestvennykh i muzeinykh uchrezhdenii* 1 (1922): 3.

22. In 1924 the section's members were F. Lekht (head), Boris Krasin (music), N. G. Vinogradov (theater), N. I. Shuvalov (music), and K. A. Vrochinskaia (secretary). As of 1924, one member of the section had to be a Party member. GARF f. 2307, op. 1, d. 32a, l. 203.

23. Tenure of the section's chair changed at least three times in the early twenties: A. M. Rodionov headed the section in 1922 and 1923, followed by Lekht in 1924 and P. I. Novitskii after April 1925. GARF f. 2307, op. 1, d. 35, ll. 4–5.

24. Musical institutions directly subordinate to Glavnauka included the research institutes GIII, GIMN, and GAKhN, as well as the Stradivarius String Quartet, the State Choirs and Philharmonias (one each in Moscow and Leningrad), the state instrument collection, and organizations such as the ASM and RAPM. Before 1924, Glavnauka also supervised the work of the academic theaters, including the Bol'shoi.

25. GARF f. 2307, op. 10, d. 60, l. 17ob.; GARF f. 2307, op. 10, d. 35, ll. 139–42; GARF f. 2307, op. 9, d. 263, l. 25ob.

26. GARF f. 2307, op. 9, d. 262, l. 4.

27. GARF f. 2307, op. 9, d. 263, l. 19ob.

28. GARF f. 2307, op. 1, d. 32a, l. 195.

29. Ibid., l. 204ob.

30. GARF f. 2307, op. 10, d. 248, ll. 54–56. "Foreign obligations" included planning for the "immortalization of Lenin," a project that Glavnauka had wanted to supervise. The art section was also told to "give up" hoping for a return of the academic theaters to its administration.

31. The council's presidium consisted of the heads of GUS and its four sections, as well as the heads of Glavnauka, Glavsotsvos (Main Administration for Schools), and Glavpolitprosvet. By 1927, delegates from Glavprofobr and Rabis had been added, and these agencies were also represented on the presidium of the scientific-artistic section. See GARF f. 298, op. 1, d. 1, l. 15; *Biulleten' GUSa* 5–6 (*Nauchno-khudozhestvennaia sektsiia*, no. 1–2) (1927): 3.

32. I.e., Glavnauka, Glavprofobr, Glavpolitprosvet, the State Publishing House, Goskino, GAKhN, and Glavrepertkom.

33. GARF f. 298, op. 1, d. 129, l. 155.

34. S., "V muzo Glavnauki," *Muzyka i Oktiabr'* 4–5 (1926): 25.

35. In October 1926, the commission included Avraamov (GUS), Nikolai Garbuzov (director of GIMN), Derzhanovskii (ASM), Ivanov-Boretskii (GUS / Moscow Conservatory),

Lebedinskii (RAPM), Shuvalov (Glavnauka), Iavorskii (GUS), and Krasin (Glavnauka/GUS). See GARF f. 298, op. 1, d. 107, l. 23.

36. GARF f. 298, op. 1, d. 128, l. 190.

37. Ibid., l. 61.

38. Ibid., ll. 62–62ob. On March 24, the art section's presidium approved the music subsection's resolution on the ASM and agreed to support sending Feinberg and Beliaev to upcoming ISCM festivals in Prague and Venice. GARF f. 298, op. 1, d. 106, l. 33.

39. GARF f. 298, op. 1, d. 128, ll. 176–77.

40. Ibid., ll. 195–195ob.; N. Malkov, "Assotsiatsiia sovremennoi muzyki," *Zhizn' iskusstva* 3 (1926): 14.

41. GARF f. 298, op. 1, d. 127, l. 129ob.

42. GARF f. 298, op. 1, d. 128, l. 191.

43. GARF f. 298, op. 1, d. 129, ll. 82–83.

44. GARF f. 298, op. 1, d. 128, ll. 58–58ob.; "Po Narkomprosu," *Sovetskoe iskusstvo* 4–5 (1925): 86.

45. GARF f. 298, op. 1, d. 128, ll. 64–64ob.

46. GARF f. 298, op. 1. d. 127, l. 128.

47. Ibid., l. 61. The following year Piatnitsky did receive the more distinguished title of "Honored Artist of the Russian Republic" in conjunction with his 25-year jubilee. See Smith, "Soviet Arts Policy, Folk Music, and National Identity," 27.

48. GARF f. 298, op. 1, d. 128, l. 26.

49. Ibid., l. 172; *Biulleten' GUSa* 5–6 (1927): 4.

50. Read, *Culture and Power*, 188; Fitzpatrick, "The Soft Line," 272; Clark, *Petersburg*, 184.

51. Alekseeva et al., *Vospominaniia o Moskovskoi konservatorii*, 548; M. Bruk, "Komsomol'tsy 20-kh godov," *Sovetskaia muzyka* 11 (1963): 9.

52. Lunacharsky took a personal interest in the initial efforts to reform the conservatories and other institutions of artistic education in 1921–22. The First All-Russian Conference on Artistic Education was held in December 1921. Iavorskii was the main architect of the regulations drawn up for the conservatory. See *Uchebnye plany muzykal'nykh-uchebnykh zavedenii RSFSR* (Moscow, 1924).

53. For Iavorskii's curriculum and reform plan for professional music schools, see GARF f. 298, op. 1, d. 382, ll. 2–7; "Uchebnyi plan muzykal'nykh-uchebnykh zavedenii RSFSR," *K novym beregam muzykal'nogo iskusstva* 2 (1923): 53–54. On the distribution of students at the Moscow Conservatory (VUZ: 38; technicum: 344; school: 517), see "Khronika," *K novym beragam muzykal'nogo iskusstva* 2 (1923): 57. See also L. S. Ginzburg et al., *Moskovskaia konservatoriia*, 294–96; Barenboim et al., *Iz istorii sovetskogo muzykal'nogo obrazovaniia*, 40–44, 49–52, 226–33.

54. GARF f. 1565, op. 1, d. 87, l. 183.

55. Ibid., l. 189ob.

56. Ibid., l. 177.

57. Ibid., ll. 186–186ob.

58. Ibid., l. 178a.

59. Ibid., l. 179.

60. Ibid., ll. 179–81.

61. L. Lebedinskii, "'Chistye teoretiki' i zhizn'," *Muzykal'naia nov'* 4 (1924): 9–10.

62. GARF f. 1565, op. 1, d. 87, l. 168.

63. Ibid., ll. 141–50.

64. Similar institutional loyalties also appear to have dominated the actions of N. S. Derzhavin, the Communist director of Leningrad University during the 1924 student purge. See Peter Konecny, "Chaos on Campus: The 1924 Student *Proverka* in Leningrad," *Europe-Asia Studies* 46 (1994): 631.

65. L. Lebedinskii, "'Chistye teoretiki' i zhizn'," *Muzykal'naia nov'* 4 (1924): 9–10.

66. According to its 1923 statute, GUS had the authority to designate and confirm professors, teachers (*prepodavateli*), and "scientific coworkers" at all VUZy and research institutes. On

retirement from one of these institutions, academic personnel addressed their request for a pension to GUS for approval. GARF f. 298, op. 1, d. 1, l. 14.

67. GARF f. 298, op. 1, d. 115, l. 66ob.

68. GARF f. 298, op. 1, d. 127, l. 80. The student purges at the conservatory are discussed in Chapter 6. Fitzpatrick notes that university "professors were untouched by the 1924 purge of students." *Education and Social Mobility*, 82. Yet both the Moscow and Leningrad conservatories dismissed professors (up to 27 percent of them) in 1924.

69. RGALI f. 658, op. 6, d. 55, l. 9.

70. GARF f. 298, op. 1, d. 127, ll. 91–97.

71. Ibid., ll. 86–88ob.

72. Ibid., ll. 84–84ob. Although this protocol is identified as "number 17," it is the only documentary evidence I found of this commission.

73. I have no information on the voice teacher, "Solina," although this may in fact refer to the soprano Nadezhda Salina (1864–1956). The careers of the remaining five after 1924 went roughly as follows: Deisha-Sionitskaia and Petrova-Zvantseva continued to teach solo voice until 1932. Sibor remained in the violin department until 1951. Kipp was awarded a pension in 1925 and died soon thereafter. Krein committed suicide in 1926.

74. GARF f. 298, op. 1, d. 127, ll. 80–81.

75. The results of the purge were published in "Moskovskaia konservatoriia," *Muzykal'naia kul'tura* 2 (1924): 151–52.

76. She remained at the conservatory until 1930, although the GUS music subsection moved to grant her a pension in January 1925 and January 1926. GARF f. 298, op. 1, d. 128, ll. 10–11; GARF f. 298, op. 1, d. 129, l. 27. In 1904 Iavorskii described her as a poor teacher, who lacked "*deiatel'nost'*" and "*umnoe rukovodstvo.*" See Iavorskii, *Stat'i, vospominaniia, perepiska*, 250.

77. GARF f. 298, op. 1, d. 127, ll. 82–83ob.

78. Of those listed, only Strakhov, Vallashek, Prokof'ev, and Shenshin were actually dismissed.

79. GARF f. 298, op. 1, d. 127, l. 83.

80. Miaskovskii letter to Iavorskii, July 16, 1924, in Iavorskii, *Vospominaniia, stat'i i pis'ma*, 510–11.

81. *Muzyka i revoliutsiia* 4 (1927). (See fig. 3.)

82. *Muzykal'noe obrazovanie* 5–6 (1926): 7. Gubert's husband had been the director of the conservatory in the 1880s.

83. V. Vinogradov, "Chetyre goda obshchestvennoi zhizni Moskovskoi gosudarstvennoi konservatorii," *Muzyka i revoliutsiia* 4 (1927): 5.

84. On the Academy of Sciences, see Graham, *The Soviet Academy of Sciences*, 82–119; Alexander Vucinich, *Empire of Knowledge: The Academy of Sciences and the USSR (1917–1970)* (Berkeley and Los Angeles, 1984), 124–32; Tolz, *Russian Academicians and the Revolution.*

85. Briusova, Nazarii Raiskii, Konstantin Igumnov, Nikolai Sherman, and the student Party member, Petr Smigla.

86. Twenty-six of ninety-four professors and teachers at the Leningrad Conservatory were dismissed. See GARF f. 298, op. 1, d. 127, l. 143ob.; ibid., ll. 140–60.

87. GARF f. 298, op. 1, d. 127, l. 157ob.

88. Ibid., l. 145.

89. GARF f. 298, op. 1, d. 117, l. 208.

90. Ibid., ll. 208–208ob.

91. GARF f. 298, op. 1, d. 129, l. 120ob. Rabkrin was also involved.

92. GARF f. 298, op. 1, d. 128, ll. 196–196ob. On the use of this strategy among the Bolsheviks, see Moshe Lewin, *The Making of the Soviet System* (New York, 1985), 22; Roy Medvedev, *Let History Judge* (New York, 1973), 47.

93. Sheila Fitzpatrick describes Narkompros's lack of a single agency for arts administration during NEP as a "historical accident." See "The Emergence of *Glaviskusstvo:* Class War on the Cultural Front, Moscow, 1928–29," *Soviet Studies* 23 (1971): 238.

94. GARF f. 1565, op. 1, d. 49, chast' 1, l. 13. Protocols of the Glavprofobr Presidium for December include excerpts of a GUS art section protocol from October 23, 1922.

95. Ibid., ll. 1–2.

96. "GPP khronika," *Khudozhnik i zritel'* 4–5 (1924): 59. In addition to Lunacharsky, the commission included V. K. Vladimirov and I. V. Ekskuzovich from Narkompros, as well as Slavinskii and P. M. Lebedev from Rabis.

97. G. Nedarov, "Glaviskusstvo," *Sovetskoe iskusstvo* 4–5 (1925): 23–26.

98. "Piatyi vsesoiuznyi s"ezd Rabis," *Sovetskoe iskusstvo* 3 (1925): 77–78.

99. On January 12, 1925, the presidium of the scientific-artistic section asked all subsections to work out a response to the "Glaviskusstvo question" in two weeks. See GARF f. 298, op. 1, d. 106, l. 43. The music subsection assigned Iavorskii, Gol'denveizer, Briusova, and Shuvalov to the commission. See GARF f. 298, op. 1, d. 128, l. 3.

100. A. Lunacharskii, "Ne pora li organizovat' glaviskusstvo?" *Iskusstvo trudiashchimsia* 1 (1924): 6.

101. A. Lunacharskii, "Ne pora *li organizoval' glaviskussto*?" *Iskusstvo trudiashchimsia* 3 (1924): 6.

102. Ibid., 4.

103. GARF f. 298, op. 1, d. 127, ll. 114–114ob.

104. N. Briusova, "Ne pora?" *Iskusstvo trudiashchimsia* 3 (1924): 8.

105. Fox, "Glavlit," 1062–63.

106. S., "V muzo glavnauki," *Muzyka i Oktiabria* 4–5 (1926): 26–27.

107. A. Solovtsov, "Ob usvoenii staroi kul'tury," *Muzyka i Oktiabr'* 1 (1926)1: 17; "Kontserty," *Muzyka i Oktiabr'* 2 (1926): 21.

108. GARF f. 298, op. 1, d. 129, l. 29ob.

109. "Zapret sniat," *Krasnaia gazeta*, October 3, 1925, 4.

110. GARF f. 298, op. 1, d. 129, l. 30ob.

111. GARF f. 298, op. 1, d. 107, ll. 131–35.

112. Ibid., l. 131.

Chapter 6

1. Vl. Fere, "Moskovskaia konservatoriia v 20-e gody," 20.

2. The terms *byvshie liudi* and *ci-devants* refer to people from the former privileged classes. See Fitzpatrick, "Ascribing Class," especially 750–52.

3. These changes are emphasized in the Soviet scholarship on the conservatory's transition to Soviet rule. See Ginzburg et al., *Moskovskaia konservatoriia*, 290–310; Keldysh, *100 let Moskovskoi konservatorii*, 97–130; *Istoriia muzyka narodov SSSR*, 177–83; *Istoriia russkoi sovetskoi muzyki*, 57–59; G. A. Pribegina, *Moskovskaia konservatoriia 1866–1991* (Moscow, 1991), 78–128.

4. Mironova, *Moskovskaia konservatoriia*, 5–19; Ridenour, *Nationalism, Modernism, and Personal Rivalry in Nineteenth-Century Russian Music* (Ann Arbor, 1981), 213.

5. Iu. Briushkov, "Vospominaniia o godakh ucheniia v Moskovskoi konservatorii," in *Vospominaniia o Moskovskoi konservatorii*, ed. Alekseeva et al., 283.

6. Ellon D. Carpenter, "The Contributions of Taneev, Catoire, Conius, Garbuzov, Mazel, and Tiulin," in *Russian Theoretical Thought in Music*, ed. McQuere, 293–313.

7. Fere, Kabalevsky, Shekhter, Starokadomskii, and Oborin joined Miaskovskii's class after Katuar's death in 1926.

8. Saradzhev was professor of conducting, and oversaw orchestra and choral classes from 1922 to 1928. He became the president of the ASM in 1927. He also conducted the premiere of Kastal'skii's "Agricultural Symphony" on December 13, 1925, at the Theater of the Revolution. Golovanov, a graduate of the Synodal school who had composed religious music before the revolution, became the chief conductor at the Bol'shoi Theater. He conducted the premieres of Miaskovskii's Fifth and Sixth Symphonies.

9. Despite the difference in creative orientation between Miaskovskii's group and the more traditional representatives of the "academic school," the composition faculty in Moscow was relatively undisturbed by the generational and philosophical tensions between "academics" and "reformers" that consumed the Leningrad Conservatory. See Haas, *Leningrad's Modernists*, 18–21.

10. Carpenter, "The Contributions of Taneev," 313.

11. Muzykal'no-nauchno-issledovatel'skoe otdelenie nauchno-kompozitorskogo fakul'tet (MUNAIS).

12. The sources (two of which cite the Party archive) agree that there were eight people in the original group, but all list different people, including E. Burtman-Astrova, V. Milovidova, V. Revich, N. Sudushkin, V. Ozol', P. Smigla, V. Vinogradov, L. Vishnevskaia, and L. Lebedinskii. See Ginzburg et al., *Moskovskaia konservatoriia*, 306; L. Veselovskaia et al., eds., *Bol'shoi put' (iz istorii partiinoi organizatsii Moskovskoi konservatorii)* (Moscow, 1966), 12; P. Smigla, "Iz vospominanii," in *Vospominaniia o Moskovskoi konservatorii*, ed. Alekseeva et al., 217; Bruk, "Komsomol'tsy 20-kh godov," 8.

13. T. Cherniakov, "Piat' let raboty iacheiki VKB(b) Konservatorii," in *K desiatiletiiu Oktiabria*, Moskovskaia gosudarstvennaia konservatoriia, 17.

14. Smigla, "Iz vospominanii," in *Vospominaniia o Moskovskoi konservatorii*, ed. Alekseeva et al., 217.

15. There were forty-seven Party members and sixty-six Komsomol'tsy. See V. Vinogradov, "Chetyre gody obshchestvennoi zhizni Moskovskoi Gosudarstvennoi Konservatorii," *Muzyka i revoliutsiia* 4 (1927): 5, 7. The conservatory even had fewer Communists than the Advanced Artistic and Theatrical Studio, which was also considered an artistic VUZ. See Hudson, *Blueprints and Blood*, 92.

16. Veselovskaia et al., *Bol'shoi put'*, 13.

17. Smigla, "Iz vospominanii," in *Vospominaniia o Moskovskoi konservatorii*, ed. Alekseeva et al., 221.

18. Bruk, "Komsomol'tsy," 8.

19. Iurii Mitianin, "Muzyka i komsomol," *Muzykal'naia nov'* 5 (1924): 19.

20. Iu. M., "Uchatsia (byt)," *Muzykal'naia nov'* 12 (1924): 30.

21. The way these anxieties about the degeneration of revolutionary purity informed public discourse and focused in sexual images is illuminated by Naiman in *Sex in Public*. See also Fitzpatrick, "The Problem of Class Identity," 21.

22. V. Vinogradov, "Chetyre gody," *Muzyka i revoliutsiia* 4 (1927): 6.

23. Smigla, "Iz vospominanii," in *Vospominaniia o Moskovskoi konservatorii*, ed. Alekseeva et al., 226.

24. For two early positions favoring close ties between the conservatory's Party organization and RAPM, see S. Krylova, "Mosk. gos. konservatoriia," *Muzykal'naia nov'* 1 (1923): 29–30; Uspenskaia, "V Moskovskoi gos. konservatorii. Ispolnitel'skii otdel," *Muzykal'naia nov'* 11 (1924): 27.

25. Veselovskaia et al., *Bol'shoi put'*, 10.

26. Ippolitov-Ivanov resigned as director over proposed staff reductions, but retained his professorship until his death in 1935. He oversaw reforms at the Tblisi Conservatory as rector of that institution in 1924–25. M. Ippolitov-Ivanov, "Iz vospominanii," in *Vospominaniia o Moskovskoi konservatorii*, ed. Alekseeva et al., 193; GARF f. 1565, op. 1, d. 49, ch. 1, l. 123.

27. In the reelection of the conservatory's adminstration in September 1924, she received a majority of "no" votes, but was appointed nonetheless at Glafprofobr's insistence. See "Moskovskaia konservatoriia," *Muzykal'naia kul'tura* 2 (1924): 151.

28. The group's first meeting took place on January 12. See RGALI f. 2009, op. 1, d. 27, l. 1.

29. "Ot initsiativnoi gruppy professorov konservatorii," *Khudozhnik i zritel'* 2–3 (1924): 56; "Obrashchenie gruppy professorov Moskovskoi gosudarstvennoi konservatorii," *Muzykal'naia nov'* 4 (1924): 21–22.

30. "Ot initsiativnoi gruppy," *Khudozhnik i zritel'* 2–3 (1924): 56.

31. "Assotsiatsiia proletarskikh muzykantov," *Muzykal'naia nov'* 5 (1924): 25–26.
32. RGALI f. 658, op. 5, d. 55, ll. 9, 14–14ob.
33. Ibid., ll. 1–8, 9–10ob., 12.
34. "Ot redaktsii." *Muzykal'noe obrazovanie* 1–2 (1926): 3.
35. Efforts to professionalize the conservatory and minimize its role in producing "amateur" music lovers in the prerevolutionary period are discussed in Mironova, *Moskovskaia konservatoriia. Istoki,* 4–19.
36. Jelagin, *Taming of the Arts,* 12–13.
37. A. V. Lunacharskii, "Osnovy khudozhestvennogo obrazovaniia," in *V mire muzyki* (Moscow, 1958), 185.
38. V. Vinogradov, "Proletarizatsiia MGK i voskresnaia rabochaia konservatoriia," in *K desiatiletiiu Oktiabria,* Moskovskaia gosudarstvennaia konservatoriia, 36.
39. S. Abakumov, "V Moskovskoi Gos. Konservatorii. Khorovoi otdel," *Muzykal'naia nov'* 12 (1924): 28; L. Lebedinskii, "Voprosy khodozhestvennogo obrazovaniia," *Muzykal'naia nov'* 6–7 (1924): 7.
40. Iavorskii, *Stat'i, vospominaniia, perepiska,* 635–36.
41. "Polozhenie o Leningradskoi i Moskovskoi Konservatoriiakh," *Muzykal'noe obrazovanie* 3–4 (1926): 126.
42. "Raboty metodicheskogo soveshchaniia po khudozhestvennomu obrazovaniiu," *Muzykal'noe obrazovanie* 1 (1928): 58.
43. S. Abakumov, "V Moskovskoi Gos. Konservatorii. Khorovoi otdel," *Muzykal'naia nov'* 10 (1924): 25.
44. M. Bruk, "O pedfake," *Proletarskii muzykant* 1 (1929): 30.
45. "Plan reformy konservatorii," in *Iz istorii sovetskogo muzykal'nogo obrazovaniia,* ed. Barenboim et al., 226, 230.
46. K., "Ispolnitel'skii otdel," *Muzykal'naia nov'* 10 (1924): 27.
47. A. Veprik, "Muzyka na zapade," *Muzykal'noe obrazovanie* 1–2 (1928): 20–21; E. Braudo, "Pobediteli na vsemirnom konkurse pianistov," *Pravda,* February 2, 1927.
48. "Ob'iasnitel'naia zapiska k uchebnym planam Moskovskoi gosudarstvennoi konservatorii," *Muzykal'noe obrazovanie* 3–4 (1926): 94–97.
49. The conservatory's contingent consisted of A. V. Aleksandrov, Aleksandr Gol'denveizer, Iosif Dubovskii, Vladimir Ziring, Sergei Evseev, Mikhail Ivanov-Boretskii, Konstantin Igumnov, Aleksandr Kastal'skii, Georgii Konius, Pavel Krylov, Maria Nemenova-Lunts, Anna Ostrovskaia, Isaak Rabinovich, Nazarii Raiskii, Sergei Rozanov, Konstantin Saradzhev, Lev Tseitlin, Nikolai Sherman, and Abram Iampol'skii. Mikhail Gnesin and Aleksandr Veprik also participated as representatives of Glavprofobr.
50. See the conference resolutions in *Muzykal'noe obrazovanie* 1–2 (1926): 55–62.
51. Iurii Shaporin, quoted in Haas, *Leningrad's Modernists,* 83.
52. At the Leningrad Conservatory these critiques were advanced by Asaf'ev and the progressives on the composition faculty, Shcherbachev, and Riazanov. During the Civil War, Kastal'skii denounced the "scholastic schemes" of "white-handed composers," a complaint that was echoed by Iavorskii and Briusova. Arthur Lourié later objected to the "scholasticism" of a system that he claimed produced "unemotional craftsmen." See Haas, *Leningrad's Modernists,* 19–26; Kastal'skii, "K voprosu," in *Muzykal'naia zhizn' Moskvy,* ed. Stepanova, 283; GARF f. 2306, op. 25, d. 163, ll. 4–5; Lourié, *Sergei Koussevitzky,* 117.
53. On the pedagogy of Shcherbachev and his followers, see Haas, *Leningrad's Modernists,* 80–104. Konius and other professors in Moscow were also proposing to introduce original composition in the first year of study in the fall of 1924. See Konius's report to the GUS music subsection, GARF f. 298, op. 1, d. 127, l. 128ob.
54. David-Fox, *Revolution of the Mind,* 120–21; Holmes, *The Kremlin and the School House,* 35; Fitzpatrick, *Education and Social Mobility,* 22–25.
55. Fitzpatrick, *Education and Social Mobility,* 68–71.

56. Debate between G. Konius and K. Milashevich at a presidium meeting of the conservatory *tvorcheskii otdel*, November 18, 1924. GARF f. 298, op. 1, d. 127, l. 172. Other courses required at all VUZy as of 1925 included "History of the Revolutionary Movement and Communist Party" and "Soviet Economics and Politics." See K. Milashevich, "K voprosu o metodakh politobrazovaniia v muzykal'nykh shkolakh," *Muzykal'noe obrazovanie* 1–2 (1926): 38–40.

57. GARF f. 298, op. 1, d. 127, l. 172.

58. Fere, "Moskovskaia konservatoriia," 20. On the shortage of teachers for courses in the "social minimum" at other educational institutions, see Fitzpatrick, *Education and Social Mobility*, 70.

59. *Muzykal'noe obrazovanie* 1–2 (1926): 58.

60. Ibid., 60.

61. Statutes for both the Moscow and Leningrad conservatories were ratified by Glavprofobr on December 5, 1925, and approved by GUS on December 19. GARF f. 298, op. 1, d. 128, l. 193.

62. "Polozhenie o Konservatoriiakh," *Muzykal'noe obrazovanie* 3–4 (1926): 126–28.

63. "Uchebnye plany Moskovskoi gosudarstvennoi konservatorii," *Muzykal'noe obrazovanie* 3–4 (1926): 100–101.

64. "Polozhenie o Konservatoriiakh," *Muzykal'noe obrazovanie* 3–4 (1926): 127.

65. GAKhN's president, Pavel Kogan, made a strong plea for GAKhN's right to head up all artistic research and theoretical work at the 1925 conference.

66. GUS confirmed the admissions of the first graduate students at the Moscow Conservatory on December 12, 1926. Iurii Briushkov recalls that there was no "clear sense" of what graduate study was about (he ended up teaching two students and practicing a lot). See Briushkov, "Vospominaniia o godakh ucheniia v Moskovskoi konservatorii," in *Vospominaniia o Moskovskoi konservatorii*, ed. Alekseeva et al., 284. A second Glavprofobr conference on artistic education in September 1927 set out guidelines for graduate programs. See *Muzykal'noe obrazovanie* 1 (1928): 58–59.

67. The exact wording and significance of these titles were debated twice at meetings of the GUS music subsection in 1925. GARF f. 298, op. 1, d. 128, l. 106; GARF f. 298, op. 1, d. 106, ll. 3–4.

68. The curriculum for architects also retained its traditional contours. See Hudson, *Blueprints and Blood.*

69. The opera studio began as the private initiative of Ippolitov-Ivanov and his wife, Varvara Zarudnaia-Ivanova, in 1917. Initially it had its own budget and statute and was run out of the Ivanovs' apartment. It was institutionalized at the conservatory in 1924. See P. Mikulin, "Vokal'naia studia imini P. I. Chaikovskogo (1917–24)," in *Vospominaniia o Moskovskoi konservatorii*, ed. Alekseeva et al., 259.

70. RGALI, f. 658, op. 6, d. 55, ll. 1–8.

71. Iurii Mitianin, "Muzyka i Komsomol," *Muzykal'naia nov'* 5 (1924): 19–20; P. Smigla, "Iz vospominanii," in *Vospominaniia o Moskovskoi konservatorii*, ed. Alekseeva et al., 216.

72. S. Krylova, "Mosk. gos. konservatoriia," *Muzykal'naia nov'* 1 (1923): 29.

73. RGALI f. 658, op. 6, d. 20, ll. 1–2. Cited in Ginzburg et al., *Moskovskaia konservatoriia*, 296–97. Published statistics contradict this source. See *K novym beregam* 2 (1923): 57, where the distribution of students is listed as follows: VUZ, 38; technicum, 344; school, 517.

74. RGALI f. 658, op. 6, d.55, l. 9.

75. Peter Konecny, "Chaos on Campus," 617–35; David-Fox, *Revolution of the Mind*, 147–60; Fitzpatrick, *Education and Social Mobility*, 97–105.

76. GARF f. 298, op. 1, d. 127, l. 104ob.

77. RGALI f. 658, op. 6, d. 55, ll. 9, 10ob., 29.

78. L. Lebedinskii, "Voprosy khudozhestvennogo obrazovaniia," *Muzykal'naia nov'* 6–7 (1924): 7; V. Vinogradov, "Chetyre godi obshchestvennoi zhizni Moskovskoi Gosudarstvennoi Konservatorii," *Muzyka i revoliutsiia* 4 (1927): 6.

79. This claim is verified by the figures cited in the documents of the 1924 student and faculty purge: In June 1924, 170 students remained in the piano department, which made up 32.8 percent of the total student body (517), a reduction of 17.2 percent. GARF f. 298, op. 1, d. 127, l. 89ob.

80. L. Lebedinskii, "Chistye teoretiki," *Muzykal'naia nov'* 4 (1924): 10; L. L., "Po muzykal'nym shkolam. V Moskovskoi konservatorii," *Muzykal'naia nov'* 8 (1924): 36.

81. L. L., "Po muzykal'nym shkolam. V Moskovskoi konservatorii," *Muzykal'naia nov'* 8 (1924): 35; "Moskovskaia konservatoriia," *Muzykal'naia kul'tura* 2 (1924): 151; GARF f. 298, op. 1, d. 127, ll. 88, 89ob., 92.

82. N. Martynov, *A. Davidenko. Tvorcheskii put', cherty stilia* (Leningrad, 1977), 13.

83. Gliere's telegram to Mosolov, Mosolov's affidavit, Krasin's petition, and supplemental documentation are published in L. B. Rimskii, "Perepiska A. V. Mosolova, materialy, i dokumenty iz ego arkhiva," in *Iz proshlogo sovetskoi muzykal'noi kul'tury*, vol. 3, ed. T. Livanova (Moscow, 1982), 55–56. Similar dynamics were at work in Leningrad, where a combined effort by Glazunov, Nikolaev, and Iavorskii overturned Gavriil Popov's expulsion. See Haas, *Leningrad's Modernists*, 24.

84. GARF f. 298, op. 1, d. 127, l. 86ob.; Konecny, "Chaos on Campus," 625.

85. "Moskovskaia konservatoriia," *Muzykal'naia kul'tura* 2 (1924): 151.

86. Worker and peasant representation at Leningrad University dropped during the fall semester as purged students from less desirable social backgrounds were reinstated. But in January 1925, workers and peasants still made up 25 percent of the student body. See Konecny, "Chaos on Campus," 627.

87. The class included six Party members and fifteen members of the Komsomol. See *Muzykal'naia nov'* 9 (1924): 30.

88. Vilkovir studied composition at the St. Petersburg Conservatory from 1910 to 1916. He left RAPM at the end of 1924. From 1925 to 1933 he worked at the State Publishing House and was active with ORK. He taught instrumentation in the program for military band directors at the Moscow Conservatory from 1933 to 1957.

89. E. Vilkovir, "Ob uchrezhdenii rabfakov pri konservatoriiakh," *Muzykal'naia nov'* 1 (1923): 19–20.

90. Ibid.; L. Lebedinskii, "Voprosy khudozhestvennogo obrazovaniia," *Muzykal'naia nov'* 6–7 (1924): 8; L. A. Averbukh, "Iavorskii v pervom Moskovskom Gosudarstvom muzykal'nom tekhnikum," in Iavorskii, *Stat'i, vospominaniia, perepiska*, 137–38.

91. Vilkovir, "Ob uchrezhdenii rabfakov," *Muzykal'naia nov'* 1 (1923): 21.

92. A. S., "Otkrytie rabfaka pri Moskovskoi Konservatorii," *Muzykal'naia nov'* 2 (1923): 25.

93. N. Savolei, "Muzo Edinogo Khudozhestvennogo Rabfaka," *Muzyka i revoliutsiia* 2 (1926): 36.

94. N. Savolei, "Muzo Edinogo Khudozhestvennogo Rabfaka," in *K desiatiletiiu Oktiabria*, Moskovskaia gosudarstvennaia konservatoriia, 38–39; V. Vinogradov, "Stranichki vospominaniia," in *Vospominaniia o Moskovskoi konservatorii*, ed. Alekseeva et al., 237–38; Ginzburg et al., *Moskovskaia konservatoriia*, 308.

95. N. Savolei, "Muzo Edinogo Khudozhestvennogo Rabfaka," *Muzyka i Oktiabr'* 2 (1926): 17–18.

96. V. M. Blazhevich, M. F. Gnesin, E. M. Guzikov, N. M. Danilin, M. A. Deisha-Sionitskaia, S. I. Druziakina, P. D. Krylov, K. G. Mostras, S. V. Rozanov, B. O. Sibor, N. I. Speranskii, M. I. Tabakov, Lev Tseitlin, Abram and Mark Iamopol'skii, and F. F. Ekkert made up the main core of teaching personnel.

97. *Muzykal'noe obrazovanie* 1–2 (1926): 59.

98. "Usloviia priema v vysshie khudozhestvenno-professional'nye uchebnye zavedeniia okhobra," in *Iz istorii sovetskogo muzykal'nogo obrazovaniia*, ed. Barenboim et al., 46. From 1921 on, a representative from the local Glavprofobr organization sat on all conservatory admissions committees.

99. Political knowledge was also tested, often with amusing results. See L., "Po muzykal'nym shkolam," *Muzykal'naia nov'* 8 (1924): 36; RGALI f. 658, op. 6, d. 55, l. 9.

100. Fitzpatrick, *Education and Social Mobility*, 106.

101. "O prieme v konservatoriiu," *Muzykal'noe obrazovanie* 3–4 (1926): 112–15.

102. Ginzburg et al., *Moskovskaia konservatoriia*, 308.

103. Memoir of former *rabfak* student Stepan Titov, in *Vospominaniia o Moskovskoi konservatorii*, ed. Alekseeva et al., 549. Titov was the father of the cosmonaut G. S. Titov.

104. Savolei, "Vtoroi god," *Muzykal'naia nov'* 9 (1924): 29.

105. Al. Mil'prud, "V plenu reaktsionnoi professory," *Komsomol'skaia pravda*, December 8, 1928, 5; "Chto pokazalo obsledovanie Moskovskoi konservatorii," *Pravda*, April 17, 1929, 2.

106. "Raboty metodicheskogo soveshchaniia po khudozhestvennomu obrazovaniiu," *Muzykal'noe obrazovanie* 1–2 (1926): 53.

107. V. Vinogradov, "Chetyre godi," *Muzyka i revoliutsiia* 4 (1927): 6. These developments were consistent with general trends in higher education, where the nomination system was abandoned and entrance examinations reinstituted in 1926. But while the percentage of white-collar students nearly doubled at the conservatory, it rose by a mere 4 percent in higher education overall (to 40 percent in 1927). See Fitzpatrick, *Education and Social Mobility*, 106–7.

108. V. Vinogradov, "Proletarizatsiia MGK," in *K desiatiletiiu Oktiabria*, Moskosvkaia gosudarstvennia konservatoriia, 36.

109. *Narodnoe prosveshchenie v RSFSR k 1928/29 godu: Otchet NKP RSFSR za 1928/28 uchebnyi god* (Moscow, 1929), 65. Cited in James McClelland, "Proletarianizing the Student Body: The Soviet Experience During the New Economic Policy," *Past and Present* 80 (1978): 131.

110. "Instruktsiia Glavprofobra o vyborakh studentov v predmetnye komissii VUZov" (1921), in *Iz istorii sovetskogo muzykal'nogo obrazovaniia*, ed. Barenboim et al., 39–40.

111. Fitzpatrick, *Education and Social Mobility*, 12.

112. GARF f. 298, op. 1, d. 127, l. 84.

113. Ibid., ll. 94–95; L., "Po muzykal'nym shkolam," *Muzykal'naia nov'* 9 (1924): 35. Prokof'ev had served in the conservatory's administration during the Civil War, and was the first dean of the *pedfak*. He was also a dedicated advocate of contemporary music. After his dismissal from the conservatory, he accepted a position at the Institute of Musical Science (GIMN), where he continued to attract negative publicity from RAPM.

114. GARF f. 1565, op. 1, d. 87, l. 33.

115. GARF f. 298, op. 1, d. 117, l. 208ob.

116. L. Kaltat, "Itogi proizvodstvennoi praktiki studentov MGK," *Muzyka i Oktiabr'* 2 (1926): 18–19.

117. Nikolai Rechmenskii, "Proizvodstvennaia praktika studentov M. G. Konservatorii," *Muzykal'noe obrazovanie* 3–4 (1926): 62; K., "V Moskovskoi gosudarstvennoi konservatorii," *Muzykal'naia nov'* 10 (1924): 26.

118. K. Uspenskaia, "V Moskovskoi gos. kons.," *Muzykal'naia nov'* 11 (1924): 27.

119. Loiter, Siver, and V. M. Kamionskaia, "Pis'mo Komsomol'tsev Konservatorii tov. A. V. Lunacharskomu," *Muzyka i Oktiabr'* 4–5 (1926): 17.

120. "Dostizheniia nashego iskusstva," *Pravda*, May 1, 1926.

121. A. V. Lunacharskii, "Otvet tov. A. V. Lunacharskogo," *Muzyka i Oktiabr'* 4–5 (1926): 17–18.

122. V. Vinogradov, "Konservatoriia i obshchestvennost'," *Muzykal'noe obrazovanie* 1–2 (1927): 190–92.

123. K. Igumnov, "K 60-i let'iu Moskovskoi gosudarstvennoi konservatorii," *Muzyka i revoliutsiia* 4 (1927): 3; S. Evseev, "Konservatoriia i sovremennost'," *Muzykal'noe obrazovanie* 5–6 (1926): 7–14.

124. "Metodicheskie pis'ma Glavprofobr," *Muzykal'noe obrazovanie* 3–4 (1926): 48.

125. N. Briusova, "Muzykal'noe prosveshchenie i obrazovanie," *Muzyka i revoliutsiia* 1 (1926): 27.

126. Sheila Fitzpatrick, "The Problem of Class Identity," 12–17; Konecny, "Chaos on Campus," 617.

127. Dan Orlovsky, "The Hidden Class: White-Collar Workers in the Soviet 1920s," in *Making Workers Soviet: Class, Power, and Identity*, ed. Lewis H. Siegelbaum and Ronald Grigor Suny (Ithaca, 1994), 239.

Chapter 7

1. Fitzpatrick, "The Emergence of Glaviskusstvo," 241.

2. Maks Zhizhmor's tragedy *Betkhoven* was put on by the *Peredvizhnoi teatr* in Leningrad under the direction of N. I. Solov'ev and P. P. Gaideburov. It was published by Modpik in a print run of 3,000. See *Zhizn' iskusstva* 5 (1927): 20, and 12 (1927): 21; Evg. Braudo, "Knigi o Betkhovene," *Pechat' i revoliutsiia* 4 (1927): 92.

3. In addition to the scholarly works discussed below, the Beethoven centennial also marked the publication of a two-volume bibliographic guide to over 600 articles, books, and source materials on the composer available in Russian. See M. P. Alekseev and Ia. Z. Berman, *Betkhoven. Materialy dlia bibliograficheskogo ukazatel'ia russkoi literatury o nem*, vols. 1–2 (Odessa, 1927–28).

4. *Muzykal'noe obrazovanie* 1–2 (1927): 7–58. The sketchbook dated to 1825 and included penciled drafts of two of the late string quartets, Op. 130 and Op. 132. It came to the attention of Mikhail Ippolitov-Ivanov in 1922 after Soviet authorities confiscated it from an émigré. Additional details are provided by M. Ivanov-Boretskii in "Moskovskaia chernovaia tetrad' Betkhovena," *Muzykal'noe obrazovanie* 1–2 (1927): 59–60; Boris Schwarz, "Beethoveniana in Soviet Russia," *The Musical Quarterly* 47 (1961): 4–10.

5. Schnabel performed all five of the Beethoven piano concertos with the Leningrad Philharmonic in two concerts (March 9 and 16). He also gave two recitals of Beethoven sonatas (March 13 and 20). Klemperer conducted the *Missa Solemnis* in Leningrad on April 19 and 20 and the Third and Fifth Symphonies in Moscow on April 25. Other foreign guests participating in various Beethoven activities included Joseph Szigeti (two performances of the Beethoven violin concerto with the Leningrad Philharmonic) and the pianists Egon Petri and Friedrich Brürer.

6. Schwarz, *Music and Musical Life*, 93. Schwarz wrote extensively on the disposition of Beethoven memorabilia and the composer's reputation in Russia. See his "Beethoveniana in Soviet Russia," 4–21; "More Beethoveniana in Soviet Russia," *The Musical Quarterly* 49 (1963): 143–49; and "A Little-Known Beethoven Sketch in Moscow," *The Musical Quarterly* 56 (1970): 539–50.

7. "K iubileinym Betkhovenskim torzhestvam," *Izvestiia*, September 22, 1926, 6. The structure and composition of the committee were as follows: Head: Lunacharsky; Executive Committee: Pavel Novitskii, chair (head of the Artistic Section of Glavnauka and rector of VKhUTEMAS), S. Bogomazov (VOKS), Lev Lebedinskii (RAPM), Mikhail Ivanov-Boretskii (GAKhN, GIMN), Nazarii Raiskii (Moscow Conservatory and Rosfil), Lev Tseitlin (Persimfans), Nikolai Shuvalov (Glavnauka), A. Iurovskii (State Publishing House, Music Division), Boleslav Iavorskii (GUS); Publication Section: Gol'denveizer, Lebedinskii, Ivanov-Boretskii, Iurovskii, Iavorskii; Agitation-Enlightenment Section: V. Blazhevich, Nadezhda Briusova, A. Gedike, A. Groman-Solovtsov, and G. Liubimov. See Nikolai Shuvalov, "Prazdnik kul'tury," *Biulleten' Betkhovenskogo Komiteta pri Narkomprose RSFSR* 1 (1927): 10.

8. "V komitete po podgotovke Betkhovenskikh torzhestv," *Muzykal'noe obrazovanie* 1–2 (1927): 168.

9. A. Lunacharsky and P. Novitskii, "Ko vsem rabotnikam muzykal'noi kul'tury v SSSR," *Biulleten' Betkhovenskogo Komiteta pri Narkomprose RSFSR* 1 (1927): 3–4.

10. Lunacharsky's various public speeches and articles were drawn from three main texts. The first, "Chto zhivo dlia nas v Betkhovene," appeared as the lead article in *Muzyka i revoliutsiia* 3 (1927): 3–8, as well as in the Leningrad Philharmonic's commemorative collection, Leningradskaia gosudarstvennaia filarmoniia, *Betkhoven (1827–1927)* (Leningrad, 1927), 5–14. The text was

modified slightly for publication as the introduction to S. M. Maikapar, *Znachenie tvorchestva Betkhovena dlia nashei sovremennosti* (Moscow, 1927), 1–19. The second text was a revision of his speech for the Persimfans Beethoven concert on February 27, 1927, published as "Pochemu nam dorog Betkhoven" in his collection *Iskusstvo i molodezh'* (Moscow, 1929), 100–118. The third, "Betkhoven i sovremennost'," appeared initially in the evening edition of *Krasnaia gazeta*, March 8, 1927, 4. All are reprinted in the 1958 collection of Lunacharsky's writings on music, *V mire muzyki. Stat'i i rechi.* Subsequent citations of these texts refer to this volume.

11. Lunacharskii, "Chto zhivo dlia nas v Betkhovene," *V mire muzyki*, 338–40.

12. Lunacharskii, "Betkhoven i sovremennost'," *V mire muzyki*, 331–33.

13. Pavel Novitskii, "Betkhoven i revoliutsiia," in *Betkhoven (1827–1927)*, Leningradskaia Gosudarstvennaia Akamedicheskaia Filarmoniia, 15.

14. Ibid., 17–19.

15. Ibid., 19.

16. Igor Glebov (Asaf'ev), "Betkhoven," *Betkhoven (1827–1927)*, Leningradskaia Gosudarstvennaia Akamedicheskaia Filarmoniia, 24–36; S. Ginzburg, "Betkhoven," *Zhizn' iskusstva* 12 (1927): 6–7.

17. E. M. Braudo, *Betkhoven i ego vremia 1770–1827. Opyt muzykal'no-sotsiologicheskogo issledovaniia* (Moscow, 1927).

18. Braudo, *Betkhoven i ego vremia*, 18.

19. Ibid., 5–6. Braudo presents the same argument in "Betkhoven—grazhdanin," *Muzyka i revoliutsiia* 3 (1927): 21.

20. The Beethoven centennial was a major event for musical communities throughout the West. For an exploration of the aesthetic roots of the Beethoven mystique and the musical qualities that have so closely linked Beethoven's music with concepts of heroism, suffering, and transcendence, as well as Western perceptions of "great" music, see Scott Burnham, *Beethoven Hero* (Princeton, 1995). For an examination of the manipulation of Beethoven as a cultural icon in Germany, see David B. Dennis, *Beethoven in German Politics, 1870–1989* (New Haven, 1996).

21. Nadezhda Briusova, "Muzykal'noe obrazavanie," in *K desiatiletiiu Oktiabria*, Moskovskaia gosudarstvennaia konservatoriia, 10.

22. M. V. Ivanov-Boretskii, *Betkhoven. Biograficheskii ocherk* (Moscow, 1927), 10.

23. Braudo, *Betkhoven i ego vremia*, 6–7.

24. "V komitete," *Muzykal'noe obrazovanie* 1–2 (1927): 169.

25. M. V. Ivanov-Boretskii, "Sovetskaia delegatsiia, Mezhdunarodnye privetstviia, Muzykal'no-istoricheskii kongress," *Muzykal'noe obrazovanie* 3–4 (1927): 47–48.

26. K. A. Kuznetsov, "Predislovie," in *Russkaia kniga o Betkhovene*, ed. K. A. Kuznetsov (Moscow, 1927), 1.

27. A. Glazunov, "Betkhoven kak kompozitor i myslitel'," *Pechat' i revoliutsiia* 3 (1927): 95.

28. See Nadezhda Briusova, "Betkhoven i sovremennost'," in *Russkaiia kniga o Betkhovene*, ed. Kuznetsev, 3–12; K. A. Kuznetsov, "'Pozdnii Betkhovene'—po ego razgovornym tetradiam," the third installment of "Tri etiuda o Betkhovene," *Muzyka i revoliutsiia* 3 (1927): 16–20.

29. In addition to the "Beethoven Week" organized by the Narkompros committee, Persimfans, the Leningrad Philharmonic, Rosfil, and many other musical institutions sponsored recitals, concerts, and lectures. Progams for these events are listed in *Biulleten' Betkhovenskogo Komiteta* 1 (1927): 21–25.

30. *Muzyka i revoliutsiia* 2 (1927): 36.

31. Adolf Weissman, "Betkhoven dlia mass," *Sovremennaia muzyka* 22 (1927): 284.

32. *Sovremennaia muzyka* 21 (1927): 258–159. The performances took place in the recital hall of the Moscow Conservatory on March 23, 24, 26, and 29.

33. *Zhizn' iskusstva* 9 (1927): 10. Roman Gruber spoke on the significance of personality (*lichnost'*) in Beethoven's music and its implications for contemporary musicology. Grachev's report on Beethoven's relationship to the German romantics used the letters of Spohr, Schubert, Schumann, and Wagner as sources. D. Iurman presented a report titled "Opyt patografii Betkhovena."

34. *Biulleten' GAKhN* 6–7 (1927): 48; Kuznetsov, *Russkaia kniga o Betkhovene.*

35. "V komitete," *Muzykal'noe obrazovanie* 1–2 (1927): 169.

36. "Nedel'ia Betkhovena," *Biulleten' Betkhovenskogo Komiteta* 1 (1927): 25.

37. "V komitete," *Muzykal'noe obrazovanie* 1–2 (1927): 168.

38. See "Betkhoven" and "Eshche o Betkhoven," in *V mire muzyki,* 77–81, 82–85. Both articles were reprinted from Lunacharsky's 1923 collection of essays, *V mire muzyki.* "Betkhoven" was first published in *Kul'tura teatra* 2 (1921): 4–7, then in *Teatr i muzyka* 8 (1922): 60–62. The article was based on a speech for a concert-meeting on January 9, 1921, dedicated to the 150th anniversary of Beethoven's birth. "Eshche o Betkhoven" originally appeared in *Kul'tura teatra* 3 (1921): 6–8. It was an amended version of Lunacharsky's address at the dedication of the Beethoven Hall of the Bol'shoi Theater.

39. Lunacharskii, "Chto zhivo dlia nas v Betkhovene," *V mire muzyki,* 335–36.

40. L. Lebedinskii, "Pod znakom Betkhovene," *Na literaturnom postu* 8 (1927): 4.

41. Kemp-Welch, *Stalin and the Literary Intelligentsia,* 43–44; Fitzpatrick, "The Emergence of Glaviskusstvo," 238–40. After years of resisting such calls, in May 1927 the artistic section of GUS acknowledged that Narkompros's organizational structure for the arts was in collapse (*proval*) and that a Glaviskusstvo "might be necessary." See GARF f. 298, op. 1, d. 5, ll. 114–18.

42. RGALI f. 658 op. 1, d. 347, ll. 5–6.

43. "Otchet RAPMa," supplement to *Proletarskii muzykant* 1 (1929): 16–18.

44. L. Lebedinskii, "Muzykal'naia zhizn' za 10 let revoliutsii," *Na literaturnom postu* 20 (1927): 71–73.

45. "Dokladnaia zapiska Narkomy Prosveshcheniia Assotsiatsii Proletarskykh Muzykantov," *Muzykal'noe obrazovanie* 1–2 (1927): 171–74.

46. As late as February 1927, *Muzyka i revoliutsiia* still listed the delegation's original personnel. See *Muzyka i revoliutsiia* 3 (1927): 37.

47. M. Ivanov-Boretskii, "Sovetskaia delegatsiia," *Muzykal'noe obrazovanie* 3–4 (1927): 47; L. Lebedinskii, "Betkhovenskie torzhestva v Vene," *Na literaturnom postu* 9 (1927): 43–46. The Soviet delegation was able to make an official presentation of a wreath at the Beethoven memorial. A photograph of this event appears in *Das neue Russland* 4 (1927): 51.

48. The most extensive discussion of Persimfans in English is found in Stites, *Revolutionary Dreams,* 135–40. See also Schwarz, *Music and Musical Life,* 46–47.

49. Stites, *Revolutionary Dreams,* 136.

50. Detailed theoretical statements on the principles and merits of conductorless performance are found in the pamphlet *Orkestr bez dirizhera* (Moscow, 1922) and in Arnold Tsukker, *Piat' let Persimfansa* (Moscow, 1927), 205–11.

51. In 1924, Vladimir Derzhanovskii described the orchestra as a symbol of the intelligentsia's move away from an attitude of "passive sabotage" toward the revolutionary government. "Operno-kontsertnyi front," *Muzykal'naia kul'tura* 3 (1924): 238.

52. See his reports to the musical subsection of GUS in October 1924 and February 1926. GARF f. 298, op. 1, d. 127, ll. 129–30; GARF f. 298, op. 1, d. 129, ll. 52–55.

53. Repertoire for concerts given from 1922 to 1927 is listed in Tsukker, *Piat' let Persimfansa,* 229–36.

54. GARF f. 298, op. 1, d.127, l. 130; GARF f. 298, op. 1, d. 129, l. 78.

55. In addition to program notes, the orchestra published a journal, *Persimfans,* which appeared irregularly between 1927 and 1929.

56. GARF f. 298, op. 1, d. 129, l. 54.

57. Tsukker, *Piat' let Persimfansa,* 235–36; GARF f. 298, op. 1, d. 129, l. 55. From a list of forty composers, working-class audiences ranked Scriabin as their favorite, followed closely by Beethoven, then Wagner, Rimsky-Korsakov, Tchaikovsky, and Prokofiev, respectively. Seventy percent indicated a preference for modern Russian and European music. W. V., "Fünf Jahre Persimfans," *Das neue Russland* 4 (1927): 75.

58. L. Sosnovskii, "Chego zhdet ot zhurnala novyi slushatel'?" *Persimfans* 2 (1927–28): 3; W. V., "Fünf Jahre Persimfans," *Das neue Russland* 4 (1927): 75.

59. Prokofiev made no mention of workers' musical preferences, claiming that the program was chosen because Persimfans was proud of its performances of these pieces. See Prokofiev, *Soviet Diary 1927*, 88–89.

60. Sergei Bugoslavskii, "K 5-letiiu Persimfansa," *Zhizn' iskusstva* 7 (1927): 14; S. Korev, "Novye metody simfonicheskogo ispol'neniia," *Sovetskoe iskusstvo* 2 (1927): 29–31; G. Polianovskii, "Rabochie kontserty Persimfansa," *Muzyka i revoliutsiia* 2 (1927): 30. Pillars of the artistic community including Mikhail Ippolitov-Ivanov (former director of the Moscow Conservatory), Pavel Kogan (president of GAKhN), and Konstantin Saradzhev (head of the ASM) also paid tribute to the orchestra. See also *Persimfans* 3–4 (1927): 3–6.

61. "Betkhovenskaia khronika," *Biulleten' Betkhovenskogo Komiteta* 1: 23. These performances featured the *Egmont* Overture, the Violin Concerto, and the Third, Fifth, and Seventh Symphonies.

62. "Khronika," *Sovremennaia muzyka* 22 (1927): 287.

63. Nikolai Mal'ko, "Zadachi Filarmonii," in Gosudarstvennaia Akademicheskaia Filarmoniia, *10 let simfonicheskoi muzyki, 1917–28* (Leningrad, 1928), 17.

64. I. M. Shillinger, "O kompozitsii simfonicheskoi rapsodii, 'Oktiabr,'" *Persimfans* 3–4 (1927–28): 12. On the rhapsody's borrowings from the cinema, see also Anton Uglov, "Dela Persimfansa," *Izvestiia*, November 26, 1927, 7.

65. Georgii Orlov, "Oktiabr' (1917–27)," *Persimfans* 3–4 (1927–28): 14–16. The only other favorable review I was able to locate was by Nikolai Malkov ("Islamei"), "Simfonicheskie novinki k Oktiabriu," *Zhizn' iskusstva* 45 (1927): 34–35.

66. D. Kabalevskii, "Persimfans," *Muzykal'noe obrazovanie* 1 (1928): 72–73; Kabalevskii, "Kontserty v Moskve," *Sovremennaia muzyka* 24 (1927): 46; "Ob"edinenie revoliutsionnykh kompozitorov i muzykal'nykh deiatel'ei," *Muzyka i revoliutsiia* 5–6 (1928): 43–44; S. Korev, "Sovetskaia simfonicheskaia muzyka," *Sovetskoe iskusstvo* 7 (1927): 48–52; *Vecherniaia Moskva*, November 24, 1927.

67. "Sovetskaia simfonicheskaia muzyka," *Sovetskoe iskusstvo* 7 (1927): 51.

68. "Kontserty v Moskve," *Sovremennaia muzyka* 24 (1927): 46.

69. "Ob"edinenie revoliutsionnykh kompozitorov i muzykal'nykh deiatel'ei," *Muzyka i revoliutsiia* 5–6 (1928): 43.

70. M. Grinberg, "Dmitrii Shostakovich," *Muzyka i revoliutsiia* 11 (1927): 18.

71. This symphony was later unpopular with the composer and Soviet musicologists. In the heydey of socialist realism official histories denounced it for formalist tendencies.

72. M. Grinberg, "Dmitrii Shostakovich," *Muzyka i revoliutsiia* 11 (1927): 20; S. Korev, "Sovetskaia simfonicheskaia muzyka," *Sovetskoe iskusstvo* 7 (1927): 48.

73. Iu. Vainkop, "Simfonicheskie novinki k Oktiabriu," *Zhizn' iskusstva* 45 (1927): 34.

74. V. Belyi, "Levaia fraza muzykal'noi reaktsii," *Muzykal'noe obrazovanie* 1 (1928): 43–47.

75. A. B., "Kantata N. Roslavetsa 'Oktiabr,'" *Sovremennaia muzyka* 24 (1927): 39. This review also includes the cantata's text on 40–43. See also S. Korev, "Sovetskaia simfonicheskaia muzyka," *Sovetskoe iskusstvo* 7 (1927): 50.

76. S. Korev, "Sovetskaia simfonicheskaia muzyka," *Sovetskoe iskusstvo* 7 (1927): 50.

77. "'Prolog' L. A. Polovinkina," *Sovremennaia muzyka* 24 (1927): 37; S. Korev, "Sovetskaia simfonicheskaia muzyka," *Sovetskoe iskusstvo* 7 (1927): 51.

78. Like Roslavets, Mosolov vanished from the Soviet musical scene in the mid-thirties, and his work was dismissed as decadent and formalist. After the composer's death in 1973, the Soviet musicologist Inna Barsova began a cautious reappraisal of his career and investigation into his ultimate fate. See Barsova, "Aleksandr Mosolov: dvadtsatye gody," 77–87. L. Rimskii edited a small portion of Mosolov's correspondence, published as "Perepiska A. V. Mosolova, materialy i dokumenty iz ego arkhiva," in *Iz proshlogo sovetskoi muzykal'noi kul'tury*, vol. 3, ed. Livanova, 53–58. In the late eighties Barsova collaborated with the composer's widow to publish many of his prose writings in *A. V. Mosolov. Stat'i i vospominaniia* (Moscow, 1986). On constructivism in Mosolov's work, see her "Tvorchestvo Aleksandra Mosolova," in *Rossiia: Frantsiia*, 202–20. In 1989 *Sovetskaia muzyka* published previously censored archival materials relating to Mosolov's

expulsion from the Composers' Union, his personal appeal to Stalin, and his fate in the purges. Barsova edited and provided commentary for both installations. See "Iz neopublikovannogo arkhiva A. V. Mosolova," *Sovetskaia muzyka* 7 (1989): 80–92, and 8 (1989): 69–75.

79. Other pieces featured on commemorative concert programs but not specifically commissioned for them included M. Gnesin's *Symphonic Monument 1905–17*, V. Deshevov's *Suite from the "Red Whirlwind,"* and Iurii Shaporin's *Funeral Procession.*

80. On the incorporation of everyday speech in opera in this period, see Clark, *Petersburg*, 225–41.

81. N. D., "Obshchestvennyi pokaz raboty Proizvodstvennogo Kollektiva studentov pri Nauchno-Kompozitorskom fakul'tete M.G.K. 18 dekabria 1927 goda," *Muzyka i revoliutsiia* 1 (1928): 31. The minutes from Prokoll's meetings indicate that there was a trial "demonstration" of the first link of the cantata on October 2, but I could find no corroborating evidence to suggest that it actually took place or that an audience was present. See GTsMMK f. 447, ed. khr. 770, l. 1.

82. All three of the group's meetings in September focused on whether to use Levina's or Chemberdzhi's setting of Gorky's *Burevestnik* for the opening selection. See GTsMMK ed. khr. 771, ll. 1–3. Sergei Riauzov, "Vospominaniia o 'Prokolle,'" *Sovetskaia muzyka* 7 (1949): 57.

83. GTsMMK f. 447, ed. khr. 771, l. 6.

84. N. Malkov, "Muzyka v kul'turnoi revoliutsii," *Zhizn' iskusstva* 45 (1927): 30. Translated in Rosenberg, *Bolshevik Visions*, 464–68.

85. A. Tsukker, "Litsom k muzkyke!" *Persimfans* 3–4 (1927–28): 7–8.

86. R. Pel'she, "Za desiat' let," *Sovetskoe iskusstvo* 5 (1927): 28–30.

87. L. Gurevich, "Na vernom puti," *Muzyka i revoliutsiia* 5–6 (1928): 13; "Konkurs garmonistov," *Muzyka i revoliutsiia* 1 (1928): 32. For statistics on participation in the competitions in Leningrad, see I. I. Zemtsovskii and V. P. Il'in, "Muzykal'naia samodeiatel'nost'," in *Muzykal'naia kul'tura Leningrada za 50 let*, ed. V. M. Bogdanov-Berezovskii, 470–71.

88. Mikh. Rozenfel'd, "Sinitsa v Kolonnom zale," *Komsomol'skaia pravda*, January 3, 1928, 3; "Konkurs garmonistov," *Muzyka i revoliutsiia* 1 (1928): 33; M. Ippolitov-Ivanov, "Voinstvuiushchaia garmoshka," *Komsomol'skaia pravda*, January 25, 1928, 3.

89. L. Gurevich, "Na vernom puti," *Muzyka i revoliutsiia* 5–6 (1928): 11.

90. A. Lunacharskii, "Garmon' na sluzhbe revoliutsii," *Komsomol'skaia pravda*, January 3, 1928, 3.

91. O. Tsekhnovitser, "Novaia muzyka i proletariat," *Novaia muzyka* 1 (1927): 13–14.

92. Viktor Beliaev, "Desiat' let russkoi simfonicheskoi muzyki," *Sovremennaia muzyka* 24 (1927): 24–25; Korev, "Sovetskaia simfonicheskaia muzyka," *Sovetskoe iskusstvo* 7 (1927): 48; Roslavets, "Muzyka," *Sovetskoe iskusstvo* 5 (1927): 74.

93. "Velikii Oktiabr'," *Muzyka i revoliutsiia* 11 (1927): 5–6.

94. Roslavets, "Muzyka," *Sovetskoe iskusstvo* 5 (1927): 74.

95. Ibid.; "Velikii Oktiabr'," *Muzyka i revoliutsiia* 11 (1927): 3–4.

96. Riauzov, "Vospominaniia o 'Prokolle,'" *Sovetskaia muzyka* 7 (1949): 57.

97. Korev, "Sovetskaia simfonicheskaia muzyka," *Sovetskoe iskusstvo* 7 (1927): 52.

98. Roslavets, "Muzyka," *Sovetskoe iskusstvo* 5 (1927): 75; I. Shillinger, "O sovremennoi muzyke," *Zhizn' iskusstva* 13 (1927): 7.

99. R. Pel'she, "Za desiat' let," *Sovetskoe iskusstvo* 5 (1927): 30–32; Igor Glebov, "Russkaia simfonicheskaia muzyka za 10 let," *Muzyka i revoliutsiia* 11 (1927): 23.

100. V. Belyii, "Akademicheskaia zhizn'," *K desiatiletiiu Oktiabria*, Moskovskaia gosudarstvennaia konservatoriia, 27; Tsukker, "Litsom k muzkyke!" *Persimfans* 3–4 (1927–28): 7; Roslavets, "Muzyka," *Sovetskoe iskusstvo* 5 (1927): 75; R. Pel'she, "Iskusstvo revoliutsii," *Muzyka i revoliutsiia* 11 (1927): 6–7; Pel'she, "Za desiat' let," *Sovetskoe iskusstvo* 5 (1927): 28–30.

101. N. Briusova, "Muzykal'noe obrazovanie," *K desiatiletiiu Oktiabria*, Moskovskaia gosudarstvennaia konservatoriia, 12.

102. Tsukker, "Litsom k muzkyke!" *Persimfans* 3–4 (1927–28): 10.

103. O. Tsekhnovitser, "Novaia muzyka i proletariat," *Novaia muzyka* 1 (1928): 16.

Chapter 8

1. The best introduction to the Cultural Revolution remains Sheila Fitzpatrick, ed., *Cultural Revolution in Russia, 1928–1931* (Bloomington, 1978).

2. Bailes, *Technology and Society under Lenin and Stalin*, 159–87; Fitzpatrick, *Education and Social Mobility*, 116–36, 184–88.

3. Fitzpatrick, "The Emergence of *Glaviskusstvo*," 243; Kemp-Welch, *Stalin and the Literary Intelligentsia 1928–1939*, 49–50.

4. Fitzpatrick, "Cultural Revolution as Class War," in *Cultural Revolution in Russia*, 15–17; Fitzpatrick, *Education and Social Mobility*, 129–30; Kemp-Welch, *Stalin and the Literary Intelligentsia*, 52–56.

5. Fitzpatrick, "Editor's Introduction," in *Cultural Revolution in Russia*, 7; Fitzpatrick, "Cultural Revolution as Class War," in *Cultural Revolution in Russia*, 28–30; Fitzpatrick, "The Emergence of *Glaviskusstvo*," 233–38.

6. See Gail Lapidus, "Educational Strategies and Cultural Revoluton: The Politics of Soviet Development," Robert Sharlet, "Pashukanis and the Withering Away of the Law in the USSR," and S. Frederick Starr, "Visionary Town Planning during the Cultural Revolution," in *Cultural Revolution in Russia*, ed. Fitzpatrick, 78–104, 169–88, 207–40; Holmes, *Kremlin in the School House*, 109–26; Peris, *Storming the Heavens;* E. Thomas Ewing, *The Teachers of Stalinism: Policy, Practice, and Power in Soviet Schools of the 1930s* (New York, 2002), 53–66.

7. On the suppressing of utopianism in this period and the thirties, see Stites, *Revolutionary Dreams*, 223–41.

8. See, for example, Lewis Siegelbaum, "Building Stalinism 1929–1941," in *Russia: A History*, ed. Gregory Freeze (Oxford, 1997), 304–6.

9. Kelly and Shepherd, *Constructing Russian Culture;* Clark, *Petersburg;* Groys, *Total Art of Stalinism;* Stites, *Russian Popular Culture;* Stites, *Revolutionary Dreams;* Brooks, *Thank You, Comrade Stalin.*

10. David-Fox, "What Is Cultural Revolution?"; David-Fox, "*Mentalité* or Cultural System?" 181–201, 210–11.

11. Amy Nelson, "The Struggle for Proletarian Music," 101–32.

12. GTsMMK f. 179, ed. khr. 48, ll. 1–4, 19, 31–32; GTsMMK f. 179, ed. khr 405, ll. 1–3.

13. Edmunds, "Music and Politics," 66–89; Taruskin, *Defining Russia Musically*, 93; Fitzpatrick, "The Lady Macbeth Affair," in *The Cultural Front*, 192–94; Haas, *Leningrad's Modernists*, 26–32; Schwarz, *Music and Musical Life*, 102–3; *Istoriia russkoi sovetskoi muzyki*, 38–39, 58–59; *Istoriia muzyki narodov SSSR*, 145–47; Leningradskaia gosudarstvennaia konservatoriia, *Sto let Leningradskoi konservatorii, 1862–1962. Istoricheskii ocherk* (Leningrad, 1962), 143–44; Ginzburg et al., *Moskovskaia konservatoriia*, 321–22.

14. David-Fox, "What Is Cultural Revolution?"; David-Fox, "*Mentalité* or Cultural System?" 198–99, 210.

15. GARF f. 298, op. 1, d. 111, l. 65. The stenogram of the session, which took place on February 23, runs from l. 64 to l. 66.

16. Nadezhda Briusova's report for the plenary session, GARF f. 298, op. 1, d. 111, l. 75.

17. Other members of the GUS plenum also asked if the real motivation for the reform was the "weakness" of the faculty. GARF f. 298, op. 1, d. 111, l. 65.

18. GARF f. 298, op. 1, d. 111, l. 66.

19. Ibid., l. 64.

20. Ibid., l. 75.

21. Ibid., l. 65. Gnesin recalls these events in "Mysli o Iavorskom," in Iavorskii, *Vospominaniia*, vol. 1 (1964), 74–75.

22. Bruk, "O pedfake," *Proletarskii muzykant* 1 (1929): 30–31.

23. Sovet RAPM, "K polozheniiu v Moskovskoi konservatorii," *Proletarskii muzykant* 1 (1929): 28–30.

24. "Chto pokazalo obsledovanie Moskovskoi konservatorii," *Pravda*, April 17, 1929, 2.

25. Sovet RAPM, "K polozheniiu v Moskovskoi konservatorii," *Proletarskii muzykant* 1 (1929): 29; B. Shteinpress, "Ob orkestrovom klasse," *Proletarskii muzykant* 1 (1929): 31–32.

26. D. Gachev, A. Groman-Solovtov, et al., "Nuzhna reforma," *Muzykal'noe obrazovanie* 4–5 (1928): 77–80.

27. A. Mil'prud, "Konservatoriia v rukakh reaktsionnoi professury," *Komsomol'skaia pravda*, December 1, 1928, 5. On the Golovanov affair at the Bol'shoi Theater, see Fitzpatrick, "The Emergence of *Glaviskusstvo*," 244–45.

28. Briusova's report on these events, RGALI f. 2009, op. 1, ed khr. 24, l. 14. See also Nelson, "Assigning Meaning to Musical Speech," 261–62.

29. "V konservatorii neblagopolucheno," *Pravda*, November 16, 1928, 5; A. Mil'prud, "Konservatoriia," *Komsomol'skaia pravda*, December 1, 1928, 5; A Mil'prud, "V plenu reaktsionnoi professury," *Komsomol'skaia pravda*, December 8, 1928, 5; "K voprosu of polozhenie v MGK," *Muzykal'noe obrazovanie* 6 (1928): 12–15; "Pis'mo v redaktsiiu," *Muzykal'noe obrazovanie* 6 (1928): 72–77; Pavel Novitskii, "Tsitadel' muzykal'noi khudozhestvennoi reaktsii," *Muzyka i revoliutsiia* 11 (1928): 18–21; K. Milashevich, "Tsitadel' golovotiapskoi kritiki," *Muzyka i revoliutsiia* 12 (1928): 17–23; Pavel Novitskii, "O pravoi opasnosti v iskusstve," *Muzyka i revoliutsiia* 12 (1928): 23–28.

A more muted campaign also began at the Leningrad Conservatory. See B. Khvatskii, "V Leningradskoi konservatorii ne blagopoluchno," *Zhizn' iskusstva* 44 (1928): 8–9; "V Leningradskoi konservatorii ne blagopoluchno," *Zhizn' iskusstva* 47 (1928): 6–9.

30. Cheliapov was a lawyer, but had studied piano at the Music and Drama School of the Moscow Philharmonic Society before the revolution. He held positions at the Communist Academy and the Red Professors' Institute. He was the first editor in chief of the Composers' Union journal, *Sovetskaia muzyka*, a position he held until he was purged in 1937.

31. Members of the commission are listed in "Khronika," *Proletarskii muzykant* 1 (1929): 34. Organizations and institutions represented included GUS, Glavprofobr, Glaviskusstvo, Rabis, and the conservatory's Party and Komsomol organizations, as well as the regional Party committee, RAPM, ORK, *Pravda*, *Komsomol'skaia pravda*, and *Rabochaia Moskva*. See also "K obsledovaniiu Moskovskoi Gosudarstvennoi Konservatorii," *Muzykal'noe obrazovanie* 1 (1929): 39.

32. Sovet VAPM, "MGK," *Proletarskii muzykant* 1 (1929): 29–30.

33. The conservatory's Communists had proposed that Ippolitov-Ivanov resume the post he had held during the Civil War as a "figurehead," comparable to Glazunov in Leningrad. See Tov. Kamionskaia, "Preniia po dokladu tov. Obolenskogo," in *Puti razvitiia muzyki. Stenograficheskii otchet pri APPO TsK VKP (b)*, Vsesoiuznaia kommunisticheskaia partiia. Tsentral'nyi komitet. Otdel agitatsii, propagandy i pechati. Soveshchanie po voprosu muzyki (Moscow, 1930), 45. Pshibyshevskii's appointment was announced in *Vecherniaia Moskva*, June 17, 1929, 1.

34. N. Briusova, "Proletariazatsiia khudozhestvennoi shkoly," *Muzykal'noe obrazovanie* 2 (1929): 6.

35. S. Dubel', "Rekonstruktivnyi period v MGK," *Muzykal'noe obrazovanie* 1 (1930): 23.

36. "Otchet RAPMa," supplement to *Proletarskii muzykant* 1 (1929): 18.

37. L. Lebedinskii, "Obshchestvennye gruppirovki muzykantov v RSFSR," *Revoliutsiia i kul'tura* 15 (1928): 61.

38. On Sviderskii's tenure as head of Glaviskusstvo, see Fitzpatrick, "The Emergence of *Glaviskusstvo*," 242–44.

39. S. Korev, "Glaviskusstvo i rukovodstvo muzykal'noi zhizni," *Proletarskii muzykant* 3 (1930): 27.

40. RGALI f. 658, op. 1, d. 347, l. 6.

41. On Blium's work with Glavrepertkom, see Richmond, "The Conditions of the Contemporary," 2–5.

42. V. Belyi, "O proletarskom tvorchestve i demogogakh iz 'Muzyka i revoliutsii,'" *Proletarskii muzykant* 3 (1929): 19.

43. "Tri dokumenty nashei epokhi," *Muzyka i revoliutsiia* 2 (1929): 3–7.

44. "Disput o RAPM (Muzykal'naia komissiia komakademii)," *Proletarskii muzykant* 3 (1929): 30–33.

45. Prokoll continued to exist, but in November 1929 it adopted a new statute that established its complete support for RAPM and its platform. See GTsMMK f. 447, ed. khr. 773, ll. 3–4.

46. E. Braudo, "Muzyka-massam," *Pravda*, March 27, 1929, 6; Veselovskaia et al., *Bol'shoi put'*, 30. The Conservatory Communists who spearheaded the organization of Music to the Masses were Cherniakov, Sherman, Milashevich, and Vinogradov.

47. "K polozheniiu v o-ve 'Muzyka-massam,'" *Proletarskii muzykant* 7 (1930): 26; "V rab. ob-ve 'Muzyka-massam,'" *Muzyka i revoliutsiia* 2 (1929): 29.

48. Lebedinskii later admitted that the very existence of Music to the Masses reflected RAPM's weaknesses. See Lebedinskii, *8 let bor'by za proletarskiiuiu muzyku*, 69–70.

49. B. Shteinpress, "Vserossiiskaia Assotsiatsiia Proletarskykh Muzykantov (RAPM) i obshchestvo 'Muzyka-massam,'" *Za proletarskuiu muzyku* 1 (1930): 8.

50. A. Avraamov, "Elektrifikatsiia muzyki," *Sovetskoe iskusstvo* 1 (1928): 66; A. Tsukker, "Litsom k muzyke," *Persimfans* 3–4 (1927–28): 10; Orest Tsekhnovitser, "Novaia muzyka i proletariat," *Novaia muzyka* 1 (1928): 16; "Pered partsoveshchaniem i konferentsiei po voprosam muzyki," *Proletarskii muzykant* 2 (1929): 1–5; "Nazrevshie zadachi," *Muzyka i revoliutsiia* 9 (1928): 3–5.

51. The stenogram of this meeting was published as *Puti razvitiia muzyki. Stenograficheskii otchet pri APPO TsK VKP (b)*, Vsesoiuznaia kommunisticheskaia partiia. Tsentral'nyi komitet.

52. Shteinpress, "Preniia po dokladu tov. Obolenskogo," in *Puti razvitiia*, 27–28; Belyi, "Preniia po dokladu tov. Obolenskogo," in *Puti razvitiia*, 33–34; Pel'she, "Preniia po dokladu tov. Obolenskogo," in *Puti razvitiia*, 43–44.

53. Revich, "Preniia po dokladu tov. Obolenskogo," in *Puti razvitiia*, 39.

54. Pshibyshevskii, "Preniia po dokladu tov. Obolenskogo," in *Puti razvitiia*, 47.

55. Chicherov, "Preniia po dokladu tov. Obolenskogo," in *Puti razvitiia*, 18.

56. Savolei, "Preniia po dokladu tov. Obolenskogo," in *Puti razvitiia*, 37; Sutyrin, "Preniia po dokladu tov. Obolenskogo," in *Puti razvitiia*, 21.

57. Vinogradov, "Preniia po dokladu tov. Obolenskogo," in *Puti razvitiia*, 35; Gachev, "Preniia po dokladu tov. Obolenskogo," in *Puti razvitiia*, 50.

58. Vinogradov, "Preniia po dokladu tov. Obolenskogo," in *Puti razvitiia*, 34; Stankov, "Preniia po dokladu tov. Obolenskogo," in *Puti razvitiia*, 32; Ia. Bauman, "Itogi I Vserossiiskoi muzykal'noi konferentsii," *Muzyka i revoliutsiia* 4 (1929): 3.

59. Rabinovich, "Preniia po dokladu tov. Obolenskogo," in *Puti razvitiia*, 17.

60. Stankov, "Preniia po dokladu tov. Obolenskogo," in *Puti razvitiia*, 32.

61. "Osnovnaia resoliutsiia konferentsii," in *Puti razvitiia*, 75–80; "Ideologicheskaia platforma VAPM," supplement to *Proletarskii muzykant* 1 (1929): 3–12.

62. L. Obolenskii, "K otkrytiiu Vserosiiskoi muzykal'noi konferentsii," in Pervaia vserossiisskaia muzykal'naia konferentsiia, *Nash muzykal'nyi front*, ed. S. Korev (Leningrad, 1929), 5.

63. Kerzhentsev, "Doklad," in *Puti razvitiia*, 6; Obolenskii, "Doklad," in *Puti razvitiia*, 10; Kerzhentsev, "Zakliuchitel'noe slovo," in *Puti razvitiia*, 52.

64. Obolenskii, "Doklad," in *Puti razvitiia*, 10.

65. Obviously the old technical specialists were more critical to socialist construction than musicians. But concern among the authorities that class war not take too many victims was common in both areas, perhaps because music and engineering are both more ideologically "neutral" than literature and art, making expertise a more critical issue. On the technical intelligentsia, see Bailes, *Technology and Society under Lenin and Stalin*, especially 69–121.

66. Kerzhentsev, "Zakliuchitel'noe slovo," in *Puti razvitiia*, 53–54.

67. Stalin personally prompted the attack on Boris Pil'niak. See Kemp-Welch, *Stalin and the Literary Intelligentsia*, 58. Edward Brown considered the persecution of Pil'niak and Evgenii

Zamiatin for collaborating with the foreign press the literary equivalents of the Shakhty Affair and the Industrial Party trial. See Brown, *Proletarian Episode in Russian Literature*, 167.

68. "Plenum Soveta Vseroskomdrama. Fragment stenogrammy, posviashchennyi muzykal'nym voprosam (18–19 dekabria 1931 goda)," *Muzykal'naia akademiia* 2 (1993): 160–77, especially 166–68.

69. S. Korev, *Muzykal'nyi front pered smotrom* (Moscow, 1929), 12.

70. Nikitina, "Muzyka i massy," in *Nash muzykal'nyi front*, ed. Korev, 13.

71. Zetkin, *My Recollections of Lenin*, 19.

72. Kerzhentsev, "Zakliuchitel'noe slovo," in *Puti razvitiia*, 54.

73. "Zaiavleniia v Assots. Prol. Muz.," *Proletarskii muzykant* 5 (1929): 39–40.

74. "V assotsiatsii proletarskykh muzykantov," *Proletarskii muzykant* 6 (1929): 39.

75. Iu. Keldysh, "D. Vasil'ev-Buglai," *Proletarskii muzykant* 8 (1930): 8–13; Iu. K., "Massovye pesni s garmon'iu Vasil'eva-Buglaia," *Za proletarskuiu muzyku* 1 (1931): 25–26.

76. Fitzpatrick, *Education and Social Mobility*, 132–33; Holmes, *Kremlin and the Schoolhouse*, 118–21.

77. David-Fox, *Revolution of the Mind*, 75.

78. L. Lebedinskii, "Vazhneishshee zveno nashei raboty," in *Dovesti do kontsa bor'bu*, 4–5; N. Briusova, "Na bor'bu s muzykal'nym durmanom," in *Dovesti do kontsa bor'bu*, 17; L. Lebedinskii, "Nash massovyi muzykal'nyi byt," *Proletarskii muzykant* 9–10 (1930): 22.

79. V. Vinogradov, "Opyt analyza 'legkogo zhanra,'" *Proletarskii muzykant* 1 (1931): 17.

80. Lebedinskii, "Nash massovyi," *Proletarskii muzykant* 9–10 (1930): 14.

81. V. Vinogradov, *Sud nad muzykal'noi khalturoi* (Moscow, 1931), 26.

82. Ibid., 26–28.

83. Maxim Gorky, "O muzyke tolstykh," *Pravda*, April 18, 1928, 4, reprinted as "The Music of the Degenerate," *The Dial* 85 (1928): 480–84; A. V. Lunacharskii, "Sotsial'nye istoki muzykal'nogo iskusstva," *Proletarskii muzykant* 4 (1929): 12–20, reprinted in Lunacharskii, *V mire muzyki*, 369–80. See also Starr, *Red and Hot*, 89–94; Stites, *Popular Culture*, 73.

84. L. Lebedinskii, "Amerikanskii tanets," in *Dovesti do kontsa bor'bu*, 20–22. Morbid imagery and concern about the psychological effects of jazz also characterized Western observers' critiques of the new dance music in these years. In 1928 the Danish composer Carl Nielson lamented that "men and women, when dancing, press their knees against one another and gyrate with glassy eyes and empty brains, the picture of nonentity. . . . My opinion is that [jazz] spoils the young musician's ear and individuality; it is a nasty and death-like music." Quoted in Starr, *Red and Hot*, 88.

85. Vinogradov, *Sud nad muzykal'noi khalturoi*, 12–13. Shostakovich reportedly used a similar "demonstration" to "reveal" the true character of a Civil War song, *Over the Seas, Over the Valleys* (*Za moriami, za dolami*). At a meeting of TRAM he conducted a duet pairing the RAPM-approved Civil War song with a traditional lullaby, *Sleep, My Lovely Child* (*Spi mladenets moi prekrasnyi*). In this rendition, the two pieces sounded identical. See Pavel Marinchik, *Rozhdenie komsomol'skogo teatra* (Moscow and Leningrad, 1963), 225–26. Quoted in Wilson, *Shostakovich*, 79.

86. Naiman, *Sex in Public*, 289.

87. V. Blium, "Ob odnom 'levom' zagibe," *Vecherniaia Moskva*, July 3, 1930, 3; Lebedinskii, "Nash massovyi," *Proletarskii muzykant* 9–10 (1930): 26–27.

88. Vinogradov, *Sud nad muzykal'noi khalturoi*, 31–48.

89. Clark, *Petersburg*, 16–20.

90. Korev, "Glaviskusstvo," *Proletarskii muzykant* 3 (1930): 29–30.

91. "Zaiavlenie 33 kompozitorov," in *Dovesti do kontsa bor'bu*, 33–37. Roslavets's efforts to rally support from MODPIK/Dramsoiuz during the Glaviskusstvo purge are also discussed in "Pozornyi dokument" and "Zaiavlenie Roslavetsa," in *Dovesti do kontsa bor'bu*, 28–33, 37–39. These materials were also published in *Proletarskii muzykant* 1 (1930): 31–34, and 2 (1930): 42–43.

92. G. Anisimov and G. Krasnukh, "Opyt letnei raboty LOVAPM," *Proletarskii muzykant* 6 (1930): 26; V. Isaenko, "Pochemy nravitsia tsyganshchina," *Za proletarskuiu muzyku* 5 (1930): 15; V. Pronin, "Za proletarskuiu muzyku,—pomog," *Za proletarskuiu muzyku* 5 (1930): 16; "Ogon' po khalturshchikam (pis'ma s mest)," *Za proletarskuiu muzyku* 8 (1930): 14–15; "Ogon' po khalturshchikam (pis'ma s mest)," *Za proletarskuiu muzyku* 9 (1930): 17–18.

93. L. Lebedinskii, "Amerikanskii tanets," in *Dovesti do kontsa bor'bu,* 20–26; Vinogradov, *Sud nad muzykal'noi khalturoi,* 14–18; M. Zarzhevskii, "Opyt izucheniia pesen na demonstratsii," *Proletarskii muzykant* 9–10 (1930): 59–60.

94. S. Korev, "Glaviskusstvo," *Proletarskii muzykant* 3 (1930): 30. Popular musical preferences also proved remarkably tenacious when Vladimir Blium instigated a "trial" of the Piatnitsky Choir in the journal *Radioslushatel'* in 1930. Despite Blium's efforts to condemn the choir's repertoire as "kulakism," letters defending the choir far outnumbered those agreeing with Blium. See Smith, "Soviet Arts Policy, Folk Music, and National Identity," 71–76.

95. RAPM's concerns over Vasil'ev-Buglai's debts to folk music are addressed in Iu. Keldysh, "Problema proletarskogo muzykal'nogo tvorchestva i poputnichestvo," *Proletarskii muzykant* 1 (1929): 15.

96. L. Lebedinskii, "Nash massovyi," *Proletarskii muzykant* 9–10 (1930): 7.

97. Ibid., 9, 22; N. Briusova, "Starinnye narodnye pesni," *Za proletarskuiu muzyku* 7 (1930): 7, 10.

98. L. Lebedinskii, "Nash massovyi," *Proletarskii muzykant* 9–10 (1930): 30.

99. Sokhor, *Russkaia sovetskaia pesnia,* 120. On Litfront, see Katerina Clark, "Little Heroes and Big Deeds: Literature Responds to the First Five-Year Plan," in *Cultural Revolution in Russia,* ed. Fitzpatrick, 196; Kemp-Welch, *Stalin and the Literary Intelligentsia,* 82–89; Brown, *The Proletarian Episode,* 156–57.

100. RAPM's songs were overwhelmingly in duple, not triple, meter. Exceptions are Belyi's *Slyshish' soldat* and Shekhter's *Traurnaya pesnia.* For another discussion of RAPM's output in this period, see Sokhor, *Russkaia sovetskaia pesnia,* 119–23.

101. L. Lebedinskii, "O proletarskii massovoi pesni," *Proletarskii muzykant* 3 (1929): 9.

102. Each issue of *Za proletarskuiu muzyku* included a short lesson on "musical literacy."

103. S. Krylova, "Kak slushat' operu," *Za proletarskuiu muzyku* 1 (1930): 8–10.

104. RAPM relied on inexpensive anthologies of (often simplified) classics and their own revolutionary compositions put out by the State Publishing House to introduce this music to the masses. See B. S., "Deshevaia notnaia biblioteka, 'muzyka-massam,'" *Za proletarskuiu muzyku* 1 (1930): 21–23. They also presented simplistic historical-ideological introductions to Beethoven and Musorgsky. See Iu. Keldysh, "Tvorchestvo Musorgskogo," *Za proletarskuiu muzyku* 2 (1930): 8–11; L. L., "Betkhoven," *Za proletarskuiu muzyku* 3 (1930): 9–16.

105. Rossiiskaia assotsiatsiia proletarskykh muzykantov, *Tvorcheskii sbornik,* vol. 1 (Moscow, 1931), 1.

106. Concerns about the skills of beginning writers and the need to reach a broad, newly literate audience also underpinned RAPP's emphasis on the literature of "small forms" in this period. At the same time, writers also wrestled with the challenge of capturing the "monumental" achievements of the First Five-Year Plan in an appropriately "revolutionary" long form. See Clark, "Little Heroes and Big Deeds," in *Cultural Revolution in Russia,* ed. Fitzpatrick, 199–200.

107. Iu. Keldysh, "Put' oktiabria," *Proletarskii muzykant* 1 (1929): 40–41.

108. A. Veprik, "Put' oktiabria," *Muzykal'noe obrazovanie* 1 (1929): 35–36; Evgenii Braudo, "Lenin v muzyke," *Pravda,* January 24, 1929, 6; "Put' oktiabria," *Vecherniaia Moskva,* January 16, 1929, 3.

109. *Proletarskii muzykant* 9 (1931), especially 9, 29, 31; *Za proletarskuiu muzyku* 21 (1931), especially 5–6.

110. V. Shebalin, "Prenia," *Proletarskii muzykant* 9 (1931): 10–12; N. Kriukov, "Prenia," *Proletarskii muzykant* 9 (1931): 19; "Plenum Soveta Vseroskomdrama," 167, 172 (speeches by

Shostakovich and Shebalin). For another derogatory assessment of the opera, see V. Kharlamov, "Slova i dela," *Govorit Moskva* 25 (1931): 14.

111. Laurel Fay, "The Punch in Shostakovich's Nose," in *Russian and Soviet Music: Essays for Boris Schwarz*, ed. Malcom H. Brown (Ann Arbor, 1984), 234.

112. D. Zhitomirskii, "'Nos'—opera D. Shostakovicha," *Proletarskii muzykant* 7–8 (1929): 33–39, especially 33, 37, 38.

113. Synopsis in Manashev Yakubov, "The Golden Age: The True Story of the Premiere," in *Shostakovich Studies*, ed. David Fanning (Cambridge, 1995), 193.

114. Sekretariat LOVAPM, "Burzhuaznuiu ideologiiu v muzyke razoblachim do kontsa," *Rabochii i teatr* 62–63 (1930): 7; D. Zhitomirskii, "'Nos'—opera D. Shostakovicha," *Proletarskii muzykant* 7–8 (1929): 33. This criticism may have motivated Shostakovich's particularly vehement denunciation of the "light genre" and his admission that orchestrating *Tahiti Trot* had been a "political mistake" in the pages of *Proletarskii muzykant.* See "Anketa 'Proletarskogo muzykanta' o legkom zhanre," *Proletarskii muzykant* 3 (1930): 25. As this episode suggests, in his music and his politics Shostakovich charted a course that conformed to neither RAPM's utilitarianism nor the "elite modernism" of the ASM. His work with the Komsomol theater troupe, TRAM, and the parody of Davidenko's mass song *They Wanted to Vanquish Us* in the incidental music he wrote for a production of *Hamlet* in 1931 offer further evidence of the ambiguity of his position in the musical scene. See Fitzpatrick, "The Lady Macbeth Affair," in *The Cultural Front*, 194–99; Taruskin, *Defining Russia Musically*, 93–94.

115. Yakubov, "The Golden Age," in *Shostakovich Studies*, ed. Fanning, 197.

116. As quoted in Wilson, *Shostakovich*, 75.

117. Fay, "The Punch in Shostakovich's Nose," 238.

118. Clark, *Petersburg*, 204–5, 212–13.

119. McQuere, "The Theories of Boleslav Yavorsky," in *Russian Theoretical Thought in Music*, 109–65; Carpenter, "Russian Music Theory," 42–51; Wehrmeyer, *Studien zum russischen Musikdenken*, 95–138.

120. His research at GAKhN yielded two scholarly articles in the twenties: "Osnovnye elementy muzyki," *Iskusstvo* 1 (1923): 185–212, and "Konstruktsiia melodicheskogo protsessa," in S. Beliaeva-Ekzempliarskaia and B. L. Iavorskii, *Struktura melodii* (Moscow, 1929), 7–36. The most complete exposition of his work was completed and published only in 1930–31 by his student, the composer Sergei Protopopov, as *Elementy stroeniia muzykal'noi rechi*, ed. B. L. Iavorskii, parts 1–2 (Moscow, 1930–31).

121. His research on these questions was published before the conference. M. V. Ivanov-Boretskii, "O ladovoi osnove polifonicheskoi muzyki (kritika odnoi skholasticheskoi teorii)," *Proletarskii muzykant* 9 (1929): 13–16.

122. "Konferentsiia po teorii ladovogo ritma," *Proletarskii muzykant* 2 (1930): 7.

123. N. A. Garbuzov, *Teoriia mnogoosnovnosti ladov i sozvuchii. Trudy GIMNa* (Moscow, 1928).

124. "K voprosu ob edinichnoi i dvoinoi sistemakh B. Iavorskogo," *Muzykal'noe obrazovanie* 1 (1930): 21. Although Garbuzov continued to maintain that his approach was superior to and proved the deficiencies of Iavorskii's system, Soviet theorists later identified similarities between the two scholars' conclusions. See Iosif Ryzhkin, "Teoriia mnogoosnovnosti (N. Garbuzov)," in *Ocherki po istorii teoreticheskogo muzykoznaniia*, ed. L. A. Mazel and I. Ia. Ryzhkin, 2d ed. (Moscow and Leningrad, 1976 [1939]), 227. Ellon D. Carpenter also notes that in the second volume of *Teoriia mnogoosnovnosti ladov i sozvuchii* (1932), Garbuzov presents a definition of mode as a dynamic process occurring in time, a position close to Iavorskii's. See Carpenter, "The Contributions of Taneev," 324.

125. "Konferentsiia," *Proletarskii muzykant* 2 (1930): 8.

126. A. Lunacharskii, "O teorii ladovogo ritma," in B. Iavorskii, *Stat'i, vospominaniia, perepiska*, 39. A condensed version of Lunacharsky's speech appeared as "Neskol'ko zamechanii o teorii ladovogo ritma," *Proletarskii muzykant* 2 (1930): 10–13.

127. Lunacharskii, "O teorii," in Iavorskii, *Stat'i vospominaniia, perepiska*, 37–38.

128. Ibid., 44.

129. Ibid., 47–48.

130. Ibid., 51.

131. Denise Youngblood uses "the middle" to describe the film directors and critics whose dissatisfaction with the commercial conditions of NEP launched the Cultural Revolution in the film industry. See Youngblood, *Movies for the Masses*, 178.

132. His biographer praises his "sober, realistic appraisal" of modal rhythm and his part in the debate. See T. Livanova, ed., *Mikhail Vladimirovich Ivanov-Boretskii. Stat'i i issledovaniia. Vospominaniia o nem* (Moscow, 1972), 40.

133. On Asaf'ev's contributions to the aesthetics of socialist realism and his debt to Iavorskii, see Malcom H. Brown, "The Soviet Russian Concepts of 'Intonazia' and 'Musical Imagery,'" *Musical Quarterly* 60 (1974): 557–67. Iavorskii's contributions to Soviet music theory and aesthetics are detailed in D. Daragan, "Odin iz samykh aktivnykh stroitelei," *Sovetskaia muzyka* 5 (1978): 83; L. Maslenkova, "B. L. Iavorskii o vospitanii slukha," *Kritika i muzykoznanie* 2 (1980): 200; L. A. Mazel and I. Ia. Ryzhkin, eds., *Ocherki po istorii teoreticheskogo muzykoznaniia* (Moscow, 1939).

134. Congress resolution quoted in Vinogradov, *Sud nad muzykal'noi khalturoi*, 3.

135. "Plenum Soveta Vseroskomdrama," 162.

136. "O proletarskoi massovoi pesne," *Proletarskii muzykant* 8 (1930): 24.

137. "Puti razvitiia muzyki—disput v komakademii o platformakh APM i OSM," *Proletarskii muzykant* 1 (1931): 21.

138. Ibid., 20.

139. L. Lebedinskii, "O vragakh i druzhiakh proletarskoi muzyki," *Proletarskii muzykant* 1 (1931): 9. Linking RAPM so directly to RAPP may have been ill advised given that the Proletarian Writers had their own opponents within the Communist Academy. See Fitzpatrick, "Cultural Revolution as Class War," in *Cultural Revolution in Russia*, 29–30; Kemp-Welch, *Stalin and the Literary Intelligentsia*, 86–89.

140. "Rech' na soveshchanii khoziaistvennikov, 23 iulia 1931g." and "O nekotorykh voprosakh istorii bolshevizma," in I. V. Stalin, *Sochineniia*, vol. 13 (Moscow, 1951), 69–73, 84–102.

141. Pervaia konferentsiia Rossiiskoi Assotsiatsii Proletarskykh Muzykantov. *Rezoliutsii* (Moscow, 1931), 3–34. See also *Proletarskii muzykant* 3–4 (1931): 73–82.

142. "Novoe tvorcheskoe ob"edinenie," *Proletarskii muzykant* 7 (1931): 51. Starokadomskii, Kochetov, Kabalevskii, Shirinskii, Shenshin, and Vladimir and Nikolai Kriukov rounded out "the nine."

143. D. Shostakovich, "Deklaratsiia obiazannostei kompozitora," *Rabochii i teatr* 31 (1931): 6.

144. See *Fakty i tsifry protiv RAPMa*, supplement to *Proletarskii muzykant* 9 (1931).

145. "Plenum Soveta Vseroskomdrama," 176.

Epilogue

1. Jelagin, *Taming the Arts*, 190.

2. Schwarz, *Music and Musical Life*, 107; Maes, *History of Russian Music*, 298–304.

3. Brooke, "Development of Soviet Music Policy," 208.

4. Barsova, "Iz neopublikovannykh arkhivov Mosolova," 70–71.

5. Feliks Aronovich Fradkin, "Soviet Experimentalism Routed: S. T. Shatskii's Last Years," in *School and Society in Tsarist and Soviet Russia*, ed. Ben Eklof (New York, 1993), 154–75, especially 169.

6. Jelagin, *Taming the Arts*, 196.

7. I. Vinokurova, "Trizhdy rasstrelianyi muzykant," *Muzykal'naia akademiia* 1 (1996): 79–84; Caroline Brooke, "Soviet Musicians and the Great Terror," *Europe-Asia Studies* 54 (2002): 397–413.

8. Hakobian, *Music of the Soviet Age*, 13; Dmitrii Paperno, *Zapiski moskovksogo pianista* (Ann Arbor, 1983), 58–59. Roy Medvedev claimed that more than 600 members (nearly one-third of the total membership) of the writers' union were "arrested and destroyed" in 1936–39. See Medvedev, *Let History Judge*, 231. See also Boris Kagarlitsky, *The Thinking Reed: Intellectuals and the Soviet State from 1917 to the Present*, trans. Brian Pearce (London, 1988), 94.

9. Detlef Gojowy, "Half-Time for Nikolai Roslavets (1881–1944): A Non-Love Story with a Post-Romantic Composer," in *Russian and Soviet Music*, ed. Brown, 215.

10. Lobanova, *Roslavec*, 90–93.

11. Ferenc, "Investigating Russian Musical Modernism," 16.

12. Tomoff, "Creative Union."

13. Schwarz, *Music and Musical Life*, 119.

14. Fitzpatrick, "The Emergence of *Glaviskusstvo*," 253; Tomoff, "Creative Union."

15. Fitzpatrick, "Shostakovich and the Cultural Puritans," in *The Cultural Front*, 183–215.

16. Nicholas Timasheff, *The Great Retreat: The Growth and Decline of Communism in Russia* (New York, 1946).

17. The work of Sheila Fitzpatrick and Vera Dunham has been central to scholarly conceptions of Stalinist culture. See Fitzpatrick's essays: "Stalin and the Making of a New Elite," "Becoming Cultured: Socialist Realism and the Representation of Privilege and Taste," and "Cultural Orthodoxies under Stalin," in *The Cultural Front*, 149–82, 216–37, 238–56. See also Vera S. Dunham, *In Stalin's Time: Middleclass Values in Soviet Fiction* (Durham, 1990 [1976]).

18. James von Geldern, "The Centre and the Periphery: Cultural and Social Geography in the Mass Culture of the 1930s," in *New Directions in Soviet History*, ed. Stephen White (Cambridge, 1992), 63.

19. On the ways in which popular appeal could operate independently from the main trajectory of Soviet politics on the variety stage, see David MacFadyen, *Songs for Fat People: Affect, Emotion, and Celebrity in the Russian Popular Song* (Montreal, 2002).

GLOSSARY

NEP	New Economic Policy

State Agencies

Narkompros	Commissariat of Enlightenment
Sovnarkom	Council of People's Commissars
Rabkrin	Workers' and Peasants' Inspectorate

Divisions of Narkompros

GUS	State Academic Council
Glavnauka	Main Administration of Scientific and Artistic Institutions
Glavprofobr	Main Administration of Professional Education
Glavpolitprosvet	Main Political Enlightenment Committee (Narkompros Agency also under the jurisdiction of the Central Committee's Agitprop Section)
Glavlit	Main Administration of Literature and Presses
Glavrepertkom	Main Committee on Repertoire
Glaviskusstvo	Main Administration of Artistic Affairs

Organizations

ASM	Association of Contemporary Music
ISCM	International Society of Contemporary Music
KNM	New Music Circle (Leningrad)
LASM	Leningrad Association of Contemporary Music
RAPM	Russian Association of Proletarian Musicians
ORK	Organization of Revolutionary Composers
Persimfans	First Symphonic Ensemble (Conductorless Orchestra)
Prokoll	Production Collective of Student Composers at the Moscow Conservatory
Proletkul't	Proletarian Culture Organizations

Rabis	Trade Union of Art Workers
Vseroskomdram (VRKD)	All-Russian Society of Composers and Dramatists

Institutions

GAKhN (RAKhN)	State (Russian) Academy of Artistic Sciences
GIMN	State Institute of Musical Science
GIII (RIII)	State (Russian) Institute of the History of the Arts

Miscellaneous

VUZ	Institution of Higher Education
pedfak	pedagogical faculty
rabfak	workers' faculty
MGPSPS	Moscow Trade Union Soviet
VTsPS	All-Russian Trade Union Soviet

WORKS CITED

Archival Sources

GARF	Gosudarstvennyi arkhiv Rossiiskoi Federatsii / State Archive of the Russian Federation
fond 298	GUS (State Academic Council)
fond 1565	Glavprofobr (Main Administration of Professional Education)
fond 2306	Narkompros (Commissariat of Enlightenment)
fond 2307	Glavnauka (Main Administration of Scientific and Artistic Institutions)
fond 2313	Glavpolitprosvet (Main Political Enlightenment Committee)
RGALI	Rossiiskii gosudarstvennyi arkhiv literatury i iskusstva / Russian State Archive of Literature and Art
fond 658	Moscow Conservatory
fond 645	Glaviskusstvo (Main Administration of Artistic Affairs)
fond 941	GAKhN (State Academy of Artistic Sciences)
fond 2004	Boris Krasin
fond 2009	Nadezhda Briusova
GTsMMK	Gosudarstvennyi tsentral'nyi muzei i muzykal'noi kul'tury im. M. I. Glinki / Glinka State Central Museum of Musical Culture
fond 179	Persimfans
fond 447	Sergei Riauzov / Prokoll
fond 473	Arsenii Avraamov

Journals

Biulleten' Betkhovenskogo Komiteta pri Narkomprose RSFSR
Biulleten' GAKhN
Biulleten' glavnogo upravleniia nauchnikh, khudozhestvennykh i muzeinykh uchrezhdenii
Biulleten' GUSa
Das neue Russland
De Musica
Gorn

Govorit Moskva
Iskusstvo
Iskusstvo trudiashchimsia
K novym beregam muzykal'nogo iskusstva
Khudozhnik i zritel'
Muzyka
Muzyka i byt
Muzyka i Oktiabr'
Muzyka i revoliutsiia
Muzykal'naia kul'tura
Muzykal'naia letopis'. Stat'i i materialy
Muzykal'naia nov'
Muzykal'noe obrazovanie
Muzykoznanie
Na literaturnom postu
Novaia muzyka
Oktiabr'
Pechat' i revoliutsiia
Persimfans
Prizyv
Proletarskii muzykant
Rabis
Rabochii i teatr
Revoliutsiia i kul'tura
Sovetskoe iskusstvo
Sovremennaia muzyka
Teatral'naia Moskva
Za proletarskuiu muzyku
Zhizn' iskusstva

Newspapers

Izvestiia
Komsomol'skaia pravda
Krasnaia gazeta
Pravda
Rabochaia gazeta
Vecherniaia Moskva

Music Anthologies

Belyi, Viktor, ed. *Antologiia sovetskoi pesni. 1917–1957*. Vol. 1. Moscow: Gosudarstvennoe muzykal'noe izdatel'stvo, 1957.

Pervyi sbornik revoliutsionnykh pesen. 10 pesen, garmonizovannykh A. D. Ch. St. Petersburg: n.p., 1906.

Pesni katorgi i ssylki. Moscow: Izdatel'stvo vse soiuznogo obshchestva politicheskikh katorzhan a ssyl'no-poselentsev, 1930.
Rossiiskaia assotsiatsiia proletarskykh muzykantov. *Tvorcheskii sbornik*. Vol. 1. Moscow: Gosudarstvennoe muzykal'noe izdatel'stvo, 1931.

Memoirs, Diaries, Document Collections, and Other Primary Sources

Aleksandrov, A. N. *Stranitsy zhizni i tvorchestva*. Ed. and comp. V. Blok and E. A. Polenova. Moscow: Sovetskii kompozitor, 1990.
Alekseev, M. P., and Ia. Z. Berman. *Betkhoven. Materialy dlia bibliograficheskogo ukazatel'ia russkoi literatury o nem*. Vols. 1–2. Odessa: n.p., 1927–28.
Alekseeva, E. N., Galina Pribegina, and Nadezhda Tumanina, eds. *Vospominaniia o Moskovskoi konservatorii*. Moscow: Muzyka, 1966.
Artizov, A. N., and O. N. Naumov, eds. *Vlast' i khudozhestvennaia intelligentsiia. Dokumenty TsK RKP(b)-VKP(b), VChK-OGPU-NKVD o kul'turnoi politike. 1917–1953 gg*. Moscow: Demokratiia. Mezhdunarodnyi fond, 1999.
Asaf'ev, Boris. *Kniga o Stravinskom*. Leningrad: n.p., 1929.
———. *Muzykal'naia forma kak protsess*. Moscow: n.p., 1930.
———. *Izbrannye trudy*. 5 vols. Moscow: Izdatel'stvo Akademii nauk SSSR, 1952–57.
Barenboim, L. A., et al., eds. *Iz istorii sovetskogo muzykal'nogo obrazovaniia. Sbornik materialov i dokumentov*. Leningrad: Muzyka, 1969.
Barsova, Inna. "Iz neopublikovannogo arkhiva A. V. Mosolova." *Sovetskaia muzyka* 7 (1989): 80–92.
———. "Iz neopublikovannykh arkhivov Mosolova (Okonchanie)." *Sovetskaia muzyka* 8 (1989): 69–75.
———, ed. *A. V. Mosolov: Stat' i i vospominaniia*. Comp. Nina Meshko. Moscow: Sovetskii kompozitor, 1986.
Beliaeva-Ekzempliarskaia, S., and B. L. Iavorskii. *Struktura melodii*. Moscow: Gosudarstvennaia akademiia khudozhestvennykh nauk, 1929.
Blok, Aleksandr. *The Spirit of Music*. Trans. I. Frieman. Westport, Conn.: Hyperion Press, 1973 [1946].
———. *Sobranie sochinenii v vos'mi tomakh*. Vol. 6. Ed. V. N. Orlov, A. A. Surkov, and K. I. Chukovskii. Moscow: Khudozhestvennaia literatura, 1962.
Braudo, E. M. *Betkhoven i ego vremia 1770–1827. Opyt muzykal'no-sotsiologicheskogo issledovaniia*. Moscow: Gosudarstvennoe muzykal'nyi izdatel'stvo, 1927.
Briusova, N. Ia. *Zadachi narodnogo muzykal'nogo obrazovaniia. Doklad prochitanyi na konferentsii kul't.-pros. proletarskykh organizatsii*. Moscow: n.p., 1919.
Bruk, M. "Komsomol'tsy 20-kh godov." *Sovetskaia muzyka* 11 (1963): 8–14.
Chaliapin, Feodor. *Man and Mask*. Trans. Phillis Megroz. New York: Garden City Publishing, 1932.
———. *Pages from My Life*. Ed. Katharien Wright, trans. H. M. Buck. New York: Harper and Brothers, 1927.
Dovesti do kontsa bor'bu s NEPmanskoi muzyki. Moscow: Gosudarstvennoe muzykal'noe izdatel'stvo, 1931.
Druskin, Mikhail. *Issledovaniia: vospominaniia*. Leningrad: Sovetskii kompozitor, 1977.

———. "Iz khroniki muzykal'noi zhizni Leningrada 20-kh godov." *Sovetskaia muzyka* 9 (1979): 113–22.

Fere, Vladimir. "Moskovskaia konservatoriia v 20-e gody." *Sovetskaia muzyka* 11 (1958): 20–24.

Fuelop-Miller, Rene. *The Mind and Face of Bolshevism*. New York: Harper and Row, 1962 [1926].

Garbuzov, N. A. *Teoriia mnogoosnovnosti ladov i sozvuchii. Trudy GIMNa*. Moscow: Gosudarstvennoe muzykal'noe izdatel'stvo, 1928.

Glikman, I. D., ed. *Pis'ma k drugu: Dmitrii Shostakovich—Isaaku Glikmanu*. Moscow: DSCH, 1993.

Goriaeva, T. M., ed. *Istoriia sovetskoi politicheskoi tsenzury. Dokumenty i kommentarii*. Moscow: ROSSPEN, 1997.

Gorky, Maxim. *Days with Lenin*. New York: International Publishers, 1932.

Gosudarstvennaia Akademicheskaia Filarmoniia. *Desiat' let simfonicheskoi muzyki, 1917–28*. Leningrad: Izdatel'stvo Gosudarstvennoi akademicheskoi filarmonii, 1928.

Got'e, Iurii. *Time of Troubles, The Diary of Iurii Vladimirovich Got'e: Moscow, July 8, 1917 to July 23, 1922*. Ed. and trans. Terence Emmons. Princeton: Princeton University Press, 1988.

Iavorskii, Boleslav. *Stroenie muzykal'noi rechi*. Moscow: n.p., 1908.

———. *Vospominaniia, stat'i i pis'ma*. Vol. 1. Ed. I. S. Rabinovich and D. S. Shostakovich. Moscow: Sovetskii kompozitor, 1964.

———. *Stat'i, vospominaniia, perepiska*. 2d ed. Vol. 1. Ed. I. S. Rabinovich and D. S. Shostakovich. Moscow: Sovetskii kompozitor, 1972.

Ippolitov-Ivanov, Mikhail Mikhailovich. *M. M. Ippolitov-Ivanov. Pis'ma, stat'i, vospominaniia*. Ed. N. N. Sokolov. Moscow: Sovetskii kompozitor, 1986.

Ivanov-Boretskii, M. V. *Betkhoven. Biograficheskii ocherk*. Moscow: Gosudarstvennoe muzykal'nyi izdatel'stvo, 1927.

Kalendar'-spravochnik Muzykal'nogo otdela Narodnogo komissariata po prosveshcheniiu na 1919-i god. Petrograd and Moscow: n.p., 1919.

Korev, S. *Muzykal'nyi front pered smotrom*. Moscow: Tea-kino-pechat', 1929.

Kriukov, Andrei. *Materialy k biografii B. Asaf'ev*. Leningrad: Muzyka, 1981.

Kuznetsov, K. A., ed. *Russkaia kniga o Betkhovene*. Moscow and Leningrad: n.p., 1927.

Lamm, O. "Druz'ia Pavla Aleksandrovicha Lamma i uchastniki muzykal'nykh vecherov v ego dome (20-e gody xx veka)." In *Iz proshlogo sovetskoi muzykal'noi kul'tury*, ed. T. N. Livanova. Vol. 1. Moscow: Sovetskii kompozitor, 1975.

———. "Pervye gody raboty Gosudarstvennogo muzykal'nogo izdatel'stva. Dela i liudi." In *Sovetskaia muzyka. Kul'tura, istoriia, traditsii, sovremennost'*, ed. D. G. Daragan. Moscow: Muzyka, 1980.

Lebedinskii, Lev. *8 let bor'by za proletarskuiu muzyku*. Moscow: Gosudarstvennoe muzykal'nyi izdatel'stvo, 1930.

———. "A. Davidenko. Materialy dlia tvorcheskoi biografii." *Sovetskaia muzyka* 4 (1935): 22–37.

Lenin, Vladimir Il'ich. *Lenin o literature i iskusstve*. Ed. N. Kriutkov. Moscow: Khudozhestvennaia literatura, 1986.

Leningradskaia gosudarstvennaia filarmoniia. *Betkhoven (1827–1927)*. Leningrad: Gosudarstvennoe muzykal'nyi izdatel'stvo, 1927.

Lourié, Arthur. "The Russian School." *Musical Quarterly* 18 (1932): 519–29.

———. *Sergei Koussevitzky and His Epoch*. Trans. S. W. Pring. New York: Alfred A. Knopf, 1931.

Lunacharskii, A. V. *Iskusstvo i molodezh'*. Moscow: Molodaia gvardiia, 1929.

———. *V mire muzyki*. Moscow: Gosudarstvennoe muzykal'nyi izdatel'stvo, 1923.

———. *V mire muzyki. Stat'i i rechi*. Moscow: Sovetskii kompozitor, 1958.

Lunacharsky, A. V. *Revolutionary Silhouettes*. Ed. and trans. Michael Glenny. New York: Hill and Wang, 1968.

———. *V mire muzyki. Stat'i i rechi*. 2d ed. Moscow: Sovetskii kompozitor, 1971.

Maikapar, S. M. *Znachenie tvorchestva Betkhovena dlia nashei sovremennosti*. Moscow: Gosudarstvennoe muzykal'nyi izdatel'stvo, 1927.

Malko, Nikolai. *A Certain Art*. New York: W. Morrow, 1966.

Martynov, N. A. *A. Davidenko. Tvorcheskii put', cherty stilia*. Leningrad: Sovetskii kompozitor, 1977.

———, comp. *Aleksandr Davidenko. Vospominaniia. Stat'i. Materialy*. Leningrad: Muzyka, 1968.

Maiakovskii, V. V. *Sochineniia v trekh tomakh*. Vol. 1. Moscow: Khudozhestvennoe literatura, 1970.

Mayakovsky, Vladimir. *Selected Works in Three Volumes*. Vol. 1. Moscow: Raduga, 1985.

Miaskovskii, Nikolai. *N. Ia. Miaskovskii. Sobranie materialov v dvukh tomakh*. Ed. S. I. Shlifshtein. Moscow: Muzyka, 1964.

Moskovskaia gosudarstvennaia konservatoriia. *K desiatiletiiu Oktiabria, 1917–1927. Sbornik statei*. Moscow: Moskovskaia gosudarstvennaia konservatoriia, 1927.

Narodnoe prosveshcheniie v RSFSR k 1928/29 godu: Otchet NKP RSFSR za 1928/28 uchebnyi god. Moscow: n.p., 1929.

Orkestr bez dirizhera. Moscow: Izdanie pervogo simfonichiskogo ansamblia, 1922.

Paperno, Dmitrii. *Zapiski moskovksogo pianista*. Ann Arbor: Hermitage, 1983.

Pervaia konferentsiia Rossiiskoi Assotsiatsii Proletarskykh Muzykantov. *Rezoliutsii*. Moscow, 1931.

Pervaia vserossiisskaia muzykal'naia konferentsiia. *Nash muzykal'nyi front*. Ed. S. Korev. Moscow: Gosudarstvennoe izdatel'stvo, 1930.

"Plenum Soveta Vseroskomdrama. Fragment stenogrammy, posviashchennyi muzykal'nym voprosam (18–19 dekabria 1931 goda)." *Muzykal'naia akademiia* 2 (1993): 160–77.

Prokof'ev, Sergei. *Materialy, dokumenty, vospominaniia*. Ed. S. I. Shlifstein. Moscow: Gosudarstvennoe muzykal'noe izdatel'stvo, 1961.

Prokofiev, Oleg, ed. and trans. *Sergei Prokofiev: Soviet Diary 1927 and Other Writings*. London: Faber, 1991.

Protokoly pervoi vserossiiskoi konferentsii proletarskykh kul'turno-prosvetitel'nykh organizatsii, 15–20 Sept. 1918. Moscow: n.p., 1918.

Protopopov, Sergei. *Elementy stroeniia muzykal'noi rechi*. Ed. B. L. Iavorskii. Parts 1–2. Moscow: Gosudarstvennoe muzykal'nyi izdatel'stvo, 1930–31.

Riauzov, Sergei. "Vospominaniia o 'Prokolle.'" *Sovetskaia muzyka* 7 (1949): 54–58.

Rimskii, L. B., ed. "Perepiska A. V. Mosolova, materialy, i dokumenty iz ego arkhiva." *Iz proshlogo sovetskoi muzykal'noi kul'tury*. Vol. 3. Ed. T. Livanova, 53–88. Moscow: Sovetskii kompozitor, 1982.

Rosenberg, William G., ed. *Bolshevik Visions: First Phase of the Cultural Revolution in Soviet Russia*. Ann Arbor: University of Michigan Press, 1990 [1984].

Roslavets, Nikolai. "O psevdo-proletarskoi muzyki." In *Na putiakh iskusstva. Sbornik statei,* ed. V. M. Bliumenfeld, V. F. Pletnev, and N. F. Chuzhak, 180–92. Moscow: Proletkul't, 1926.

Sabaneev, Leonid. *Muzyka posle Oktiabria.* Moscow: Rabotnik prosveshchenie, 1926.

———. "Three Russian Composers in Paris." *Musical Times* (1927): 882–84.

Sbornik dekretov, postanovlenii i rasporiazhenii po muzykal'nomu otdelu Narkomprosa. Petrograd: n.p., 1919.

Shcherbachev, Vladimir. *V. V. Shcherbachev. Stat'i materialy, pis'ma.* Ed. A. Kriutkov, comp. R. Slonimskaia. Leningrad: Sovetskii kompozitor, 1985.

Shebalin, Vissarion. *Literaturnoe nasledie: Vospominaniia, perepiska, stat'i, vystupleniia.* Moscow: Sovetskii kompozitor, 1975.

Shul'gina, Elena, comp. *L. V. Shul'gin. Stat'i, vospominaniia.* Moscow: Sovetskii kompozitor, 1977.

Sollertinsky, Dmitrii, and Liudmilla Sollertinsky. *Pages from the Life of Dmitrii Shostakovich.* Trans. Graham Hobbs and Charles Midgley. New York: Harcourt Brace Jovanovich, 1980.

Stalin, I. V. *Sochineniia.* Vol. 13. Moscow: Gosudarstvennoe izdatel'stvo politicheskoi literatury, 1951.

Stepanova, Svetlana Romanova, ed. *Muzykal'naia zhizn' Moskvy v pervye gody posle Oktiabria.* Moscow: Sovetskii kompozitor, 1972.

Taneev, Sergei. *Podvizhnoi kontrapunkt strogogo pis'ma.* Moscow: n.p., 1909.

"Tezisy ob osnovakh politiki v oblasti iskusstva." *Vestnik rabotnikov iskusstv* 2–3 (1920): 65–66.

Trotsky, Leon. *Problems of Everyday Life and Other Writings on Culture and Science.* New York: Monad Press, 1973.

Tsukker, Arnol'd. *Piat' let Persimfansa.* Moscow: Izdatel'stvo Pervogo simfonicheskogo ansamblia Mossoveta, 1927.

Uchebnye plany muzykal'nykh-uchebnykh zavedenii RSFSR. Moscow: n.p., 1924.

Vinogradov, V. *Sud nad muzykal'noi khalturoi.* Moscow: Gosudarstvennoe muzykal'noe izdatel'stvo, 1931.

Volkov, Solomon. *Testimony: The Memoirs of Dmitrii Shostakovich as Related to and Edited by Solomon Volkov.* Trans. Antonina W. Boius. New York: Harper and Row, 1979.

Vsesoiuznaia kommunisticheskaia partiia. Tsentral'nyi komitet. Otdel agitatsii, propagandy i pechati. Soveshchanie po voprosu muzyki. *Puti razvitiia muzyki. Stenograficheskii otchet pri APPO TsK VKP (b).* Moscow: n.p., 1930.

Wells, H. G. *Russia in the Shadows.* Westport, Conn.: Hyperion Press, 1973 [1921].

Wilson, Elizabeth. *Shostakovich: A Life Remembered.* Princeton: Princeton University Press, 1994.

Zetkin, Klara. *My Recollections of Lenin.* Moscow: Foreign Languages Publishing House, 1956.

Zharov, A. *Krasnaia garmoshka.* 2d ed. Moscow: Novaia Moskva, 1925.

Zhitomirskii, Daniil V. "O Davidenko i Prokolle." In *Aleksandr Davidenko. Vospominaniia. Stat'i. Materialy,* comp. N. A. Martynov. Leningrad: Muzyka, 1968.

———. "O proshlom bez prikras." *Sovetskaia muzyka* 2 (1988): 96–105.

———, ed. *A. D. Kastal'skii. Stat'i, vospominaniia i materialy.* Moscow: Gosudarstvennoe muzykal'noe izdatel'stvo, 1960.

Secondary Sources

Ament, Suzanne. "Russian Revolutionary Songs of 1905 and 1917: Symbols and Messengers of Protest and Change." M.A. thesis, Georgetown University, 1984.

Bailes, Kendall E. *Technology and Society under Lenin and Stalin: Origins of the Soviet Technical Intelligentsia, 1917–1941*. Princeton: Princeton University Press, 1978.

———. *Science and Russian Culture in an Age of Revolutions: V. I. Vernadsky and His Scientific School, 1863–1945*. Bloomington: Indiana University Press, 1990.

Barsova, Inna. "Aleksandr Mosolov: dvadtsatye gody." *Sovetskaia muzyka* 12 (1976): 77–87.

———. "Tvorchestvo Aleksandra Mosolova v kontekste sovetskogo muzykal'nogo konstruktivizma 1920-kh godov." In *Rossiia: Frantsiia*, ed. I. E. Danilova. Moscow: Gosudarstvennyi muzei izobrazitel'nykh iskusstv imeni A. S. Pushkina, 1988.

Bartlett, Rosamund, ed. *Shostakovich in Context*. Oxford: Oxford University Press, 2000.

Blium, Arlen. *Za kulisami "Ministerstva pravdy": Tainaia istoriia sovetskoi tsenzury, 1917–1929*. St. Petersburg: Akademicheskii proekt, 1994.

———. *Sovetskaia tsenzura v epokhu total'nogo terrora, 1929–1953*. St. Petersburg: Akademicheskii proekt, 2000.

Bogdanov-Berezovskii, V. M. *Muzykal'naia kul'tura Leningrada za piat'desiat let. Muzykal'no-istoricheskie ocherki*. Leningrad: Muzyka, 1967.

———, ed. *V pervye gody sovetskogo muzykal'nogo stroitel'stva*. Leningrad: Sovetskii kompozitor, 1959.

Bogdanova, A. *Muzyka i vlast' (poststalinskii period)*. Moscow: Nasledie, 1995.

Bonnell, Victoria E. *Iconography of Power: Soviet Political Posters under Lenin and Stalin*. Berkeley and Los Angeles: University of California Press, 1997.

Born, Georgina. *Rationalizing Culture: IRCAM, Boulez, and the Institutionalization of the Musical Avant-Garde*. Berkeley and Los Angeles: University of California Press, 1995.

Bowers, Faubion. *Scriabin: A Biography of the Russian Composer, 1871–1915*. Vol. 2. Palo Alto: Kodansha International, 1969.

Brandenburger, David. "The 'Short Course' to Modernity: Stalinist History Textbooks, Mass Culture, and the Formation of Russian Popular Identity, 1934–1956." Ph.D. diss., Harvard University, 1999.

Bronfin, E. *Muzykal'naia kul'tura Petrograda pervogo poslerevoliutsionnogo piatiletiia, 1917–1922*. Leningrad: Sovetskii kompozitor, 1984.

Brooke, Caroline. "The Development of Soviet Music Policy, 1932–1941." Ph.D. diss., Cambridge University, 1999.

———. "Soviet Musicians and the Great Terror." *Europe-Asia Studies* 54 (2002): 397–413.

Brooks, Jeffrey. *When Russia Learned to Read: Literacy and Popular Literature, 1861–1917*. Princeton: Princeton University Press, 1985.

———. *Thank You, Comrade Stalin! Soviet Public Culture from Revolution to Cold War*. Princeton: Princeton University Press, 2000.

Brown, Edward J. *The Proletarian Episode in Russian Literature, 1928–1932*. New York: Octagon Books, 1971.

———. *Russian Literature Since the Revolution.* Rev. ed. Cambridge, Mass.: Harvard University Press, 1982 [1963].
Brown, Malcom H. "The Soviet Russian Concepts of 'Intonazia' and 'Musical Imagery.'" *Musical Quarterly* 60 (1974): 557–67.
Burnham, Scott. *Beethoven Hero.* Princeton: Princeton University Press, 1995.
Carpenter, Ellon D. "Russian Music Theory: A Conspectus." In *Russian Theoretical Thought in Music*, ed. Gordon McQuere. Ann Arbor: UMI Research Press, 1983.
———. "The Contributions of Taneev, Catoire, Conius, Garbuzov, Mazel, and Tiulin." In *Russian Theoretical Thought in Music*, ed. Gordon McQuere. Ann Arbor: UMI Research Press, 1983.
Chamberlin, William Henry. *The Russian Revolution 1917–1921.* Vol. 1. Princeton: Princeton University Press, 1987 [1935].
Clark, Katerina. "The 'Quiet Revolution' in Soviet Intellectual Life." In *Russia in the Era of NEP: Explorations in Soviet Society and Culture*, ed. Sheila Fitzpatrick et al. Bloomington: Indiana University Press, 1991.
———. *Petersburg: Crucible of Cultural Revolution.* Cambridge: Cambridge University Press, 1995.
Claudin-Urondo, Carmen. *Lenin and the Cultural Revolution.* Atlantic Highlands, N.J.: Humanities Press, 1977.
Daragan, D. "Odin iz samykh aktivnykh stroitelei." *Sovetskaia muzyka* 5 (1978): 81–83.
David-Fox, Michael. *Revolution of the Mind: Higher Learning Among the Bolsheviks.* Ithaca: Cornell University Press, 1997.
———. "*Mentalité* or Cultural System? A Reply to Sheila Fitzpatrick." *Russian Review* 58 (April 1999): 210–11.
———. "What Is Cultural Revolution?" *Russian Review* 58 (1999): 181–201.
Dennis, David B. *Beethoven in German Politics, 1870–1989.* New Haven: Yale University Press, 1996.
Dreiden, Simon. *Muzyka—revoliutsii.* 3d ed. Moscow: Sovetskii kompozitor, 1981.
Dunham, Vera S. *In Stalin's Time: Middleclass Values in Soviet Fiction.* Durham: Duke University Press, 1990 [1976].
Eastman, Max. *Artists in Uniform: A Study of Literature and Bureaucratism.* New York: Octagon Books, 1972 [1934].
Edmunds, Neil. "Alexander Davidenko and Prokoll." *Tempo* 182 (1992): 1–5.
———. "Music and Politics: The Case of the Russian Association of Proletarian Musicians." *Slavonic and East European Review* 78 (2000): 66–89.
———. *The Soviet Proletarian Music Movement.* Bern: Peter Lang, 2000.
Ermolaev, Herman. *Soviet Literary Theories, 1917–1934: The Genesis of Socialist Realism.* Berkeley and Los Angeles: University of California Press, 1963.
Eroshkin, N. P. *Vysshie organy gosudarstvennoi vlasti i organy tsentral'nogo upravleniia RSFSR (1927–1967gg.).* Moscow: Tsentral'nyi gosudarstvennyi arkhiv RSFSR, 1971.
Ewing, E. Thomas. *The Teachers of Stalinism: Policy, Practice, and Power in Soviet Schools of the 1930s.* New York: Peter Lang, 2002.
Fanning, David, ed. *Shostakovich Studies.* Cambridge: Cambridge University Press, 1995.
Fay, Laurel. "Shostakovich versus Volkov: Whose Testimony?" *Russian Review* 39 (1980): 484–93.

———. "The Punch in Shostakovich's Nose." In *Russian and Soviet Music: Essays for Boris Schwarz*, ed. Malcolm H. Brown. Ann Arbor: UMI Research Press, 1984.
———. *Shostakovich: A Life*. Oxford: Oxford University Press, 2000.
Ferenc, Anna. "Reclaiming Roslavets: The Troubled Life of a Russian Modernist." *Tempo* 182 (1992): 6–9.
———. "Investigating Russian Musical Modernism: Nikolai Roslavets and His New System of Tone Organization." Ph.D. diss., University of Michigan, 1993.
Figes, Orlando. *A People's Tragedy: The Russian Revolution 1891–1924*. New York: Penguin Books, 1996.
Figes, Orlando, and Boris Kollonitsky. *Interpreting the Russian Revolution: The Language and Symbols of 1917*. New Haven: Yale University Press, 1999.
Fitzpatrick, Sheila. *The Commissariat of Enlightenment: Soviet Organization of Education and the Arts Under Lunacharsky. October 1917–1921*. Cambridge: Cambridge University Press, 1970.
———. "The Emergence of *Glaviskusstvo:* Class War on the Cultural Front, Moscow, 1928–29." *Soviet Studies* 23 (1971): 236–53.
———. "The Soft Line on Culture and Its Enemies." *Slavic Review* 33 (1974): 267–87.
———. *Education and Social Mobility in the Soviet Union, 1921–1934*. Cambridge: Cambridge University Press, 1979.
———. "The Problem of Class Identity in NEP Society." In *Russia in the Era of NEP: Explorations in Soviet Society and Culture*, ed. Sheila Fitzpatrick et al. Bloomington: Indiana University Press, 1991.
———. *The Cultural Front: Power and Culture in Revolutionary Russia*. Ithaca: Cornell University Press, 1992.
———. "Ascribing Class: The Construction of Social Identity in Soviet Russia." *Journal of Modern History* 65 (1993): 745–70.
———. "Cultural Revolution Revisited." *Russian Review* 58 (1999): 202–9.
———, ed. *Cultural Revolution in Russia, 1928–1931*. Bloomington: Indiana University Press, 1978.
Fitzpatrick, Sheila, Alexander Rabinowitch, and Richard Stites, eds. *Russia in the Era of NEP: Explorations in Soviet Society and Culture*. Bloomington: Indiana University Press, 1991.
Fox, Michael S. "Glavlit, Censorship, and the Problem of Party Policy in Cultural Affairs, 1922–1928." *Soviet Studies* 44 (1992): 1045–68.
Fradkin, Feliks Aronovich. "Soviet Experimentalism Routed: S. T. Shatskii's Last Years." In *School and Society in Tsarist and Soviet Russia*, ed. Ben Eklof. New York: St. Martin's Press, 1993.
Frank, Stephen P. "Confronting the Domestic Other: Rural Popular Culture and Its Enemies in Fin-De-Siècle Russia." In *Cultures in Flux: Lower-Class Values, Practices, and Resistance in Late Imperial Russia*, ed. Stephen P. Frank and Mark D. Steinberg. Princeton: Princeton University Press, 1994.
Frumkin, Vladimir. "Tekhnologiia ubezhdeniia: zametki o politicheskoi pesne." *Obozrenie* 6 (1983): 17–25.
Fussell, Paul. *The Great War in Modern Memory*. Oxford: Oxford University Press, 1975.
Gen-Ur, U., ed. *Aktual'nye voprosy muzykal'nogo obrazovaniia na sovremennom etape i nasledie B. V. Asaf'ev*. Petrozavodsk: 1984.

Gilman, Chris. "The Fox-Trot and the New Economic Policy: A Case Study in 'Thingification' and Cultural Imports." *Experiment* 2 (1996): 443–75.

Ginzburg, L. A., et al., eds. *Moskovskaia konservatoriia, 1866–1966.* Moscow: Muzyka, 1966.

Gleason, Abbott, Peter Kenez, and Richard Stites, eds. *Bolshevik Culture: Experiment and Order in the Russian Revolution.* Bloomington: Indiana University Press, 1985.

Glinsky, Albert. *Theremin: Ether Music and Espionage.* Urbana: University of Illinois Press, 2000.

Gojowy, Detlef. *Neue sowjetische Musik der 20er Jahre.* Laaber: Laaber-Verlag, 1980.

———. "Half-Time for Nikolai Roslavets (1881–1944): A Non-Love Story with a Post-Romantic Composer." In *Russian and Soviet Music: Essays for Boris Schwarz,* ed. Malcolm H. Brown. Ann Arbor: UMI Research Press, 1984.

———. *Arthur Lourié und der russische Futurismus.* Laaber: Laaber-Verlag, 1993.

Gooderham, Peter. "The Komsomol and Worker Youth: The Inculcation of 'Communist Values' in Leningrad during NEP." *Soviet Studies* 34 (1982): 506–28.

Gorbunov, V. V. "Bor'ba V. I. Lenina s separatistskimi ustremleniiami Proletkul'ta." *Voprosy istorii KPSS* 1 (1958): 29–40.

———. "Kritika V. I. Leninym teorii Proletkul'ta ob otnoshenii k kul'turnomu naslediiu." *Voprosy istorii KPSS* (1968): 83–93.

———. *V. I. Lenin i Proletkul't.* Moscow: Politizdat, 1974.

Gorsuch, Anne E. *Youth in Revolutionary Russia: Enthusiasts, Bohemians, Delinquents.* Bloomington: Indiana University Press, 2000.

Gorzka, Gabriele. *A. Bogdanov und der russische Proletkul't.* Frankfurt: Campus-Verlag, 1980.

Graham, Loren. *The Soviet Academy of Sciences and the Communist Party, 1927–1932.* Princeton: Princeton University Press, 1967.

———. *Science in Russia and the Soviet Union: A Short History.* Cambridge: Cambridge University Press, 1993.

Groys, Boris. "The Birth of Socialist Realism from the Spirit of the Avant-Garde." In *The Culture of the Stalin Period,* ed. Hans Günther. New York: St. Martin's Press, 1990.

———. *The Total Art of Stalinism: Avant-Garde, Aesthetic Dictatorship, and Beyond.* Princeton: Princeton University Press, 1992.

Günther, Hans, ed. *The Culture of the Stalin Period.* New York: St. Martin's Press, 1990.

Haas, David. *Leningrad's Modernists: Studies in Composition and Musical Thought, 1917–1932.* New York: Peter Lang, 1998.

Hakobian, Levon. *Music of the Soviet Age, 1917–1987.* Stockholm: Melos Music Literature, 1998.

Hatch, John. "The Politics of Mass Culture: Workers, Communists, and Proletkul't in the Development of Workers' Clubs, 1921–25." *Russian History / Histoire Russe* 13 (1986): 119–48.

———. "The Formation of Working Class Cultural Institutions during NEP: The Workers' Club Movement in Moscow, 1921–1923." *Carl Beck Papers in Russian and East European Studies* 806 (1990).

———. "Hangouts and Hangovers: State, Class, and Culture in Moscow's Workers' Club Movement, 1925–28." *Russian Review* 53 (1994): 97–117.

Hayward, Max, and Leopold Lebedz, eds. *Literature and Revolution in Soviet Russia, 1917–1962*. Oxford: Oxford University Press, 1963.

Hingley, Ronald. *Russian Writers and Soviet Society, 1917–1978*. New York: Weidenfeld and Nicolson, 1979.

Ho, Allan, and Dmitry Feofanov. *Shostakovich Reconsidered*. London: Toccata Press, 1998.

Holmes, Larry E. *The Kremlin and the School House: Reforming Education in Soviet Russia, 1917–1931*. Bloomington: Indiana University Press, 1991.

Hudson, Hugh D. *Blueprints and Blood: The Stalinization of Soviet Architecture, 1917–1937*. Princeton: Princeton University Press, 1994.

Husband, William B. *"Godless Communists": Atheism and Society in Soviet Russia, 1917–1932*. DeKalb: Northern Illinois University Press, 2000.

Istoriia muzyki narodov SSSR. Vol. 1. Ed. Iurii Keldysh. Moscow: Sovetskii kompozitor, 1970.

Istoriia russkoi sovetskoi muzyki. Vol. 1. Ed. A. D. Alekseev. Moscow: Gosudarstvennoe muzykal'noe izdatel'stvo, 1956.

Jelagin, Juri. *Taming of the Arts*. Trans. Nicholas Wreden. New York: E. P. Dutton, 1951.

Johnson, James H. *Listening in Paris: A Cultural History*. Berkeley and Los Angeles: University of California Press, 1995.

Kagarlitsky, Boris. *The Thinking Reed: Intellectuals and the Soviet State from 1917 to the Present*. Trans. Brian Pearce. London: Verso, 1988.

Kassoff, Brian. "The Knowledge Front: Politics, Ideology, and Economics in the Soviet Book Publishing Industry, 1925–1935." Ph.D. diss., University of California, Berkeley, 2000.

Kats, B., and R. Timenchik. *Anna Akhmatova i muzyka: Issledovatel'skie ocherki*. Leningrad: Sovetskii kompozitor, 1989.

Keldysh, Iurii. *Sto let Moskovskoi konservatorii*. Moscow: Muzyka, 1966.

———, ed. *B. V. Asaf'ev i sovetskaia muzykal'naia kul'tura: materialy Vsesoiuznoi nauchno-teoreticheskoi konferentsii*. Moscow: Sovetskii kompozitor, 1986.

Kelly, Catriona, and David Shepherd, eds. *Constructing Russian Culture in the Age of Revolution: 1881–1940*. Oxford: Oxford University Press, 1998.

———. *Russian Cultural Studies: An Introduction*. Oxford: Oxford University Press, 1998.

Kemp-Welch, A. "New Economic Policy in Culture and Its Enemies." *Journal of Contemporary History* 13 (1978): 449–65.

———. *Stalin and the Literary Intelligentsia, 1928–1939*. New York: St. Martin's Press, 1991.

Kenez, Peter. *Birth of the Propaganda State: Soviet Methods of Mass Mobilization, 1917–1928*. Cambridge: Cambridge University Press, 1985.

Kepley, Vance, Jr. "Cinema and Everyday Life: Soviet Worker Clubs of the 1920s." In *Resisting Images: Essays on Cinema and History*, ed. Robert Sklar and Charles Musser. Philadelphia: Temple University Press, 1990.

Khentova, Sofiia. *Molodye gody Shostakovicha*. Leningrad: Sovetskii kompozitor, 1975.

———. *D. D. Shostakovich v gody Velikoi Otechestvennoi voiny*. Leningrad: Muzyka, 1979.

———. *Shostakovich, zhizn' i tvorchestvo*. 2 vols. Leningrad: Sovetskii kompozitor, 1985.

———. *Shostakovich v Moskve.* Moscow: Moskovskii rabochii, 1986.
———. *Udivitel'nyi Shostakovich.* St. Petersburg: "Variant," 1993.
Kirschenbaum, Lisa A. *Small Comrades: Revolutionizing Childhood in Soviet Russia, 1917–1932.* New York: Routledge, 2000.
Koenker, Diane P., William G. Rosenberg, and Ronald Grigor Suny, eds. *Party, State, and Society in the Russian Civil War: Explorations in Social History.* Bloomington: Indiana University Press, 1989.
Konecny, Peter. "Chaos on Campus: The 1924 Student *Proverka* in Leningrad." *Europe-Asia Studies* 46 (1994): 617–35.
———. *Builders and Deserters: Students, State, and Community in Leningrad, 1917–1941.* Montreal: McGill-Queens University Press, 1999.
Koval'skii, K. "B. B. Krasin." *Sovetskaia muzyka* 7 (1936): 106–7.
Krasovitskaia, T. Iu., and A. P. Nenarokov. "Protokoly Kollegii Narkomprosa RSFSR kak istoricheskii istochnik." In *Sovetskaia kul'tura. 70 let razvitiia,* ed. B. B. Piotrovskii, 353–62. Moscow: Nauka, 1987.
Krebs, Stanley Dale. *Soviet Composers and the Development of Soviet Music.* New York: W. W. Norton, 1970.
Lahusen, Thomas. *How Life Writes the Book: Real Socialism and Socialist Realism in Stalin's Russia.* Ithaca: Cornell University Press, 1997.
LaPasha, Robin C. "From Chastushki to Tchaikovsky: Amateur Activity and the Production of Popular Culture in the Soviet 1930s." Ph.D. diss., Duke University, 2001.
Leningradskaia gosudarstvennaia konservatoriia. *Sto let Leningradskoi konservatorii. 1862–1962. Istoricheskii ocherk.* Leningrad: Gosudarstvennoe muzykal'noe izdatel'stvo, 1962.
Leonard, Richard Anthony. *A History of Russian Music.* Westport, Conn.: Greenwood, 1977 [1957].
Leonova, M. F. *Dmitrii Pokrass.* Moscow: Sovetskii kompozitor, 1981.
Leppert, Richard, and Susan McClary, eds. *Music and Society: The Politics of Composition, Performance, and Reception.* Cambridge: Cambridge University Press, 1987.
Lewin, Moshe. *Lenin's Last Struggle.* New York: Monthly Review Press, 1968.
———. *The Making of the Soviet System.* New York: Pantheon, 1985.
Lidtke, Vernon. *The Alternative Culture: Socialist Labor in Imperial Germany.* New York: Oxford University Press, 1985.
Livanova, Tamara Nikolaevna, ed. *Mikhail Vladimirovich Ivanov-Boretskii. Stat'i i issledovaniia. Vospominaniia o nem.* Moscow: Sovetskii kompozitor, 1972.
———. *Iz proshlogo sovetskoi muzykal'noi kul'tury.* Vols. 1–3. Moscow: Sovetskii kompozitor, 1975–82.
Lobanova, Marina. "L'eredita di N. A. Roslavec nel campo della teoria musicale." *Musica / Realta* 4 (1983): 41–65.
———. *Nikolaj Andreevic Roslavež und die Kultur seiner Zeit.* Frankfurt: Peter Lang, 1997.
Lokshin, D. L. *D. S. Vasil'ev-Buglai.* Moscow: Sovetskii kompozitor, 1958.
MacDonald, Ian. *The New Shostakovich.* London: Fourth Estate, 1990.
MacFadyen, David. *Songs for Fat People: Affect, Emotion, and Celebrity in the Russian Popular Song.* Montreal: McGill-Queens University Press, 2002.

Maes, Francis. *A History of Russian Music: From Kamarinskaya to Babi Yar.* Trans. Arnold J. Pomerans and Erica Pomerans. Berkeley and Los Angeles: University of California Press, 2002.

Maguire, Robert A. *Red Virgin Soil: Soviet Literature in the 1920s.* Evanston: Northwestern University Press, 2000 [1968].

Maksimenkov, Leonid. *Sumbur vmesto muzyki. Stalinskaia kul'turnaia revoliutsiia, 1936–1938.* Moscow: Iuridicheskaia kniga, 1997.

Mally, Lynn. "Intellectuals in the Proletkul't: Problems of Authority and Expertise." In *Party, State, and Society in the Russian Civil War: Explorations in Social History*, ed. Diane Koenker et al. Bloomington: Indiana University Press, 1989.

———. *Culture of the Future: The Proletkult Movement in Revolutionary Russia.* Berkeley and Los Angeles: University of California Press, 1990.

———. *Revolutionary Acts: Amateur Theater and the Soviet State.* Ithaca: Cornell University Press, 2000.

Maslenkova, L. "B. L. Iavorskii o vospitanii slukha." *Kritika i muzykoznanie* 2 (1980): 198–207.

Mazel, L. A., and I. Ia. Ryzhkin, eds. *Ocherki po istorii teoreticheskogo muzykoznaniia.* 2d ed. Moscow and Leningrad: Gosudarstvennoe muzykal'noe izdatel'stvo, 1976 [1939].

McAuley, Mary. "Bread Without the Bourgeoisie." In *Party, State, and Society in the Russian Civil War: Explorations in Social History*, ed. Diane Koenker et al. Bloomington: Indiana University Press, 1989.

McBurney, Gerard. "The Resurrection of Roslavets." *Tempo* 173 (1990): 7–9.

McClelland, James C. "Proletarianizing the Student Body: The Soviet Experience During the New Economic Policy." *Past and Present* 80 (1978): 122–48.

———. "Utopianism versus Revolutionary Heroism in Bolshevik Policy: The Proletarian Culture Debate." *Slavic Review* 39 (1980): 403–25.

———. "The Professoriate in the Russian Civil War." In *Party, State, and Society in the Russian Civil War: Explorations in Social History*, ed. Diane Koenker et al. Bloomington: Indiana University Press, 1989.

McQuere, Gordon D., ed. *Russian Theoretical Thought in Music.* Ann Arbor: UMI Research Press, 1983.

Medvedev, Roy. *Let History Judge.* New York: Vintage Books, 1973.

Minor, N. N. *N. Ia. Briusova i ee shkola muzykal'nogo obrazovaniia.* Saratov: Izdatel'stvo Saratovskogo pedagogicheskogo instituta, 1994.

Mironova, N. A. *Moskovskaia konservatoriia. Istoki.* Moscow: Moskovskaia gosudarstvennaia konservatoriia, 1995.

Montague, Stephen. "Rediscovering Leon Theremin." *Tempo* 177 (1991): 18–23.

Naiman, Eric. *Sex in Public: The Incarnation of Early Soviet Ideology.* Princeton: Princeton University Press, 1997.

Nelson, Amy. "Assigning Meaning to Musical Speech: The Theories of Boleslav Yavorsky in the Cultural Revolution." In *Intersections and Transpositions: Russian Music, Literature, and Society*, ed. Andrew Baruch Wachtel, 253–73. Evanston: Northwestern University Press, 1998.

———. "The Struggle for Proletarian Music: RAPM and the Cultural Revolution." *Slavic Review* 59: 1 (2000): 101–32.

Nest'ev, I. V. "Muzyka Betkhovena v sovetskoi Rossii." *Betkhoven. Sbornik statei.* Vol. 2. Ed. N. L Fishman. Moscow: Muzyka, 1972.

———. "Iz istorii russkogo muzykal'nogo avangarda." *Sovetskaia muzyka* 1 (1991): 75–87.

Neuberger, Joan. *Hooliganism: Crime, Culture, and Power in St. Petersburg, 1900–1914.* Berkeley and Los Angeles: University of California Press, 1993.

Norris, Christopher, ed. *Shostakovich: The Man and His Music.* London: M. Boyars, 1982.

———. *Music and the Politics of Culture.* New York: St. Martin's Press, 1989.

Olkhovsky, Andrei. *Music under the Soviets: The Agony of an Art.* Westport, Conn.: Greenwood, 1975 [1955].

"Organizator zvukov." *Muzykal'naia gazeta* 6 (1990): 4.

Orlova, Elena. *B. V. Asaf'ev: put' issledovatelia i publitsista.* Leningrad: Muzyka, 1964.

Orlova, Elena, and Andrei Kriukov. *Akademik Boris Vladimirovich Asaf'ev: Monografia.* Leningrad: Sovetskii kompozitor, 1984.

Orlovsky, Dan. "The Hidden Class: White-Collar Workers in the Soviet 1920s." In *Making Workers Soviet: Class, Power, and Identity,* ed. Lewis H. Siegelbaum and Ronald Grigor Suny. Ithaca: Cornell University Press, 1994.

Peris, Daniel. *Storming the Heavens: The Soviet League of the Militant Godless.* Ithaca: Cornell University Press, 1998.

Petrone, Karen. *Life Has Become More Joyous, Comrades: Celebrations in the Time of Stalin.* Bloomington: Indiana University Press, 2000.

Pinegina, L. A. *Sovetskii rabochii klass i khudozhestvennaia kul'tura, 1917–1932.* Moscow: Izdatel'stvo Moskovskogo universiteta, 1984.

Plaggenborg, Stefan. *Revolutionskultur. Menschenbilder und kulturelle Praxis in Sowjetrussland zwischen Oktoberrevolution und Stalinismus.* Cologne: Böhlau, 1996.

Poliakova, Liudmila. *Soviet Music.* Trans. Xenia Danko. Moscow: Foreign Languages Publishing House, n.d.

Pribegina, G. A. *Moskovskaia konservatoriia 1866–1991.* Moscow: Muzyka, 1991.

Prieberg, Fred K. *Musik in der Sowjetunion.* Cologne: Verlag Wissenschaft und Politik, 1965.

Raynor, Henry. *Music and Society Since 1815.* New York: Schocken Books, 1976.

Read, Christopher. *Culture and Power in Revolutionary Russia: The Intelligentsia and the Transition from Tsarism to Communism.* London: Macmillan, 1990.

Richmond, Steven. "'The Conditions of the Contemporary': The Censors and Censoring of Soviet Theater, 1923–1927." *Russian History* 27 (2000): 1–56.

Ridenour, Robert C. *Nationalism, Modernism, and Personal Rivalry in Nineteenth-Century Russian Music.* Ann Arbor: UMI Research Press, 1981.

Roberts, Peter Deane. *Modernism in Russian Piano Music: Skriabin, Prokofiev, and Their Russian Contemporaries.* 2 vols. Bloomington: Indiana University Press, 1993.

Robinson, Harlow. *Sergei Prokofiev: A Biography.* New York: Viking, 1987.

Rosen, Charles. *Arnold Schoenberg.* New York: Viking Press, 1975.

Rothstein, Robert. "The Quiet Rehabilitation of the Brick Factory: Early Soviet Music and Its Critics." *Slavic Review* 29 (1980): 373–88.

———. "Popular Song in the NEP Era." In *Russia in the Era of NEP,* ed. Sheila Fitzpatrick et al. Bloomington: Indiana University Press, 1991.

———. "Death of the Folk Song?" In *Cultures in Flux: Lower-Class Values, Practices, and Resistance in Late Imperial Russia*, ed. Stephen P. Frank and Mark D. Steinberg. Princeton: Princeton University Press, 1994.

Rowney, Don K. *Transition to Technocracy: The Structural Origins of the Soviet Administrative State*. Ithaca: Cornell University Press, 1989.

Schwarz, Boris. "Beethoveniana in Soviet Russia." *The Musical Quarterly* 47 (1961): 4–21.

———. "More Beethoveniana in Soviet Russia." *The Musical Quarterly* 49 (1963): 143–49.

———. "A Little-Known Beethoven Sketch in Moscow." *The Musical Quarterly* 56 (1970): 539–50.

———. *Music and Musical Life in Soviet Russia, 1917–1981*. Bloomington: Indiana University Press, 1983 [1972].

Shaverdian, A. I., ed. *Puti razvitiia sovetskoi muzyki. Kratkii obzor.* Moscow: Gosudarstvennoe muzykal'noe izdatel'stvo, 1948.

Shepherd, John. *Music as Social Text*. Cambridge: Polity, 1991.

Siegelbaum, Lewis. "Building Stalinism 1929–1941." In *Russia: A History*, ed. Gregory Freeze. Oxford: Oxford University Press, 1997.

Sitsky, Larry. *Music of the Repressed Russian Avant-Garde, 1900–1929*. Westport, Conn.: Greenwood, 1994.

Slonimsky, Nicolas. "The Changing Style of Soviet Music." *Journal of the American Musicological Society* 3 (1950): 236–55.

Smith, Gerald Stanton. *Songs to Seven Strings: Russian Guitar Poetry and Soviet Mass Song*. Bloomington: Indiana University Press, 1984.

Smith, Susannah Lockwood. "Soviet Arts Policy, Folk Music, and National Identity: The Piatnitskii State Russian Folk Choir, 1927–1945." Ph.D. diss., University of Minnesota, 1997.

Soboleva, G. *Russkii-sovetskii romans*. Moscow: Znanie, 1985.

Sochor, Zinovia. *Revolution and Culture: The Bogdanov-Lenin Controversy*. Ithaca: Cornell University Press, 1988.

Sokhor, Arnol'd. *Russkaia sovetskaia pesnia*. Leningrad: Sovetskii kompozitor, 1959.

Sokolov, Iurii. *Russian Folklore*. Trans. Catherine Ruth Smith. New York: Macmillan, 1950.

Starr, S. Frederick. *Red and Hot: The Fate of Jazz in the Soviet Union*. New York: Oxford University Press, 1983.

Steiner, Evgeny. *Stories for Little Comrades: Revolutionary Artists and the Making of Early Soviet Children's Books*. Trans. Jane Ann Miller. Seattle: University of Washington Press, 1999.

Stites, Richard. *Revolutionary Dreams: Utopian Vision and Experimental Life in the Russian Revolution*. Oxford: Oxford University Press, 1989.

———. *Russian Popular Culture: Entertainment and Society Since 1900*. Cambridge: Cambridge University Press, 1992.

Subotnik, Rose. *Developing Variations: Style and Ideology in Western Music*. Minneapolis: University of Minnesota Press, 1991.

Swift, E. Anthony. *Popular Theater and Society in Tsarist Russia*. Berkeley and Los Angeles: University of California Press, 2002.

Tarakanov, Mikhail, ed. *Istoriia sovremennoi otechestvennoi muzyki.* Vol. 1. Moscow: Muzyka, 1995.

Taruskin, Richard. Review of *Modernism in Russian Piano Music: Skriabin, Prokofiev, and Their Russian Contemporaries*, by Peter Deane Roberts. *Slavic Review* 53 (1994): 866.

———. *Defining Russia Musically: Historical and Hermeneutical Essays.* Princeton: Princeton University Press, 1997.

Theremin: An Electric Odyssey. Directed by Steven M. Martin. MGM Home Entertainment, 1995.

Thorpe, Richard G. "The Management of Culture in Revolutionary Russia: The Imperial Theaters and the State, 1897–1928." Ph.D. diss., Princeton University, 1991.

Timasheff, Nicholas. *The Great Retreat: The Growth and Decline of Communism in Russia.* New York: E. P. Dutton, 1946.

Tolstoy, Vladimir, Irina Bibikova, and Catherine Cook, eds. *Street Art of the Revolution: Festivals and Celebrations in Russia, 1918–33.* New York: Vendome Press, 1990.

Tolz, Vera. *Russian Academicians and the Revolution: Combining Professionalism and Politics.* New York: St. Martin's Press, 1997.

Tomoff, Kiril. "Creative Union: The Professional Organization of Soviet Composers, 1939–1953." Ph.D. diss., University of Chicago, 2001.

Tsivian, Yurii. "The Tango in Russia." *Experiment* 2 (1996): 307–35.

Veselovskaia, L., et al., eds. *Bol'shoi put' (iz istorii partiinoi organizatsii Moskovskoi konservatorii).* Moscow: n.p., 1966.

Vinokurova, I. "Trizhdy rasstrelianyi muzykant." *Muzykal'naia akademiia* 1 (1996): 79–84.

Vlasova, Ekaterina. "Venera Milosskaia i printsipy 1789." *Muzykal'naia akademiia* 2 (1993): 154–60.

von Geldern, James. "The Centre and the Periphery: Cultural and Social Geography in the Mass Culture of the 1930s." In *New Directions in Soviet History*, ed. Stephen White. Cambridge: Cambridge University Press, 1992.

———. *Bolshevik Festivals, 1917–1920.* Berkeley and Los Angeles: University of California Press, 1993.

von Geldern, James, and Richard Stites, eds. *Mass Culture in Soviet Russia: Tales, Poems, Songs, Movies, Plays, and Folklore, 1917–1953.* Bloomington: Indiana University Press, 1995.

von Hagen, Mark. *Soldiers in the Proletarian Dictatorship: The Red Army and the Soviet Socialist State, 1917–1930.* Ithaca: Cornell University Press, 1990.

Vucinich, Alexander. *Empire of Knowledge: The Academy of Sciences and the USSR (1917–1970).* Berkeley and Los Angeles: University of California Press, 1984.

Walker, Barbara. "*Kruzhok* Culture: The Meaning of Patronage in the Early Soviet Literary World." *Contemporary European History* 11 (2002): 107–8.

Weber, William. "Wagner, Wagnerism, and Musical Idealism." In *Wagnerism in European Culture and Politics*, ed. David Large and William Weber. Ithaca: Cornell University Press, 1984.

Wehrmeyer, Andreas. *Studien zum russischen Musikdenken um 1920.* Frankfurt: Peter Lang, 1991.

Weiner, Douglas R. *Models of Nature: Ecology, Conservation, and Cultural Revolution in Soviet Russia.* Bloomington: Indiana University Press, 1988.

Young, Glennys. *Power and the Sacred in Revolutionary Russia: Religious Activists in the Village*. University Park: Pennsylvania State University Press, 1997.
Youngblood, Denise. *Soviet Cinema in the Silent Era, 1918–1935*. Ann Arbor: UMI Research Press, 1985.
———. *Movies for the Masses: Popular Cinema and Soviet Society in the 1920s*. Cambridge: Cambridge University Press, 1992.
Zarudko, Valentina. "Istoriia muzyki. Iz proshlogo sovetskoi muzykal'noi kul'tury." In *Moskovskii muzykoved*. Vol. 1. Ed. M. E. Tarakanov, 5–19. 1990.
Zelenov, M. V. "Glavlit i istoricheskaia nauka v 20–30-e gody." *Voprosy istorii* 3 (1997): 21–35.
Zemtsovskii, I. I., and V. P. Il'in. "Muzykal'naia samodeiatel'nost'." In *Muzykal'naia kul'tura Leningrada za 50 let*, ed. V. M. Bogdanov-Berezovskii. Leningrad: Muzyka, 1967.
Zil'berbrandt, M. I. "Pesnia na estrade." In *Russkaia sovetskaia estrada 1917–1929 gg. Ocherki istorii*, ed. E. Uvarova. Moscow: Iskusstvo, 1976.

INDEX

Made in the USA
Middletown, DE
21 December 2016